Remnants of Meaning

Remnants of Meaning

Stephen Schiffer

A Bradford Book
The MIT Press
Cambridge, Massachusetts
London, England

This book was set in Palatino by Asco Trade Typesetting Ltd., Hong Kong, and printed and bound by Halliday Lithograph in the United States of America.

Library of Congress Cataloging-in-Publication Data

Schiffer, Stephen R.
  Remnants of meaning.

  "A Bradford book."
  Bibliography: p.
  Includes index.
  1. Semantics (Philosophy)   2. Meaning (Philosophy)   I. Title.
B840.S33   1987   121'.68   86-31112
ISBN 0-262-19258-6

To Michele,
for whom nothing was precluded

Contents

Acknowledgments

Discussion with many people helped to shape this book, but I can actually locate the influence of Anita Avramides, Paul Benacerraf, Akeel Bilgrami, John Carroll, Stewart Cohen, Arthur Collins, Paul Coppock, Dan Dennett, Richard Feldman, Jerry Fodor, Graeme Forbes, Alvin Goldman, Mike Harnish, Jeff Hershfield, Jerry Katz, Jody Kraus, Keith Lehrer, Ernie LePore, David Lewis, Colin McGinn, Chris Peacocke, John Pollock, Keith Quillen, Mark Sainsbury, Chris Shields, Holly Smith, Bob Stalnaker, Neil Tennant, Peter Unger, and Richard Warner.

Hartry Field, Brian Loar, and Steve Stich read the entire penultimate draft of this book, and each gave me several pages of extremely helpful comments on it. Their comments, in fact, secured that the draft they read was penultimate.

I started talking philosophy with Brian Loar in Oxford in 1964 and have not stopped yet. These conversations, and Loar's own written work, have had an inestimable impact on my thought. Hartry Field, through his writings and in the numerous discussions I have had with him over the past eleven years, has also been a huge influence. To both of these friends I am extremely grateful.

Raymond Saunders, the painter, has been my friend for nearly twenty-five years; I am touched and delighted by his gift to me of the front cover art.

The person to whom I am most indebted is my wife, Michele. She has had the best influence on my life, and this influence has very much affected this book.

Preface

In 1957 the then Oxford philosopher H. P. Grice published a short article in the *Philosophical Review* called "Meaning," in which he did the following:

1. He distinguished the sense of 'meaning' applicable to speakers, as in

In uttering 'Il pleut', Pierre meant that it was raining,

from the sense of 'meaning' applicable to marks and sounds, as in

'La neige est blanche' means that snow is white.

2. He proposed a definition of *speaker-meaning* (as we may call it) that had this feature: if correct, it showed that speaker-meaning could be defined in wholly psychological terms, independently of any other *semantic* notions.

3. He suggested that *expression-meaning*—the meaning of marks and sounds—could then be defined in terms of the defined notion of speaker-meaning, but made no serious effort to show how this could be done.

As a graduate student at Oxford in the sixties, I was much taken with Grice's program. I thought that his actual account of speaker-meaning was inadequate (it was best viewed as a first shot at a definition of *telling*); but I was taken with the idea of *reducing* the semantic to the psychological by first defining speaker-meaning in terms of a certain species of intentional behavior whose specification did not itself involve anything semantical, and then defining expression-meaning in terms of the reduced notion of speaker-meaning. In my book *Meaning* (1972) I tried to carry forward the Gricean program, which I now call 'intention-based semantics' (IBS), by offering a more adequate account of speaker-meaning and by showing how expression-meaning and other semantic notions, such as Austin's (1962) notion of an illocutionary act, could be defined in terms of speaker-meaning. However, the account of expression-meaning was in important ways incomplete and, apart from its incompleteness, defective in ways that made it at best a first step in what one might have hoped to be the right direction. So when I finished my book, I regarded the need to provide a complete and fully adequate account of expression-meaning as very much a part of the continuing IBS agenda. At the same time I thought that there were no insuperable obstacles to getting such an account, and was encouraged by work of David Lewis's (1975) to suppose that I knew the lines along which to get it. I thought that the real challenge to the IBS program was the one that I am about to describe. This optimism, I later came to realize, was naive; but this was not something that I could realize until it became clear to me why the challenge just alluded to could not be met.

The IBS program of reducing the semantic to the psychological was attractive to me for several reasons, but one very important reason was this. First, I was a physicalist as regards the semantic and the psychological and felt, with Quine and others, that we could not be assured that there *were* semantic and psychological facts unless it could be shown that these facts were identical to physical or topic-neutral facts—facts, that is, statable in sentences devoid of semantic, mentalistic, and intentional idioms. Second, I felt that the program of reducing the semantic and the psychological to the physical would be considerably aided if we could first reduce the semantic to the psychological. Certainly I felt that the project of defining the semantic in terms of the psychological was fairly pointless if one was then going to view propositional attitudes as primitive and inexplicable. IBS seeks to explain the fact that a certain sequence of sounds means that such and such among a certain population of speakers by virtue of the sequence being correlated with the belief that such and such by communicative practices that prevail in the population. What could be the point of trading in facts about *meaning* for facts about the *content of beliefs* if one ends up with nothing to say about the latter? (Cf. Block 1986.)

Both mental states and sentences have what is called *intentionality* or *representational content*: a particular sentence means *that worms do not have noses*, and a particular state is a belief *that worms do not have noses*. What the theorist ultimately wants, of course, is a general theory of content, a theory of linguistic *and* mental representation. Now in *Meaning* it was argued that all questions about linguistic representation reduce to questions about mental representation, but no attempt was made there to account for mental representation—to account, that is, for the content of mental states. This meant that the IBS program, as I construed it, and as tied to physicalism, would not be complete until an account of propositional attitudes was given that satisfied the following two conditions.

A. It showed, in conformity with the IBS program of *reducing* semantic facts to propositional-attitude facts, that propositional-attitude facts, such as the fact that Ralph believes that worms do not have noses, could in their turn be explicated without recourse to the semantic features of sentences. Here it was assumed that believing was a *relation* to things believed, and the task was to find objects of belief that were consonant with the IBS program. In other words, what entity can *the IBS theorist* take to be the referent of 'that worms do not have noses' in the sentence that ascribes to Ralph his belief? This was a substantial challenge, because many philosophers were skeptical of the possibility of accounting for the content of beliefs in a language-independent way.

B. It showed, in conformity with my physicalism, that propositional-attitude facts were facts statable in sentences devoid of mentalistic and intentional idioms.

In the years following the publication of *Meaning* I tried to come up with a theory of propositional attitudes that satisfied these two constraints. But without success. I used to joke that I was able to refute all of the theories compatible with my presuppositions, until one day in 1982 I finally decided that I probably was not joking. Conditions A and B could not be satisfied. But that was not the end of it, was in fact only the beginning. In trying to deal with the negative conclusions thus reached, and to trace out their consequences for the philosophy of language and mind, I came gradually to give up virtually all of what I used to accept, and a good deal of what most philosophers still accept. Believing is not, after all, a relation that relates a believer to what she believes; natural languages do not, after all, have compositional meaning theories; and not only is IBS a hopeless endeavor, but there can be no significant reduction or "explication" of our semantic or propositional-attitude notions; and in the end one is left with the no-theory theory of meaning, the deflationary thought that the questions that now define the philosophy of meaning and intentionality all have false presuppositions. It was thus that I came to write *Remnants of Meaning*.

I want now to make explicit the structure and drift of this book.

In chapter 1, "Starting Points: The Semantic, the Psychological, and the Physical," a hypothetical philosopher is implicitly defined by nine hypotheses that he holds, most of which are held in common with many other philosophers. The "implicit philosopher" is pretty close to myself, before reaching philosophical maturity, and the rest of the book in effect traces the steps by which he came to abandon his old views and take on certain new ones. This autobiographical insight is, however, irrelevant to an understanding of this book, which presupposes no interest whatever in my intellectual development (or its opposite).

The first hypothesis is that there are semantic facts: some marks and sounds have *meaning*, some are *true*, some *refer* to things, and so on.

The second hypothesis is that every natural language has a compositional meaning theory: a finitely statable theory that specifies the meaning of each word and syntactic construction of the language in a way that determines the meaning of every expression of the language.

The third hypothesis is that a correct compositional meaning theory for a language is also a compositional truth-theoretic semantics for the language: that is, it determines a truth condition for every utterance in the language that has one.

The fourth hypothesis gives the reason for supposing that natural languages have compositional semantics: namely, it would not be possible to account for a human's ability to understand utterances of indefinitely many novel sentences of a language without the assumption that the language had a compositional semantics.

The fifth hypothesis corresponds to the first, and is merely that humans have beliefs and other propositional attitudes with content.

The sixth hypothesis expresses the "token-token identity theory": your present belief that you are reading is a neural state-token of yours.

The seventh hypothesis is what I call the relational theory of propositional attitudes: believing is a relation to things believed, to values of the variable 'y' in the schema 'x believes y', which things have features that determine the intentional features of beliefs (for instance, my present belief that snow is white is true just in case what I believe—the referent of the singular term 'that snow is white'—is true). Naturally the big question here, which the rest of the book makes much of, is, What are these "things believed"? Here, too, one is reminded of the connection between the relational theory of propositional attitudes and the hypothesis that every natural language has a compositional semantics: if English has a correct compositional semantics, then 'believes' must be treated in that semantics as a semantic primitive, and it is arguable that the only tenable way this can be done is to treat 'believes' as a relational predicate true of a believer and what he believes.

The eighth hypothesis is that semantic and psychological facts are not irreducibly semantic or psychological, but can be revealed to be facts statable in sentences devoid of semantic, mentalistic, and intentional idioms. This hypothesis goes beyond the token-token physicalism of the sixth hypothesis in its refusal to recognize anything, of any ontological category, that is irreducibly semantic or psychological.

The ninth hypothesis is that the Gricean program, Intention-Based Semantics, is essentially correct, and thus the semantic reduces to the psychological in the style of that program.

Thus our hero, the hypothetical philosopher implicitly defined by these nine hypotheses, accepts the relational theory of belief and so must say what the objects of belief are. Here, fortunately, it is possible to get an exhaustive partition of the positions in logical spaces; for whatever the "objects of belief" are, they must be things that can have truth values and stand in logical relations to one another. Evidently, then, things believed (the values of 'y' in 'x believes y') must either be propositions (of one stripe or another), sentences or utterances of a public language, or formulae in the brain's "language of thought." But the philosopher is also an IBS theorist, and this means that he cannot accept that believing is a relation to sentences or utterances of a public language. For on that view it is precisely the *meaning* of the sentence or utterance believed that determines the content of a belief, and this fact would defeat his attempt to reduce the meaning of marks and sounds to propositional-attitude content. The IBS theorist who accepts the relational theory must choose between propositions and mental representations as the objects of belief. But the theorist is also a physicalist in the strong sense of the eighth hypothesis, and this means that, whatever he selects as the relata of propositional-attitude relations, he must show that propositional-attitude facts reduce, on that selection, to facts statable in physicalistic or "topic-neutral" terms.

In chapter 2, "Functionalism and Propositions," it is argued that our hero will have a hard time satisfying his physicalism if he opts for propositions as the objects of belief. For if believing is a relation to propositions, then it would seem that *functionalism* is the best way to get a physicalistically creditable account of the belief relation, and in this chapter it is argued that functionalism cannot be correct.

In chapter 3, "The Real Trouble with Propositions," it is argued that, for reasons that have nothing to do with the mind-body problem, believing cannot be a relation to propositions. For consider Tanya's belief that Gustav is a dog. If the propositionalist theory of believing is correct, then the proposition that provides the complete content of Tanya's belief either contains (so to say) doghood or else contains a mode of presentation of it; but there are arguments to show that neither of these alternatives pans out. The IBS theorist who subscribes to the relational theory of belief must turn to neural sentences of the inner system of mental representation.

In chapter 4, "Intentionality and the Language of Thought," it is argued that believing cannot be a relation to formulae in a language of thought. The case against that view is overdetermined, but one problem made much of in this chapter is that (a) it does not appear possible to obtain a correct naturalistic account of what determines the truth conditions of Mentalese formulae, and (b) without such a naturalistic account the hypothesis that believing is a relation to neural sentences has no credibility. Of course it is made clear that in rejecting mental representations as the objects of belief one is not thereby rejecting the empirical hypothesis that the brain is an information processor and thus processes in a neural machine language. Since propositional attitudes are relations neither to propositions nor to mental representations, the end of this chapter also concludes that IBS cannot be correct if the relational theory of propositional attitudes is.

At this point we know that if the relational theory of propositional attitudes is correct, then believing is a relation to a sentence or utterance of a public language, and it is the meaning of the sentence or utterance that determines the content of any belief having that sentence or utterance as its object. In chapter 5, "Sententialist Theories of Belief," it is argued that no sententialist theory of belief can be correct. It is also argued, as a corollary to the main argument, that no extensionalist account of compositional semantics can be correct. Much of this chapter focuses on Davidson's paratactic theory of propositional-attitude ascriptions.

At the end of this chapter it is clear that the relational theory of propositional attitudes is false, if what has gone before is correct. The falsity of the relational theory, we have already noticed, threatens the hypothesis that every natural language has a correct compositional semantics, and this is the topic of chapter 7. The next chapter deals with the by now evident falsity of physicalism.

Chapter 6, "Ontological Physicalism and Sentential Dualism," begins with the realization that the physicalism of the eighth of the initial hypotheses cannot be correct: if it is a fact that I believe that worms do not have noses, then that fact is not one statable in nonmentalistic and nonintentional terms. But what is our hero now to do? Is he to accept eliminativism and deny that we have beliefs with content and words with meaning, or, even worse, to renounce the scruples of the natural scientist and "just surface listlessly to the Sargasso Sea of mentalism" (Quine 1975, p. 91)? Neither, I maintain: we can find a way between eliminativism and dualism by denying the existence of genuinely objective, language-independent belief properties (believing that such and such, being a belief that such and such) and facts. This nominalism then allows one to embrace both Ontological Physicalism, the thesis that there are no extralinguistic irreducibly psychological entities of any ontological category, and Sentential Dualism, the thesis that there are true but irreducible belief-ascribing sentences. In arguing for this solution to the mind-body problem, "token-token physicalism" (the sixth of the initial hypotheses) is tentatively accepted, and the solution is brought to bear on, and to solve, the paradox Kripke (1982) has located in the work of Wittgenstein.

In chapter 7, "Compositional Semantics and Language Understanding," I turn to a tension that has existed since the conclusion of chapter 5. On the one hand, it would appear that if, as many suppose, natural languages have compositional truth-theoretic semantics, then the relational theory of propositional attitudes must be correct; while, on the other hand, I have argued that the relational theory is false. I must therefore deny that the relational construal of 'believes' is required by its accommodation within a compositional semantics, or else deny that natural languages have compositional semantics. I opt for the latter course. I do not think that there is any better way of treating propositional-attitude verbs in compositional semantics, but argue in this chapter that the reason usually given for supposing that natural languages have compositional semantics—viz., that it would not otherwise be possible to explain language understanding (the fourth of the initial hypotheses)—is not a good reason. I describe a possible world in which a certain person, Harvey, understands spoken English, but in which, thanks to the "conceptual roles" of certain expressions in his neural *lingua mentis*, the complete explanation of his language understanding ability does not presuppose that the language he understands has a compositional semantics.

Chapter 8, "Compositional Semantics, Meaning Theories, and Ontology," is a continuation of the preceding chapter, and in it the following two questions are considered. First, let it be granted that compositional semantics is not needed to explain language understanding. Might it not be needed for some other reason—say, just to explain how the semantic features of a sentence depend on those of its parts? Second, let it be granted that natural languages do not have compositional truth-theoretic semantics. Might they not nevertheless have finitely statable meaning theories that are not compositional truth-theoretic semantics, a meaning theory for a particular language being a theory that "explicitly states something knowledge of which would suffice for interpreting utterances of speakers of the language to which it applies" (Davidson 1976, p. 171)? Both questions are answered negatively, and a lengthy discussion of Michael Dummett's anti-realism and verificationist semantics figures into the discussion of the second. In the chapter's last section an important connection is forged between my nominalism and my denial of compositional semantics.

In chapter 9, "Intention-Based Semantics and the Analysis of Meaning," I return to that which, in its way, began this whole discussion. After reviewing the nature of the IBS program and problems with its account of speaker-meaning, I try to explain its failure to account for expression-meaning, the meaning of marks and sounds. It turns out that not only does an IBS account of expression-meaning presuppose semantic compositionality and the relational theory of propositional attitudes, but it also presupposes that understanding utterances is an inferential process of a certain dubious sort. It is this last presupposition that requires the IBS account of expression-meaning to require language users to have propositional knowledge which they seem pretty clearly not to have. In the end the whole business of "analysis" is disparaged.

Now the patient reader wants to know what my theory of meaning and intentionality is. What is the correct, positive theory of meaning and content that is to take the place of those against which I have argued? In chapter 10, "The No-Theory Theory of Meaning," I give my answer: There is none. Given the conclusions already reached in this book, there is nothing (at least nothing that has not already been given) that could *count as* a correct theory of meaning or content. The questions that now define the philosophy of language have false presuppositions. The no-theory theory of meaning is not a defeatist program; I am less certain if it is not despairing.

Remnants of Meaning

Chapter 1

Starting Points: The Semantic, the Psychological, and the Physical

---

1.1 Introduction

There are four things that I hope to do in this book. I want to begin by listing all of the facts about language and thought which, in a philosophical study of them, may be taken as uncontroversial starting points. Then I want to describe certain hypotheses that many are inclined to find supported by this firm foundation; next, to argue that most of these hypotheses are not supportable; and finally, of course, to give the true theory of linguistic and mental representation.

1.2 The Bedrock Data

Here are those facts whose sum total may be taken as our uncontroversial starting point in the proper study of language and thought: we humans have noise- and mark-making proclivities, and, like earthworms and flounders, we survive for some finite period of time in the environments into which we are born.

1.3 Some Widely Held Hypotheses

Mme S, confronting M. A, utters the sequence of sounds

[*]   Monsieur, votre fille a mordu mon singe.

Given relevant background information, many, perhaps most, philosophers of language and mind would be willing to subscribe to the following hypotheses pertaining to, or encompassing, this incident—hypotheses, it should be said, formulated now with only that degree of precision appropriate to a first chapter.

1. The first hypothesis is that *there are semantic facts*: the sequence [*] and certain of its parts have semantic features. For example:

   a. [*] is a sentence of a natural language which *means* that the hearer's daughter bit the speaker's monkey.

b. In uttering [∗] S *said that* A's daughter bit her, S's, monkey.

c. Consequently, what she said, and so the utterance of [∗], is *true* just in case the girl bit the monkey.

d. The occurrences of 'votre fille' and 'mon singe' in the utterance of [∗] *refer* respectively to a certain girl and a certain monkey.

e. The sequence 'a mordu' *applies to*, or *is true of*, a pair of things just in case the first bit the second.

Someone who accepts (a)–(e), but is impressed with the fact that noises merely qua noises do not have any semantic features, may be tempted to ask, What makes it the case that [∗] means what it does? By virtue of what does any mark or sound, or sequence of them, come to have a given meaning? What makes it the case that an utterance of 'mon singe' refers to a certain monkey, or, for that matter, that 'Ronald Reagan' refers to Ronald Reagan? Someone who is inclined to ask such questions most likely supposes, however tacitly, that these semantic facts cannot be brute, primitive, irreducible facts but must *somehow* be explicable in terms of more basic facts, facts that are statable in a nonsemantic idiom but determine all of the semantic facts there are.

Quine, in his Indeterminacy Thesis, has denied that there is any determination of the semantic by more basic facts and has looked sourly on the semantic because of that.[1] This notwithstanding, the philosophical literature of this century is replete with attempts to answer the foregoing sorts of questions. Whether this is a legitimate or worthwhile enterprise is another matter, one to which I shall return.

2. Quite likely [∗] was a *novel* sentence both for Mme S and for M. A; that is to say, a sentence neither of them had encountered before its spontaneous utterance by Mme S. Yet they both understood the sentence and S's utterance of it. Now, in encountering a novel but understood sentence, one is being confronted not with novel words but with familiar words put together, via familiar constructions, in a novel way. This strongly suggests that there can be no explaining one's mastery of a natural language independently of the specification of compositional mechanisms that generate the meanings of complex expressions out of the meanings of simpler ones.

It suggests, moreover, a second hypothesis held by most philosophers of language, that *every natural language has a compositional meaning theory*— a compositional meaning theory for a language L being a finitely statable theory of L which specifies the meanings of all the primitive vocabulary in L and specifies compositional rules showing how these meanings determine the meanings of the infinitely many complex expressions in L.

Writing in 1967, Donald Davidson observed what can still be observed today:

> It is conceded by most philosophers of language ... that a satisfactory theory of meaning must give an account of how the meanings of sentences depend upon the meanings of words. Unless such an account could be supplied for a particular language ... there would be no explaining the fact that we can learn the language: no explaining the fact that, on mastering a finite vocabulary and a finitely stated set of rules, we are prepared to produce and to understand any of a potential infinitude of sentences. (1967a, p. 17)

Davidson went on in that celebrated article to make his famous proposal about the form that such a theory should take. That proposal has had a tremendous impact, but an impact less than that of the question he raised. I think it is fair to say that the single most dominant topic in the philosophy of language for at least fifteen years following the appearance of Davidson's seminal article was the form that a compositional meaning theory for a particular language should take. If that question no longer engages philosophers of language in quite the way it used to, it is not because the question has been answered.

3. Pending clarification of what meanings are supposed to be, the foregoing characterization of a meaning theory is pretty vague. But of course that is as it should be, for the question of how 'meaning' is to be understood in this context just is the hotly debated question of the form that a theory of meaning for a particular language should take. Still, there is a further assumption shared by most philosophers of language that would constrain a little the possible answers to these questions. This further hypothesis is that, whatever form a meaning theory for a natural language L takes, it must at least yield a determination of the *truth conditions* for utterances in L that have truth conditions. After all, it is a fact about the *meaning* of [*] that an utterance of it would be true just in case the hearer's daughter bit the speaker's monkey; furthermore, in order to understand an utterance of [*] one would have to know that the speaker said that his or her indicated monkey was bitten by the hearer's indicated daughter, and that, therefore, what was said, and so the utterance of [*], is true just in case the girl bit the monkey. In other words: To understand a language is to have the ability to understand utterances in it; and to understand an utterance in the assertive mode is to know that it is true provided that such and such is the case, where what the speaker said in the utterance was precisely that such and such was the case. All this, it is commonly held, does motivate the assumption that a meaning theory for L must also be, in the sense indicated, a truth theory for L.

Thus, the third widely held hypothesis is that *every correct compositional meaning theory for a language L is also a compositional truth-theoretic semantics for L.* Here it is possible to be precise, but we may say that a correct compositional truth-theoretic semantics for a language L is a finitely statable theory that ascribes properties to the finitely many words and expression-forming operations of L in such a way as to determine, for each of the infinitely many sentences of L that can be used to say something true or false, the condition, or conditions, under which an utterance of that sentence would be true.[2]

This characterization does not entail that a compositional truth-theoretic semantics for L will be a meaning theory for L, but a meaning theory for L may well be at least a compositional truth-theoretic semantics for L (and more); and the present hypothesis, in maintaining that a correct meaning theory for a language will be, inter alia, a compositional truth-theoretic semantics, voices the sentiment of the many for whom "semantics with no treatment of truth conditions is not semantics" (Lewis 1970b, p. 190).

Of course, from the fact (if it is one) that a compositional meaning theory must also be a compositional truth-theoretic semantics, nothing very specific follows about the form that such a theory would have to take. In particular, this hypothesis by no means endorses Davidson's suggestion that a meaning theory for L should take the form of an extensional, finitely axiomatized theory of truth for L in the style of Tarski, somehow relativized to utterances of sentences. Indeed, for all that has so far been said, the required compositional truth-theoretic semantics might directly take the form of a recursive axiomatization of the Gricean facts about the sentences of the language used by a given population (see Davies 1984).

4. There is, evidently, an important connection between the theory of meaning and the theory of language understanding. For Michael Dummett, a theory of meaning *is* a theory of understanding,[3] although his understanding of the theory of understanding may be less than transparent. Davidson believes that every natural language has a compositional truth-theoretic semantics because he believes that otherwise there would be no explaining the fact that we can learn those languages, and he has written that "the main, if not the only, ultimate concern of philosophy of language is the understanding of natural languages" (1973a, p. 71). Others in the Davidsonian tradition have also expressed a keen appreciation of the connection between meaning and understanding:

> However elaborate its philosophical ramifications, however lofty its ontological representation, meaning resides in just those facts about a language which its mastery implicitly recognizes. (Foster 1976, p. 1)

Any philosophy of language must exhibit the central role of meaning, and that notion critically interacts with that of *understanding*. The meaning of an expression in a language is what a competent speaker of the language understands by that expression.... [A]ny theory of meaning must be assessed for the plausibility of the account it issues in of speakers' understanding. (Platts 1979, p. 43)

It is, I have said, widely believed among philosophers of language that every natural language has a compositional truth-theoretic semantics. Later it will be clear that there is more than one conceivable reason for thinking that natural languages require such semantics. But it is also clear that virtually the only reason to be discerned in the literature for this supposition is the belief, shared by Frege,[4] Davidson, and numerous others, that

[U]   It would not be possible to account for a human's ability to understand utterances of indefinitely many novel sentences of a language without the assumption that that language had a compositional truth-theoretic semantics.

This is the fourth of the widely held hypotheses I am in the midst of listing.

We have already informally glossed some motivation for supposing [U]: to understand a language is to have the finitely based ability to understand a potential infinitude of utterances in it, and to understand an utterance is to know what speech acts, with what truth conditions, were performed in it. But what exactly does [U] require? That is to ask, how would a compositional truth-theoretic semantics for *L* figure into the theory of understanding *L* if it were to be indispensable to it?

Mme S utters the sentence [*]. M. A hears S's utterance of [*] and, even though he has never before encountered [*], instantaneously forms the correct belief that S, in uttering [*], said that A's daughter had bitten S's monkey, and that, therefore, what she said, and thus her utterance of [*], is true provided that his daughter did bite that monkey. In the event, A understands, or knows the meaning of, [*], understands S's utterance of [*], and manifests his understanding of the language to which [*] belongs. A theory of A's understanding of that language would be at least a theory of A's language *processing*: it would be a theory that explains how A can go from

[1]   his auditory perception of S's utterance of [*]

to

[2]   his belief that S said that her monkey was bitten by A's daughter, and thus what she said, and so her utterance, is true just in case his daughter did bite the monkey.

Evidently, if [U] is correct, then a compositional semantics for French would have to enter into the complete account of this processing. But how? Few theorists who have endorsed [U] have paused to speculate on this,[5] but the following is the beginning of an obvious first thought.

The process that begins with [1], A's auditory perception of S's utterance, and terminates with [2], his belief about what S said in that utterance, is mediated by a sequence of internal states, some of which will be representational states—states that represent external states of affairs—although only some of these states need be thought of as actual belief states.[6] What [U] suggests is that some of these states represent segments of S's utterance as having certain semantic properties, and that, on the basis of this, and in accordance with a certain compositional truth-theoretic semantics for French, some state later in the comprehension sequence represents S's entire sound sequence, the utterance of [∗], as having a certain semantic property. This representation may then be thought of as interacting with other states representing, inter alia, S as having certain intentions that determine references for indexical elements in [∗], to produce in A the belief state that represents S as having said what she said. Theorists may at this point be expected to differ on the further, empirical question of whether the compositional semantics for French already adverted to will itself be internally represented or whether it is merely needed to describe the algorithms followed by the transformations among A's inner representational states.

Naturally this is the barest sketch. Just to begin, one wants to be told the nature of the "semantic properties" ascribed to the smallest semantical units discerned in [∗], and the form that the compositional semantics which ascribes them will take. Nonetheless, the language-processing picture implicit in [U] has exercised a strong grip on the philosophical imagination of the past couple of decades. Later I shall try to loosen this grip.

5. A fifth hypothesis is that *humans have beliefs (and other propositional attitudes) with content*. Thus, Mme S, in uttering [∗], was, we may suppose, giving voice to her belief *that her monkey had been bitten by A's daughter*. No doubt she also believes that De Gaulle is dead, and that at least some snow is white. There would appear to be many such psychological facts.

6. Given that S consciously believes that the girl bit S's monkey, most philosophers would agree that *there is some internal state of S's—in particular, some neural state-token*[7]—*that is that belief*. Let n be the neural state-token that happens to be Mme S's present belief that the girl bit the monkey. Someone who accepts that n is that belief, and is impressed with the fact that neural states qua neural states do not have any psychological or intentional features, is apt to raise two questions, and to feel that there

have *got* to be answers to them:

What makes *n* a belief?

What makes *n* a belief *that the girl bit the monkey*?

Someone who is inclined to ask these questions most likely supposes, however tacitly, that the fact that the *neural* state *n* happens to be a belief, let alone a belief that a certain child bit a certain monkey, cannot be a brute, primitive, irreducible fact but must *somehow* be one that is explicable in terms of more basic facts, facts that are statable in a nonmentalistic and nonintentional idiom but determine all of the psychological facts there are.

Quine, recognizing the application of his Indeterminacy Thesis to propositional attitudes, has denied that there is any determination of the psychological by more basic facts, and has taken such a skeptical view of propositional attitudes because of this as to propose that the canonical scheme for those concerned to limn "the true and ultimate structure of reality" should be "the austere scheme that knows ... no propositional attitudes but only the physical constitution and behavior of organisms" (1960, p. 221). This notwithstanding, the philosophical literature of this century is replete with attempts to answer the foregoing sorts of questions. Whether this is a legitimate or worthwhile enterprise, and whether, if it is not legitimate, we should share Quine's skepticism, are other matters, ones to which we shall later return.

7. A seventh widely held hypothesis is one I shall call *the relational theory of propositional attitudes*. Stated with respect to believing, it is, nearly enough, the hypothesis that believing is a relation to things believed, to values of the variable '*y*' in the schema '*x* believes *y*', to things having truth-valuational properties that determine the truth-valuational properties of beliefs. My present belief that snow is white is true, this hypothesis has it, just in case what I believe—the referent of the singular term 'that snow is white'—is true.[8] Needless to say, the big question for those who accept this hypothesis is, What are these "things believed," and how are we to account for their semantic—that is, truth-theoretic—properties?

Why suppose that the relational hypothesis is true? The classical answer, which derives from Frege (1892), is alluded to in a nicely confident proclamation from Tyler Burge:

The most elementary point about the semantics of sentences about propositional attitudes is that such sentences have the form of a *relational* propositional-attitude predicate with singular argument places for at least a subject (e.g., a person) and something believed (thought, desired, intended, said). This latter ... is, with some qualification, the semantical value of the grammatical object of the propositional-attitude verb. (Burge 1980)

Suppose one takes it for granted that a natural language such as English has a compositional truth-theoretic semantics. Then it may well seem to be an "elementary point about the semantics of sentences about propositional attitudes" that propositional-attitude verbs are *relational predicates*. For if σ is any well-formed indicative sentence of English, then ⌜believes that σ⌝ is a well-formed predicate phrase. Since there are infinitely many such predicate phrases, no compositional truth-theoretic semantics, being finitely statable, can treat them as semantically primitive. A compositional truth-theoretic semantics must therefore treat 'believes' (or 'believes that') as semantically primitive; and it is arguable that the only tenable way this can be done is to treat 'believes' as a relational predicate; that is, as a predicate with argument places for singular terms. In a word, the classical motivation for the relational theory of propositional attitudes is just that the relational construal of propositional-attitude verbs is the only feasible construal of them *relative to the assumption that natural languages have compositional truth-theoretic semantics.*[9]

If the relational theory of propositional attitudes is correct, then one should expect what indeed are familiar grammatical and logical facts: quantifier expressions and paradigm singular terms can occur as grammatical complements of 'believes', as in 'believes everything that Harry says' and 'believes your theory', and inferences such as the following are patently valid:

Alfred and Donald both believe that snow is white.
So there is something which they both believe.

But can one reverse the last conditional and argue that these familiar facts prove the relational theory of propositional attitudes? That would be precipitate. For one can infer the relational theory from the meaningfulness of quantified sentences such as

[i]   There is something which Alfred believes

only after it has been established that the quantification here ('there is something which') is to be read *objectually* rather than *substitutionally*. On the objectual reading, [i] is true just in case the open sentence 'Alfred believes *x*' is true of some *object*, and if this is the correct reading, then the relational theory of believing does indeed follow. On the substitutional reading, however, [i] is true just in case some *substitution-instance* of 'Alfred believes that *S*' (e.g., 'Alfred believes that snow is white') is true, and this does not imply the relational theory, for it is consistent with *any* account of the logical form of the substitution-instances that make the quantification true.[10] The only deep reason for preferring the relational theory of 'believes' is that it is needed to account for the logical form of sentences like 'Alfred believes that snow is white'.

My gloss of the relational theory has been relaxed, and if precision were now important, it would need to be qualified in several respects. In particular, proponents of the hypothesis that I suppose to be widely held are not *committed* to either of these claims:

(a)   That 'believes' is unambiguous and always dyadic.

Thus, a theorist who would represent

[1]   Ralph believes that God exists

as

   B(Ralph, the proposition that God exists)

might recognize a different, triadic belief relation at work in

[2]   Ralph believes that that dog has fleas,

to be represented as

   B'(Ralph, the property of having fleas, the relevant dog).

(Of course, this would not preclude the theorist from then seeking to reduce B' to B.)

(b)   That in sentences of the form 'x believes that σ', when 'believes' is functioning as a dyadic predicate, the sentence σ, or clause $\ulcorner$that $\sigma\urcorner$, always functions as a singular term whose referent is the thing which x is being said to believe.

One famous way of not being committed to this is Davidson's (1969) proposal, later to be scrutinized, that [1] is correctly paraphrased as

   Ralph believes that. God exists.

where 'that' is a demonstrative whose referent is the utterance of the sentence following it. A less exotic exception would be a theorist who would represent [2] as

   ($\exists m$)(m is a mode of presentation under which that dog is presented to Ralph & B(Ralph, the proposition that m has fleas)),

that proposition being one that is true, at least in the actual world, just in case that dog has fleas.[11] On this way of representing [2], the 'that'-clause, 'that that dog has fleas', is not itself a singular term which refers to what Ralph believes, but rather provides an *indirect* and *partial* characterization of what he believes.

Still, notwithstanding these qualifications, my rough initial statement of the relational theory is not too far from the mark. For, as will become clear as we proceed, every relational theorist maintains that for each belief which has content, there is some entity (which may itself be a sequence of entities) whose properties determine the complete content of that belief; and the most interesting respect in which relational theorists may differ is in what they take those entities to be—propositions, sentences, mental representations, or whatever. There is much more that will be said on these matters.

1.4 Some Less Widely Held Hypotheses

Philosophers holding the following hypotheses may be taken, at least provisionally, also to hold the hypotheses of the preceding section, and the overall position defined by all these hypotheses will be what is put to the test in the first part of this book.

8. Earlier hypotheses recognized the existence of semantic and psychological facts. This eighth hypothesis is that *these semantic and psychological facts are not irreducibly semantic or psychological but can be revealed to be facts statable by sentences devoid of semantic or psychological terms; and if these facts, like functional facts, are not themselves physical facts, then they, like functional facts again, are at least realized by physical facts.*

This assumption, which goes beyond hypothesis 6 in its insistence that there is *nothing* that is irreducibly mental, need reflect no confidence in the enterprise known as conceptual analysis, but merely the inability to accept that semantic and psychological properties, being irreducible, are primitive and inexplicable. The sentiment here is that, surely, somewhere down the line such facts must cash out into a basis of physical facts that determine all of the semantic and psychological facts there are. Clearly, the feeling is, the fact that, say, 'Saul Kripke' refers to Saul Kripke cannot be accepted as a brute, primitive, irreducible fact; surely that thought violates those physicalistic scruples which ought to guide any rational inquiry into our nature and that of the world we inhabit. This conviction even leads some to urge that one should not undertake to maintain that there *are* semantic or psychological facts unless one is prepared to maintain that such facts are reducible to physical facts.

There is more than one way of trying to motivate a reduction of semantic and psychological properties to properties specifiable in an untainted idiom, and some of these will be the topic of later discussion; but it may be worth noticing now how easily a reductionist stance is insinuated by what may well seem to be the most reasonable response to questions already raised. The sequence of marks [∗] means that, and is true just in case, the hearer's daughter bit the speaker's monkey; and some neural state-token n is Mme S's present belief that her monkey was bitten by A's daughter. Acceptance of this generates the questions

What makes it the case that [∗] means what it does?

What makes it the case that n is a belief that the girl bit the monkey?

Evidently, these are genuine questions; they have answers. One possible answer, looking just at the second question, is that nothing makes it the case that n is a belief that the girl bit the monkey other than its simply being the case that n has the primitive and irreducible property of being a belief that that particular girl bit that particular monkey. Perhaps having that property necessitates having certain other properties, but having those other properties cannot itself account for what makes it the case that n is a belief that the girl bit the monkey.

This answer may strike one as not merely obscurantist but magical: it makes n's being a belief that the girl bit the monkey nothing short of magical. One may reasonably feel that the only nonmagical, naturalistically respectable response to the question is to suppose that there must be naturalistic facts—facts, no doubt, detailing head-world causal relations and n's potential to control behavior—that make it the case that n is a belief with the content it has. This must mean that n has certain naturalistic properties which constitute its being a belief that that particular girl bit that particular monkey, and no one who accepts this can coherently deny the adumbrated reductionist hypothesis.

(I sympathize with the reader who is impatient for clarification of the key notions being bandied, and ask her or him not to despair of eventual relief.)

9. *The Gricean program, Intention-Based Semantics (IBS), is essentially correct, and the semantic reduces to the psychological in the style of that program.* Up to now we have in effect been imagining a philosopher who begins with the conviction that there are semantic and psychological facts only if they are physicalistically reducible, and with the belief that there are semantic and psychological facts. This philosopher, in wondering how the semantic and the psychological reduce to the physical, faces a prior question: How is the semantic related to the psychological? Many, especially nowadays, who are drawn to the Gricean program IBS are attracted to it because they are inclined to suppose, first, that the only feasible reduction of the semantic and the psychological to the physical is via the reduction of the semantic to the psychological, and, second, that the Gricean program is the only feasible program for reducing the semantic to the psychological.[12]

The essence of IBS is that it takes a certain notion of communication, or speaker-meaning, to be foundational in the theory of meaning by (1) defining it, without reference to anything semantic, in terms of acting with the intention of producing belief or action in another, and then (2) defining all other public-language semantic notions—sentence and word meaning, reference, and so on—in terms of the reduced notion of speaker-meaning.[13]

Thus, the IBS theorist's reductionist enterprise consists of two stages. In the first stage he seeks to identify speaker-meaning—a person's meaning that such-and-such, or that so-and-so is to do such-and-such—with a species of intentional behavior that does not itself presuppose any of the semantic concepts in question. Here one will find the theorist offering a completion of the schema

> In uttering x, S means that p iff, for some A, S utters x intending in way ... to activate in A the belief that p

that not only is free of any overt presupposition of public-language semantic notions but provides as well a suitable basis for the definitions in terms of it of the various concepts of expression-meaning, the meanings of marks and sounds.

In the second stage the theorist seeks to define the meaning of linguistic items in terms of speaker-meaning, thereby completing the reduction of the semantic to the psychological. Here the theorist will avail himself of an ancillary concept of *convention*, itself already defined, in wholly nonsemantic terms, as various kinds of self-perpetuating regularities in behavior (see Lewis 1969, 1975; Schiffer 1972, 1982). With this in hand he will then attempt to define a sentence σ's meaning q in a population P in terms of there prevailing in P a certain type of conventional correlation between the utterance-type σ and the act-type of meaning that q, a correlation that will render uttering σ an especially efficacious device in P for meaning that q. Perhaps as a crude first shot the theorist will suggest that

> Utterance-type σ means q in population P iff there prevails in P a system of conventions conformity to which requires one not to utter σ unless one means thereby that q.

Then the meanings of words and syntactic formations would be explained in terms of their contributions, as determined by the system of conventions, to the meanings of the sentences in which they occur. This system of conventions may itself be identified with the language of the population P, and we should expect the main effort of the IBS theorist to be directed toward a detailed account of the sort of system of conventions that must obtain in a population in order for the population to have a natural language with the richness of ours. In the end, the theorist will have offered his own detailed account of the form that a meaning theory for a particular language should take. However, no such detailed account has yet been offered by any IBS theorist, and later I shall try to show why.

I have said that IBS is a reductionist program: it seeks to *reduce* the semantic to the psychological. For this it is not enough that semantic notions be correctly defined in terms of belief and intention. It is also required that the explication of belief and intention does not in its turn require reference to the very semantic notions that the IBS theorist is attempting to reduce to them; otherwise the IBS project would spin for eternity in a vicious circle.

Now the IBS theorist has been represented as holding the relational theory of propositional attitudes: 'p' in his definitions, as in his construal of the schema 'x believes p', is an *objectual* variable, its values the things believed, intended, and meant. (Later we shall inquire whether IBS can be divorced from the relational theory of propositional attitudes—and find that it cannot be; but for now I can best illuminate the way IBS constrains the theory of propositional-attitude content by taking IBS in tandem with the relational theory.) Consequently there are two places in the explication of belief where the IBS theorist's reductionist hopes might be frustrated.

First, it might be that 'p' ranges over sentences or utterances and that it is precisely the *meaning* of these sentences or utterances that determines the content of the beliefs which are relations to these linguistic items. The IBS theorist owes an account of believing which shows that it is not a relation to sentences or utterances that obtains by virtue of their public-language semantic features.

Second, it might be that even if the objects of belief are wholly language-independent entities, the belief relation that obtains between believers and those objects can only be understood in tandem with meaning relations that obtain between the believer's words and the meanings they express. The IBS theorist owes an account of the belief relation that shows it not to presuppose *any* public-language semantic concepts.

It is the first possibility that is the most respected in the IBS tradition, the feeling being that the belief relation will provide no further threat once it is shown that the content-determining features of the objects of belief are not public-language semantic features. It is important that we see just what theories of the objects of belief can cohere with the reductionist program of Intention-Based Semantics.

1.5 Intention-Based Semantics and the Possible Objects of Belief

Beliefs have *content*: one of Mme S's beliefs is *that her monkey was bitten by M. A's daughter*. Part of what is involved in a belief's having content is its having semantic properties—in particular, truth-valuational properties: perhaps Mme S's belief is *true*.

According to the relational theory of propositional attitudes, believing is a relation to objects of beliefs, values, so to say, of the "propositional" variable 'p' in the schema 'x believes p', and the semantic properties of beliefs are determined by semantic properties of these belief objects: Mme S's belief is true just in case what she believes is true.

IBS constrains the nature of the semantic features of belief objects: the content-determining semantic properties of the objects of belief must not, on pain (to the IBS theorist) of circularity, be public-language semantic properties. It will be useful, then, explicitly to distinguish between

> *non*–public-language semantic properties, which do *not* entail meaning in a public, communicative language,

and

> *public-language* semantic properties, which, of course, do have that entailment.

We then know that

> IBS is true only if the semantic properties of belief objects that determine the semantic properties of beliefs are *non*–public-language semantic properties.

It is time we asked, presupposing the correctness of the relational theory of belief, what the objects of belief might be and how these candidates fare with respect to the IBS constraint.

As regards the possible objects of belief, we get, at the most general level of abstraction, what, simplifying only a little, would appear to be an exhaustive and exclusive division into *propositionalist* and *sententialist* theories of belief. *Either* belief objects

(a)   *are* contents—propositions of one kind or another, abstract, objective, language-independent entities that have essentially the truth conditions they have,

or else they

(b)   are things that *have* content—sentences (or possible utterances of them), either of a public language or of an inner language of thought—things that only contingently have the truth conditions they happen to have.

The propositional theory is prima facie very appealing to the IBS theorist. Not only are the semantic properties of propositions clearly non–public-language semantic properties, but, as propositions are contents, no further theory of content is needed for them: because they are things that are represented, and not themselves representations, one needs no theory of their contingent representational features—they do not have any.

Sententialist theories of belief may be divided into those that are compatible with IBS and those that are not. To the latter belong the famous theories of Carnap (1947) and Davidson (1969), for they take believing to

be a relation to a public-language sentence or utterance—of the belief
ascriber's language, for Davidson; of the believer's language, for Carnap—
and they take the content-determining semantic properties of those sentences or utterances to be their public-language semantic properties.

Brian Loar (1981) has elaborated an ingenious theory according to which
belief is a relation to a sentence in the belief ascriber's language, but in
which the content-determining semantic features of the sentence are not its
public-language semantic features but ones defined in the style of Tarski.[14]
Loar's view, however, requires that beliefs be individuated on the basis of
interpersonally ascribable functional states, and, as I shall argue in the next
chapter, it is doubtful that this can be done.

This leaves as the only sententialist theory compatible with IBS the
topical hypothesis that believing is a relation to a mental representation, a
"sentence" in one's neural "language of thought." The plan here is to
reduce à la IBS the contents of marks and sounds (i.e., public-language
semantic features) to the contents of mental states (i.e., their intentional
features, ones ascribed in 'that'-clauses) and then to reduce the contents of
mental states to the non—public-language semantic properties of the mental
representations which realize those mental states. But the non—public-
language semantic properties of formulae in the inner code are contingent
properties of them, and they require a substantial theory, one that tells us,
especially, what determines the truth conditions of sentences in the language of thought.

So we may imagine a theorist who accepts the widely and less widely
held hypotheses of 1.3 and 1.4. He believes, qua theorist of IBS, that the
semantic reduces to the psychological, that all questions about meaning
or reference in a public language are really, at root, questions about
belief, desire, and intention. This theorist has incurred a clamorous debt: to
produce a correct theory of belief and the other propositional attitudes
that is consonant with the reduction to them of public-language semantic
properties. But the task of explicating belief is to be guided by a further,
physicalist constraint, a constraint that underlies and motivates his adherence
to the IBS program: facts statable by belief-ascribing sentences must be
revealed to be facts also statable by sentences devoid of psychological or
intentional terms. Nothing is to be countenanced that is irreducibly mental;
belief states, types as well as tokens, must be shown to be identical to states
that are intrinsically specifiable in a nonmentalistic, nonintentional idiom.
Where n is a belief that p, for any p, it must be possible to show that there
is a physicalistically respectable fact that makes it the case that n is a belief
that p.

The imagined theorist is also a relationalist as regards belief: that Mme
S can be correctly described as believing that her monkey was bitten by

M. A's daughter is a matter of her standing in the belief relation to some object with features, some of them truth-theoretic, that makes that belief ascription true. These semantic, content-determining features of belief objects must be non–public-language semantic features if the theorist's attempt to reduce the semantic features of marks and sounds to the intentional, or representational, features of beliefs is to succeed. That means (*pace* Loar) that he must choose between mental representations, formulae in the believer's *lingua mentis,* and propositions, of one stripe or another, as the proper objects of belief.[15]

If the theorist maintains that believing is a relation to sentences in a language of thought, then—after getting clear about what exactly that should be taken to mean[16]—he has these tasks:

1. To say what features of inner formulae are determinative of belief content. "Conceptual roles" and referential, truth-theoretic properties are likely candidates here.

2. To show that those of these features that are semantic—namely, the referential, truth-theoretic ones—are non–public-language semantic features.

3. To show that these content-determining features, and thus the intentional features of beliefs, are amenable to naturalistic explication in a way that satisfies the theorist's physicalist constraint. This will amount, we shall see, to showing how physical facts can determine the truth conditions of the infinity of formulae in the inner system of mental representation.

4. To show that there is some physical, or functional, or computational relation—that is, some relation intrinsically specifiable in nonmentalistic terms—to formulae of the neural code that *is* the belief relation.

If, on the other hand, the theorist maintains that believing is a relation to propositions, things that *are* contents, then his major tasks will be these:

1. To say what exactly he takes propositions to be—sets of possible worlds, say, or perhaps finer-grained, structured abstract entities[17]—and how truth and falsity are to be defined for them. (However, as propositions are wholly language-independent and have their truth conditions essentially—the proposition that snow is white, unlike the sequence of marks 'snow is white', has its truth condition in every possible world—the theorist will not have to allay the fear that the semantic properties of propositions are public-language semantic properties.)

2. To show that that relation between persons and propositions that is the belief relation can be revealed to be a relation intrinsically specifiable in functional, or other physicalistically reputable, terms.

In the next chapter I give reason to doubt that the propositionalist can achieve task 2, and in the chapter after that I argue that, quite apart from any need to conform to naturalistic scruples, belief cannot be a relation to propositions. In chapter 4 I try to show that the prospects are at least as dim for the mental representation hypothesis, thus, it would seem, leaving the IBS theorist without a theory of belief that is consistent with his program, and thus without a program. Subsequent chapters are equally uncharitable to other points of view.

Chapter 2
Functionalism and Propositions

2.1 Introduction

The theorist defined by the nine hypotheses of chapter 1 holds the relational theory of belief, and therefore needs to say what the objects of belief are. He also subscribes to IBS, and so must say what the objects of belief are in a way that does not imply that their content-determining features are public-language semantic features. This theorist will therefore have some attraction to the view that believing is a relation to propositions, that they are the values of 'y' in the schema 'x believes y'. But he is also a physicalist, and if he holds that believing is a relation to propositions, then he must show that that relation is identical to a relation that is intrinsically specifiable in nonmentalistic and nonintentional terms.

Now the functionalist claims that what makes a physical state-token a belief that such-and-such is its being a token of a physical state-type that has a certain functional role. And Brian Loar has shown that the way to combine this with the idea that believing is a relation to propositions is to construe believing as a function (in the set-theoretic sense) that maps propositions onto internal physical states having functional roles indexed by those propositions in ways determined by some psychological theory in which belief, desire, and so on are theoretical constructs (Loar 1981). Most of this chapter is about this functionalist way of reconciling the view that believing is a relation to propositions with physicalism, that is, the physicalism of the eighth of the widely held hypotheses of the preceding chapter.

The next section is concerned with certain preliminaries; then 2.3 sets up the form of a functionalist account of belief, when believing is taken to be a relation to propositions. This form requires the belief relation to be functionally defined via its role in some psychological theory, and the propositional-functionalist must say what that theory is. Sections 2.4, "Commonsense Functionalism," and 2.5, "Psychofunctionalism," explore the possibilities, and conclude that neither works. The last section asks where in logical space the erstwhile propositional-functionalist might move to next.

2.2 *Functional Roles and Functional Properties*

There are three mind-body problems.

The first concerns the nature of *minds*, things satisfying open sentences like

[1] x is in pain
[2] x believes that God is good.

The *dualist* with respect to minds joins with Descartes in claiming that no mind satisfies any physical predicate which, like 'x weighs 117 pounds', entails being an occupier of space. One way of being an *antidualist* with respect to minds is to be an eliminativist with respect to the mental and thus to claim that as nothing satisfies mental predicates like [1] and [2], there are no minds. The more common way of being an antidualist is to claim that minds are also occupiers of space.

The second mind-body problem concerns the nature of *mental state* (event, process) *tokens*, datable occurrences satisfying open sentences like

[3] x is a pain
[4] x is a belief that God is good.

The dualist with respect to pains, beliefs, desires, and all other mental state-tokens claims that no mental state-token is identical to any other kind of state-token; in particular, not identical to any physical state-token, to something that satisfies an open sentence like

   x is an instance of blah-blah pattern of neural activity.

The antidualist with respect to mental state-tokens who is not an eliminativist about them will insist that mental state-tokens are physical state-tokens and that in human beings, at least, pains and beliefs are states of the nervous system.

The third mind-body problem concerns the nature of *mental properties*, properties expressed by open sentences like [1]–[4] (the properties expressed by [3] and [4] are mental state-*types*). The dualist here claims that these properties are irreducibly mental and thus not identifiable with properties expressed by predicates devoid of mental terms. This is precisely what is denied by the noneliminativist antidualist about properties. Forty years ago this antidualist argued that mental properties were identical to certain kinds of behavioral properties, namely, dispositions to behave in certain ways; but it proved difficult to say in behavioral terms what those ways were. Twenty years ago he argued that mental properties were physical properties, or, what comes to the same thing, that mental state-types were physical state-types. But this "type-type identity theory" was thought to founder on the phenomenon of multiple realization: surely we must not, by an identification of belief properties with neurophysiological properties, preclude machines from having beliefs, and it is not, we know, very plausible to suppose that the physical property that realizes pain in a person also realizes pain in a rat. Nowadays a noneliminativist antidualist about mental properties is most likely to claim that they are properties of a kind that I shall now call *functional properties*, using that expression in the broadest possible way.[1]

The notion of a functional property is to derive from that of a functional role.

A *functional role* is simply *any* second-level property of first-level state-types possession of which entails that the state-type possessing it is causally or counterfactually related in a certain way to other state-types, to outputs, to inputs, or to distal objects and their properties.[2] Thus, the property expressed by the following open sentence is a functional role:

> x is a first-level state-type such that one's being kicked causes x to be tokened in one, which in turn causes one to wince.

More apposite examples are much more difficult to give, for they will take the form of an open sentence

> Tx,

where substituends for the free variable 'x' will produce very complex *theories* about the behavior of very complex systems, such as computers, or even persons. Still, the very simple example illustrates two important features of all functional roles:

First, a given physical state-type can, and invariably will, have indefinitely many functional roles. This is just to say that a state-type can stand in numerous distinct causal (or transitional) relations to numerous other states or to outputs, inputs, and so on.

Second, two distinct physical state-types can have the same functional role: a state-type that figures in the etiology of my behavior can have a causal property that is also had by a different state-type that figures in the etiology of the behavior of a computer.

Now each functional role determines a unique *functional property*, viz., the property of having some property which has that functional role; since the properties which have functional roles are state-types, the functional property determined by a functional role is the property of being a token of a state-type which has that functional role. In other words, if F is a functional role, then the property expressed by the open sentence

> x is a token of some state-type which has F

is a functional property.

A few comments should prove useful.

a. A first-level physical state-type may be said *to realize a functional property* just in case it has the functional role determinative of that functional property. Then it follows that a functional property can be *multiply realized*: many different physical properties can realize the same functional property.

b. One reason why it is important clearly to distinguish functional properties and functional roles is that, as belief properties such as *being a belief that snow is white* are properties of state-tokens, they could not coherently be identified with functional roles, but only with functional properties.

c. I began this excursion into functional properties with the claim that contemporary noneliminativist antidualists about belief properties would identify them with functional properties, in the sense just explained. But of course this needs qualification, as it could only apply to those belief properties, like the one expressed by [4], that are state-types, and not to those, like the one expressed by [2], that are properties of persons. However, the latter can be defined in terms of the former in the style of

x believes that such-and-such iff *x* has a belief that such-and-such.

The more cautiously worded statement of the contemporary view is, then, that each belief state-type is identical to some functional property,[3] while for each belief property of persons there is some functional property such that the belief property is identical to the property of having some state-token which has that functional property. This is how I should be understood when I write without qualification of the view that belief properties are functional properties.

d. Functional roles are properties of state-types, but this should be understood as relativized to organisms and times: state-type N has functional role F in x at t—thus leaving open the possibility that N might not have F in y at t'. Suppose, for example, that neural state-type H realizes hunger in both Al and Bob, and that only in Al is it the case that the smell of pizza always causes a tokening of H. This would be a theoretically uninteresting example of H's having a functional role in Al which it did not have in Bob; the possibility of theoretically interesting examples of this phenomenon is discussed below in connection with "Twin Earth" counterexamples to functionalism.

e. The nebulous label 'functionalism' will nowadays support nearly any antimentalist, physicalistically creditable theory of belief properties, but I nevertheless decline to apply the label 'functionalism' to the position that belief properties are functional properties. For any theorist who claims that each belief property is identical to some functional property owes an account of what it is that determines *which* functional property a given belief property is identical with. As will later be apparent, there is more than one way in which a theorist might seek to discharge this debt. One of them is to claim that there is some psychological theory such that the identification of each belief property with a given functional property is determined by the role that the notion of belief plays in that theory, and I think that, given the history of our subject, 'functionalism' finds its most felicitous application here—as a label not just for the thesis that belief properties are functional properties, but for that thesis *together with* a certain thesis about the way in which the pairing of belief properties with functional properties is determined. I do not, however, pretend that this is anything more than a terminological point.

One can be an antidualist about minds and a dualist about mental states, or an antidualist about mental states and a dualist about mental properties. The most thoroughgoing antidualism, or physicalism, is one that is anti-dualistic with respect to all three kinds of mental entities. It will not countenance anything, of any ontological category, that is irreducibly mental, neither minds nor mental states nor mental properties.

The theorist defined by his subscription to the nine hypotheses of chapter 1 is a noneliminativist physicalist of the highest degree. He will therefore want to take seriously the thought that belief properties are functional properties, in the sense explained. At the same time, he is a theorist of IBS who holds the relational theory of belief and so is drawn to the view that belief is a relation to propositions. Putting this all together, we get the well-known thought that

> For each proposition p there is some functional role F such that being a belief that p = being a token of a state-type that has F.

If this is true, then there must be *some* principled way of correlating propositions with functional roles that determines an identification of each belief property with some functional property. This chapter is mostly about functionalist ways this might be done. But before getting down to that, it will be helpful to introduce the notion of a *functional theory* and to discuss the way propositions might enter into such theories.

There is one other preliminary matter. We know that two theorists might agree that believing is a relation to propositions and that propositions are abstract, objective, language-independent things that have essentially the truth conditions they have, but might still disagree over the proper objects of belief: sets of possible worlds, say, or entities with as much structure and as many components as the sentences that express them. This issue will matter in the next chapter, but not in this one: the reader should see the propositional-functionalist as helping himself to whatever style of proposition he thinks will be most useful to him. That will make no difference to the objections I shall level against him.

2.3 Functional Theories and Propositions

We might have a *black-box problem*: we are given an input/output system (the black box) whose outputs are a function of its inputs and its internal, physical states; we have access to the inputs and outputs but know nothing about the nature of the internal states or of the causal laws governing them. Nevertheless, we seek a theory that will be explanatory and predictive of the outputs. To provide such a theory is to solve the black-box problem.

We might be able to solve the problem by devising a correct *functional theory* of the system: we might theorize that there are so many internal state-types the system might be in, which are related to one another, to inputs, and to outputs in such-and-such causal or transitional ways. If this theory is correct and detailed enough, it could enable us to predict the system's outputs on the basis of its inputs, just as knowledge of a computer's program may provide us with the ability to predict its outputs, even though we know next to nothing about its internal hardware. (It ought to be clear that there is a big difference between functio*nal* theories and functional*ist* theories: the former are empirical theories about the behavior of I/O systems, whereas the latter are philosophical theories about the identification of mental properties and functional properties. There are an enormous number of true—although perhaps unformulated—functional theories, but I doubt that there is even one true functionalist theory.)

What form will a functional theory take? If it needs only to quantify over a relatively small number n of internal state-types, it can take the form of a straightforward existential generalization over them:

[i] $(\exists S_1), \ldots, (\exists S_n)(T(S_1, \ldots, S_n))$.

Here the open sentence

[ii] $T(S_1, \ldots, S_n)$

expresses an n-ary relation among state-types and will relate them to one another and to possible inputs and outputs. The theory [i] will be true, of course, provided there is an n-tuple of physical state-types that satisfies [ii]. Each member of this n-tuple will have the *functional role* determined for it by the open sentence (i.e., it will be, for some i, the ith member of an n-tuple of physical state-types that satisfies a certain complex causal or transitional relation). These physical state-types that realize the theory will be the ones that enter into the causal laws whose unavailability defined the black-box problem. We are about to see that a functional theory might not be able to take the simple, straightforward form of a quantification over the causally operative, internal, physical state-types of the system. In other words, [i] is not the only form that an explicitly functional theory might take.[4]

How might *propositions* enter into a functional theory providing the solution to a black-box problem?

Suppose that in order to solve a given black-box problem we needed, somehow, to ascribe functional roles to indefinitely many internal, physical state-types. This would preclude our functional theory from taking the form [i], where we quantify directly over the physical state-types to which functional roles are being ascribed. How, then, are we to devise a theory that ascribes functional roles to each of indefinitely many physical state-types?

Well, as a first step, we might hypothesize that the causal, or transitional, relations that obtain among the system's internal states *mirror* certain logical (or other) relations that obtain among propositions. Then we might hope to ascribe functional roles to internal state-types via a quantification over functions that map propositions onto state-types whose causal relations to one another, to inputs, and to outputs mirror the relevant logical (or other) relations in which their correlated propositions stand to other propositions. This is what we would be doing if our speculation were to take a form such as the following:

$(\exists f)(\exists g)(p)(q)(r)(s)$ (if p is true and condition C_1 obtains, then one is in $f(p)$; if one is in $f(q$ only if $r)$ and in $g(q)$, then one is in $g(r)$; if one is in $g(s)$ and condition C_2 obtains, then s becomes true).

(The resemblance between this and a rudimentary belief (f) / desire (g) theory, with C_1 a perceptual input condition and C_2 an output condition, is not accidental, but is inessential to the illustration.) This theory says that there is a pair of functions from propositions to internal states having the functional roles dictated by the theory's content. In a functional theory of this sort propositions are exploited as *external indices* of the functional roles one wishes to ascribe to possible physical states of the system in question. So this, as Loar has made clear, is how propositions might enter into a functional theory: as objects wholly external to the system and its workings, to which we refer in order to ascribe functional roles to unknown physical state-types of the system—unavailable state-types that enter into unavailable causal laws that are explanatory of the system's behavior at a deeper level than that to which the functional theory aspires.

It will help to solidify the intuitive idea just invoked by remarking on the analogous way in which physical properties can be indexed by numbers. The analogy has been well expressed by Robert Stalnaker:

What is it about such physical properties as having a certain height or weight that makes it correct to represent them as relations between the thing to which the property is ascribed and a number? The reason we can understand such properties—physical quantities—in this way is that they belong to families of properties which have a structure in common with the real numbers. Because the family of properties which are *weights* of physical objects has this structure, we can ... use a number to pick a particular one of the properties out of the family. (1984, p. 9)

Stalnaker then suggests an analogous explanation of how a person can be related to a proposition:

The analogy suggests that to define a relation between a person or physical object and a proposition is to define a class of properties with a structure that makes it possible to pick one of the properties out of the class by specifying a proposition. (1984, p. 11)

What we have learned from Brian Loar is that an explicitly functional theory which exploits propositions in the way just adumbrated will take the form

[iii] $(\exists f_1), \ldots, (\exists f_n)(T(f_1, \ldots, f_n))$,

where the quantified variables (the 'f_i's) range over functions that map propositions onto physical state-types of the system, and where, if the theory is true, these state-types will have the functional roles the theory determines.

Theories of types [i] and [iii] are functional theories.[5] *Functional* theories— to repeat what was earlier said—are empirical theories about the causal (or transitional) organization of the internal states of I/O systems; they are not philosophical theories and imply nothing whatever about the nature of propositional attitudes. *Functionalism* is a philosophical theory about the nature of propositional attitudes, and it will be convenient to reserve the rubric 'functionalist theories of propositional attitudes' for philosophical theories of belief and desire that are of that persuasion. What makes a functionalist a functionalist is the way he explicates propositional attitudes in terms of functional theories.

Our present concern is with functionalists who hold that propositions are indeed the objects of propositional attitudes. By stipulation, the propositional-functionalist holds that

Some psychological theory determines a correlation of each proposition p with a functional role indexed by p in that theory in such a way that being a belief that p = the functional property of being a token of some (first-level, physical) state-type that has that functional role.

This raises two questions: (1) *What* psychological theory does this? (2) *How* does it do it? That is, given that we have a psychological theory which we know "defines" belief, how should we go about constructing that "definition"? (The scare quotes indicate that a "definition" which determined the identification of each belief property with a given functional property need not give the *meaning* of 'believes'; the importance of this to be manifested in the later discussion of Psychofunctionalism.)

Brian Loar, improving on the work of F. P. Ramsey and David Lewis, has proposed an answer to question 2 that, I hazard, would have to be the right sort of answer, if functionalism were true (see Ramsey 1929; Lewis 1970a, 1972; Loar 1981). The issues here are actually many, subtle, and technical, but I hope that for our purposes the following will suffice.

Suppose that one has a psychological theory T involving the theoretical constructs *belief* and *desire*, that T "defines" those notions, and that, for simplicity, there is no question of the theory's reducing, or defining, any other notions in tandem with them. Now, to form the Loar-style "definition" of belief with respect to T, write out T as a single sentence, replacing all occurrences of the "theoretical" predicates 'x believes p' and 'x desires p' with functional (in the set-theoretic sense) expressions of the form

x is in (a member of the set of first-level state-types) $Bel(p)$,

thus yielding as our representation of T,

[1] $T(Bel, Des)$,

wherein, if [1] is true, 'Bel' and 'Des' are names of functions that map propositions onto sets of neurophysiological state-types having functional roles determined by the roles of 'Bel' and 'Des' in [1].[6] By two applications of existential generalization, [1] yields its Ramsey-sentence,

$(\exists f)(\exists g)T(f,g)$,

which is an explicitly functional theory of form [iii]. This we get trivially whether or not [1] defines Bel and Des. But *if* [1] does define them, then the idea, roughly speaking, is that [1] is *equivalent* to

There are functions f and g that uniquely are such that $T(f,g)$,

and that one gives the desired functionalist reduction of Bel and Des thus:

$Bel =_{df}$ the first member of the unique ordered pair of functions that satisfies '$T(f,g)$'.

$Des =_{df}$ the second member, etc.[7]

For *any* theory T containing the constructs *belief* and *desire* (and any others, such as *intention*, that we think should be co-defined with them—a qualification I shall continue to ignore), we can form *the Loar-style definition of Bel and Des with respect to T*—that is, the definitions those functions would have *if* they were correctly defined by *T*. (*Bel* and *Des*, it should be kept in mind, are simply believing and desiring construed as functions from propositions to (sets of) internal state-types.) Each such definition may be construed as the *stipulative* definition of the function Bel_T, with respect to which one can always ask, Is it the case that $Bel = Bel_T$? This is just to ask if believing is functionally defined by the theory *T*.

Now, for each proposition *p* in the domain of Bel_T, there is a functional role *F* such that it *follows from the definition of Bel_T* that

$Bel_T(p) =$ the set of first-level, physical state-types that have *F*.

Then we may say that *F* is *the T-correlated functional role of $Bel_T(p)$* (intuitively, the functional role determined by the role of the belief that *p* in the generalizations of *T*), and know that

$Bel = Bel_T$ iff, for each *p*, one believes *p* just in case one is in a token of a state-type which has the *T*-correlated functional role of $Bel_T(p)$.

In other words, if $Bel = Bel_T$, then *the criterion* for a state-token *n*'s being a belief that *p* is that *n* be a token of a state-type which has the functional role that the definition of Bel_T correlates with *p*.

In light of this resolution of question 2, the claim of the propositional-functionalist is just this:

For some theory *T*, $Bel = Bel_T$.

Question 1 is then, What theory is that?

2.4 *Commonsense Functionalism*

Functionalism is the theory that, for some *T*, $Bel = Bel_T$; functionalists may differ on what they take that theory to be. *Commonsense* functionalism (CSF) is the theory that $Bel = Bel_{T*}$, *T** being folk psychology, that commonsense psychologcial theory which embeds our concepts of belief and desire and is common knowledge among those who have them.

Perhaps no one today is a commonsense functionalist, but that (if one will overlook the anachronism of my Loarian formulation) was not so a few years ago, most thoroughgoing materialists then being functionalists, and CSF the dominant functionalism. And David Lewis taught us the reason for this (see Lewis 1966, 1970a, 1972).

Scientists, in articulating new theories, often do so using new terms that are not explicitly defined by them but just show up working in the statement of the theory. It is convenient to think of terms like 'electron', 'mass', 'gravity', 'quark', 'gene', 'id', 'phlogiston', and others as having been given life in this way. If so, then it is plausible to suppose that these "theoretical terms" derive their meanings from their roles in the theories that introduce them. But how? David Lewis, furthering work of Ramsey's, offered a theory that purported to show how we could derive explicit definitions of a theory's theoretical terms in terms of the roles they play in the theory (Ramsey 1929; Lewis 1970a). It was then tempting to conjecture that psychological terms such as 'believes' and 'desires' were theoretical terms of our commonsense psychological theory, defined by their roles in it. CSF was then simply a consequence of this, the Loar-style definition now viewed as an improved suggestion about the style of theoretical definition involved.

Of course, if propositional-attitude verbs have their *meanings* determined by theoretical roles they play, then the theory in which they play those roles must be one available to those who understand those terms, and that could only be the folk theory. An advantage, therefore, of CSF vis-à-vis alternative functionalist theories is that it is the only one that can offer an account of the meanings of psychological terms, and thus of our *concepts* of belief and desire. I am inclined to think that this is an important point, and will later use it to the disadvantage of both CSF and its functionalist competitor.

In any event, CSF is false; there simply is no commonsense belief/desire psychological theory with the wherewithal for defining those notions. The reasons for this are, by and large, known, but I think worth rehearsing.

1. It is in the first place not entirely clear that there *is* a folk psychological theory. The commonsense psychological theory is supposed to be that system of lawlike generalizations using the notions *belief* and *desire* that is known, or "used," by plain folk who possess those concepts. *But can anyone state so much as a single generalization that fills that bill?* Certainly, the *raison d'être* of our common concepts of belief and desire is their interlocking role in the explanation of behavior, a role exemplified when John explains that Mary raised her arm because she wanted the waiter's attention and believed that that was a good way of getting it. What is far from obvious, however, is that to explain John's explanatory ability we must credit him with implicit knowledge of, or see him as somehow employing, a system of generalizations involving the constructs *belief* and *desire* which, when conjoined with circumstantial facts, yields explanations of behavior.

When we explain a person's behavior in terms of his beliefs and desires, we do not advert to psychological laws; we simply ascribe to him particular beliefs and desires. David Lewis noticed this, and asked, "How can my behavior be explained by an explanans consisting of nothing but particular-fact premises about my present state of mind? Where are the covering laws?" (1972, p. 213). Thinking that there had to be some, he answered his own question with the claim that the covering laws were implied by

ascriptions of particular beliefs and desires, the mechanism of this implica-
tion revealed by the definitions of belief and desire with respect to folk
psychology. But if we cannot find these "covering laws"—and I am about
to suggest that we cannot—then we should wonder whether the covering-
law model of explanation is the correct model for commonsense, belief/
desire explanations of behavior. It *might* just be a fact about our internal
processing that we ascribe beliefs and desires under certain conditions, and
draw behavioral conclusions from those ascriptions under certain other
conditions, even when none of this allows us to recover anything that
looks like a lawlike generalization. Later, in chapter 6, I shall try to suggest
how our propositional-attitude concepts can function in an explanatory and
predictive way even if no folk *theory* embeds them; now I want to consider
the less than conclusive reasons for doubting the availability of folk psychological generalizations.

The folk theory is commonly thought to contain at least three kinds of
generalizations: those determinative of what might be called *internal functional roles*, which describe how beliefs determine or constrain beliefs, and
how beliefs and desires generate further desires; *perceptual input conditions*,
which take us from certain observable states of affairs to beliefs that they
obtain; and *output conditions*, generalizations that take us from beliefs and
desires, or intentions, to basic acts.

As regards *internal functional roles*, I am unaware that anyone has ever
revealed a true, commonsense law that shows how beliefs and desires
determine further desires. One wants to say,

> If x believes (p only if q) and desires p and ..., then x desires q.

But how is this to be completed, especially without recourse to anything
better than very rough ways of capturing *degrees* of belief and desire? (I
trust that it is clear that the indented sentence would be false without the
dots. One may very much desire to be rich, believe that one will be rich
only if one murders one's parents, and yet not desire to murder one's
parents. Or, to use another kind of exception, if a person believes that (she
will gorge herself on chocolate only if she craves chocolate) and desires to
gorge herself on chocolate, it does not follow that she desires to crave
chocolate. Her desire to gorge may be an unwilling capitulation to a
craving she desires not to have.) Turning to rationality constraints among
beliefs, one naturally thinks of generalizations such as

> If x believes (p and q), then x believes p;
> If x believes ((if p, q) and p), then x believes q;
> If x believes p, then x does not believe not-p.[8]

Yet it is doubtful that any of these is either true or part of the folk lore.
Perhaps the last is the most conservative; but it cannot be part of the

folk psychology, because that is defined by what the folk believe, and I am one of the folk and do not believe it. The generalization fails in the light of unconscious belief, self-deception, and compartmentalized, irrational thought; and it is far from certain that it applies to beliefs ascribable with 'that'-clauses containing indexicals or demonstratives (for, notoriously, it may be true both that Ralph believes that you are a pervert and that you are not a pervert—he may mistakenly think that 'she' in his two utterances 'She is a pervert' and 'She (unlike that other one) is not a pervert' refer to different people).

Perceptual input conditions may well be in the worst shape. Surely, if any belong to a folk theory, then that theory ought to dish up some sort of completion, probabilistic or otherwise, of this:

[P]   If there is a red block directly in front of x and ..., then x will believe that there is a red block in front of x.

If a completion of [P] is to be common knowledge, it will have to fill the gap with conditions that entail that x is "well enough" sighted, is not colorblind, has his eyes open and the block in his line of vision, is attentive to color and shape, has experienced red and square things, is a human being above a certain age, is normal to a certain extent, is sober and undrugged, is in circumstances that satisfy such-and-such lighting conditions, and is not possessed of any beliefs that would defeat the prima facie evidence of his sense experience. It is not obvious to me that I could ever succeed in completing this in a way that would yield a truth, nor, if I could, that it would not be of a complexity that defied its being commonly believed and thus of the folk theory.

Similar remarks are in order for attempts to state true and interesting output conditions and input conditions for desires that are not derived from beliefs and other desires.

2. Suppose we understand the notion of *a* folk psychology as *any* untaught belief/desire *theory* implicitly held by *any* ordinary people. Then I have just argued that there is reason to doubt that there is *any* folk psychology. A different point is this: CSF is correct only if there is a folk theory held by *all* who have the concepts of belief and desire that is adequate for their definition; but it is obvious that nothing rich enough to define belief is held by all the folk.

If the *meaning* of 'believes' is determined by a folk psychology expressed by its use, then that theory must be one implicitly held by everyone who has the concept *belief*. But there cannot be such a commonly held theory for this reason: if a belief/desire theory is to have any chance of defining our concept of belief, it will have perceptual input conditions; but it is clear on reflection that no such condition is common knowledge, however implicitly, among all who have the concept *belief*. Consider in this regard the mooted completion of [P], as good a candidate for a folk psychological input condition as one can hope to find. It is simply obvious that there could be humans, blind or sighted—not to mention extraterrestrials and machines—who have the concept of belief, yet fail to know or use any theory to which a completion of [P] belongs. At the same time we must notice (a) that the perceptual input conditions (if any) that belong to the "commonsense" belief/desire theory (if any) that most sighted people know seem to consist almost exclusively of *visual* input conditions, and (b) that insofar as we have perceptual input conditions for nonvisual sensory modes, the point made with respect to [P] can be made with respect to them: there can be people who have the concept *belief* but, owing to their own sensory deprivations (they are deaf, have no sense of smell or touch, etc.), are ignorant of perceptual conditions satisfied by those who have the sensory capacities they lack.

It is not just that sighted people rely mostly on sight for their worldly knowledge, but also that most sighted people are extremely ignorant about the perceptual input conditions appropriate to blind people, let alone people like Helen Keller. It might of course be suggested that no one who was ignorant of the perceptual input conditions that we know could have the same concept of belief that we have. However, to mention just one problem with this suggestion, it seems clear to me that when Ray Charles says, "I believe that Count Basie is dead," he means just what I mean when I say, "Ray Charles believes that Count Basie is dead"—even if Ray Charles knows no completion of [P].

The dilemma for CSF is thus apparent. On the one hand, the *point* of being a *commonsense* functionalist is that it allows one to say that folk psychology *defines* 'belief' (as opposed to merely determining its extension). On the other hand, if folk psychology contains [P], then it cannot *define* 'belief' (for there will be people with our concept of belief who know no theory containing [P]); and if it does not contain [P], then it will contain very few and meager perceptual input conditions and so, once again, cannot define 'belief'.

Notice that the problem just generated derives from the fact that there can be those who have our concept of belief while being *ignorant* of our folk theory (assuming that there is such a theory); the fact that our folk theory *fails* relevantly *to apply* to those people is the basis for a different objection, to be made shortly.

3. Now let us assume that there is a folk psychology, a commonsense belief/desire psychological theory, that it is suitably regimented, fully stated, and as rich as one might reasonably hope it to be;.let T^* be that folk theory. T^* defines belief only if $Bel = Bel_{T^*}$, and $Bel = Bel_{T^*}$ only if, for

each p, the T^*-correlated functional role of $Bel_{T^*}(p)$ provides a *sufficient* condition for believing p; that is, only if a sufficient condition for believing p is that one is in a state having the T^*-correlated functional role of $Bel_{T^*}(p)$. But the T^*-correlated functional role of $Bel_{T^*}(p)$ will not in general provide a sufficient condition for believing p, and one reason (there are others) this is so is that T^* will often determine the same T^*-correlated functional roles for distinct beliefs; it will sometimes follow from the definition of Bel_{T^*} that $Bel_{T^*}(p) = Bel_{T^*}(q)$, when believing p and believing q are in no sense equivalent.[9]

Consider the "theory"

$[T^{\#}]$ $(p)(q)(x)$ (if x believes p & x believes q, then x believes $(p$ & $q)$).

Even without having a settled format for specifying the functional definition of 'believes' with respect to a given theory, it ought to be intuitively clear that one reason why $T^{\#}$ cannot define 'believes' is that it determines the same functional role for all nonconjunctive beliefs: in the relevant sense, it distinguishes no role for the belief that snow is white that it does not also distinguish for the belief that grass is green. Certainly with the Loarian format it can be shown that it follows from the definition of $Bel_{T^{\#}}$ that $Bel_{T^{\#}}$(that snow is white) = $Bel_{T^{\#}}$(that grass is green); that is, that both belief$_{T^{\#}}$'s have the same $T^{\#}$-correlated functional roles. The moral, then, is this. If T^* is to define belief, then, for each p, the T^*-correlated functional role of $Bel_{T^*}(p)$ must be *unique*, in this sense: there is no q such that both (i) the belief that p and the belief that q are nonequivalent beliefs and (ii) $Bel_{T^*}(p)$ and $Bel_{T^*}(q)$ have the same T^*-correlated functional roles. But how is T^* to satisfy this uniqueness constraint?[10]

a. If there is a folk theory, it will contain generalizations determinative of internal functional roles; but they will fare no better with respect to the uniqueness constraint than $T^{\#}$: as propositional variables occur in these generalizations only within belief contexts and not outside of them, these generalizations will assign the same functional roles to all beliefs of the same logical form.

b. Since we are allowing optimism to run unbridled, we may suppose that the folk theory has an output component that takes us from beliefs and desires to intentions to perform basic acts, and from them to basic acts. Perhaps the final output condition will be a completion of this:

[O] If x intends to do A now, A is a basic act-type, and ..., then x does A now.

As the act-type variable 'A' occurs here both within *and without* content clauses, it is reasonable to suppose that unique T^*-correlated functional roles are assigned to at least some beliefs whose contents are specifiable using substituends of '*A*'. However, [O] together with the generalizations determinative of internal functional roles will at best still only assign unique functional roles to some beliefs about basic act-types. If T^* consisted only of these two components, the T^*-correlated functional role of Bel_{T^*}(that snow is white) would be the same as that of Bel_{T^*}(that grass is green), and thus it would not be the case that $Bel = Bel_{T^*}$.

c. If T^* is to define belief, it must *at the least* have a fairly vast array of perceptual input conditions, and if there are any such conditions, some completion of [P] would certainly be among them. If a proposition p occurs in the antecedent of an input condition, then $Bel_{T^*}(p)$ will have a unique T^*-correlated functional role. However, only a very restricted range of propositions will enter into the perceptual input conditions. If T^* consists only of the foregoing constraints on internal functional roles, output conditions, and perceptual input conditions, it cannot possibly satisfy the uniqueness constraint; that tripartite theory will determine no functional role for the belief that dinosaurs are extinct that it does not also determine for the belief that fleas are mortal.

Might T^* reasonably be thought to include generalizations that are not of the three sorts reviewed and that would assure unique functional roles for beliefs not affected by the output or perceptual input conditions? It seems unlikely that such generalizations would take the form of nonperceptual input conditions; for even if we could find a few, it seems unlikely that we could find enough to make any appreciable headway.

Loar has suggested that T^* will contain generalizations, reminiscent of Carnap's "meaning postulates" (Carnap 1947), that are partially constitutive of interbelief content relations. He calls them *M-constraints* and gives as an example

If x believes that y is north of z and that u is north of y, then x believes that u is north of z.

The thought occurs that T^* could satisfy the uniqueness constraint if the M-constraints linked each proposition not occurring in an input condition to a proposition occurring in one in a unique way. But the folk theory, *ex hypothesi*, is one available to all the folk, and it seems obvious to me that no such theory contains nearly enough M-constraints to do the job in question. One needs only to consider the belief that the government of New Zealand is not a dictatorship, and to ask what "observational belief," or set of observational beliefs, that belief is functionally related to in a way that no other belief is. Nor can I think of what else the folk theory might include to secure satisfaction of the uniqueness constraint. I am therefore inclined to suppose that folk psychology cannot provide the functionalist reduction of belief.

4. The preceding objection was that because T^* could not satisfy the uniqueness constraint, there would be some p such that the T^*-correlated functional role of $Bel_{T^*}(p)$ did not provide a sufficient condition for believing p. The present objection offers a different reason why T^*-correlated functional roles will not in general yield sufficient conditions for being in the belief states associated with them. The argument is very familiar, so I may be very brief: CSF is false because one can always construct a Twin Earth or Burge-type example in which, for some p, (a) someone does not believe p even though (b) he is in a state that has the T^*-correlated functional role of $Bel_{T^*}(p)$. Well, perhaps I should not be quite *that* brief.

Twin Earth is *exactly* like Earth except for the following difference and whatever it entails: although the things they call 'cats' on Twin Earth look and behave exactly like cats, they are not cats but have a radically different genetic make-up and comprise a wholly disparate biological species. Anyway, Earthling Ralph utters 'There are cats' and, in doing so, expresses his belief that there are cats. That belief is realized in Ralph by a token of the neural state-type N that has the T^*-correlated functional role of Bel_{T^*}(that there are cats), F^c. Twin-Ralph is a molecule-for-molecule duplicate of Ralph, and so he too utters 'There are cats' and he too is in a token of N. The problem for CSF is that its falsity is evidently entailed by these two truths:

(1)   Since N in Ralph has F^c, so too does N in Twin-Ralph;

but, notwithstanding this,

(2)   Twin-Ralph does not believe that there are cats.

The truth of (1) is not really debatable. Although a specification of F^c might conceivably require a reference to cats (and not to their Twin Earth lookalikes, tcats), the *counterfactual* nature of F^c would secure that it was satisfied by N in Twin-Ralph. Perhaps the point here can be most clearly made by changing the example slightly. Suppose that the T^*-correlated functional role of Bel_{T^*}(that one is looking at a cat) is such that a state-type has that functional role only if the presence of a cat in one's line of vision would under such-and-such conditions cause that state-type to be tokened in one. If that functional role is possessed by the neural state-type N' that realizes Ralph's belief that he is looking at a cat, then it is clearly also possessed by N' in Twin-Ralph; for if there *were* a cat in his line of vision (etc.), then N' *would* be tokened in him. (*Ex hypothesi*, cats and tcats are distinguishable only at the chromosomal level, a level we may assume to be unavailable to ordinary people.) The general point, then, is that T^*-correlated functional roles will invariably be counterfactual in a way that entails their possession by Twin-Ralph's states, assuming their possession by Ralph's states.

It is important, however, to be clear that the truth of (1) follows not from a truth about *functional roles* but from a truth about *T*-correlated* functional roles. It is, we know, perfectly possible for a neural state-type to have a functional role in Ralph that it does not have in Twin-Ralph. For example, the functional role expressed by

Every token of x in y is caused by y's looking at a cat

might well be satisfied by the pair $\langle N, \text{Ralph} \rangle$, but not by the pair $\langle N, \text{Twin-Ralph} \rangle$. The reason Twin Earth is a problem for CSF is that the functional role determined for the belief that there are cats by the folk theory will, by virtue of its counterfactual nature, be satisfiable in a world in which there are no cats (cf. Owens 1983).[11]

There are two ways in which one might think to deny (2). One might claim (a) that the creatures on Twin Earth really are cats, there then being no reason to deny that Twin-Ralph believes that there are cats; or (b) that Twin-Ralph has that belief even though there are not cats, but only tcats, on Twin Earth.

It is difficult to take either of these responses seriously. What would the proponent of (a) say about the bizarre mutant offspring of two turtles that ended up looking and behaving exactly like a cat though it was genetically a turtle? If he should insist that it was a cat, then we should have to agree to disagree; if he agreed that it was not a cat, then he would owe a reason for supposing that the creatures on Twin Earth are cats. As regards (b), it is just absurd to suppose that in using 'cat' Twin-Ralph is not talking and expressing beliefs about the tcats he thinks he is talking and thinking about, but is really talking and thinking about cats, none of which he has ever encountered or even heard of. Twin-Ralph, by parity of reason, has as much right as Ralph does to be said to be expressing a true belief about the thing he is looking at when he says, "I'm looking at a cat," in which case we cannot say that he believes that he is looking at a cat, since *that* belief, unlike the one he expresses, is false.

There is an inclination even among philosophers, who ought to know better, to disparage Twin Earth arguments because of their science fiction flavor. That really is to miss the point. Twin Earth is simply a fanciful way of making a plain point: in order to have beliefs with contents ascribable with sentences containing 'cat', one must have had some sort of contact, direct or indirect, with cats; but that evident platitude would be a falsehood if CSF were true.

There is one reply that the commonsense functionalist might make to the Twin Earth counterexample that we should briefly consider before turning to the similar, and at the same time interestingly different, counterexample of Tyler Burge.

The commonsense functionalist might try to hold a *description theory* of natural-kind concepts and argue that the truth of (1) and (2) does not refute his functionalism. He will first of all point out that in presenting a simplified account of his position, we have oversimplified. The *Bel* function should be represented not as a unary function but, at the minimum, as a dyadic function of the form

$Bel(x, p)$,

which maps a person x and a proposition p onto states of x's having the functional role indexed by p in the folk theory. Without this minor refinement CSF would be all too easily refutable: the neural state-type that realizes my belief that *I* am phlegmatic has exactly the same T^*-correlated functional role as your belief that *you* are phlegmatic; and if belief were simply represented as the unary function, then that common functional role would, on the simplified characterization of CSF, entail that we believed the same proposition (which, of course, we do not, as your belief is true iff *you* are phlegmatic, mine iff *I* am phlegmatic). When belief is correctly represented as the dyadic function, then we may see the definition of Bel_{T^*} as yielding, for some F,

x is in $Bel_{T^*}(x,$ that x is phlegmatic) iff x is in a state having functional role F,

from which we would get the right result.

His theory aligned, the functionalist may then try to explain the truth of (1) and (2) thus: "The concept *cat* is the same on Earth and Twin Earth—roughly, the concept expressed by 'those creatures that are conspecific with the such-and-such looking creatures I have encountered'. As such, 'cat' would refer to cats on Earth, to tcats on Twin Earth. When Ralph says 'That's a cat,' he is expressing his belief that the creature before him is conspecific with such-and-such creatures in his environment, and when Twin-Ralph says 'That's a cat,' he is expressing his belief that ... in *his* environment. These are different though analogous beliefs, each determined by the T^*-correlated functional role shared by the same neural state-type that realizes both their beliefs, all this in accord with its being the case that $Bel = Bel_{T^*}$."

The trouble with this reply, as we shall see in 3.5, is that the implicit description-theoretic account of natural-kind concepts is as demonstrably false as philosophical theories of that status can be.

So much for the Twin Earth counterexample. Burgian counterexamples to CSF are more interesting than Twin Earth ones; for while they share the same intuitive force, they differ in these two important respects:

i. They also constitute a very strong prima facie objection to IBS, as they appear to show that the content of one's belief is sometimes a function of the meanings of words in one's linguistic community.

ii. Let us say that a functional role F is *environment-invoking* if we cannot know whether a system is in a state of a type that has F without knowing details about the physical environment in which that system is located (thus the functional role expressed by 'Every token of x is caused in so-and-so by his looking at a cat' is environment-invoking). The Twin Earth objection to CSF works because T^*-correlated functional roles are *not* environment-invoking, and this might engender a non-commonsense functionalist hope that $Bel = Bel_T$, for some T whose T-correlated functional roles *are* environment-invoking. The second reason Burgian examples are of interest is that they seem to show that *no* functional role can determine what one believes.

The now classic example unfolds as follows (Burge 1979; see also Burge 1982a, 1982b). Alfred's use of 'arthritis' encompasses more than the correct use of that term, which is limited to inflammation of the joints; Alfred also applies the word to rheumatoid ailments not in the joints. So it is not surprising that, noticing an ailment in his thigh which seems to him symptomatically like the disease in his hands and ankles, Alfred says to his doctor, "I have arthritis in the thigh." Here Burge claims, and I think rightly, that Alfred has the false belief that he has arthritis in the thigh. Calling the world we have in mind 'w', we may therefore say,

In w Alfred has the belief that he has arthritis in his thigh.

We next consider a possible world w' that differs from w in just one respect (and whatever it entails): in w' Alfred's use of 'arthritis' is the *correct* use; it is the accepted usage of that term in Alfred's linguistic community. *Ex hypothesi*, all other facts about Alfred are the same; his physical environment and functional organization are unchanged. Since Alfred's use of 'arthritis' in w' is entirely correct, it seems clear that the belief Alfred expresses in w' when he says "I have arthritis in the thigh" is *true*. But then,

In w' Alfred does *not* have the belief that he has arthritis in his thigh,

for that belief is false (arthritis being, by definition, an inflammation of the joints), whereas the one he has is true.

Now, by construction, Alfred in w' is in exactly the same T^*-correlated functional states as Alfred in w; therefore, if CSF were correct, he would be expressing the same belief by his two utterances. He is not; therefore, CSF is false.[12]

But also, by construction, Alfred in w' is in *all respects* functionally equivalent to himself in w, and that was the point made in (ii).[13]

But also, since (a) Alfred believes that he has arthritis in his thigh only in w, and not in w', and since (b) the only difference between w and w' is in the meaning of 'arthritis' in Alfred's linguistic community, then (c)—and this was the point made in (i)—the contents of one's beliefs must, in contradiction with IBS, sometimes be partly a funcion of the meanings of one's words in one's linguistic community.

5. If $Bel = Bel_{T*}$, then, for each p, the $T*$-correlated functional role of $Bel_{T*}(p)$ must provide a *necessary condition* for believing p; it must be a necessary condition for one's believing p that one be in a token of a state-type that has the $T*$-correlated functional role of $Bel_{T*}(p)$. But it is doubtful that such *necessary* conditions could be provided by any folk theory that was even remotely a candidate for providing *sufficient* conditions.

If there is a folk theory that defines my use of 'believes', then it is one that I know. If there is such a theory and it is to have any chance of defining anything, it must have perceptual input conditions. These perceptual input conditions will partly determine $T*$-correlated functional roles for the beliefs that enter into them. But there will be people who have those beliefs but are not in states with those $T*$-correlated functional roles. Therefore, those functional roles do not provide necessary conditions for having the beliefs they are correlated with, and CSF is false.

The dilemma for CSF—for that is one way of seeing this objection—may be put thus. Consider my belief that there is an apple in my hand. Either there is an input condition applicable to this belief, or there is not. If there is not, CSF cannot begin to get off the ground: there simply will not be a folk theory rich enough to define anyone's concept of belief. If there is a perceptual input condition for my belief, it will be visual, of the form

If there is an apple in x's hand and x is sighted and ..., then x will believe that there is an apple in x's hand.

For that is the only input condition, if any, that I know, and CSF is supposed to tell me how to explicate *my* concept of belief. But my concept of belief allows me to say of a blind person that she believes that there is an apple in her hand, and I assume that such ascriptions can be literally true. I assume, too, that many blind people can discern by touch and smell that they are holding an apple, but I do not know how they do this and certainly do not know any perceptual input condition applicable to them for such beliefs.

Now let F^a be the $T*$-correlated functional role of Bel_{T*}(that there is an apple in x's hand), $T*$ being the folk theory that I know. Suppose that Sally is a blind person who presently believes that there is an apple in her hand, and let N be the neural state-type that realizes her present belief that she is holding an apple. *Must we suppose that N has the functional role F^a?* To say that N has F^a is to say that if Sally *were* sighted, and there were an apple in her hand, and ..., then N would be tokened in her. It seems to me absurd, however, to suppose that this must be the case, and doubtful that it is the case. Quite likely, if Sally were sighted, some *other* neural state-type would realize her belief that she was holding an apple. But CSF is true only if the possession by N of F^a is a necessary condition for its realizing a belief that Sally has an apple in her hand. Therefore, CSF, once again, is false.

The moral of the last objection is really this: If CSF is true, then there is a folk theory with perceptual input conditions applicable to all believers. But there is obviously no such theory.

2.5 Psychofunctionalism

The functionalist says that, for some theory T, $Bel = Bel_T$. T is not, we now know, any commonsense psychological theory; but perhaps it is a *scientific* psychological theory, cognitive psychology the science. Ned Block (1980a) has called the philosophical theory that affirms this 'Psychofunctionalism', and we may turn straightway to some reasons for doubting it.

1. If, as Psychofunctionalism claims, there is a scientific psychological theory that determines the identity of each belief property with some functional property, then that theory is neither known, formulated, nor conceived. Evidently, the position must be that there is some true but yet unthought-of scientific psychological theory T^s such that $Bel = Bel_{T^s}$. T^s, it would have to be conceded, could not *define* 'believes', but the idea would be that it does reveal that term's reference. The idea would be that, for each p,

> being a belief that p = being a token of a state-type that has the T^s-correlated functional role of $Bel_{T^s}(p)$ (i.e., the functional role indexed by p in T^s),

where this would be a necessary truth but one that is only knowable *a posteriori* after scientific investigation had unearthed T^s.

Now how on earth can the reference, or extension, of 'a belief that bedbugs are mortal' in my mouth be revealed by a theory that no one knows? I know that some will want to respond: in just the same way that scientists can discover that being a dog = being of such-and-such genotype. But this response is not altogether unproblematic.

First of all, *scientists* cannot discover that being a dog = being of a certain genotype. Scientists can perhaps discover that all and only past, present, and future *actual* dogs are of that genotype, and that properties of that genotype account for the phenotypical and behavioral features by which we identify dogs as dogs; but to deduce the property identity, we should need a *philosophical* theory that (a) entailed a completion of

> Being a dog = being of such-and-such genotype if ... ,

and that (b) in conjunction with the scientific discovery entailed that

Being a dog = being of such-and-such genotype.

If there is a philosophical theory with this power, I am ignorant of it.

If there were such a philosophical theory, it could take the form of a theory of the meaning or reference of 'dog', and some will look here to the seminal work of Kripke, Putnam, and others (Kripke 1980; Putnam 1975; Devitt 1981; Salmon 1981). That work is indeed suggestive, although it is not obvious what philosophical theory of the sort needed it suggests. In any event—and I suppose this is the most important point apropos of Psychofunctionalism—the intuitive picture suggested by the Kripke/Putnam line on natural-kind terms seems inapplicable to belief predicates.

"The original concept of [dog]," Kripke has written, "is *that kind of thing,* where the kind can be identified by paradigmatic instances" (1980, p. 122). It is as if the word 'dog' got introduced by our coming across certain hitherto unknown creatures, which we assumed to belong to a single biological species, and our saying, "Let's call something a 'dog' if it belongs to the species of those creatures—whatever that species turns out to be"; scientists then prepared ultimately to reveal, in genetic terms, what this species is. But what analogous caricature is there that is both helpful to the Psychofunctionalist and possessed of a shred of plausibility?

I can summarize my first doubt thus: (a) Psychofunctionalism has no greater plausibility than the plausibility of there being a correct semantic theory of belief predicates that in conjunction with a scientific psychological theory T^s entails that $Bel = Bel_{T^s}$; but (b) no one has given us the slightest reason to think that this semantic theory exists.

2. (This and the next objection are merely to remind the reader of a couple of points that I shall not take the space properly to develop, but that are forcefully argued for in the literature and will spawn topics for later discussion.) In order for a psychological theory to determine the extension of 'believes', it must be possible to state the theory using that word. But it is by no means to be assumed that the correct and suitably powerful information-processing theories of cognitive science will be statable using folk psychological idioms. The functional architecture postulated by such an information-processing theory might simply be too rich and fine-grained to enable one to identify beliefs with functional states invoked by the theory (Churchland 1981; Stich 1983; Dennett 1986). It may turn out that a term of the vernacular like 'believes' is just too blunt a tool to serve the purposes of a fully adequate scientific theory; 'believes' and 'desires' may do fine for our quotidian needs without being up to snuff for rigorous scientific theorizing. (Some may be tempted to conclude that if this is so, then we ought to be reluctant to suppose that there really are beliefs; but, as I suggest in 6.4, this may be to miss the point of our commonsense psychological concepts.)

3. Even if a scientific functional theory will need to quantify over belief states, there remains reason to doubt that it would need to consture believing as a *relation to propositions*. Scientific psychological theories will be the sorts of complex functional theories that quantify over functions from external indices of functional roles to inner physical states having them. To say that believing is both a relation to propositions *and* "defined" (i.e., reduced) by such a theory would seem to imply that these external indices could only be propositions. But this seems implausible on two counts.

First, it seems obvious that if propositions were suitable indices for a functional theory, then so would be sentences or interpreted formulae of a formal language.[14]

Second, it is not even clear that the external indices need be anything more than *uninterpreted* formulae. In other words, even if a scientific functional theory will need to quantify over belief states, there remains reason to doubt that it will need *to assign content to those states*; cognitive psychology may have no need for intentionality. In fact, it would seem that in this regard we are in a position to say something fairly strong: to the extent that it is clear to us what theories in cognitive psychology should be theories of, it is clear that the objects of belief need be nothing more than uninterpreted sentences. The essential point has been well expressed by Hartry Field:

> If the task of psychology is to state (i) the laws by which an organism's beliefs and desires evolve as he is subjected to sensory stimulations, and (ii) the laws by which those beliefs and desires affect his bodily movements, then semantic characterizations of beliefs and desires are irrelevant to psychology: one can state the laws without saying anything at all about what the believed or desired sentences mean, or about what their truth-conditions are or what their subject matter is. (1978, p. 102)[15]

That is the essential point, but it might be well to work our way back to it along a route of mostly familiar points.

The one thing we clearly want from cognitive psychology is a functional theory that solves the black-box problem we humans pose: a theory that, by specifying functional properties of inner states, is explanatory and predictive of bodily movements in the light of sensory stimulations and other inputs. Given the complexity of our internal structure, this theory will entail a quantification over functions from external indices of functional roles to physical state-types having them. Propositions, we have seen, might be those external indices, but *they need not be*. What is now generally appreciated is that *uninterpreted formulae can fulfill that function just as well*. In using propositions to index functional roles, we would be exploiting logical relations among them, but we could use uninterpreted formulae to index the same functional roles by exploiting formal, or syntactic, relations among those formulae. Instead of a law of the form

If x is in $f(p$ and $q)$, then x is in $f(p)$

we could have a law of the form

If x is in $f(\ulcorner \sigma\ \&\ \sigma'\urcorner)$, then x is in $f(\sigma)$,

the utility of this last in no way requiring that the values of these sentential variables be semantically interpreted.

If we want to make sense of there being an *unformulated* theory, it is useful to identify it with the equivalence class of sentences that would formulate it. If the theory is a functional theory of us, one of these formulations will contain no propositional-attitude terms but will simply be an existential quantification over functions from external indices of functional roles to state-types to which those roles are being ascribed. To say that a yet unthought-of scientific theory will need to invoke notions of belief and desire is just to say that a formulation of the theory using the Loarian '*Bel*' and '*Des*' will belong to the equivalence class of formulations of that theory; by existential generalization on these functors we get that other member of the class which explicitly quantifies over functions of the sort described. Combining the points just made, we can see how a functional theory of us might be formulated using '*Bel*' and '*Des*', covenient technical reconstructions of our 'belief' and 'desire', but in which the functions expressed by those terms had in their domain uninterpreted formulae rather than propositions.

The foregoing is a partial vindication of the claim that, to the extent that it is clear to us what theories in cognitive psychology should be theories of, it is clear that objects of belief need be nothing more than uninterpreted sentences. For we have seen that one sort of theory we clearly expect from cognitive psychology can get along with meaningless symbols as the objects of propositional attitudes. But a full vindication would need to show that *no* strictly legitimate theory of cognitive psychology will need to assign content to belief states, and I have no idea of how one would hope to show that. At the same time, it is true, I think, that—*pace* Jerry Fodor and Tyler Burge—we cannot yet say clearly (or perhaps even unclearly) what sort of scientific theory would need contentful objects of belief.[16]

If a functional theory may be indifferently formulated using propositions, sentences, or uninterpreted formulae as external indices of functional roles (so that the difference between them is like the difference between Fahrenheit and Celsius scales), then its formulation using '*Bel*' can be construed as having any one of those sorts of indices constituting the *Bel* function's domain of arguments. It is therefore hard to see how its one arbitrary formulation which does use propositions to index functional roles can be regarded as fixing the extension of ordinary-language 'believes'. But to this the propositionalist who is also a Psychofunctionalist may seem to have a reply. He may say that the fact that 'believes' expresses a relation to propositions is not determined by any scientific psychological theory (perhaps, he might say, it is determined just by the fact that *we* use 'that'-clauses to refer to propositions); what the yet unconceived scientific theory determines is *which* relation to propositions the belief relation is. It is thus irrelevant that a given functional theory may enjoy equivalent formulations only some of which use propositions; it is the one that does which yields the functionalist reduction of that relation between people and propositions that is the belief relation.

The trouble with this reply is that, as the scientific theory which determines the belief relation has itself no need to ascribe propositional content to those states to which it ascribes functional roles, it makes it a mystery why our 'that'-clauses should be construed as referring to propositions.

4. It is absurd to a degree to suppose that there could be a single belief/desire scientific psychology that was both applicable to all possible believers and powerful enough to determine a functional property for each belief property to be identical with. If there were such a theory, it would have to include *perceptual input conditions* applicable not just to fully normal university graduates but to very young children, Helen Keller, the most primitive and culturally remote tribesman, extraterrestrials with undreamt-of perceptual faculties, and certain machines. Nothing could be such a theory; anything that purported to be would at best be a motley disjunction of distinct theories, each applicable to a limited range of believers. If this is right, then there is no scientific psychological theory T^s such that $Bel = Bel_{T^s}$; for $Bel = Bel_{T^s}$ only if, for each p, the T^s-correlated functional role of $Bel_{T^s}(p)$ provided a necessary condition for believing p, and that would require the applicability of T^s to all possible believers.

5. $Bel = Bel_{T^s}$ only if, for each p, the T^s-correlated functional role of $Bel_{T^s}(p)$ provides a sufficient condition for believing p. For T^s to satisfy this "sufficiency constraint," its T^s-correlated functional roles would have to be possessed by Alfred's inner state-types but not by Twin-Alfred's, and not by Alfred's in the possible world in which his use of 'arthritis' is correct. The claim that $Bel = Bel_{T^s}$ must, in other words, be immune to Twin Earth and Burge-type counterexamples, and who can give any ground for confidence on this score?

2.6 Functionalism Extended

'Functionalism', I have stipulated, is to be our label for the philosophical thesis that

> Some psychological theory determines a correlation of each proposition p with a functional role indexed by p in that theory in such a way that being a belief that $p =$ the functional property of being a token of some state-type that has that functional role.

This is then perspicuously recast as the thesis that

> For some psychological theory T, $Bel = Bel_T$.

But it is, for the reasons just rehearsed, doubtful that there is such a theory; doubtful, therefore, that functionalism is true.

There are two positions in logical space either of which the erstwhile propositional-functionalist might next seek to occupy, without ceasing to hold that belief is a relation to propositions and without just surfacing listlessly to the Sargasso Sea of mentalism.[17] The first is very close to what we have been considering. It concedes that there is no *single* psychological theory that determines the functionalist reduction of belief properties, but supposes that there is one for each thing capable of having beliefs. That is, so to say,

> For each possible believer x there is some psychological theory T such that, for each proposition p, x believes p iff x is in $Bel_T(p)$.

Now this would be an exceedingly puzzling and unhelpful suggestion in the absence of some proposal as to the conditions that a psychological theory of a thing would have to satisfy in order to determine that thing's belief properties. So a fuller characterization of the proposal would be that

> For each possible believer x there is some psychological theory T that satisfies ——— condition, such that, etc.

The filling for the blank would then, in effect, provide a necessary and sufficient *metacondition* for a psychological theory's "defining" belief for a particular believer. The challenge, of course, would be to produce a persuasive metacondition, one immune to the objections already leveled against mundane functionalism.

Brian Loar has proposed a theory along the foregoing lines,[18] but I find it unconvincing, in part for the following reasons:

1. Loar does not give a fully general proposal. The only metacondition he considers is one provided by a commonsense theory that is applicable only to perceptually normal adults in our society, and I can see no obvious way of generalizing Loar's proposal to yield a metacondition applicable

to all believers. Moreover, it is a consequence of Loar's theory that the predicate 'believes that *The New Yorker* publishes Ved Mehta' in my idiolect is partially defined by a commonsense theory that is false of each blind person, and that, consequently, as I use that predicate, the sentence 'Ved Mehta believes that *The New Yorker* publishes Ved Mehta' cannot be true, as Ved Mehta is blind. This I cannot support.

2. Loar's theory is not immune to Twin Earth and Burge-type counter-examples; and although he is aware of their threat, I find inadequate his description-theoretic way of countering it.

There are, I think, other problems with the Loarian proposal. As I cannot consider it properly here, I urge anyone interested in functionalism to give it careful study and to decide for himself if it offers the propositionalist a viable form of materialism.

The second position in logical space to which the frustrated propositional-functionalist might move offers a more radical departure from function-alism. The theorist occupying this position concedes that no psychological theory will in itself provide any sort of definition, or reduction, of predicates such as

> x believes that some dogs have fleas,

but he does think that a functionalist definition is available for the predicate

> x is a belief.

He therefore proposes the following strategy:

First, find a psychological theory with respect to which one can function-ally define the *monadic predicate* 'x is a belief'. Second, determine a function-al property for each composite belief property via a *nonfunctional*, explicit definition of the form

[R] x believes p iff ($\exists s$) (s is a belief; x is in s; & $R(s, p)$),

for a given specified relation R.

Robert Stalnaker sees hope in this approach; adapting an idea of Dennis Stampe's, he has in effect suggested that a promising approach to com-pleting [R] would be via a refinement of the idea that

[FG] x believes p iff x is in a belief state that, under optimal conditions, x would not be in unless it were the case that p.

(Stalnaker 1984. See also Dretske 1986; Fodor, unpublished; Stampe 1977; and the discussion of these issues in chapter 4.)

We might call the intuitive idea expressed by [FG] the "fuel gauge model of mental representation".[19] If a neural state-token n is a belief that it is raining, then n represents the proposition, or possible state of affairs, that it is raining. Now representation is not just a feature of mental states: the position of a needle on the dashboard of your car can represent your gas tank as being ¾ full. How is it that the position of the needle has this representational power? Because of the capacity of the fuel gauge to be a reliable indicator of the amount of fuel in the gas tank, surely; because, under optimal conditions, the needle is where it is (viz., pointing at '¾') only when the tank is ¾ full of gasoline. The idea, then, is that representation *in general* derives from the capacity of a system to be a reliable indicator of its context; what accounts for the gas gauge's representational features also accounts for those of my belief that it is raining: under optimal conditions, I would not be in that belief state unless it were raining. It is because being in that belief state is in that way a reliable indicator of the weather that it is a belief *that it is raining.*

However promising the strategy of [R], and however promising the fuel gauge model, [FG] can be no more than a first stab. Among several other problems,[20] it implies that under optimal conditions one has no false beliefs. That may be, but then one wonders what these never satisfied "optimal conditions" are, and, especially, how they might be specified without rendering [FG] viciously circular by presupposing the very intentionality it is supposed to explicate.

In any event, [FG] is merely one suggested way of completing [R], and [R]—and the strategy that is supposed to culminate in a completion of it—is really best pursued in connection with attempts to say what determines the truth conditions of formulae in a system of mental representation. Consequently, I shall postpone further consideration of this quasi-functionalist position until chapter 4. In the meantime I shall try to show that for reasons that are entirely independent of the mind-body problem, believing cannot be a relation to propositions. The upshot of the present chapter is modest: if believing is a relation to propositions, and if there is a specification of that relation in nonmentalistic terms, then that specification is not the product of any functionalist theory considered in this chapter.

Chapter 3
The Real Trouble with Propositions

3.1 Introduction

The theorist defined by the nine hypotheses of chapter 1 holds the relational theory of propositional attitudes and is looking for entities to be the relata of those relations. His quest is constrained by his need to find objects for the attitudes that will cohere with his commitment to IBS and to physicalism, construed as the identification of propositional-attitude facts with facts statable in a nonmentalistic and nonintentional idiom. Qua theorist of IBS, he sees propositions as well suited to be the objects of propositional attitudes, for their semantic, contentful features are not public-language semantic features. Functionalism looked to be the way to wed the propositional theory of propositional attitudes to physicalism, but the last chapter put a damper on that thought; it now looks as if it might well be difficult to subscribe both to physicalism and to the propositional theory. This chapter raises a difficulty for the propositional theory quite apart from any concern with the mind-body issue.

For a long time I believed that if there were propositions they were ideally suited to be the objects of propositional attitudes. I thought that the only serious problem unique to the propositional theory of propositional attitudes was that, being creatures of darkness, propositions were hard to believe in. I now realize that I was wrong: the real trouble with propositions is that, even granted that they exist, propositional attitudes cannot be relations to them.

There is, I believe, more than one way of constructing an argument against the theory that believing is a relation to propositions—which should not be surprising if that theory is indeed false; but this chapter is concerned with only one of those ways.[1] I shall argue that the propositional theory founders on beliefs involving natural-kind concepts. First, however, there are some preliminary points to be made by way of cleaning up the area of the argument.

1. The theory in question is that propositional attitudes are relations to propositions. To say that believing (which will serve as my exemplar) is a

relation to a proposition is to say two things: first, that the letter 'p' in the schema

    x believes p

is a genuine objectual variable; and second, that propositions are the values of that variable. Propositions, I have said, are abstract, objective, language-independent entities that have essentially the truth conditions they have.

They are abstract in that they are not in space or time: the proposition that snow is white is not anywhere, and although it really exists, there is no time at which it began to exist and none at which it will cease to exist. The abstractness of propositions does not, however, preclude them from having concrete particulars as constituents—the Empire State Building, according to certain propositionalists, is a constituent of the proposition expressed by 'The Empire State Building is in Tacoma, Washington'.

They are objective in contrast to the subjectivity of pains and mental images, which can have no existence apart from the minds that have them. Propositions are not mental entities and would have existed even if there had never been people to conceive them.

They have their truth conditions essentially, in contrast to the contingent way in which sentences and other representations have them. It is a contingent fact, and so might well have been otherwise, that the sequence of marks 'snow is white' is true if and only if snow is white, but the proposition that snow is white has that truth condition in every possible world.

The language independence of propositions is perhaps their most important feature. For the propositionalist, the proposition that snow is white is as ontologically and conceptually distinct from the *sentence* 'snow is white' as Carlos Lopes is from the name 'Carlos Lopes'; a proposition, Frege wrote, "is like a planet which, already before anyone has seen it, has been in interaction with other planets," and "when one apprehends or thinks a [proposition] one does not create it but only comes to stand in a certain relation ... to what already existed beforehand" (1967, pp. 29–30; Frege's word for proposition was 'thought'). The importance of this independence is, of course, that if it were not the case, one could not explain the meaning of 'snow is white' in terms of its standing in a certain contingent relation to the proposition that snow is white; and if one could not do that, one would be without motivation for being a propositionalist with respect to propositional attitudes. For the theorist of IBS this is especially so.

Most of what can be said of propositions can also be said of the properties and relations that help to compose them. They, too, for the propositionalist are abstract, objective, and, especially, language independent. There is no objective and language-independent proposition to be expressed by 'snow is white' unless there is an objective and language-independent property of whiteness to be expressed by 'white'. The ontological commitment to propositions carries with it a general commitment to Platonic Realism, which is why so many people object to it. One reason I am emphasizing the language independence of propositions and properties is that unless it is kept in mind, propositions are apt to seem more readily available than they may in fact be. The problem is that there is a risk that a certain *pleonastic* use of 'property' will precipitately seduce one into thinking that language-independent properties, and thus the propositions they determine, exist. Suppose, to approach what I mean, one were concerned to construct a correspondence theory that required that there were *facts* that were language independent in just the way that propositions are supposed to be. Then one would take no comfort in the utterly pleonastic sense of 'fact' that enabled one to move back and forth between 'Michele is funny' and 'It's a fact that Michele is funny'. Likewise, if one's concern were the existence of *language-independent* properties, one would take no comfort in the pleonastic sense of 'property' that enabled one to move back and forth between 'Michele is funny' and 'Michele has the property of being funny'. The full import of these remarks will be made manifest later, when they are put to use; in the meantime I should reiterate that in making my *primary* objection to the propositional theory of propositional attitudes I shall not be taking issue with the existence of propositions. I shall express doubt, however, about the existence of certain nonpleonastic properties and thereby give voice to a further reason for doubting the propositional theory. The case against that theory may well be overdetermined.

2. Different sorts of things can count as propositions in the sense glossed— functions from possible worlds into truth values, or fine-grained complexes containing individuals and properties, such as the situation-types of Barwise and Perry (1983; see also Adams 1974; Bealer 1982; Lewis 1970b; Loar 1981; Plantinga 1974). I shall not be an interloper in this family affair; my intention is to raise a problem for the propositional theory of propositional attitudes, whatever kind of proposition is involved. I shall, however, in the ensuing discussion avail myself of a certain simplifying assumption.

Suppose that

[a]   Ralph believes that snow is white,

and that two propositionalists agree that this may be represented as

[b]   B(Ralph, the proposition that snow is white).[2]

Then, even if they disagree about what sort of thing that proposition is, they will at least agree that the expression 'that snow is white' functions in [a] as a complex singular term which refers to that proposition, and that the reference of that singular term is determined by the references of its semantically relevant parts. Perhaps 'snow' there refers to the stuff snow,

'is white' to the property of being white; and the proposition thus determined is one that, necessarily, is true just in case snow is white. Still,
the two theorists may at this juncture differ over whether or not the
proposition *contains* those referents as *constituents*. If propositions are taken
to be functions from possible worlds into truth values, then they do not
contain the entities that determine them. Our mooted proposition would
not be a complex containing snow and the property of being white, but,
say, that partial function which maps a possible world w onto truth iff snow
exists and is white in w, onto falsity iff snow exists and is not white in w,
and which is undefined otherwise. To many, this conception of unstruc-
tured propositions seems ill suited to the provision of objects of belief, for
it entails that necessarily equivalent propositions are identical and that,
therefore, one believes all mathematical and logical truths if one believes
any, there being only one to begin with. For this reason, and some others,
other theorists, seeking more finely individuated entities, construe propositions as structured entities the constituents of which are the objects,
properties, operators, and so forth, that determine them. Although it will
soon be evident that structured propositions stand a better chance of
surviving the argument I shall aim at all propositions, I do not, as I have
said, wish to take sides in intrapropositionalist disputes. However, for
expository reasons I propose harmlessly to *represent* propositions, of whatever stripe, as ordered n-tuples of the things that determine them. Thus, if
in [a] 'snow' refers to snow, and 'is white' to the property of being white,
then I would represent the proposition referred to in [a] and [b] as the
ordered pair

[c]   ⟨snow, the property of being white⟩.

The possible-worlds theorist obviously cannot identify his proposition
with this ordered pair, and the advocate of structured propositions may
well wish to treat his complexes as irreducible entities, not definable in
terms of any set-theoretic apparatus. But neither should object to our style of
representation: the possible-worlds theorist can construe [c] as representing
the function it determines, and the theorist of fine-grained propositions can
construe [c] as standing in for his irreducible complex, which has just the
same constituents as our ordered pair. And in the same unpolemical vein, I
shall allow myself to speak of the constituents of propositions, rather than
speaking periphrastically of the constituents of the ordered n-tuple that
represents the proposition in question.

3. The theory in question holds that 'believes' in sentences of the form 'x
believes that σ' expresses a relation which relates believers to propositions.
This, however, does not entail that substituends for 'that σ' *must* refer to
propositions. Thus consider an utterance of

[i]   Henry believes that that girl is clever.

A propositionalist might, consistently with his being a propositionalist, hold that the occurrence of 'that girl' refers to a certain girl and that the occurrence of 'is clever' refers to the property of being clever, but deny that the occurrence of 'that that girl is clever' refers to the proposition ⟨that girl, cleverness⟩, and thus deny that [i] is representable as

B(Henry, ⟨that girl, cleverness⟩).

He might—still consistently with his propositionalism—hold that the correct representation of [i] is

[ii]   (∃m)(m is a mode of presentation of that girl & B(Henry, ⟨m, cleverness⟩)).

This does not tell us what proposition Henry believes, but merely that he believes *some* proposition which contains *some* mode for presentation of the girl in question. On this way of representing [i], the 'that'-clause in [i], 'that that girl is clever', does not refer to what Henry believes, but rather provides an indirect and partial characterization of that proposition, if any, believing which makes [i] true, if it is true.

   The representation of [i] as [ii] is a familiar propositionalist move. What we must next note is that it is equally *consistent* with the propositional theory to represent [i] as

(∃m)(m is a mode of presentation of cleverness & B(Henry, ⟨that girl, m⟩))

(or as '(∃m)(∃m')(m is a mode of presentation of that girl, m' of cleverness & B(Henry, ⟨m, m'⟩))—I am now unconcerned with the role in [i] of 'that girl'). This is not a familiar propositionalist move, and I think for good reason; but the issues that are about to confront us require that we see it as a possible move, one available to the propositionalist.

3.2 The Structure of the Argument

Toby is known to have a pet named Gustav, and Tanya, to relieve curiosity about the kind of animal Gustav is, says,

[1]   Gustav is a dog,

thereby· revealing that

[2]   Tanya believes that Gustav is a dog.

If the theory that believing is a relation to a proposition is true, then there is some proposition *p* that is the content of the belief expressed by Tanya when she uttered [1], and it is the fact of Tanya's believing *p*, perhaps together with some other fact, that makes [2] true. My objection to this theory is that it cannot be right because there is no plausible account of the proposition that is supposed to be the content of Tanya's belief, and this because there is no plausible account of the role that 'dog' plays in [2] in the determination of that proposition.

Our question is to be what contribution 'dog' makes to the content of Tanya's belief. Happily, therefore, we may ignore for a while the vagaries of the so-called *de re/de dicto* distinction as regards singular terms, and harmlessly pretend that the only semantically relevant role of the name 'Gustav' in [2] is to refer to the creature Gustav and introduce him directly into the proposition that is the content of Tanya's belief that Gustav is a dog. So, relative to this simplifying assumption, the proposition that provides the complete content of Tanya's belief is some completion of the proposition-frame

⟨Gustav, ?⟩,

and the question confronting the propositionalist is just this: What is to take the place of '?'? That is, *what proposition* is (relative to the simplifying assumption) the content of Tanya's belief?

There are two possible answers available to the propositionalist, and they are, I believe, mutually exclusive and jointly exhaustive of the answers available to him.

First, he may hold that the proposition that provides the complete content of Tanya's belief is (given the simplifying assumption about 'Gustav') the proposition

[3]   ⟨Gustav, the property of being a dog⟩,

which proposition is true in any given possible world just in case Gustav exists and is a dog in that world. On this view the correct representation of [2] would be

[4]   *B*(Tanya, ⟨Gustav, doghood⟩).

This would be the natural position to take if one thought that the 'that'-clause in [2], 'that Gustav is a dog', was a singular term which referred to what Tanya believed, [2] thus enjoying the representation

B(Tanya, the proposition that Gustav is a dog).

For the belief ascribed to Tanya is, evidently, one that is true in any given possible world just in case Gustav has in that world the property of being a dog. I shall call this answer to our question—that [3] is the content of Tanya's belief—the *classical* propositional position; basically, it is the position that predicates in 'that'-clasues simply refer to the properties and relations they express and introduce them directly into the propositions believed.

Second, the propositionalist may hold, refinements apart, that the proposition that provides the complete content of Tanya's belief contains not doghood but a *mode of presentation* of doghood that is not explicit in [2] but that is how Tanya conceives of doghood. This line is, we shall see, best thought of as developing out of the failure of the classical response, and it takes its cue from a familiar Fregean way of treating beliefs that are *de re* with respect to ordinary physical objects. Someone taking this line would want to deny that the 'that'-clause in [2] referred to the complete content of Tanya's belief. He would want to say (refinements still apart) that [2] would be best represented as

$$(\exists m)(m \text{ is a mode of presentation of doghood } \& B(\text{Tanya}, \langle \text{Gustav}, m \rangle)).$$

In this way *different* propositions, containing *different* ways of thinking of doghood, different modes of presentation of it, can be the content of a belief ascribed by [2]; [2] does not give the proposition believed, but only gives a partial characterization of it, as a proposition containing some mode of presentation of doghood. This response will be more fully motivated and carefully set up later, when the need for it arises.

My main objection to the classical theory, which I make in the next section, is that, given the only plausible account of what the property of being a dog might be, it is clear that [3] cannot be the content of Tanya's belief.

My objection to the mode-of-presentation account, which I develop in sections after the next, is that there seems not to be any credible account of what the mode of presentation of doghood might be.

A further objection whose validity would sink any propositionalist account of beliefs involving the concept *dog* is briefly entertained at the close of this chapter, when I suggest that there might not be a genuinely nonpleonastic, language-independent property of being a dog.

3.3 The Classical Theory: ⟨Gustav, Doghood⟩ as the Content of the Belief That Gustav Is a Dog

The proposal before us, the classical theory of Tanya's belief, holds that the complete content of her belief that Gustav is a dog is proposition [3], ⟨Gustav, doghood⟩—relative, still, to our simplifying assumption about 'Gustav', which I shall not continue to mention. But I think that we can show that this cannot be right once we see what property the property of being a dog would be, if there really is a genuinely language-independent, nonpleonastic property of being a dog.

The classical theory has it that the sole function of 'is a dog' in [2], 'Tanya believes that Gustav is a dog', is to introduce doghood into that proposition that is the content of the belief that Gustav is a dog. The question now to be addressed is, Exactly what property is this property of being a dog? Of course, one possible response to this question is to reject it, protesting that the property of being a dog is primitive and irreducible, that it cannot be specified in any other terms: it is the property of being a dog, and there is an end to it. This has not in fact been a line advocated or implied by any historical personage, and we would be well advised to consider it later, after more familiar lines have been exhausted.

It is not, we shall soon see, at all plausible that doghood is primitive and irreducible; hence, if there is such a property, it is one specifiable in other terms, without using the word 'dog'. What might this other way of specifying the property be? One venerable answer, hobbled by Wittgenstein, demolished by Kripke and Putnam, is that 'dog' is somehow definable in terms of those more or less observable properties by which, in a paradigm observational case, one identifies a thing as a dog (Wittgenstein 1953; Kripke 1980; Putnam 1975). It is in fact difficult to construct a verbal definition of 'dog' along these lines, for we lack neat expressions for ascribing the doggy appearance and demeanor; but it is more or less clear what the intended properties are. Nor is it hard to fathom the appeal which this account has for the theorist who would represent [2] as [4]: they are properties by which we identify a thing as a dog, and their possession by a creature does not seem to be merely evidence or a symptom of its having the further property of being a dog; most importantly, they are properties with which, in Russell's sense, we are "acquainted" (Russell 1959), if any properties are, which makes them eminently suitable as constituents of belief contents.

Nevertheless, these properties are neither separately necessary nor jointly sufficient for being a dog. None of them is necessary, for we can imagine a creature that looked and behaved quite unlike a dog, but that we classed as one anyway because it was the offspring of paradigm dogs and was relevantly like them genetically; or, to echo Kripke, we might learn that, owing to certain optical distortions, dogs did not really have the doggy appearance that, under the illusive conditions, we took them to have. And the conjunction of these observational properties fails to provide a sufficient condition for being a dog, for, as Kripke and Putnam have taught us, we can easily imagine a thing of another species (a reptile, say), or of no recognizable biological species at all, having just the appearance and demeanor of paradigm dogs, and this thing would not be a dog.

Many philosophers have joined Kripke and Putnam in taking such counterexamples to show that, for any possible world w, a thing is a dog in w just in case it belongs in w to the natural kind to which in the actual world all and only dogs belong. This natural kind, if it exists, is reasonably taken to be the species *Canis familiaris*, to which dogs in the actual world belong. It is as if the word 'dog' got introduced as a rigid designator of the species, its reference fixed by the description 'the species of those things', where 'those things' referred to some privileged sample of the things we call 'dog'.

If this is correct, then the property of being a dog is the property of belonging to *Canis familiaris*, and [3] is now revealed to be

[5]   《Gustav, *Canis familiaris*》, the kind-membership relation〉,

which proposition is true in any given possible world just in case in that world Gustav belongs to the species *Canis familiaris*, to which all dogs in *the actual world* belong (cf. Salmon 1981, pp. 42–76).

Even this will admit of further reduction, if there really is the species *Canis familiaris*; that is, if dogs really do constitute a natural kind. It seems reasonable to suppose that membership in the species is itself to be determined by a certain empirically discoverable internal structure; that is, most plausibly, a certain complex genetic property, a genotype common to all and only dogs.[3] Whether or not the natural kind is to be individuated wholly in terms of genetic properties does not really matter for our purposes. What does matter is that the natural kind, the abstract entity *Canis familiaris*, if it exists, is not anything with which we are directly acquainted. It remains to be discovered by science what that natural kind is; at present we have only "knowledge by description" of the kind, as the natural kind, whatever it turns out to be, to which paradigm dogs belong. What we do not have at present is knowledge of the internal properties that constitute, or define, the species.

Let us suppose that there really is a definite abstract entity that is the species, the natural kind, to which all and only dogs belong, and that '*Canis familiaris*' names it, thus removing any doubt about the *existence* of proposition [5], 《Gustav, *Canis familiaris*》, the kind-membership relation〉. Nonetheless, we cannot plausibly suppose that [5] is the complete content of Tanya's belief. For suppose that we came across a race of dogs whom we mistakenly supposed not to be dogs, and in our ignorance decided that 'shmog' would stand for any creature of the same biological species as those creatures. In that event, [2] could be true while

[6]   Tanya believes that Gustav is a shmog

was false: Tanya, like us, may fail to believe that shmogs are dogs. But if the content sentence in [2] refers to [5], then so must the one in [6].

We do not need shmogs to make the point. Suppose that scientists discovered that a certain complex genotype G was in fact constitutive of the species of dogs. G would be a property that enjoyed an intrinsic description couched wholly in biochemical terms, daunting words like 'nucleotide', 'deoxyribose', and 'adenine'. Now Tanya might, in principle, be acquainted with G under its biochemical description, know that it was constitutive of some natural kind, but not know that that natural kind was the species of dogs. She might say, "There is some natural kind constituted by G, and I hereby rigidly designate that natural kind 'Oscar'." Then it might further happen that, as regards a certain creature Lulu,

[7]   Tanya believes that Lulu belongs to Oscar

was true, while it was not true that

[8]   Tanya believes that Lulu is a dog.

This might be the case if Tanya's acquaintance with Lulu was limited to a microscopic examination of certain of her cells. But if [5] were the complete content of Tanya's belief that Gustav is a dog, then, by parity of reasoning, it would also have to be held that [7] and [8] were logically equivalent, 'believes' in both serving to relate Tanya to the proposition

$$\langle\!\langle \text{Lulu, } Canis\ familiaris\ [= \text{Oscar}]\rangle, \text{the kind-membership relation}\rangle.$$

It seems clear that the complete content of the belief Tanya expresses when she says 'Lulu belongs to Oscar' is not the complete content of the belief that she would express were she then also to say 'Lulu is a dog'.

This is by no means to suggest that the species of dogs is not a constituent of the proposition believed when one has a belief whose content can be specified using the word 'dog'. But it does suggest that if the natural kind does enter into those contents, it does so only under a mode of presentation that makes that content ascribable using 'dog'. This suggestion—that beliefs such as Tanya's are of natural kinds under modes of presentation—will presently be critically examined. Before that we must complete the case against the classical theory by considering the remaining possible way of holding it.[4]

I am thus led to conclude that [3], $\langle$Gustav, doghood$\rangle$, is not the content of Tanya's belief that Gustav is a dog, if doghood is not a primitive and irreducible property. For if there is a nonpleonastic property of being a dog, and it is identical to a property specifiable in other terms, then that property would most plausibly be the biological species, the natural kind, of dogs, and [3] would be [5]; but, we have seen, [5] cannot be the content of Tanya's belief.

Therefore, [3] is the content of Tanya's belief only if doghood is primitive and irreducible. But this is why I think that if there really is an objective, language-independent property of being a dog, it is not irreducible. Suppose that God were to tell you absolutely everything that could possibly be relevant to Gustav's being a dog, other than that Gustav had the property of being a dog, or other things trivially tantamount to that, such as that Gustav was of the same species as something that was a dog. God's description would apprise you of every morphological and behavioral, every phenotypic and genetic fact about Gustav; and it would tell you with what things, likewise described, he was conspecific and from what things he had descended; it would even tell you that Gustav was of the same species as the such-and-such animals with respect to which the word 'dog' was first introduced. Now anyone who thinks that there really is a property of being a dog but denies that it is identifiable with any property specifiable in genetic (or other "biological") terms must insist that there is an entirely determinate and objective, but irreducible, property of being a dog such that the fact that Gustav has that property is an objective fact distinct from and over and above all of these other facts about him. Presumably one could know absolutely everything about Gustav without knowing, or even believing, that he had this further, irreducible property of being a dog. But *how*, if this is what being a dog really consists in, could one ever come to know or believe, after being graced with the God-given knowledge, that Gustav was a dog? The property of being a dog could not be an observable property; we know all of them. By what means, then, could we apprehend, in the situation imagined, that Gustav had this irreducible property? Are we supposed to have some special faculty, akin perhaps to moral intuition, for discerning it? Are we somehow to *infer* the possession of the irreducible property of being a dog from the possession of some other, more tangible properties? If so, how again? What would be the nature of the inference, or the source of its validation?

Matters are exacerbated when we recall the shmog example, and the fact that Tanya fails to believe that Gustav is a shmog, even though shmogs and dogs comprise a single biological species. For if one were to claim that 'dog' expressed a primitive and irreducible property, then one would be further constrained to hold that 'shmog' expressed a *different* primitive and irreducible property. Are there, then, in Plato's Heaven infinitely many primitive and irreducible properties just like doghood but for their being uninstantiated?

Surely we must not suppose that Gustav, in addition to having a certain appearance, demeanor, morphology, ancestry, genetic structure, and so on, also has, over and above all these properties, the entirely distinct, primitive, and irreducible property of being a dog.[5]

In this way I am led to conclude that the classical theory of Tanya's belief is false: the complete content of her belief, when she believes that Gustav is a dog, is not ⟨Gustav, the property of being a dog⟩. For the best candidate for being the property of being a dog (if there really is such a property) is the property of belonging to *Canis familiaris*, the biological natural kind to which all and only dogs belong (if there really is such a natural kind); but ⟪Gustav, *Canis familiaris*⟫, the kind-membership relation⟩ cannot, we have seen, be the complete content of Tanya's belief.

To say that [3] is not the content of Tanya's belief is by no means to say that the propositionalist cannot account for it, or for [2], the sentence that ascribes it. But what moves has this theorist now at his disposal? To answer this we must first take stock of what is left to the propositionalist and then see his plight on analogy with the problem he faces as regards modes of presentation and the complete contents of *de re* beliefs about material particulars. This deserves its own section.

3.4 Beliefs about Natural Kinds

Assume that belief contents are propositions. Then there is some proposition that is the content of the belief Tanya expressed when she uttered [1], and this proposition may or may not be the referent of 'that Gustav is a dog' as it occurs in [2]. At all events, we know that, even given our ongoing simplifying assumption about the role of 'Gustav', proposition [3], ⟨Gustav, doghood⟩, is not the content of Tanya's belief. At the same time we are still justified—given the assumption that the propositional theory of belief is true!—in maintaining, first, that 'is a dog' in [2] occurs there as *at least* referring to doghood, and, second, that the best candidate for doghood (given that there is such a property) is belonging to the natural kind *Canis familiaris*. We have just finished the case for the second position, but it may be worth rehearsing the case for the first. Here the point is simply this: on a propositionalist rendering of [2], 'Tanya believes that Gustav is a dog', each semantically relevant constituent of the content sentence 'Gustav is a dog' is referential; 'is a dog' is clearly a semantically relevant constituent; and its reference must at least include doghood, since [2] is true in any given possible world only if Tanya has in that world a belief that is true only if Gustav has the property of being a dog (although, as I shall later observe, this does not entail that the proposition that is the content of Tanya's belief either contains doghood or entails that Gustav is a dog). What all this suggests is, so to say, that [2] ascribes to Tanya a belief that is *de re* with respect to *Canis familiaris*, and that the proposition which is the complete content of her belief contains a *mode of presentation* of that species, whether or not it also includes the species. The proper amplification of these dense words requires us now to change the subject a little.

Suppose that Ralph says, quite sincerely,

[a]   She's clever,

'she' there referring to Emily. The propositionalist, by definition, holds that there is some proposition p that is the complete content of the belief Ralph expressed in uttering [a]; p must be such that in this the actual world it is true just in case Emily is clever, but it will presently be evident that that need not be its truth condition in all possible worlds. In fact it is clear that the complete content of Ralph's belief cannot be the singular proposition

[b]   ⟨Emily, cleverness⟩,

which proposition is true in any given possible world just in case Emily is clever in that world. For as regards the complete content of the belief expressed by Ralph in uttering [a], it is clear that he does not both believe and disbelieve it: *nothing* will induce Ralph sincerely to utter 'She is not clever' in the very circumstances in which he utters [a]. And yet, Ralph might encounter Emily in a new circumstance and, failing to recognize her as the subject of his earlier judgment, now pronounce,

[c]   She (unlike that other one) is not clever.

If the content of the belief Ralph expressed in uttering [c] were ⟨Emily, non-cleverness⟩, then we should, contrary to hypothesis, have to say that Ralph both believed and disbelieved that proposition which was the complete content of the belief he expressed in uttering [a]. Of course, to anticipate the point we are coming to, the propositionalist wants here to borrow a move from Frege and say that there are distinct modes of presentation, m and m', such that Ralph believes Emily to be clever under m but believes her not to be clever under m', m and m' being constituents of the propositions providing the contents of the beliefs expressed in the two utterances. Thus Ralph, in his utterance of [c], is not expressing disbelief in that proposition in which he expressed belief by his utterance of [a], but rather is expressing disbelief in a quite distinct proposition, one that contains m', a distinct mode of presentation of Emily from m, the one contained in the content of the belief expressed in [a] (Frege 1892; Schiffer 1977, 1978, 1981b).

Imagine now a slightly changed scenario, in which, in place of [a] and [c], we have utterances, in different circumstances, of

[a']   I believe that she's clever

and

[c']   I believe that she's not clever,

both occurrences of 'she' referring, unbeknown to Ralph, to one and the same person, Emily. Imagine further that both utterances are true and that 'believes' in [a'] and [c'] expresses the dyadic belief relation between an agent and a proposition, that relation B such that if $B(x, p)$, then p is the complete content of x's belief that p.[6] Then, needless to say, [a'] and [c'] can*not* be correctly represented respectively as

B(Ralph, ⟨Emily, cleverness⟩)

and

B(Ralph, ⟨Emily, non-cleverness⟩).

Yet 'she' in both [a'] and [c'] *does* refer to Emily. How, then, is the propositionalist to account for the logical forms of these utterances?

Well, he might appeal to "modes of presentation" and represent [a'] as

[d] $(\exists m)$ (m is a mode of presentation of Emily & B(Ralph, ⟨m, cleverness⟩)).

This does not identify for us the proposition providing the complete content of the belief Ralph expressed when he uttered [a]; it merely tells us that that proposition contains *some* mode of presentation of Emily. The proposition ⟨m, cleverness⟩ is true in a possible world w just in case whatever m is a mode of presentation of in w is clever in w.[7] Since m is in fact a mode of presentation of Emily, we know that ⟨m, cleverness⟩ is true in the actual world if and only if Emily is clever; perhaps—a point to be touched on later (but not one of much importance to present issues)—in other possible worlds m is not a mode of presentation of Emily, and in those worlds the truth of ⟨m, cleverness⟩ will be independent of the existence of Emily in them.

Suppose now that m^* is the mode of presentation that makes [d] true; that is to say, that ⟨m^*, cleverness⟩ is the complete content of the belief Ralph expressed in uttering [a]. Then we know that Ralph does not also believe ⟨m^*, non-cleverness⟩. But that of course will not preclude our theorist from representing [c'] as

[e] $(\exists m)$ (m is a mode of presentation of Emily & B(Ralph, ⟨m, non-cleverness⟩)),

for the mode of presentation that makes [e] true will be a different mode of presentation of Emily from the one that makes [d] true.[8]

What are these "modes of presentation"? That is, what sort of thing constitutes the range of values of the objectual variable 'm'? 'Mode of presentation' is a theoretical term, defined by its role in the theory of belief that has recourse to it. There may not be any modes of presentation—there may not be things that have the roles determined by 'mode of presentation' in the theory that speaks of modes of presentation—and if there are modes of presentation, we certainly do not yet know what they are; we do not, that is, know what things, if any, play the roles that must be played if there are to be modes of presentation. For the propositionalist, a mode of presentation is whatever language-independent entity completes the content of a *de re* belief when all that one is given initially is that a certain thing is believed by so and so to be such and such. As such, it must satisfy certain constraints, paramount among them being one that I have elsewhere called Frege's Constraint, a constraint that any candidate must satisfy if it is to qualify as a mode of presentation, namely:

> Necessarily, if *m* is a mode of presentation under which a minimally rational person *x* believes a thing *y* to be *F*, then it is not the case that *x* also believes *y* not to be *F* under *m*. In other words, if *x* believes *y* to be *F* and also believes *y* not to be *F*, then there are distinct modes of presentation *m* and *m'* such that *x* believes *y* to be *F* under *m* and disbelieves *y* to be *F* under *m'*. (Schiffer 1978, p. 180)

Since singular propositions such as ⟨Emily, cleverness⟩ cannot be complete contents, it is crucial to the propositional theory of propositional attitudes that there be modes of presentation satisfying Frege's Constraint. But it is a substantial question whether there are any. Actually, I am nowadays very doubtful that there are things suitable to the propositionalist that can serve as modes of presentation to enter into the complete contents of our *de re* beliefs about material particulars.[9] But that is not our present concern, which is to challenge the propositionalist to provide a plausible account of beliefs involving natural-kind concepts such as *dog*. Still, I should like briefly to rehearse one famous possible answer to the question of what modes of presentation for material particulars might be; this not for its own sake but for its relevance to the forthcoming question of what might, for the propositionalist, be the mode of presentation of *Canis familiaris* that enters into the complete content of Tanya's belief that Gustav is a dog.

The famous view I allude to is the one associated with Frege and Russell, that modes of presentation are *individual concepts*, typically "indexicalized" by irreducible occurrences in their specifications of 'I' and 'now'. If *P* is any property, then it determines the individual concept **the P**, which is the property of having *P* uniquely; so, a thing *x* instantiates **the P** provided that *x* has *P* and nothing else does. The general property *P* might contain, so to speak, oneself and the present moment; it might be the property of being now related to oneself in way *R*, whence the individual concept it determined would be that expressed by the definite description 'the thing that is *R* to me now'. On this Frege-Russell, description-theoretic reduction of *de re* thought, [d], the canonical representation of [a'], gives way to

[f]   (∃P)(Emily instantiates **the P** and B(Ralph, ⟨**the P**, cleverness⟩)).

Here the *general* proposition

[g]   ⟨**the P**, cleverness⟩

contains not the *P*, which is Emily, but the uniqueness property, **the P**, which she instantiates; and the proposition is true in a possible world *w* iff whatever instantiates **the P in w** is clever in *w*. Typically, individual concepts—**the president of France in 1984, the woman with whom I am now speaking, the husband of Nancy**—are contingent properties of the things that instantiate them. Thus, not only does [g] not contain Emily, but, if *P* is a contingent property of hers, as it almost certainly would be, then it does not even entail that Emily is clever (since [g] will be true in possible worlds in which Emily is not clever but the *P* in that world is). At the same time, if we assume that 'Emily' and 'Ralph' in [f] are rigid designators, then [f] (and thus [a']) will be true in a possible world *w* only if Ralph believes in *w* a proposition that is true in *w* just in case Emily is clever in *w*.

For the propositionalist whom we have brought to this point, there is a striking parallel between [2], 'Tanya believes that Gustav is a dog', and [a'], 'I believe that she's clever'. For as regards [2], the theorist wants to say that whereas 'is a dog' in [2] refers to doghood, the singular proposition ⟨Gustav, doghood⟩ is not the complete content of Tanya's belief. And as regards [a'], the theorist wants to say that whereas 'she' in [a'] refers to Emily, ⟨Emily, cleverness⟩ is not the complete content of Ralph's belief. The propositionalist is now motivated to find a mode of presentation for doghood to enter into the proposition that is the complete content of Tanya's belief. But the property of being a dog has, for the propositionalist, in the meantime turned out to be the property of belonging to *Canis familiaris*, the natural kind to which, in fact, all and only dogs belong. The theorist's recourse to modes of presentation will thus be manifested, roughly speaking, in his representation of [2] as

[A] $(\exists m)(m$ is a mode of presentation of *Canis familiaris* & B(Tanya, ⟪Gustav, *m*⟫, the kind-membership relation⟩)).

This is speaking roughly because the theorist, mindful of maintaining a certain position about the possible-worlds truth conditions of natural-kind beliefs, might prefer

[B] $(\exists m)(m$ is a mode of presentation of *Canis familiaris* & B(Tanya, ⟪Gustav, ⟨*m*, *Canis familiaris*⟩⟫, the kind-membership relation⟩))

to [A], as the proposition believed in [B] contains the species along with the mode of presentation of it.[10] Fortunately, however, the subtleties introduced by [B] can safely be ignored, and the pretense safely maintained that [A] is the only relevant option; for we shall be able to argue against candidate modes of presentation for the species of dogs quite independently of the question whether they would best be housed in a format of the type of [A] or of the type of [B].

So, let us suppose that the propositionalist, in recognizing the failure of the classical theory of Tanya's belief, recognizes (subject to the foregoing simplification) that the representation of [2] as [A] is his last remaining hope. What, then, might the mode of presentation of the species of dogs be that is supposed to be a constituent of that proposition which is the complete content of Tanya's belief that Gustav is a dog?

I can think of only two possible proposals.[11]

The first would be a description-theoretic account of Tanya's concept *dog*, a view which holds that in believing that Gustav is a dog, she believes of the species, under some individual concept, that Gustav belongs to it. Curiously, a description-theoretic approach to beliefs about natural kinds is the sort of positive account suggested by the informal glosses of Kripke and Putnam, official pronouncements against the decried description theory notwithstanding.

The second proposal is that the mode of presentation entering into Tanya's belief is the *stereotype* of dogs—roughly, the doggy *Gestalt*, or, to give it a topically "scientific" gloss, a *prototype* of dogs (see, for example, the discussion and references in Smith and Medin 1981).

Let us begin with the description-theoretic treatment of Tanya's belief.

3.5 Individual Concepts as Modes of Presentation of Doghood

Earlier I said that, refinements apart, recourse to modes of presentation would be manifested in the representation of [2], 'Tanya believes that Gustav is a dog', as

$(\exists m)(m$ is a mode of presentation of *Canis familiaris* & B(Tanya, $\langle\langle$Gustav, $m\rangle$, the kind-membership relation$\rangle$)).

The description-theoretic proposal, then, refinements still apart, is that the correct representation of [2] is

[P] $(\exists P)$(*Canis familiaris* instantiates **the P** & B(Tanya, $\langle\langle$Gustav, **the P**$\rangle$, the kind-membership relation$\rangle$)).

In other words, there is some individual concept **the P** such that the species of dogs, *Canis familiaris*, instantiates **the P** and Tanya believes *that Gustav belongs to the P*. This proposition, *that Gustav belongs to the P*, is the complete content of Tanya's belief; it is true in a possible world w iff Gustav belongs in w to whatever in w instantiates **the P**; as it happens, in this world **the P** is instantiated by *Canis familiaris*, the natural kind to which all of our dogs (and nothing else) belong, and therefore [2] is true. In believing that Gustav is a dog, Tanya believes of the species *Canis familiaris*, under the mode of presentation **the P**, that Gustav belongs to it.

Now let us put in a refinement that was momentarily put aside.

It is not *sufficient* for believing that Gustav is a dog that, for some mode of presentation **the P**, one believes of the species dog, under **the P**, that Gustav belongs to it. This is evident from the fact that one can believe that Gustav is of such-and-such a biochemically described genotype without believing that he is a dog, even though the genotype is the one constitutive of the species (recall the Lulu example of 3.3). Or, to take another example, if one believes that Gustav belongs to the same species as the species of George's pet, and George's pet is a dog, it does not follow that one believes that Gustav is a dog.

To correct for the failure of [P] to provide a sufficient condition for the truth of [2], the description theorist now needs to claim that

[P′]   There is a certain class C of individual concepts such that [2] is logically equivalent to

$(\exists P)$(*Canis familiaris* instantiates **the P** & B(Tanya, $\langle\!\langle$Gustav, **the P**$\rangle$, the kind-membership relation$\rangle$) & **the P** *belongs to* C).

His task then is to specify C. This may not be the easiest of tasks in view of the fact that Irish wolfhounds, German shepherds, poodles, chihuahuas, and dachshunds are all dogs, while timber wolves, coyotes, and jackals are not, and in view of the fact that in Tanya's place we may have any one of the following: Helen Keller; a man who, though he has seen a few dogs, is as ignorant about them as Putnam is about elms and birches; a person who has never encountered a dog but has read about them; a child who has no biological sophistication whatever and would obdurately persist in calling a Twin-Earth doglike non-dog a dog even after having been apprised of the creature's genetic dissimilarity to our dogs.

I really do not know how the description theorist would try to delimit the class C of individual concepts whose occurrence in beliefs would allow the use of 'dog' in ascribing content to them. So, in fairness to him, I shall ask an easier question: What might the description theorist of modes of presentation have in mind as the individual concept under which Tanya, who is one of us, has her belief about the species of dogs?

It will not do to say that it is the individual concept expressed by 'the kind to which those creatures belong', where 'those creatures' refers to some paradigmatic dogs; for there will be several kinds to which those creatures belong—*animal, mammal, canine, dog, cocker spaniel, male,* and so on. A more plausible suggestion is that it is the individual concept expressed by 'the species of those things', 'those things' understood as before, the idea being that the content of Tanya's belief is that Gustav belongs to the species of such-and-such creatures. But this, as it stands, will not do either: even supposing the role of 'those creatures' to be fixed and unproblematic, the term 'species' in ordinary language is vague and ambiguous, and consequently the phrase 'the species of those things' determines no individual concept independently of some specified reading of 'species'. It would seem that the intended reading of 'species' must be 'biological species', if we can momentarily pretend that that expression succeeds in introducing a definite property. (And it is far from clear that it does: see Kitcher, 1984.) It is most implausible, however, that Tanya believes that Gustav belongs to the biological species of such-and-such creatures when she believes that Gustav is a dog. One reason is that we must not suppose her to be in any way sophisticated about biology; but an even better reason emerges as follows.

Consider

[i]   Tanya believes that Henry is a rabbit,

which belief happens to be true: Henry is a rabbit. If it is plausible to construe [2] in the way under consideration, then, by parity of reasoning, the complete content of Tanya's belief about Henry should be given by

[ii]   Tanya believes that Henry belongs to the biological species of those creatures,

the reference here being to a fairly comprehensive sample of paradigm rabbits. But this cannot be right, as [i] ascribes to Tanya a true belief, whereas [ii] ascribes to her a false belief: rabbits do not constitute a single biological species, but rather an assortment of animals of the biological family *Leporidae* for which there is no better taxonomic term than 'rabbit'.

Perhaps, more promisingly, what Tanya really believes about Gustav is that he shares the internal properties, whatever they turn out to be, that causally account for such-and-such observable characteristics commonly found among so-and-so creatures, the latter reference again being to a wide assortment of paradigm dogs. There are, however, two problems with this suggestion. First, it is absurd to suppose that this could represent the belief of a nine-year-old child, or even of an ordinary, but biologically unreflective, adult. Second, the suggestion presupposes, in effect, that there is a complex genetic property, a genotype, common to all and only dogs; but this, I think, is also doubtful. A German shepherd and a timber wolf are capable of interbreeding and having fertile offspring; they also look very much alike, much more alike than, say, a German shepherd and a French poddle. It is a good bet that there is no genotype that is shared by the German shepherd, the French poodle, and all other dogs but excludes the timber wolf, not to mention the coyote, the dingo, and the jackal.

I dare say that the prospects are looking bleak for [P']. We are assuming that there ia a natural kind to which all and only dogs belong, and [P'] requires us to find a property P such that, first, P is uniquely instantiated by that kind and, second, P might reasonably be thought to be a constituent of the content of an ordinary person's belief that … dog …. But I believe that the foregoing reveals the questionableness of there being any non-metalinguistic property that satisfies both these requirements. Might there, however, be a *metalinguistic* individual concept that does the description theorist's trick? The thought will already have occurred to this theorist in connection with beliefs whose contents are specifiable with words like 'arthritis', 'felony', 'elm', and 'electron'. Now it is surely preposterous to think that *all* kind concepts are metalinguistic; yet that is what we would clearly be driven to if we were to suppose that the complete content of Tanya's belief *had* to include a metalinguistic individual concept that was instantiated by *Canis familiaris*. At any rate, here is (1) another reason for scotching the description theorist's final, desperate effort, followed by (2) a further reason for rejecting in this area any sort of recourse to individual concepts of natural kinds.

1. Exactly *what* metalinguistic individual concept is supposed to enter into that proposition that is the complete content of Tanya's belief? Certainly not **the kind the experts call 'dog'**; at least not until we are told what experts (experts in animals? or in animal speciation? or in what?), and what semantic relation is to be introduced by the infirm verb 'call' (*denotes*? *is true of*? and what relations do these terms introduce, anyway?). I seriously doubt that there exists any clearly specifiable metalinguistic property that is uniquely true of the kind *dog*; but that is not a line I wish now to pursue. Instead, I shall let this be my first objection: if one were ever to succeed in specifying clearly and precisely a metalinguistic individual concept instantiated by the kind to which all and only dogs belonged, that concept would be such that no ordinary person's semantic and technical expertise would be sufficient to enable its entry into the contents of his or her beliefs about dogs.

2. Let us, following Russell, say that one is *acquainted* with a property Q if Q occurs unaccompanied by a mode of presentation of it in some proposition that is the complete content of one of one's beliefs; perhaps redness and squareness are objects of acquaintance. Then the objection may be put thus. Assume that **the P** is an individual concept instantiated by the species of dogs. Then P will itself be a logically complex property concocted out of properties such as *natural kind, animal, expert, denotes, genotype*, and so on. Now if doghood cannot be a constituent of a belief content but must have in its place an individual concept that it instantiates, then that must surely be true also of at least some of the properties out of which P is concocted. Therefore, **the P** could not occur in the proposition that was the content of one's belief that so-and-so was a dog, for certain properties in P would no more be items of acquaintance than doghood is, and would require their own modes of presentation. Therefore, if one's belief about the species of dogs is under an individual concept, then that individual concept

must be composed wholly of properties with which one is acquainted. Now *what on earth* could even be a candidate for such a mode of presentation?

Several philosophers, thinking themselves well defended against the sallies from The New Theory of Reference, have remained attracted to the Frege-Russell description theory of beliefs that are *de re* with respect to material particulars other than oneself (see, for example, Lewis 1983a; Loar 1976b; Schiffer 1978; Stalnaker 1981 and 1987). For such philosophers, a description-theoretic treatment of beliefs involving natural-kind concepts is a natural temptation; but the considerations adduced in this section show not only that that is a temptation to be resisted, but also that one cannot rest content with a description-theoretic reduction of beliefs about material particulars independently of a plausible line on the properties that are supposed to compose the individual concepts, of particulars, to which the theorist makes appeal. We are in the midst of seeing that this is no easy task.

3.6 Stereotypes as Modes of Presentation of Doghood

Here the suggestion is that, in a paradigmatic case such as Tanya's, we might take the "concept" (insidious word!) *dog* to be an observational concept in the visual mode and, in line with this, take the mode of presentation under which Tanya has her belief about the species to be her "stereotype" of the species, her "prototype" of it, something like the doggy *Gestalt*. Let D be such a stereotype for Tanya; the suggestion is, then, that D enters directly into the proposition that is the content of her belief that Gustav is a dog. It should be noticed that for this hypothesis to have any chance of success, it must not be required that Gustav fit D, for Tanya can believe him to be a dog even if he is an egregious mutant. Nor must it be required that she believe that D is in any way *uniquely* true of dogs; for if that were required, then we should merely have another version of the already discredited description theory. The idea must simply be that the presence of D in the content of Tanya's belief secures its satisfaction of Frege's Constraint and somehow makes the belief, or helps to make it, about *Canis familiaris*. I have been charitable to this hypothesis in not trying to state it precisely (what, precisely, are these "stereotypes" supposed to be, anyway?[12]), but here are two reasons for doubting it even as stated.

1. The proponent of this hypothesis will need an account of what makes D a mode of presentation *of the species of dogs*. He needs, in other words, a relation R such that

D is a mode of presentation of *Canis familiaris* iff $R(D, Canis\ familiaris)$.

R cannot, we have noticed, be an instantiation relation. Evidently, one will seek some suitable *causal* relation. But what suitable causal relation? This may not be such an easy thing to find if one keeps rabbits in mind. For suppose that Tanya has seen only cottontail rabbits. How can the resultant *Gestalt*, or stereotype, then succeed in being of the larger natural kind that includes hares? But that is precisely what it must do if we are to account on the proposed lines for her belief that Henry is a rabbit.

2. No matter; it is doubtful in any event that *D* can satisfy Frege's Constraint, which really provides *the* motivation for the introduction of modes of presentation. It seems clear that, in principle, *D* could be a mode of presentation of more than one natural kind; after all, my Twin-Earth counterpart's stereotype of the non-dogs he calls 'dogs' will be the same as mine, and there is nothing to prevent tdogs from inhabiting Earth, which could certainly lead to my dog-stereotype being of two distinct zoological species. But then I might become aware that there were two distinct species sharing my stereotype. And if this were possible, then it is difficult to see what could prevent my believing and disbelieving the species of dogs to be such and such under one and the same mode of presentation (namely, *D*), thus violating Frege's Constraint. For if I can believe that dogs but not tdogs are *F*, then I can certainly misidentify dogs as tdogs and believe of the species to which they (the dogs misidentified as tdogs) belong, under *D*, that its members are not *F*, when I already believe of the species, also under *D*, that its members are *F*. Actually, it is only the great familiarity of dogs that drives me to Twin Earth. The point about stereotypes and Frege's Constraint is better made simply by changing the example: ornithological ignoramus that I am, the stereotype that I associate with 'goldfinch' is the same as the one I associate with 'bullfinch' and several other terms for birds. But that does not prevent me from believing that there are goldfinches in America.

If we are ever to take seriously the idea that beliefs such as Tanya's are made complete by the presence in them of doggy stereotypes, we shall certainly require an articulation and treatment of that intuition that elevates it into a hypothesis worth considering.

That concludes my argument against the propositional theory of belief, which may be summarized as follows.

If that theory were true, then some proposition would be the content of Tanya's belief that Gustav is a dog, and that proposition would either contain doghood itself or a "mode of presentation" of it. But if there really is a genuinely language-independent property of doghood, then doghood is the property of belonging to the biological natural kind to which all and only dogs belong (if there is such a natural kind); and once this is appreciated it is easy to show, with examples like the "shmog" example, that doghood cannot itself be the propositional constituent we seek. Then there is the problem of modes of presentation. The theory that the contents of natural-kind beliefs contain modes of presentation of the kinds is credible only if there is a credible specific proposal as to what those modes of presentation might be. But the only two specific proposals that seemed initially to have some degree of promise were found not to be satisfactory. As far as I can tell, then, there is no proposition that can plausibly be taken to be the content of a belief such as Tanya's; I conclude that the propositional theory of propositional attitudes is false.

I have a further reason for thinking that there is no proposition to be the content of Tanya's belief. There is one only if there really exists a non-pleonastic, genuinely language-independent property of being a dog; but there is no such property. I will not now set out the argument for denying that there is a property of being a dog, but it in no way proceeds from nominalist premises, and its gist may be conveyed thus. (1) If there were a (nonpleonastic, language-independent) property of being a dog, it would not be irreducible: we are not to suppose that Gustav, in addition to having a certain appearance, demeanor, morphology, ancestry, genetic structure, and so on, also has, over and above all these properties, the quite distinct, primitive, and irreducible property of being a dog. (2) If there were a reducible property of being a dog, there would be some property, however logically complex, specifiable in phenotypic and/or genetic and/or evolutionary, etc., terms which *was* the property of being a dog. (3) But there is no such property which is the property of being a dog; none of Gustav's properties, however complex, is such that, necessarily, a thing is a dog if and only if it has that property (part of my reason for thinking this is the point made in 3.5, that there is, evidently, no gene pool common to all and only dogs). The existence of doghood is, for me, of little moment; the issue is raised now for its foreshadowing effect with respect to the issue, later to be pressed, of the existence of objective, language-independent belief properties, properties such as being a belief that Gustav is a dog. Anyway, as I said at the start of this chapter, the case against the propositional theory of propositional attitudes may be overdetermined.

Chapter 4
Intentionality and the Language of Thought

4.1 Introduction

We are assuming that believing is a relation, in this sense: that 'y' in the schema 'x believes y' is an objectual variable whose values have features that determine the intentional, or contentful, features of beliefs. If IBS is true, these content-determining features of the objects of belief must not be public-language semantic features, features that presuppose meaning in a public, communicative language. This means, I argued in 1.5, that if IBS is true, then the objects of belief are either propositions or else mental representations. But the objects of belief, we know now, cannot be propositions. They must therefore be mental representations, sentences in one's language of thought, if IBS is true.

For the IBS theorist who takes this line, the thought is that the content of formulae of the inner code can be accounted for without presupposing anything about the intentional features of mental states or the meanings of linguistic items, and that it is this content, it is meaning in the language of thought, that determines the content of beliefs and thence the meaning of public-language items. "The picture, then," as neatly drawn by Colin McGinn, "is that the inner sentences are the basic objects of interpretation; their content confers content upon thoughts; and thoughts transmit their content to outer speech" (1982a, p. 70). And Jerry Fodor, the grand guru of Mentalese, has himself said that his "strategy is to view the intentional properties of mental states as inherited from the semantic properties of the mental representations which are implicated in their tokening" (unpublished; see also Fodor 1987).

I have spoken of mental representations and of sentences in a language of thought; some gloss is required, but, happily, our purposes can be served without much precision.

Ralph, it happens, is so benighted as to believe that James and Marilyn Monroe were man and wife. It is plausible that there is some internal state of Ralph's which is his belief about the two Monroes, and that this state is a physical state, no doubt a neural state of a certain kind. Let *n* be the neural state-token which happens to be that belief. The neural state *n* is a *mental representation*: being a belief that James and Marilyn Monroe were married, it, or a component of it, represents its being the case that the two Monroes were married. The representational state *n*, being a belief that James and Marilyn Monroe were married, is true if and only if they were married. Mental representations, then, are easily purchased.

To say that there are mental representations is not yet to say that there is a *system* of mental representation, let alone one that is sufficiently languagelike to warrant metaphorical talk of a language of thought. And yet, the hypothesis that our internal states of representation "have elements and structure in a way that is analogous to the way in which sentences have elements and structure" is not without plausibility (Harman 1978, p. 58). After all, if *n* represents the two Monroes as having been married, then it is reasonable to suppose that there is a part or aspect of *n* that in some way represents James Monroe, another that represents Marilyn Monroe, and another that represents having been married; and that it is because these parts are related in a certain way that the whole represents James and Marilyn Monroe as having been married. Thus, to say that we think in a language of thought is to say that our mental representations, the neural states that realize our beliefs, can be viewed, like sentences of a natural language, as organized structures, the representational features of the whole derived from the representational features of its constituent parts and structure. Even better, to say that we think in a language of thought is to say, first, that the brain is a computer, an information processor, and thus processes in an inner machine language, a neural code processed directly by our neural hardware; and, second, that our particular thoughts are realized by occurrences of formulae of this code. One's language of thought, one's *lingua mentis*, is precisely one's "brain's language of synaptic interconnections and neural spikes" (Lewis 1983a, p. 346).

The empirical hypothesis that we think in a language of thought is considerably weaker than the hypothesis we are interested in—the hypothesis that, in the sense explained, propositional attitudes are relations to mental representations, formulae of the inner code. For the former hypothesis is consistent with *any* hypothesis about the objects of propositional attitudes: someone who holds that believing is a relation to propositions, or to public-language sentences, can allow that the neural states that realize our beliefs have a sentencelike structure. I emphasize this obvious point because the literature has been ambiguous in its talk of belief being a relation to sentences in one's language of thought. Sometimes what is meant by saying that believing is a relation to a mental representation is not what I have meant—that mental representations are the values of '*y*' in the schema '*x* believes *y*'—but rather something along the lines of this:

There is some computational relation R such that x believes p iff, for some formula σ of x's inner code, $R(x, \sigma)$ and σ "means" p.

But this is little more than a restatement of the view that we think in a language of thought, and is consistent with any view about the values of 'p'. I have no interest at all in a verbal dispute about what it might or might not "really mean" to say that believing is a relation to blah-blahs; but it is amusing to notice that if the foregoing captured what that meant, then we could, by parity of reasoning, say that the *father of* relation was a relation between a man and a woman.

In any case, the thesis that concerns us, and that I shall call the *strong* language-of-thought hypothesis (SLT, for short), is a conjunction of two hypotheses. The first, which concerns the logical form of belief-ascribing sentences, is this:

[LF] Believing is a relation to mental representations in the sense that they are the values of 'y' in the schema 'x believes y'.

The second is the "inheritance thesis" glossed earlier, that the intentional features of mental states are inherited from, or reduce to, the semantic features of mental representations.

We can of course speak of the "semantic features" of mental representations whether or not the intentional features of beliefs reduce to them. Trivially, the neural sentence σ "means" for one that flounders snore if the belief that flounders snore would be realized in one by an occurrence of σ. To know the meaning of a mental representation σ is to know *what* one believes when σ is stored in one as a belief, where what one believes, the content of one's belief, is what is conveyed by the 'that'-clauses of the belief predicates true of one, predicates such as 'believes that flounders snore'. Two theorists can agree on this while disagreeing on the direction of analysis, one claiming that the "semanticity" of mental representations derives from the intentionality of mental states, the other, the SLT theorist, claiming the reverse. Thus, the second part of SLT is the hypothesis

[IT] There are features of mental representations that (a) determine the intentional features of beliefs (those features ascribed in 'that'-clauses) and (b) are themselves explicable without reference to the contents, the intentional features, of mental states, or to the semantic features of public-language expressions.

My first objection to SLT is that there is no way of satisfying LF consistently with IT;[1] my second, that there is no way of satisfying IT—no way, that is, of accounting for the representational features of neural states from scratch.

4.2 Mental Representations as Referents of 'That'-Clauses

Suppose that

[1]   Ralph believes that flounders snore.

If believing is a relation (if 'believes' in [1] is a dyadic predicate), then it is plausible that the content clause 'that flounders snore' refers in [1] to that which Ralph believes: to a neural sentence, if SLT is true. But how could the occurrence of 'that flounders snore' in [1] refer to a neural sentence? Clearly, if this is to be answerable, we must suppose, with Fodor (1981), that we are referring to the mental representation *indirectly*, via some relation to the sentence 'flounders snore', which functions in [1] to *index* the mental representation believed.

In other words, we must suppose, again with Fodor (1981), that there is some function f from English indexing sentences to mental representations such that [1] may be represented as

$B(\text{Ralph}, f(\text{'flounders snore'}))$,

$f(\text{'flounders snore'})$ being the mental representation believed by Ralph whose semantic features make it the case that Ralph believes that flounders snore rather than, say, that people who stick their chewing gum under theater seats are uncouth.

That is what we must suppose if the content clause in [1] is a singular term referring to the object of belief; but that construal is not mandatory, and all that SLT is really committed to is that there be some relation R holding between mental representations and English indexing sentences such that [1] enjoys the representation

[2] $(\exists \sigma)(R(\sigma, \text{'flounders snore'}) \ \& \ B(\text{Ralph}, \sigma))$,

'σ' here understood to range over formulae in Ralph's inner code.

But what relation is R? It is here that a problem arises. For (a) if [1] is to be represented by a substitution-instance of [2] in a way that is consistent with IT, then R must be specifiable without essential reference to the meaning of the English sentence 'flounders snore'; but (b) the only prima facie plausible way of achieving such a nonsemantic specification of R cannot work.

For, as regards (a), suppose that the best we can do in specifying R is something whose yield is on the order of this:

$R(\sigma, \text{'flounders snore'})$ iff σ means in Mentalese what 'flounders snore' means in English.

Then it would seem that IT is violated; for that thesis, in conformity with IBS, has it that public-language semantic features are inherited from the intentional features of mental states, and they in turn from the non–public-language semantic features of mental representations. Thus, the meaning of 'flounders snore' is to be explicated in terms of its potential for expressing the belief that flounders snore, and that project will spin for eternity if [1] can in turn only be explicated by reference to the meaning of 'flounders snore'. We need, as Fodor himself is well aware, a nonsemantic specification of R.[2] What might it be?

One wants a nonsemantic relation between mental representations and public-language sentences that will in fact secure that the formulae related by this relation will have the same content. Now one naturally thinks to exploit the fact that each Mentalese sentence will be uniquely correlated with a "synonymous" public-language sentence via a potential causal chain that contains the mental representation, stored as a belief, and terminates in an assertive utterance of the spoken sentence. Fodor suggests this tack, and it has been independently elaborated by Stich (Fodor 1981; Stich 1982, 1983). Fortunately for the plausibility of SLT, the implementation of this idea need not actually mention the inner code and, in the first instance, can take the form of an account of what would be asserted by an utterance of [1]:

[3]   In uttering [1] a speaker S asserts that Ralph is in a belief state that has the same content as the belief state S would be in if he were to utter 'flounders snore' sincerely and assertively.[3]

This is good for SLT because no reference is made to the content of the *sentence* 'flounders snore'. If [3] were correct, one could then define R of [2] in terms of the counterfactual causal relation between mental representations and spoken sentences determined by [3]. But [3] is not correct. For [3] is true only if Ralph's believing that flounders snore is entailed by his being in a belief state with the same content as the belief state S would be in if he were to utter 'flounders snore' sincerely and assertively. But it is very clear that this is not entailed: it might be a peculiar fact about S that, for some reason or other, he would not utter 'flounders snore' sincerely and assertively unless it meant that the flamingos were flying south early this year. What is needed to patch [3] up is precisely a reference to the content of 'flounders snore', precisely what the SLT theorist cannot have. I strongly suspect that *any* attempt to concoct a nonsemantic specification of R would founder on this problem, and therefore doubt that LF can be cashed out in a way that is consistent with IT.

So much for LF. I turn now to IT, to the problem of providing a semantics for the language of thought. It will be apparent as we proceed that this is a problem of interest to any physicalistic friend of the language of thought, whether or not he or she accepts LF.

4.3 Truth Conditions for the Language of Thought

According to SLT, there is some (no doubt complex) property Φ, which determines whatever has Φ to mean that flounders snore, such that

> Ralph believes that flounders snore iff $(\exists\sigma)(\sigma$ is a sentence of Ralph's language of thought & $\Phi\sigma$ & $B(\text{Ralph}, \sigma))$,

and likewise for anything else that Ralph might believe. In conformity with IT, Φ must not presuppose anything about the intentional features of mental states or about the meanings of public-language items. But then there is a further constraint that the naturalistically minded philosopher will want Φ to satisfy: it must not appeal to *any* irreducibly semantic or intentional properties but must be specifiable in naturalistically respectable terms. Jerry Fodor has expressed the point well:

> Anybody who jibs at intentionality as an irreducible property of the mental is likely to be equally distressed by semanticity as an irreducible property of the symbolic. The explanation of intentionality by reference to internal representations looks like a serious intellectual advance only if there is some prospect of a correspondingly serious theory about what bestows semantic properties upon mental symbols. (unpublished)

The content-determining features of mental representations must, that is, be part of the natural order.

Since the publication of Hartry Field's "Logic, Meaning, and Conceptual Role" (1977), the dominant idea among SLT theorists has been that the meaning of a mental representation is determined by two factors: its *conceptual role* and its *truth condition*.[4] Neither factor determines the other, and both together are needed to determine content. Thus, a correct semantics for a language of thought will be a two-component theory: one component will assign to each inner sentence a truth condition, and the other will assign to each inner sentence a conceptual role. The idea is that if we get both assignments right, then we will know the contents of the beliefs one's mental representations realize; for any mental representation σ, one will know exactly what one believes in believing σ. The conceptual-role component is the subject of section 4.6; this one and the next two are about the truth-condition component.

For our purposes, the truth-theoretic component of a meaning theory for a Mentalese language M may be viewed as the specification of a function that maps each sentence of M onto a possible (or impossible) state of affairs which is the sentence's truth condition; that is, the truth condition of the belief one has when that sentence is stored in one's head as a belief.[5]

Our question is this: What makes a given state of affairs the truth condition of a given mental representation? But this is best put in other terms. So let us first say that

> For any Mentalese language M, an *M-function* is any function from the sentences of M to possible (or impossible) states of affairs.

For each system of mental representation there will be infinitely many M-functions. If M is Ralph's language of thought and σ the neural formula that realizes his belief that flounders snore, then one M-function will map σ onto the possible state of affairs that flounders snore, another onto the state of affairs that pigs do not think in Hebrew, and so on. Thus, let us further say that

> An M-function f is *the TC function* for M iff, for every sentence σ of M, $f(\sigma)$ is σ's truth condition.

If our beliefs have determinate content, then, for each system of mental representation M, *just one* of the infinitely many M-functions is the TC function for M. The demand for a naturalistic account of the semantic features of mental representations requires the theorist to specify a physicalistically creditable condition C such that

> An M-function f is the TC function for M iff f satisfies C.

Now what is C?

One wants a neat and simple intuitive idea to exploit, and there is one at hand, the "fuel gauge" model of representation of 2.6. If in believing a neural sentence σ one believes that flounders snore, then σ represents the possible state of affairs that flounders snore and therefore has that state of affairs as its truth condition. So we are really looking for a theory of *representation*, of which *mental* representation is a special case. Now we have already noticed that representation is not just a feature of mental states, and that the position of a needle on the dashboard of your car can represent your gas tank as being ¾ full. And it is no mystery how the position of the needle can have this representational power: the latter derives from the capacity of the fuel gauge to be a reliable indicator of the amount of fuel in the gas tank. More exactly, *the position of the needle represents the gas tank as being ¾ full because under optimal conditions the needle is where it is (viz., pointing at '¾') when, and only when, the gas tank is ¾ full of gasoline.* This suggests that representation *in general* derives from the capacity of a system to be a reliable indicator of its context, and that what accounts for the fuel gauge's representational features also accounts for those of a person's mental representations.

The generalization appropriate to mental representation is clear and, evidently, not uncompelling:

[a]   An M-function f is the TC function for x's *lingua mentis* M iff: for every sentence σ of M, under optimal conditions x believes σ when, and only when, $f(\sigma)$ obtains.

In other words:

α is the truth condition of σ in x's inner code iff under optimal conditions x believes σ when, and only when, α obtains.

By this formula we could discover that a certain sequence of neural spikes in a frog's brain represented that there was a fly in its visual field, and that a mental representation of mine is true just in case it is raining—for when my cognitive system is working optimally, that mental representation will be stored as a belief when it is in fact raining, and if it is stored as a belief, then it is in fact raining. I say that [a] is evidently not uncompelling because it was, nearly enough, the theory of Jerry Fodor (see Fodor unpublished but also 1987, where he retreats somewhat). But is [a] true?

I cannot resist a methodological reflection. It may happen that one is committed to delivering a paper and that one discovers, at the last minute and to one's horror, that one's theory has an absurd consequence, a consequence so absurd that if it is pointed out by a critic it will, without further ado, be taken as a refutation of one's position. Now the best thing to do in this deplorable situation is to point out the disastrous consequence oneself, before anyone else can notice it, and to embrace it. That way one cannot be refuted simply by having the consequence spotted; an elaborate argument is now required. I cannot, however, claim to have discovered this methodological gem, for I suspect its employment in Jerry Fodor's cheerful acknowledgment that his theory entails that, under optimal conditions, everyone is omniscient and infallible. Omniscient because if any state of affairs obtains (and one is functioning as well as possible), then one believes, and presumably knows, it; infallible because, under the ideal conditions, one has no false beliefs. Prima facie, this is implausible: suppose that Nancy Reagan sneezed exactly three times on the morning of May 11, 1938, and now assume that your cognitive system is functioning as well as it can possibly function and that you are situated in the world as well as you might hope to be; this—*pace* Fodor—is still no guarantee that you will believe that Nancy Reagan sneezed exactly three times on the morning of May 11, 1938.

Whatever these Fodorian "optimality conditions" are, it is clear that (1) they never obtain; (2) we do not have a clue as to what they are; (3) if they are to be serviceable to SLT, they must be specifiable without mention of anything semantic or intentional; and (4) while unsatisfied, they are satisfiable; otherwise [a] would be incoherent. So [a] really comes to this:

[b]   There is some ("optimality") condition *D*—unsatisfied, but satisfiable, and specifiable in naturalistic terms—such that

An *M*-function f is the TC function for x's *lingua mentis* *M* iff: for every sentence σ of *M*, were *D* to obtain x would believe σ when, and only when, $f(\sigma)$ obtained.

But what might *D* be? Noticing that 'x' ranges over all believers, including dogs, one might reasonably decline to wait for an answer. I think that the deep problem with [b] is that it offers a false and blasphemous version of Genesis. It is blasphemous because it implies that God is an imperfect engineer. On the Fodorian version of Genesis, God set Himself the engineering task of creating little duplicates of Himself; He wanted to design creatures with cognitive systems such that, if things went as intended, these creatures too would be omniscient and infallible. Obviously, God failed; were it not for God's incompetence, we would be as omniscient and infallible as He. On the correct version of Genesis, there is no incompetence (or at least not very much). God did think that it would be nice to populate the earth with information processors and, being omnipotent and omniscient Himself, of course could have made these created systems omniscient and infalliable. But God did not want any competition: He *liked* being the only omniscient and infallible I/O device on the scene. The engineering task He set Himself was to give His creations a cognitive system that was pretty good of its kind, but *limited*. These created I/O systems were to have limited input access, limited memory storage, limited deductive and inductive abilities. Under optimal conditions they might succeed in not breaking a leg, but they would not be omniscient or infallible.[6]

The intuitive idea with which we started our search for a naturalistic determination of Mentalese truth conditions was that representation in general derives from the capacity of a system to be a reliable indicator of its context. The thought occurs that Fodor's account is not the best application of the intuitive idea.

There is another problem with Fodor's approach, noticing which might help to put us on a more promising track. Any reliability theory of mental content must take account of the fact that we are reliable indicators of our environment only with respect to *some* of our beliefs. If Ralph is looking at a dog, then it is a good bet that he believes that he is; and if he believes that he is looking at a dog, then it is again a good bet that he is. But this reliability does not extend to Ralph's belief that Jesus Christ was a deity, and if I have exactly eleven dollars in my wallet there is no reason to suppose Ralph will believe that. So if we are to account for Mentalese truth conditions in terms of reliability, we cannot hope to proceed, as it were, belief by belief, but must see reliability considerations working through the *systematic connections* that obtain among Mentalese expressions. In other words, if we are to make something of a reliability account of truth conditions for the language of thought, we had better be approaching this from the point of view of the language *as a whole* and not proceeding, as Fodor does, mental representation by mental representation. This need for a more holistic, or system-oriented, application of reliability considerations is satisfied in the next suggestion, which tries to improve on Fodor.

For any mental representation σ and state of affairs α, we can speak of

the probability that α obtains given that one believes σ,

and of

the probability that one believes σ given that α obtains.

Distinct M-functions may then be compared with respect to what we might call *head-world* (H-W) and *world-head* (W-H) reliability.

The *H-W* reliability of x (thinking in M) with respect to an M-function f measures, for each σ of M, the likelihood that $f(\sigma)$ obtains given that x believes σ.

The *W-H* reliability of x (thinking in M) with respect to an M-function f measures, for each σ of M, the likelihood that x believes σ given that $f(\sigma)$ obtains.

The thought then to be refined would be that

[c]   An M-function f is the TC function for x's *lingua mentis* M iff (some favored balance of) the H-W and W-H reliability of x (thinking in M) with respect to f is greater than that with respect to any other M-function.[7]

One might try to motivate this in the following sort of way. Suppose that Ralph thinks in English[8] and that, therefore, the TC function for his language of thought is, so to say, the "homophonic" one that maps 'snow is white' onto snow's being white, 'Richard Milhous Nixon is retired' onto Nixon's being retired, and so forth. One might then find that it was very likely that Ralph believed 'I am looking at a dog' given that he was looking at a dog; and one might find that it was very likely that Ralph was looking at a dog given that he believed 'I am looking at a dog'. At the same time, one might also find that, however optimally Ralph's cognitive system was functioning, it was very unlikely that Ralph would believe 'there were 5,983 dogs born in Kadiyevka in 1973' given that there were 5,983 dogs born in Kadiyevka in 1973, and very unlikely that all Pisces are great intellects given that Ralph believes 'all Pisces are great intellects'. Now what [c] entails is that Ralph's H-W and W-H reliability relative to the TC function for English is greater than that relative to any other E-function.

For *most* (so to speak) E-functions that is obviously correct, and to see this one needs only briefly to consider any random E-function—say, one that is just like the homophonic TC function except that it derives from a compositional semantics for E that assigns coal to 'snow', and thus maps 'snow is white' onto the state of affairs that coal is white, and so on. If an E-function is to test [c], it must be a more studied sort of systematic departure from the TC function; but in considering such departures one might come to think that none captures the reliability of Ralph as well as the TC function. In this light one might consider the E-function which is determined by a compositional semantics for English that is exactly like the compositional semantics determining the TC function, except that it assigns to 'dog' the property of being a canine, as opposed to the property of being a dog. Now the likelihood that the creature before Ralph is a canine given that he believes 'that is a dog' may well be greater than the likelihood that the creature before Ralph is a dog given that he believes 'that is a dog'; but the balance significantly favors the TC function when one considers what will cause Ralph to believe 'that is a dog', or what state of affairs is most likely to obtain given that Ralph believes 'some canines are not dogs'.

Anyway, one might think that some refinement of [c] was the way to capture the intuitive idea that content is determined by one's barometric qualities, and one might *try* to motivate [c] in the foregoing sort of way. I do not, however, think that any such attempt can succeed. My objection to [c], and to natural refinements of it, is simply that it is unlikely that there is a uniquely most reliable M-function.

If we assume that our thoughts have determinate truth conditions, then my objection is that the right-hand side of [c] fails to state a necessary condition: there will be M-functions other than the TC function for M that capture one's reliability as well as the TC function does. As regards Ralph, still thinking in English, the point is that E-functions other than the TC function will capture Ralph's H-W and W-H reliability as well as the TC function does. Why think that this is so?

1. Why think that this is *not* so? Surely the burden of proof is on the proponent of the reliability strategy to show that there will always be a *unique* M-function such that one's reliability with respect to that function is greater than one's reliability with respect to any other M-function. But I do not have a clue as to how one would even begin to try to establish this.[9]

2. Ralph, we lately noticed, is H-W or W-H reliable with respect to certain matters but not others. If Ralph drank coffee this morning, then it is a good bet that he believes that he did; but it is unlikely that he will have any belief about the exact number of hydrogen molecules in his first cup of coffee. If Ralph believes that his middle name is 'Ignatz', then it very

probably is; but if he believes that Fodor's theory of psychosemantics is correct, then . . . . Intuitively it seems that there *could* be studied departures from the TC function for E that left Ralph's reliability undiminished. Perhaps E-functions *f* and *g* derive from compositional semantics that make the same assignments to all of the "observation" terms in Ralph's idiolect but differ in their assignments to certain of his "theoretical" terms: perhaps *f* assigns to 'pound' a certain unit of *weight*, i.e., the force due to gravity on a body, whereas *g* assigns to 'pound' a certain unit of *mass*. Yet might not the external and internal reliability of Ralph be the same with respect to *f* and *g*? And if that is possible, then the way is evidently open for much more interesting and radical differences between E-functions with respect to which Ralph is equally reliable. In this context one naturally thinks of Quine's (1970) argument about the indeterminacy of theory-formulating sentences when there are two or more empirically adequate theories with respect to which those sentences could be interpreted.

3. Tyler Burge's Alfred certainly challenges the correctness of [c]. His use of 'arthritis', it will be recalled (see chapter 2, section 2.4), encompasses more than the correct range of application of that term (which is limited to inflammation of the joints), to include rheumatoid ailments not in the joints; it does not preclude him from expressing the (false) belief that he has arthritis in the thigh when he says to his doctor, "I've got arthritis in the thigh." The problem Alfred poses for [c] emerges clearly if we suppose that Alfred thinks in his spoken idiolect, E. The TC function for E will be determined by a compositional semantics for E that assigns the condition *arthritis* to 'arthritis' and thus maps 'I've got arthritis in the thigh' onto the state of affairs of Alfred's having arthritis in his thigh. Now let *g* be an E-function that is just like the TC function, except that it is determined by a compositional semantics for E that assigns to 'arthritis' the condition we may call *shmarthritis*, which is just any arthritis-like rheumatoid ailment. Thus *g* maps 'I've got arthritis in the thigh' *not* onto Alfred's having arthritis in the thigh but onto the state of affairs of his having *shmarthritis* in the thigh. (So 'Alfred has arthritis in his thigh' is *false* with respect to the TC function but *true* with respect to *g*.)

The problem for [c] is that it seems a good bet that the H-W and W-H reliability of Alfred with respect to *g* will be no less than that with respect to the TC function. First, the probability that Alfred has shmarthritis given that he believes 'I have arthritis' will be greater than the probability that he has arthritis given that he believes 'I have arthritis'. This is clear from the fact that often Alfred will not have arthritis (in a particular place, at a given time) when he believes 'I have arthritis', but he nearly always will have shmarthritis. Second, the probability that Alfred believes 'I have arthritis' given that he has shmarthritis should be the same as the probability that Alfred believes that sentence given that he has arthritis: typically,

Alfred will believe 'I have arthritis' if he really has arthritis or merely has shmarthritis.

Nor is it likely that this balance between g and the TC function will be offset by taking into account Alfred's beliefs about the "arthritis" of others or his general and molecular beliefs involving 'arthritis'. Typically, Alfred will believe 'Jones has arthritis' just in case he has heard Jones say, "I've got arthritis." In that event, the probability that Jones has shmarthritis given that Alfred believes 'Jones has arthritis' will be no less than the probability that Jones has arthritis given that Alfred believes 'Jones has arthritis', but the probability that Alfred believes that sentence given that Jones has arthritis will most likely be greater than the probability that Alfred believes that sentence given that Jones has shmarthritis—for presumably Jones is more likely to say "I've got arthritis" if he really has arthritis than if he merely has shmarthritis. Yet this last fact can hardly show that Alfred's overall reliability is better captured by the TC function than by g; for Alfred's reliability under both functions will be much greater with respect to his own bodily states than with respect to those of others. I will not go into detail about Alfred's general and molecular beliefs, but here we should probably expect a standoff. It is true that the probability that arthritis is correctly called 'arthritis' in English given that Alfred believes 'arthritis is correctly called "arthritis" in English' is greater than the corresponding probability with respect to shmarthritis; but it is also true that the situation is reversed when we consider what is likely to obtain given that Alfred believes 'arthritis is not confined to the joints'.

In this way we have a counterexample to the purported *necessity* of [c]; for we have an example in which a function satisfies the left-hand side of [c] but not its right-hand side. It is easy to see how the example also seriously challenges the purported *sufficiency* of [c]. For, given the facts about Alfred, it is quite likely that while g does not satisfy the left-hand side of [c] (i.e., it is not the TC function for E), it *does* satisfy the right-hand side.[10]

4. Another prima facie counterexample to the putative necessity of [c] is suggested by Saul Kripke's (1982) presentation of a Wittgensteinian paradox. Consider again Ralph, ever thinking in English. Now the symbol ' + ' (and the word 'plus') in E, Ralph's *lingua mentis*, stands for the addition function, and f^*, the homophonic TC function for E, is cognizant of that fact: $f^*('33 + 52 = 85')$ is the state of affairs that $33 + 52 = 85$. At the same time there is the E-function g, which is just like f^* except in what it determines for ' + '/'plus'. Let ' # ' stand for some extremely large number—a number too large for Ralph's brain to grasp, too large to be involved in any computation that Ralph could make—and let 'quaddition' stand for that mathematical function that agrees with the addition function for pairs

of numbers smaller than $\#$ but has 5 as its value when one of its arguments is at least as great as $\#$; that is, in symbols,

$$x \, \$ \, y = x + y, \text{ if } x, y < \#$$
$$= 5 \text{ otherwise.}$$

Then the E-function g is just like f^* except that the compositional semantics that determines g assigns quaddition to '+'/'plus', so that $g('17 + \# = 5')$ is the state of affairs that $17 \, \$ \, \# = 5$, which state of affairs, of course, actually obtains.

Now we are in a position to construct a counterexample to [c] in which Ralph's internal and external reliability with respect to g is no less than that with respect to f^*, the TC function for Ralph's language of thought. The simplest, and I think most convincing, way of getting such a counter-example is to suppose that although Ralph has mastered addition (in that he can add tolerably well), he has virtually no general beliefs about addi-tion—such as, for example, a belief that the sum of two numbers is always equal to or greater than either one of them—and that if he were to form such general beliefs, they would most likely be false. To make things really firm, we can just suppose that poor Ralph's brain renders him incapable of forming any such beliefs (presently we will consider the prospects of constructing a quaddition-type counterexample for a more normal Ralph). Given this assumption, it is now easy to show that Ralph is as reliable under g as he is under f^*.

First, consider sentences of the form '$x + y = z$' that Ralph *could* believe (given the constraints imposed by his brain). None of them will be about a number as large as $\#$, for such numbers are too large to grasp. So the probability that Ralph believes such a sentence given that g(that sentence) obtains is the same as that given that f^*(that sentence) obtains, for both functions yield the same value for that sentence. Next consider sentences of the form '$x + y = z$' where one of the numerals flanking '+' refers to a number at least as great as $\#$; by hypothesis, the probability of Ralph's believing any such sentence given that either g(that sentence) or f^*(that sentence) obtains is 0 (or pretty close to it). But what of the relevant conditional probabilities given that Ralph believes a sentence of the form '$x + y = z$'? Well, that is not really the question we need to be asking, for if σ_+ is any sentence of the form '$x + y = z$', the probability that $f^*/g(\sigma_+)$ obtains is 0 or 1 no matter what sentence Ralph believes. The relevant question (if I may be allowed to change relevant questions in midstream) as regards Ralph's arithmetical reliability must surely be something like this: For any σ_+, which is greater, the probability that (Ralph believes σ_+ & $f^*(\sigma_+)$ obtains) or the probability that (Ralph believes σ_+ & $g(\sigma_+)$ obtains)? But we already know that the probabilities will be the same for σ_+'s that Ralph *might* compute; and as regards those that his brain lacks the capacity to compute—because they contain numerals that refer to numbers larger than #—there clearly cannot be any difference betwen g and f^*.

There is, then, no relevant reliability difference between g and f^* as regards Ralph's believing sentences of the form '$x + y = z$', and we have assumed that he is incapable of believing (or of being reliable with respect to) general arithmetical sentences containing '$+$'. Since it is certainly *possible* that there is a person satisfying the description of Ralph, we have a counterexample to [c].

Nevertheless, the question arises whether a quaddition-type counterexample could be constructed for a more mathematically sophisticated Ralph, one who believes the sentence 'for any x, y, $x + y \geq x$' and others like it. It might be thought that such a counterexample could be constructed by altering the description of g so that it yields nonstandard interpretations of the quantifiers, '$=$', or '$>$' to fit the nonstandard interpretation of '$+$' (cf. Kripke 1982, p. 16, n. 12). The task here would be to give nonstandard interpretations of these expressions that preserved Ralph's reliability with respect to *all* of his potential beliefs involving these expressions. Perhaps this can be done, but I have not been able to satisfy myself that it can be. Still, a counterexample is a counterexample.[11]

The SLT theorist must specify some set of constraints that pick out, for any internal system of mental representation M, just one of the infinitely many M-functions as capturing the truth conditions of M and thus being the TC function for M. But these constraints, for this theorist, must be ones that are naturalistic and presuppose nothing intentional or semantic; principles of "charity" or "humanity," being explicitly framed in terms of propositional attitudes, will therefore be unavailable to him (which is not to say that they would help anyway). The strategy of trying to capture adequate constraints in terms of an agent's reliability, at least as embodied in [c] (and obvious refinements of it), seems not to work. Is there some related line to be explored?

There is one that is close to the approach that seeks to exploit one's barometric qualities, but different enough to warrant comment. It is an approach suggested by the correct, nonblasphemous version of Genesis. There, one may recall, God's goal was the creation of information processors who (a) were *limited* in certain important ways concerning memory storage, inductive and deductive reasoning abilities, and range and kind of inputs (sensory stimulations) and outputs (basic acts), but (b) were so causally connected to the environment into which God intended to place them that (c) their chances of surviving and flourishing—anyway, of having their needs and basic desires taken care of—were maximized relative to the limitations alluded to in (a). Picturesquely put, God's design task was to solve for (b) given the constraints imposed by (a) and (c). God, being God, of course solved His problem, and we are hooked up to our environment as well as we can hope to be, given our design limitations and basic desires. Now the thought likely to titillate the SLT theorist is that God could not have solved His design problem without securing that Mentalese expressions were causally related to objects and properties in the extracranial world in such a way as to determine a certain *unique* correlation of internal sentences with external states of affairs, this being the TC function.

Getting rid of God, the idea to be entertained is that

[d]   What makes an M-function f the TC function for M is that f is, in some relevant sense, uniquely determined by the correct account of the actual, or ideal, functioning of one's cognitive system *with respect to one's survival in the world.*

Perhaps a fanciful story will give content to the intuition that [d] is gesturing toward.

We are presented with a human, Ubu, who survives quite well in an environment W and thinks in a neural machine language N. We know nothing, initially, about the referential or truth-conditional features of the expressions of N, but we are given a complete *formal* description of N; that is, we know how to define well-formedness for N and thus know exactly which of the infinitely many possible neural configurations in Ubu's head would be well-formed sentences of N (I am of course cheating like crazy, *but on the side of SLT*). We also kow that believing is a certain (computational) relation to inner formulae, desiring another such relation; and we know that, simplifying a little, all of Ubu's behavior is determined by certain of his desires (which we might call *intentions*). In addition, we are given Ubu's inner belief- and desire- and behavior-forming mechanisms, which may be glossed in the following way.

We know that, roughly speaking, what Ubu believes at a given time t is determined by his sensory stimulations and what he believes at times immediately preceding t; in knowing Ubu's belief-forming mechanisms we know, for each sentence σ of N, exactly what it would take by way of sensory stimulations and/or sentences already believed for Ubu to believe σ. (So, for example, we come to know, *inter alia*, that if Ubu believes $\ulcorner \sigma @ \sigma' \urcorner$, then he also believes both σ and σ'; that if he believes $\ulcorner \sigma * \sigma' \urcorner$ and believes σ, then he also believes σ'; and that if he believes σ, then he does not also believe $\ulcorner \S\sigma \urcorner$—facts that might later lead us to translate '@', '*', and '$\S$' as 'and', 'if ..., then ———', and 'not' respectively. Note that the belief-forming mechanisms are "inner" in that they take no account of distal causes but have as their sole inputs things already in the head.) Likewise, we know that, roughly speaking, what Ubu desires at a given time t is determined by his bodily states (in particular, states of deprivation) together with what he believes and desires at times immediately preceding t; in knowing Ubu's desire-forming mechanisms we know, for each sentence σ of N, exactly what it would take by way of bodily states and/or sentences already believed and desired for Ubu to desire σ. In the same way, we know that, roughly speaking, what motor responses (or—extending this a little—bodily movements) Ubu exhibits at t is determined by what he desires immediately preceding t; in knowing his behavior-forming mechanisms we know, for each sentence σ, whether or not desiring σ could lead directly to a motor response, and, if it could, which ones, and under what conditions, it would lead to. In knowing all of this we may say that we know the "conceptual role" of each sentence of N; we also know the "conceptual role" of each subsentential expression of N, for the conceptual role of an expression may be taken to be the contribution that the expression makes to the conceptual roles of the infinitely many sentences in which it occurs.

We now know an awful lot about N and about Ubu's information processing in N; but we know nothing about the causal connections between the primitive, nonlogical vocabulary of N (roughly, the names and predicates) and distal objects and properties in W, Ubu's environment, and so do not know enough to recover the truth conditions of his inner sentences. Now what [d] in effect suggests is that if we add to what we already know certain salient facts about how N's names and predicates are causally related to objects and properties in W, then we will have both a complete account of Ubu's survival in W and enough to recover, somehow, the TC function for N.

The use of 'somehow' in the last sentence is pointed: no matter how many causal, nonsemantic facts we know, we cannot determine that a certain N-function is the TC function for N unless we also know a completion of

An N-function f is the TC function for N if . . .

that, together with the nonsemantic facts we know, entails that that function is the TC function for N. The problem is to see how this might be completed consonantly with [d], to see how the provision of a correct causal/explanatory theory of Ubu's ability to survive in W could select a *unique* N-function as *the TC function* for N.

Intuitively, one survives as well as one does because the beliefs that enter into one's survival-relevant behavior—behavior that satisfies what is needed for survival—are highly reliable: one's beliefs about how to get food and shelter tend to be true, at least often enough for one to survive. This might suggest the following direction for converting [d] into something testable. Let us think of the infinitely many N-functions as being that many different possible interpretations of N, thus enabling us to say that σ is *true under f* just in case $f(\sigma)$ obtains. Then we could compare N-functions with respect to "survival value" thus:

> N-function f has greater survival value than N-function g for Ubu in W iff Ubu is more likely to survive in W given that he tends to form beliefs that are true under f than he is given that he tends to form beliefs that are true under g.[12]

Thus suppose that the truth condition of σ in N happens to be that there is a banana in front of Ubu. If Ubu becomes hungry and reaches forward because he believes σ, then it is clearly important that σ be true if Ubu's behavior is to result in the satisfaction of his hunger. But suppose that for wild N-function g, σ is true under g just in case Albert Einstein was a terrible pinochle player. Obviously, the truth or falsity of σ under g is altogether irrelevant to Ubu's satisfying his hunger.

So perhaps the intuition leading to [d] could be refined in the hypothesis that

[e]   An M-function f is the TC function for x's *lingua mentis* M iff f has greater survival value for x in x's environment than any other M-function has.

But [e], alas, will fare no better than its reliability predecessor [c], and for pretty much the same reasons: different M-functions will converge on beliefs that matter to survival but will differ on the others (the "quaddition" example, applied now to [e]); and M-functions that differ in their assignments to survival-relevant beliefs will still manage equally to preserve survival value (the "pound" and "arthritis" examples, applied now to [e]).

The SLT theorist needs to find a way of determining truth conditions for the language of thought that will not founder on the fact that M-functions other than the TC function might maximize relevant reliability as well as it does. I turn to what promises to be such a way.

4.4 A Different Tack on Truth Conditions for the Language of Thought

Our task, in which we have yet to succeed, has been to say in naturalistically acceptable terms what determines the truth conditions of mental representations, and therewith the truth conditions of the beliefs that those mental representations realize. For convenience I have, in effect, conceptualized the task thus: to find a function g, intrinsically specifiable in wholly nonintentional terms, such that

> An M-function f is the TC function for x's *lingua mentis* M iff $g(x, M) = f$.

In other words, we seek a replacement for the letter 'g' in the indented sentence-form that contains only terms suitable to the reduction of the intentional to the nonintentional and turns the sentence-form into a non-trivial truth.

The efforts considered in the last section may suggest, and are certainly consistent with, the following two assumptions: first, that the truth we seek is *a priori* (and thus something that the philosopher can think up in his armchair); second, that it will somehow directly involve the reliability of belief states as indicators of what states of affairs obtain in the world at large. If one accepts these assumptions together with the preceding section's objections, one may be inclined to conclude that the truth in question does not exist.

But what if one rejects these two assumptions? If we reject the first, "*a prioricity*," assumption, the task of saying what determines Mentalese truth conditions will look more like scientific theorizing, and it will not be surprising that it has not yet been accomplished. If we reject the second, reliability, assumption, we shall be free to say that, while it is the need to exploit one another's head-world and world-head reliability correlations that may explain, or help to explain, why we ascribe truth-theoretic con-tent to belief states, it is nevertheless a mistake to think that we can explicate that truth-theoretic content directly in terms of those reliability correlations.

Suppose that we think in English. Then we know that the sentence of inner English

[S]   Snow is not white

has as its truth condition the (nonactual) state of affairs that snow is not white. The last section presented a general question whose application to [S] implied the question, What makes it the case that [S] has that truth condition? One answer implied that [S] had snow's not being white as its truth condition because under optimal conditions someone thinking in English would believe [S] when and only when that state of affairs ob-tained; another answer implied that [S]'s truth condition was that snow was not white because that was the state of affairs assigned to the sentence by that E-function which maximized reliability.

But in pondering these answers a reader may wonder why I did not go for the following different answer:

We may assume that [S]'s truth condition is determined by [S]'s syntax and the semantic values of its constituent words: 'snow' refers to the stuff snow; 'is white' is true of each white thing; 'not' expresses negation; and the particular arrangement of those words in [S] is an instance of a type of arrangement that expresses a function that when applied to the foregoing semantic values in the relevant order yields the state of affairs that snow is not white. Thus, [S]'s syntax and each of its semantically relevant parts have correlated with them particular semantic values (a stuff, a set of things, a truth function, and so on), each of which plays its part in the determination of [S]'s truth condition. If there are naturalistically acceptable facts (roughly, physical or topic-neutral facts) that make it the case that [S]'s words and syntactical type have their semantic values, then surely one ought to expect the following sort of story to be sort of right.

In the case of [S]'s syntax (that is, the particular configuration type that makes [S] a sentence) and the word 'not', semantic import is determined by conceptual role. Conceptual role (about which more will be said in 4.6) is an abstraction from functional role: to know the conceptual role of a neural sentence σ is just to know the functional role of believing σ, desiring σ, intending σ, and so on; and to know the conceptual role of a subsentential expression or construction is to know its contribution to the conceptual role of each sentence in which it occurs. What makes it the case that 'not' in inner English expresses negation is facts, roughly speaking, such as these: if you believe σ, then you do not also believe $\ulcorner$not $\sigma\urcorner$; if you believe $\ulcorner$if σ, then $\sigma'\urcorner$ and $\ulcorner$not $\sigma'\urcorner$, then you also believe $\ulcorner$not $\sigma\urcorner$; if you desire σ and believe $\ulcorner$if σ', then not $\sigma\urcorner$, then you also desire $\ulcorner$not $\sigma'\urcorner$. Another, but more complicated, story is available to explain the semantic import of the relevant syntactical type to which [S] belongs.

But while it is plausible that some expressions and constructions have their semantic import determined by their conceptual roles, this cannot be true of all meaningful expressions. Conceptual role is internal to the head; the expressions in the neural language of my Twin-Earth counterpart have the same conceptual roles as those in my neural language; but it is not plausible that very many names or predicates have their semantic import determined merely by what is in the head. In seeking to explain what makes it the case that 'Mia Farrow' and 'snow' have the references they have, qua terms in the language of thought, one should look to *causal* relations that run from the references to the head containing those terms. Likewise for most general terms—'dog', 'brutal', 'to kiss', and probably even 'white' (only now the world end of the causal relation is probably best thought of as being anchored at the crucial juncture not by the term's denotation but by a property correlated with the term, as another of its semantic values, which determines its denotation: doghood for 'dog', whiteness for 'white', and so on). If one could say what these causal relations were in nonintentional terms, then one would have reduced the semantic relations of reference and denotation (as those relations apply to the language of thought) to physicalistically acceptable relations. Such a reduction is just what one should expect if physicalism is true and our thoughts have truth-theoretic content.

Thus, the "different answer" to the question, By virtue of what does [S] have as its truth condition the state of affairs that snow is not white?, is that it has it by virtue of (1) the conceptual roles of certain of its parts and features and (2) certain causal relations, explicative of reference and denotation, that obtain between other of its constitutive parts and things or properties outside the head.

Of course, this conceptual-role/causal-relation answer is not inconsistent with the answers implied by the various sorts of reliability theories considered in the preceding section. The maximal reliability theorist, for example, will say that [S] has as its truth condition the state of affairs that snow is not white because that is the state of affairs correlated with [S] by that E-function which maximizes reliability, but he will not deny that [S] *also* has that truth condition because it has a certain package of conceptual-role and causal-relation features. Rather, he will hold, first, that [S] stands in the relevant reliability relation to the state of affairs that happens to be its truth condition *because* the relevant conceptual-role/causal-relation package applies to [S]; and, second, that it is *because* the conceptual-role/causal-relation package plays the role that it does in maximizing reliability that it is determinative of [S]'s truth condition.

Someone who accepts the objections brought against the reliability theorist in the last section is free to agree that (a) there is a conceptual-role/causal-relation package that is determinative of [S]'s truth condition, and even that (b) that package is adequate to explain the nature of the agent's reliability. He needs only to deny that (c) the conceptual-role/causal-relation package is determinative of [S]'s truth condition *by virtue of its role in accounting for reliability*. (He must disagree with (c) because he agrees with the objection lately made to the reliability theory of truth conditions—namely, that M-functions other than the TC function for M may maximize the relevant sort of reliability as well as the TC function does. The reliability facts cannot explain what makes the conceptual-role/causal-relation package determinative of the truth condition because they will not *uniquely* select that package but will apply equally to conceptual-role/causal-relation packages that are not determinative of [S]'s truth condition.)

Nothing, then, has so far been advanced to preclude one from entertaining the thought that

> there is a single package of conceptual roles and causal reference relations that determines the TC function for every system of mental representation,

although

we neither know what that package is nor have any *a priori* way of determining it (we cannot, for instance, say that it is whatever package accounts in such-and-such a way for such-and-such reliability facts).

But the position implied by this thought will be worth taking seriously only if we have something that looks like a viable strategy for finding that package, and I turn now to one such possible strategy. The strategy that I shall discuss, and especially the way I have chosen to develop it, is to some extent my own invention; it is an attempt to say what would be the *best* strategy to pursue at this stage of the game, given that one believes that there is a correct and naturalistically adequate account of what determines truth conditions in the language of thought. But the essential aspects of the strategy were suggested to me by remarks made in conversation by Hartry Field, and by ideas expressed in some of his articles (see especially 1975, 1986b).

The crux of the strategy is best presented if we begin with the simplifying assumption that we think in nonindexical, unambiguous English. The payoff of this simplifying assumption is that it allows us to bypass some very difficult questions and begin with the assumption that we know what the TC function is for our own system of mental representation: namely, the "homophonic" E-function determined by the disquotational schema

'σ' is true iff σ.

This TC function, familiar from the last section, is the one that maps 'snow is white' onto snow's being white, 'Ronald Reagan is Chinese' onto Reagan's being Chinese, and so forth. The difficult questions being bypassed have to do with how we might arrive at a correct syntactic description of our neural language and how we might determine which neural sentences have the same truth conditions as which sentences of the public language. But we are justified in bypassing these difficult questions because the strategy has no chance if they cannot be answered and because the simplifying assumption will not be taken back when I later object to the strategy.

Let us suppose that $f*$ is the TC function for E, which is our Mentalese system, inner English, and let 'Joe' stand for any paradigm user of this system, such as you or me. Then the Field-inspired strategy, blurted out without qualification or refinement, is as follows.

First, we use conceptual roles and causal relations that *fit* E, in a sense presently to be explained, to get a naturalistically acceptable fuction g such that $g(\text{Joe}, E) = f*$. (The idea here is that we begin with a language for which we know in advance what its TC function is, and then look for naturalistic conditions satisfied by the user of that language which uniquely select that function which we already happen to know is in fact the TC function.)

Second, we apply g to other systems of mental representation to test the following hypothesis against certain intuitive constraints:

An M-function f is the TC function for x's *lingua mentis* M iff $g(x, M) = f$.

If the hypothesis satisfies these constraints, then we are justified in tentatively accepting it.

So, in the first stage of the two-stage strategy we look for a conceptual-role/causal-relation package for inner English *as a whole* that will determine that E-function, f^*, which is in fact its TC function. We shall find such a package if we can find one that *fits E* in the sense now to be explained—after a couple of needed preliminaries.

A *reference scheme* for a language L is a function that maps each name in L onto an object (I shall ignore vacuous names as well as ambiguity) and each n-place predicate in L onto a set of ordered n-tuples. Each language will have indefinitely many reference schemes, so a reference scheme for L may or may not correlate L's names and predicates with their actual denotations. But in the case of our own language, just as we may use the disquotational truth schema to determine the TC function for English, so we may use the disquotational reference schemas,

'n' refers to n

and

'F' is true of Fs,

to determine the reference scheme for English that succeeds in correlating terms with their actual denotations. This will be the "homophonic" reference scheme that correlates 'Mia Farrow' with Mia Farrow, 'Woody Allen' with Woody Allen, 'white' with the set of white things, and so forth.

A system of *projective rules* for a language L is a system of rules that work in conjunction with a reference scheme for L to determine truth conditions for the sentences of L. Examples of projective rules are rules such as

If n is a name and F is a predicate, then $\ulcorner Fn \urcorner$ is true iff $(\exists x)(n$ refers to x and F is true of x)

and

If σ is a sentence, then $\ulcorner -\sigma \urcorner$ is true iff σ is not true.

There is no trivial, disquotational way of arriving at all the projective rules for our own language; if we knew how to state them we would know how to state an adequate grammar for English, and that is not anything that anyone knows how to do.[13] Still, let us make a further concession to the strategy I am trying to adumbrate, and pretend that in addition to knowing the correct reference scheme for inner English, we also know its correct system of projective rules. The homophonic reference scheme together with the projective rules for English would generate the disquotational assignment of truth conditions to the sentences of English and would in that way determine the TC function for inner English (cf. Field 1975, especially p. 377).

I am now in a position to explain the needed sense in which a conceptual-role/causal-relation package may be said to fit E. Quite roughly speaking, such a package P fits E just in case

1. for every E expression or construction Φ that gets its semantical import from its role in a projective rule (e.g., 'not', 'and', subject-predicate concatenation), P contains a conceptual role paired with a semantic value (e.g., negation) such that, first, Φ has both the conceptual role and the semantic value, and, second, the conceptual role is not had by any other expression or construction in E that differs from Φ in semantical import;

2. P contains a causal relation R, intrinsically specifiable in wholly physicalistic or topic-neutral terms, such that an E name n refers to a thing x iff $R(n, x)$;

3. P contains a causal relation R', intrinsically specifiable in wholly physicalistic or topic-neutral terms, such that an n-ary E predicate F is true of an n-tuple $\langle x_1, \ldots, x_n \rangle$ iff $R'(F, \langle x_1, \ldots, x_n \rangle)$.

If P is a conceptual-role/causal-relation package that satisfies these conditions for Joe's inner English, E, then it can be used to define a function g^P, the intuitive gist of which is as follows (an L-item is any expression or construction that gets its semantical import via its role in a projective rule):

$$g^P(x, M) = \begin{cases} f \text{ if } f \text{ is the } M\text{-function determined for } x\text{'s } lingua\ mentis \\ \quad M \text{ when each } L\text{-item in } M \text{ has a conceptual role} \\ \quad \text{contained in } P; \text{ each name in } M \text{ bears } R \text{ to some} \\ \quad \text{unique thing; and each } n\text{-ary predicate in } M \text{ bears} \\ \quad R' \text{ to each } n\text{-tuple of things in some set of } n\text{-tuples} \\ \quad \text{of things;} \\ \text{nothing otherwise.} \end{cases}$$

Clearly, if P is a package that satisfies (1)–(3) for Joe's language of thought E, then $g^P(\text{Joe}, E) = f^*$.

Suppose that we are lucky enough to have discovered for E a conceptual-role/causal-relation package P' such that $g^{P'}(\text{Joe}, E) = f^*$, where f^* continues to be the TC function. Then we are in a position to move to the second stage of the two-stage strategy. Here there are two questions to ask about P':

a. Is $g^{P'}$ defined for each person's language of thought? That is, is it the case that $(x)(M)(\exists f)(g^{P'}(x, M) = f)$? It will be useful to have an expression for the relation that a package P bears to x and M when P attaches to x's inner system M in the way indicated by the foregoing definition of the function g^{P}. So, when that relation obtains, I shall say that P is *appropriate to* x's system M. There is some M-function f such that $g^{P}(x, M) = f$ just in case P is appropriate to x's system M. Consequently this first question may be recast thus: Is P' appropriate to each person's language of thought? (I have already used the word 'fit' in a way that implies that P *fits* x's system M just in case P is appropriate to x's system M *and* the M-function thus determined is the TC function for x's system M. If P is appropriate to M in x, then, for some M-function f, $g^{P}(x, M) = f$; but f need not be the TC function.)

b. Given that (a) is answered affirmatively, is the following also the case?

An M-function f is the TC function for x's *lingua mentis* M iff $g^{P'}(x, M) = f$.

(In other words, given that P' is appropriate to each person's language of thought, does it also fit each person's language of thought?)

It can by no means be assumed that any package fits our own language, inner English. And if a package does happen to fit E, it can by no means be assumed that it is appropriate to any other system of mental representation. But let us assume that all of the preconditions for asking (b) have been satisfied. How are we then to go about answering (b)? Well, that is pretty easy to do if we stay with the assumption that each person thinks in his public language. For surely we should accept that a conceptual-role/causal-relation package P' determines the TC function for each system of mental representation if, and only if, the M-function that it determines for each M accords with our accepted translation manuals. If P' does that, then we should fully expect it to account for why people are reliable in the ways they are, and that is perhaps a further constraint that we should also want to see satisfied (the ability of P' to do this would not rule out the ability of other, perhaps quaddition-like, packages also to account for reliability). And if P' delivers M-functions that accord with our pretheoretic judgments and accepted translation manuals for French, Italian, and so on, then we should also expect it to accord with the belief ascriptions that we would be inclined to make about counterfactual cases in which the language involved was not one for which we had an accepted translation manual. This is a further constraint that we would certainly want to impose.

Anyhow, after all this, the hypothesis that we are invited to entertain is just the following:

[H]   It is true that we cannot now say what determines truth conditions in
      the language of thought; cannot, that is, give the desired completion
      of the sentence-form

      An M-function f is the TC function for x's *lingua mentis* M iff
      $g(x, M) = f$.

      But that is because the conceptual-role/causal-relation package that
      is determinative of truth conditions is not something that we can
      discover in an armchair; scientific investigation is needed to give us an
      adequate theory of conceptual roles and to tell us the relevant ways
      in which our brain states are causally related to things and proper-
      ties outside the head. Nevertheless, we are justified in thinking that
      some still-to-be-discovered conceptual-role/causal-relation package P
      is such that

      an M-function f is the TC function for x's *lingua mentis* M iff
      $g^P(x, M) = f$,

      and we have something of a strategy for using disquotational facts
      about our own language to discover what that package is. At all
      events, no reason has yet been given for thinking that no such
      account is true.

4.5 *Problems with the Different Tack*

It is time to be critical. In trying to find a manageable expository route to
the essence of the Field-inspired strategy, I simplified and idealized at
nearly every turn, and made some assumptions that were clearly false. This
would have to be corrected in a more down-to-earth treatment: it could not
be assumed, for example, that the languages of thought and of speech were
the same, or that we had access to a Tarskian description of our own
language. Most important, it could not be assumed that a conceptual-
role/causal-relation package that fit our language of thought might *also*
fit the systems of mental representation of all actual and possible people,
animals, extraterrestrials, and machines capable of having true or false
thoughts. This is the only simplifying assumption that I shall take back
in a challenging way; for all the others, I shall assume (for the sake of
argument) that they can be unsimplified in unproblematic ways.

I shall raise three problems for [H] and the story behind it. The first has
to do with a problematic consequence of the account when it is revised to
accommodate the projectability point just mentioned. The second is an
objection to the theory even as revised, which objection turns on the need
to construe the causal relations explicative of reference as functional relations. And the third concerns the theory's motivation.

The Projectability Problem

Suppose we find a conceptual-role/causal-relation package P that fits E and is appropriate to all languages of thought that are structurally very similar to E, such as Luigi's inner Italian and Odile's inner French. Now consider all actual and possible systems of inner representation of all people, animals, extraterrestrials, and machines that we credit, pretheoretically, with having true or false beliefs. In considering this variegated array it may come to seem unlikely that P is appropriate to all of its members; at the least, some degree of skepticism is in order, the need felt for a reason to think that P *is* projectable in the way in question. In fact, we can do better. We can imagine there being a system of mental representation whose formulae had truth values, but which was based on a logic somewhat different from ours and contained connectives or quantifiers that matched none of ours. P would not be appropriate to this language, for there would be connectives or quantifiers in the language that did not have any of the conceptual roles in P.[14]

How might the advocate of [H] react to this?

He might argue that it was really *indeterminate* what were the truth conditions of the sentences of these languages. This would allow the theorist to hang on to [H] in its present form: if P was not appropriate to L, then g^P would not be defined for L, and therefore no L-function would be the TC function for L. I do not doubt that this move could be encapsulated in a motivated theoretical position;[15] but it seems to me unduly chauvinistic. It seems to me that to hold that it was indeterminate what the truth-theoretic properties were for systems of mental representation structurally dissimilar to ours, because there was no single reduction for those properties and ours, would be like holding that our language of thought had no determinate truth-theoretic properties if it were discovered that no conceptual-role/causal-relation package fit it. If I were to discover such a thing, I would not conclude that I had no beliefs with determinate content; I would conclude that any premises which led to that conclusion were false. (This is not unrelated to the motivation problem—touched on below and pressed in chapter 6—as regards the physicalism that drives the Field-inspired theorist.)

Rather than push indeterminacy, the theorist might concede that a system of mental representation could have a TC function even if no single package fit both it and our system. The idea would be to individuate systems of mental representation by relevant types and argue that for each such type of system there was some conceptual-role/causal-relation package that fit it. This would mean that there was a class of functions— g^P, $g^{P'}$, and so on—determinative of TC functions for languages of thought. An adequate development of this idea would include a strategy for arriving at these functions for inner languages dissimilar to our own.

The main problem with this proposal is that it leaves us without any evident way of explaining what two diverse content-determining packages have in common. Suppose that our finished theory tells us that there are seventeen (or five or thirty-three) relevant types of systems of mental representation and the same number of content-determining packages, so that

> An M-function f is the TC function for x's *lingua mentis* M iff M is of type A and $g^{Pa}(x, M) = f$; or M is of type B and $g^{Pb}(x, M) = f$; or ....

This listlike reduction would be very unsatisfactory. It could not be left as a brute fact; we should want to know what all of these seventeen (or five or thirty-three) packages had in common by virtue of which they determined the truth conditions of the languages of thought to which they applied. But what could the [H]-theorist say? If he could say what made each of these packages content-determining, he would have an *a priori* account to rival those of 4.3; he could say that

> An M-function f is the TC function for x's *lingua mentis* M iff $g^{P}(x, M) = f$, for some package P that satisfies blah-blah condition.

But it is definitive of [H] that there is no such condition. Perhaps this helps to explain the feeling that if there is a correct and naturalistically acceptable account of what determines truth conditions in a language of thought, then that account is something discoverable by a philosopher.

The Causal-Relation Problem

This is an objection to [H] that may be put as the following argument.

If [H] is correct, then there is a conceptual-role/causal-relation package that fits E, inner English. If there is such a package, then it contains a causal relation that fits the disquotational "true-of" relation that relates general terms in E to the things they apply to (R *fits* the true-of relation for E just in case an E expression x is true of y iff $R(x, y)$). But it is arguable, and will now be argued, that no causal relation will fit the true-of relation.[16]

If there is a causal relation that fits the true-of relation, then it is a physical relation, a disjunction of physical relations, or a functional relation; my strategy will be to consider each of these in turn and show why no causal relation of that type can fit the true-of relation. I shall take the notion of a physical relation for granted, as its vagueness will not affect the argument. The notion of a functional relation may be explained in terms of notions familiar from chapter 2.

A *functional role*, it may be recalled (see 2.2), is a second-level property of first-level physical properties which entails that any property having it plays a certain causal/explanatory role in the functioning of a certain system. And each functional role F determines a *functional property*: the first-level property of having some (first-level physical) property or other that has F. Now the notion of a functional property is really just the limiting case, when $n = 1$, of an n-ary functional relation. So we may say that an n-ary relation R is an n-ary *functional relation* provided that, for some functional role F,

$R(x_1, \ldots, x_n)$ iff for some (first-level physical) relation S, $S(x_1, \ldots, x_n)$ & S has F.

In other words, a functional relation is a relation among things that obtains when those things are related by some relation that has a certain functional role. Notice that a functional relation can be realized, even within a single system, by several distinct physical relations (if R is the functional relation of being related by some relation that has such-and-such functional role, then R is *realized* by any relation that has that functional role).

Functional roles, when they are rich enough to be interesting, are determined by open sentences that become true or false theories when turned into closed sentences. One way of obtaining such an open sentence is to take a theory and replace certain of its theoretically primitive property or relation terms with variables, thus obtaining an open sentence of the form

[a] $T(\Phi_1, \ldots, \Phi_n)$,

which may or may not be satisfied by a given n-tuple of first-level physical properties or relations. For each $i \leq n$, [a] determines a functional role: the second-level property that any property or relation must have if it is to be the ith member of an n-tuple that satisfies [a]. This allows for the possibility of giving *functional definitions* of the theoretical primitives whose replacements by variables resulted in the open sentence [a]. For example, if 'R' and 'S' are theoretical relation terms (say, 'refers' and 'is true of'), and

    $T(R, S)$

is the theory in which they occur, then they can be functionally defined in tandem, as interlocking theoretical constructs, thus:

$R(x, y)$ iff $P(x, y)$, for some (first-level physical) relation P that is the first member of an ordered pair of (first-level physical) relations that satisfies '$T(x, y)$'.

$S(x, y)$ iff $P(x, y)$, for some relation P that is the second member etc.[17]

If the true-of relation is a functional relation, then it will be "defined" in this sort of way, no doubt in tandem with the reference relation that relates a name to its bearer—the scare quotes a reminder that such a "definition" purports only to identify a relation with a given functional relation, and makes no claim of meaning analysis.

Now let us see why the true-of relation for E will be fit neither by (1) a physical relation, (2) a disjunction of physical relations, nor (3) a functional relation.

1. The disquotational true-of relation for E will have in its domain such terms as 'dog', 'goldfinch', 'supercilious', 'aluminum', 'electron', 'leaf', 'betel', 'to walk', 'to sneeze', 'seltzer', 'to marry', 'unicorn', 'paca', 'leprous', 'lethargic', 'to use', 'emu', 'birch', 'to liberate', 'to believe', 'to massacre', 'ultraviolet', 'beige', and 'Hungarian'. Can it seriously be supposed that there is a single *physical* relation P such that an E expression x is true of y iff $P(x, y)$? First, it is hard to see how a single physical relation could cover all these examples. Second, even if there were a physical relation that related each of these terms to each thing it was true of, it seems likely that it would be so attenuated that it would also relate terms to things they were not true of: it would relate 'arthritis' to both arthritis and shmarthritis.

2. It might be thought that the true-of relation could be explicated as a disjunction of distinct physical relations, one for each relevant kind of general term. But this will not work, for it is not even plausible that there will be such physical relations for each kind of general term. For consider just the one for animal natural-kind terms; and then consider the quite different ways in which you are related to dogs, goldfinches, emus, etc.; and then consider the other quite different ways in which, say, blind people who also think in inner English are related to those things; or think of Helen Keller. If there is a disjunctive relation, it will have to be a really motley thing having numerous strands even for terms of semantically unified categories, such as animal natural-kind terms. The problem with such a motley disjunctive relation is that (a) if it is to fit the true-of relation for E, then each of its component nondisjunctive physical relations P must be such that, for any E expression x, if $P(x, y)$, then x is true of y; but (b) there is no reason to suppose that this requirement would be met. Suppose, for example, that P is the physical relation that seems to work for 'rabbit', 'lion', 'tiger', 'horse', and a few others, or that P' is the physical relation that seems to work for 'polio', 'herpes', 'bulimia', and a few others. It seems to me that there is absolutely nothing to rule out the very real possibility that P would relate 'dog' to wolves and coyotes (as well as to dogs) or that P' would relate 'arthritis' to shmarthritis (as well as to arthritis). (Another problem with the motley-disjunction solution is that it would greatly exacerbate the projectability problem; but I shall not pursue this point.)

3. It is, I submit, overwhelmingly plausible that if a conceptual-role/causal-relation package fits E, then its causal relations will be functional relations; they will, like functional properties generally, describe causal connections, but they will do so in a way that allows them to be multiply realized by distinct physical relations. Unfortunately, functional relations will not do the trick either.

If reference relations are functional relations, then there is some theory that can be stated using 'is true of' and 'refers' as theoretical primitives and with respect to which those terms (perhaps along with others, such as 'true') can be functionally defined in the way sketched above. There are two cases to consider: (a) that in which the defining theory does *not* utilize the disquotational reference scheme for E and (b) that in which it does. A theory utilizes the disquotational reference scheme for E if it has for each general term in E an axiom such as

'Dog' is true of x iff x is a dog.
'Red' is true of x iff x is red.
'Loves' is true of x and y (in that order) iff x loves y.

(Likewise, *mutatis mutandis*, for names, which I shall continue to ignore.)[18]
   a. Let T be a theory applicable to thinkers in E that contains 'refers' and 'is true of' as applied to systems of mental representation. Further, let 'R be the functional relation determined for the true-of relation by T. If T utilizes the disquotational reference scheme for E and 'R is realized, then 'R will fit the true-of relation for E, because any relation that realizes 'R would relate the E expressions in its domain only to things it was true of (this gets elaborated in (b) below). But this is not secured if T does *not* utilize the disquotational reference scheme for E; and in that case, as we are about to see, the considerations adduced against the reliability proposals of 4.3 show that 'R would *not* fit the true-of relation for E, because 'R would have realizations that related E expressions to things they were not true of. I shall elaborate this in a slightly roundabout way.
   Toward the end of his well-known article "Mental Representation," Hartry Field (1978) briefly entertains (but does not really endorse) a certain way of explicating the semantical notions of truth and reference for the language of thought. The hypothesis entertained there is *not* the Field-inspired [H] that I have been discussing but one that is very close to the reliability-based explications of 4.3; so close to them that, as we shall see, it is subject to the same objection that did them in. Appreciation of this objection may be seen as part of the motivation underlying the strategy that I have been discussing. My reason for now discussing Field's old reliability-based proposal is its bearing on the proposal now under consideration, that the causal relations contained in a conceptual-role/causal-relation package that fits E are functional relations.
   Field's reliability proposal was this. If (i) we had a suitably articulated *reliability theory* (very roughly, a theory that could be used in conjunction with facts not stated by the theory to say in a systematic way what things a person was reliable about and why he was reliable about them—see Field 1978, pp. 103–104, and 1986b; Schiffer 1981a; Stich 1983, pp. 198–207), then (ii) 'true', 'refers', and the like, applied to systems of internal repre-

sentation, would be primitives of the theory, and (iii) "we could then use this theory to give a functional account of truth and reference for systems of internal representation." Field adds that such a functional account would be desirable "for the reason that functional accounts are always desirable: it would allow for the possibility that the reference relation is realized by different physical relations in different organisms" (1978, p. 104).

Suppose we have a reliability theory for thinkers in E that uses 'refers' and 'is true of' as theoretical primitives. Suppose, too, that the theory does not utilize the disquotational reference scheme for E and that therefore the theory itself does not entail anything about what E expressions refer to or are true of.[19] Then the considerations adduced against the reliability proposals of 4.3 show it to be inevitable that if the reference relations are realized at all, they will be realized by physical relations that relate E expressions to things they do not denote. If, for example, Burge's Alfred is among the people the theory is about, then the functional relation correlated with 'is true of' by the reliability theory in question will have as one of its realizations a relation that relates 'has arthritis' to having shmarthritis.

To see this point clearly, let us consider still another hypothesis that would have been at home among the reliability proposals of 4.3:

[R]   An M-function f is the TC function for M iff f plays a distinguished role in the reliability theory for thinkers in M,

where to say that f plays a distinguished role in a theory T' means not only that the role played by f in T' is indispensable to the explanatory power of T' but also that it is a role that could not be played by any other M-function. An advocate of [R] would be someone who felt that there was no hope of *systematically* exploiting reliability correlations with respect to M without assigning references to expressions in M and then going on to devise a recursively specifiable M-function. But he would know that different M-functions would yield different reliability correlations: the probability that $f(\sigma)$ obtains given that x believes σ may be quite different from the probability that $f'(\sigma)$ obtains given that x believes σ. He would also know, however, that with a suitable M-function f^* we could say things like

> the probability that $f^*(\sigma)$ obtains given that
> x believes σ
> and (simplifying a little) that
> $f^*(\sigma)$ is about the stock market
> is very high,

and other very useful things like that. (A "reliability theory" for x thinking in M would at least be a theory that enabled us to derive knowledge of that sort; perhaps, too, it would explain *why* x was reliable in the ways thus captured. *How* it would do all this is another matter.) This advocate of [R] would be motivated by the idea that (i) we shall have no need for a theory that uses an M-function that does not directly or indirectly use the function to exploit reliability facts; (ii) there will be a *unique* M-function that enters into the correct and fully adequate reliability theory for M (and thus a unique M-function that enters into all of the correct and fully adequate theories for which an M-function is needed); and (iii) it is plausible to identify the TC function for M with that uniquely needed M-function.

Now the trouble with [R] should be clear: if the objections to the "maximal reliability" account [c] of 4.3 are correct, then they carry over to [R]. Those objections seem to show that there would be no uniquely distinguished M-function utilized by the reliability theory for thinkers in M, but that any number of distinct M-functions would do equally well. If we assume (what I would deny) that the reliability theory for thinkers in M would have to be constructed using some M-function, then our interest in an M-function would be dictated by *how* reliable it makes thinkers in M and *what* it makes them reliable about. But the moral of the case against [c] is that quite distinct M-functions will capture interesting reliability to equal degrees; there will be no *most* interesting M-function. And, of course, if this is right, then [R] fails to state a necessary condition (and as we have seen nothing to rule out the possibility that some M-function other than the TC function for M will be more interesting than it, we have no good reason not to suppose that [R] also fails to state a sufficient conditon).

The same problem of no most interesting M-function threatens Field's reliability proposal. If reference relations for the language of thought are functional relations defined by a reliability theory, and that theory does not utilize the disquotational reference scheme for E, then those functional relations will be realized by physical relations that relate E expressions to some things they are not true of. One such realization will assign arthritis to 'arthritis', but another will assign it shmarthritis; one such realization will assign addition to 'plus', but another will assign it quaddition; and so on. This means that no functional relation 'R will fit the true-of relation for E if 'R is determined by a reliability theory that does not utilize the disquotational reference scheme for E.

What if 'R were determined by a theory that was not a reliability theory? But what sort of theory might that be? If reference relations for the language of thought are functional relations, then Field is surely right that the defining theory would be a reliability theory. Anyway, the onus clearly must be on the advocate of [H] to show that some nonreliability theory could both functionally define reference relations and be immune to the promiscuous-realization problem.

b. Now suppose that the theory T containing 'refers' and 'is true of' as applied to languages of thought does utilize the disquotational reference scheme for E. Let "'R'" continue to stand for the functional relation determined by T for the true-of relation. 'R will fit the true-of relation for E if, *but only if,* 'R is realized. *But in showing that no physical relation or disjunction of physical relations could fit the true-of relation for E, we have already shown that* 'R *would not be realized.* By hypothesis, T contains for each general term of E an axiom of the form '"F" is true of x iff x is F' (e.g., '"dog" is true of x iff x is a dog'). It is therefore clear that a physical relation, or disjunction of physical relations, P could realize the functional relation determined by T for the true-of relation only if each substitution instance of the schema

'F' bears P to x iff x is F

were true. If there were such a realization, it would fit the disquotational true-of relation for E. But, I have already argued, it is most unlikely that there would be such a realization (if there were such a realization, we could have used it in the conceptual-role/causal-relation package for E in the first place and would not have needed recourse to functional relations). And if 'R is not realized, then it will have as its extension the null set and therefore cannot fit the disquotational true-of relation for E.

I therefore conclude that [H] is unlikely to be correct; for it is unlikely that any conceptual-role/causal-relation package would fit E. It is unlikely that any such package would fit E because it is unlikely that any physical relation, disjunction of physical relations, or functional relation would be a causal relation that fit the disquotational true-of relation for E.

The Motivation Problem
The proposals considered in 4.3 actually offered to say what determines the TC function for any system of mental representation; they offered naturalistically acceptable completions of

An M-function f is the TC function for x's *lingua mentis* M iff $g(x, M) = f$

that they further claimed were true (which is where they went wrong). [H] is not a proposal of that sort; it offers no such completion. [H] is merely the claim that there is an unknown true completion, together with a partial characterization of what the completion would be like, and something to say about how to find it. I should not pretend to have *shown* that no interesting version of [H] is true. The issues are too vague and my arguments too complex for that. But maybe this is now evident, that there is no reason for accepting [H] other than whatever reason there may happen to be for accepting the conjunction of these three propositions: (1) that the physicalism of 1.4, which holds that there are no irreducibly intentional facts, is true; (2) that we have mental representations with truth-theoretic content; (3) that no non-[H]-type reduction is correct.

Now I accept (2) and (3), and wish merely to remind the reader that we have yet to say hardly anything about the motivation for (1). [H] can be no better motivated than the physicalism that drives it, and that physicalism has not yet received any serious justification. Later I shall argue, first, that (1) is true only if Platonic realism (as opposed to nominalism) with respect to intentional properties and facts is correct, and, second, that there is no good reason to think that that realism is correct. In other words, there is no good reason to think that there are intentional truths only if they are reducible to physical or topic-neutral truths. It simply does not *matter* (I shall later argue) whether there is a conceptual-role/causal-relation package that fits E, because the legitimacy of intentional facts in no way requires that.

So much for the SLT theorist's attempt to provide a naturalistically adequate account of Mentalese truth conditions. I have hardly proved that the SLT-desired reduction cannot be had, but these futile efforts, the best I know, at least explain why in my own IBS-induced odyssey I could not rest with SLT. I turn now to the conceptual-role component in the SLT theorist's theory of meaning for languages of thought.

4.6 Conceptual Role and Mentalese Meaning

According to SLT, there is some (no doubt complex) property Φ, which determines whatever has Φ to mean that flounders snore, such that

> Ralph believes that flounders snore iff $(\exists\sigma)(\sigma$ is a sentence of Ralph's language of thought & $\Phi\sigma$ & $B(\text{Ralph}, \sigma))$,

and likewise for anything else that Ralph might believe. According to the two-factor theory still under consideration, Φ will be a conjunctive property, one of the conjuncts being that naturalistic property that determines σ's truth condition, that is, the truth condition of Ralph's belief that flounders snore. We had trouble finding these truth-condition-determining naturalistic properties; but let us now suppose that they exist, and see why they cannot suffice to determine the contents of beliefs, and thus why the second, conceptual-role factor is thought to be needed.

The reason why the truth-condition factor does not suffice to determine intentional content is the obvious reason that two inner sentences might have the same truth condition—and even the parts of those sentences might have the same extensions—but realize different beliefs.[20] So one might believe that Hesperus is Hesperus but not believe that Hespersus is Phosphorus even though (*pace* the description theory) the mental representations realizing those beliefs have the same truth condition. Whence the need for something else to take up the slack between "referential meaning" (the truth condition of a sentence together with the extensions of its semantically relevant parts) and complete content. That something else, the second property making up the content-determining, conjunctive Φ, is supposed to be the *conceptual role* of a mental representation.[21]

The rough intuitive idea, familiar by now, is that a theory of conceptual role for one's system of mental representation would tell us how sensory stimulations influence what sentences of the system one believes, how one's beliefs influence each other, and how beliefs and desires lead to further desires, to intentions, and, eventually, to bodily movements.[22] The conceptual role of a mental representation, then, is the counterfactual role of that formula in perceptual belief formation and in theoretical and practical reasoning. Or, again, there is the gloss given earlier. The brain, being a computer, is endowed with certain belief-forming mechanisms. These mechanisms determine the conditions under which a given sentence of a person's inner code will be stored as a belief. Suppose you know that x's belief-forming mechanisms are such that whether or not x believes σ at time t depends just on x's sensory stimulations and what x believes at times immediately preceding t, but you do not know *how* x's believing σ is determined by those variables. Then what you are ignorant of (disregarding now the role of σ in practical reasoning) is the conceptual role of σ. Thus, for every mental representation σ of x's inner code, x's belief-forming mechanisms determine a very complex counterfactual property that details the way in which x's believing σ is determined by sensory stimulations and other mental representations believed, and this complex, counterfactual property of an inner sentence is (subject to the foregoing qualification about practical reasoning) its conceptual role.

Vague though it be, the foregoing gloss reveals the following about those counterfactual properties of inner sentences that are conceptual roles:

1. They are *formal* properties, so to speak, in that they can be specified without reference to any truth-theoretic properties their bearers might have. For to specify the conceptual role of a neural formula, one need only say how it is causally or transitionally related to sensory stimulations and other neural formulae, and for this one need not say what the truth conditions of those formulae are or what their parts refer to.

2. The conceptual role of a mental representation does not in general determine its truth condition. For Ralph and his Twin-Earth twin both believe the neural sentence σ, which has the same conceptual role in both of them, even though σ in Ralph is true just in case water ($=H_2O$) is wet, whereas σ in Twin Ralph is true just in case twater ($=XYZ$) is wet. (Thus, not only does SLT semantics need a conceptual-role component in addition to a truth-condition component, it also needs a truth-condition component in addition to a conceptual-role component.)

However the notion of conceptual role is refined, it must for the SLT theorist be such that we can determine what a person believes—*that flounders snore, that Hesperus is Phosphorus*—just from knowing the conceptual role and the truth condition of the neural formula believed. Now to know what a person believes is to know the 'that'-clauses, the content specifications, that characterize his belief; it is to know, for example, that he believes *that flounders snore*. Consequently the conceptual-role component of the theory of meaning for a language of thought *M* must do this:

[CR] It must assign to each sentence σ of *M* a conceptual role *c* and specify some principle *P* of belief-content specification such that, for any state of affairs α, from *P* together with the knowledge that (σ has *c* and α is σ's truth condition) one can deduce what a person believes when σ is tokened in him as a belief.

I shall close my discussion of the conceptual-role component of Mentalese meaning with two comments.

First, no one to my knowledge has made *any* proposal as to how [CR] is to be achieved, nor is it in any way clear to me what form a theory would need to take in order to satisfy the requirements imposed by [CR].[23]

Second, even though I am unclear as to how precisely one would hope to achieve a conceptual-role component for Mentalese semantics adequate to the needs of SLT, there is a reason I am doubtful the theorist can deliver a correct theory that satisfies the demands of [CR]. All of the following people can believe that flounders do not snore: you, Helen Keller, a person who cannot distinguish a flounder from a sea bass, a person who has never seen a fish but has heard about them. It is a good bet that no two of the mental representations realizing the belief in these people have the same conceptual role. This means that the correlation of the predicate 'is a belief that flounders do not snore' with a conceptual role cannot be effected by some psychological theory applicable to all believers. One then wonders how on earth this correlation will be effected.

I conclude that SLT looks most unpromising. That position has two parts, LF, which claims that mental representations are the values of '*y*' in the schema '*x* believes *y*', and the inheritance thesis, IT, which claims that one can account for the content-determining features from scratch, without presupposing anything about the content of beliefs or the meaning of public-language expressions. But both parts seem false. I further conclude that IBS looks most unpromising. For (a) that program stands or falls on the possibility of accounting for the content of propositional attitudes without appeal to the public-language semantic features of linguistic items; (b) that evidently requires that the content-determining features of the objects of belief (that is, the objects in the range of the belief relation) not be public-language semantic features;[24] (c) the only theories consonant with the foregoing constraint are SLT and the propositional theory of propositional attitudes; and (d) each of those theories looks most unpromising.

If believing is a relation, then—we can now say—it is a relation to sentences or utterances in a public language; and it is the public-language semantic features of those sentences or utterances that determine the intentional, or contentful, features of beliefs. This hypothesis is the next topic.

Chapter 5
Sententialist Theories of Belief

5.1 Introduction

Donald Davidson is the creator of two justly famous theories. The first is about the form that a compositional semantics, or meaning theory, for a particular language should take; and the second—what will presently be our main concern—is about the logical form of propositional-attitude ascriptions. The two theories are very intimately connected, and, I shall argue, problems that infect their intersection make it doubtful that either of them can be true. More than this, I shall argue that the problem for Davidson generalizes. *Sententialist* theories of propositional attitudes go hand in hand with *extensionalist* accounts of compositional semantics. One cannot coherently be a sententialist with respect to the belief relation unless one supposes that the correct meaning theory, or compositional semantics, for a given natural language is extensionalist; and one who supposes that natural languages have extensionalist meaning theories is constrained to be a sententialist as regards the belief relation. The primary conclusion of this chapter will be that (a) no sententialist account of propositional-attitude relations can be correct; but in showing this I believe I shall also show that (b) no extensionalist account of compositional semantics can be correct.

The interest of (b) should be manifest, but (b) also has interest because of its relation to another conclusion that I shall later reach: that natural languages do not have compositional semantics. The interest of (a) is as follows.

We are still entertaining the relational theory of propositional attitudes, which requires us to find objects of belief—values of 'y' in 'x believes y'—that have truth values and other features that determine the intentional, or contentful, features of beliefs. But now we know, I think, that the content-determining features of the relata of the belief relation cannot be non–public-language semantic features (and that, consequently, IBS cannot be true if the relational theory is correct). If the relational theory of propositional attitudes is correct, then, we may now say, the content-determining features of beliefs must be public-language semantic features, and things believed must be sentences of a public language, or utterances of them. By a *sententialist theory of the belief relation* I mean any theory (or any refinement of any theory) which holds that believing is a relation between a believer and a sentence or utterance of a public language that obtains by virtue of the meaning or content of the sentence or utterance in the language. So if I am right that no such theory can be correct, and if I am right that no nonsententialist theory is correct, then it follows that the relational theory of propositional attitudes cannot be correct.

In section 1.3 we noticed that there was an important connection between the relational theory of propositional attitudes and the hypothesis that every natural language has a correct compositional truth-theoretic semantics: namely, that the relational theory has arguably got to be true if the compositionality thesis is correct. For, to repeat what was earlier said, if σ is any well-formed indicative sentence of English, then ⌐believes that σ⌐ is a well-formed predicate phrase. Since there are infinitely many such predicate phrases, no compositional truth-theoretic semantics, being finitely statable, can treat them as semantically primitive. A compositional truth-theoretic semantics must therefore treat 'believes' as semantically primitive; and it is arguable that the only tenable way this can be done is to treat 'believes' as a relational predicate—to treat, refinements aside, 'y' in 'x believes y' as an objectual variable. As I, too, believe that the relational theory must be correct if natural languages have compositional truth-theoretic semantics, this chapter also concludes that natural languages do not have such semantics; but the full defense of this further claim must await a later chapter.

The widely held hypothesis that every natural language has a compositional truth-theoretic semantics is, we also noted in 1.3, inextricably related to another widely held hypothesis: that every natural language has a compositional meaning theory, a finitely statable theory of the language which shows how each of its sentences owes its meaning to the meanings of its parts and its syntax. For it is a fact about the *meaning* of a sentence that utterances of it have the truth conditions they have, and there can be no understanding an utterance in the assertive mode without knowing what statement, with what truth conditions, was made in it. I agree that if natural languages have compositional meaning theories, then those meaning theories must also be compositional truth-theoretic semantics; must also, that is, determine a correct truth condition for every utterance in the language that has one. I am therefore further constrained to deny that natural languages have compositional meaning theories, and that denial is also something I shall later try directly to defend.

Now, however, I want to set up the discussion of sententialist theories of propositional attitudes by reviewing some already familiar connections between the theory of language understanding and the theory of meaning;

by noting a curious feature of Davidson's own proposal about the form that a correct meaning theory for a natural language must take; and by elaborating a little on the connection between extensionalist meaning theories and sententialist theories of belief.

5.2 Language Understanding and Semantics

M. A, strolling with his daughter in the Bois de Boulogne, is again confronted by Mme S,[1] who utters the sequence of sounds

[i]   Monsieur, votre fille a mordu mon singe encore une fois.

Now M. A has an auditory perception of these sounds and, even though he has never before encountered [i], forms the correct belief that Mme S, in uttering [i], said that A's daughter had again bitten S's monkey, and that, therefore, what she said, and so her utterance, is true provided that his daughter did once again bite the monkey. In the event, A understands, or knows the meaning of, [i]; understands S's utterance of it; and again manifests his understanding of the language to which [i] belongs.

Davidson has written, and I would agree, that "the main, if not the only, ultimate concern of philosophy of language is the understanding of natural languages" (1973a, p. 71). To understand a natural language is to understand utterances in it, and to understand an utterance is to know what was said in the production of it. A theory of understanding for a language L would explain how one could have an auditory perception of the utterance of a novel sentence of L and know what was said in the utterance of that sentence. A theory of M. A's understanding of French, for example, would account for how, even though he had never before encountered [i], he knew, upon hearing Mme S's utterance of it, that she said that his daughter had again bitten her, S's, monkey.

It may seem obvious that A understands S's utterance because he knows the meanings of the words contained in it and knows a rule for determining the meaning of the sentence on the basis of its syntax and the meanings of its words. Now this has in fact seemed obvious to most, if not all, theorists of language, and I have already said (in 1.3) that it is widely held that every natural language has a *compositional semantics*. A compositional semantics, or meaning theory, for a language L would be a finitely statable theory of L that gives the meaning of each of the finitely many words in L and describes compositional rules that show how these meanings determine the meanings of the infinitely many complex expressions in L. It is thought that without the assumption that natural languages have compositional semantics there would be no explaining the ability to understand them.

The rough picture thus suggested of A's understanding of S's utterance of [i] is as follows. A hears the utterance of [i], and because he is somehow related to a correct compositional semantics for French (perhaps he has an internal representation of it) he is somehow able to ascribe properties to the sentence-type [i] that are in some sense constitutive of its meaning. This knowledge of the meaning of [i] then interacts with knowledge that A has about the context of the utterance, knowledge about Mme S, and knowledge of general psychological, or psychosemantical, truths applicable to speakers of any language; and this interaction in turn yields the knowledge that S, in uttering [i], said that her monkey was once again bitten by A's daughter.

The characterization of a compositional semantics that I have given is not ideal: it uses the insidious notion "meaning." It is not merely that the characterization in terms of "meaning" carries the suggestion, which the compositional semanticist may well want to resist, that a meaning theory must issue in theorems of the form 'σ means in L that . . .'. It is also the case that using the notion of meaning to characterize a compositional semantics puts things the wrong way round; for what we should say is that "meaning" is, as it were, whatever must be ascribed to a sentence in order to explain one's ability to understand utterances of it—to explain, that is, how one can go from an auditory perception of an utterance of the sentence to the knowledge of what was said in that utterance.

In this light one can appreciate Davidson's favored gloss of a meaning theory for a particular language: it is a finitely statable theory that "explicitly states something knowledge of which would suffice for interpreting utterances of speakers of the language to which it applies" (1976, p. 171).

Well, what form should a meaning theory for a particular language take? Since our present concern is the relational theory of propositional attitudes, and since it is doubtful that one can so much as make sense of the claim that propositional-attitude predicates are relational other than in terms of their playing a certain role in the determination of the truth conditions of the sentences in which they occur, we may for present purposes take the answer to the question just asked to be constrained by the assumption that, whatever else a compositional meaning theory will be, it will also be a compositional truth-theoretic semantics.

This understood, we may distinguish two sorts of theories about the form that a meaning theory for a particular language should take. (To keep matters as simple as possible, I shall ignore indexicality, ambiguity, and moods other than the indicative.)

A compositional semantics for a language L is *intensionalist* if its theorems somehow correlate each sentence of L with an *intension*—an abstract meaning, a proposition of one kind or another—that determines a truth value for the sentence in the actual world and every other possible world. These entities would be the contents of the sentences mapped onto them.

Such an account could take the form of a theory that explicitly maps each sentence onto a proposition, or it could take the form of a possible-worlds semantics that assigns to each sentence and possible world the condition under which the sentence is true in the possible world, thereby correlating with each sentence as its meaning, or intension, the set of possible worlds in which it is true.

A compositional semantics for a language L is *extensionalist* if its compositional component is a finitely axiomatized truth theory for L. What is meant here is absolute truth, truth in the actual world, rather than truth relative to a model or truth in an arbitrary possible world. The theorems of such a truth theory would not, of course, correlate the sentences of L with anything that could be taken to be the contents of the sentences, but would have the familiar extensionality of, say,

'La neige est blanche' is true in French iff snow is white.

I said that the *compositional component* of an extensionalist meaning theory would be an extensional truth theory for the language because, as is well known, merely to know a correct truth theory for L would not in itself suffice to enable one to interpret speakers of L. (See, for example, Kripke 1976; Loar 1976a; Foster 1976; Davidson 1976.) For the theorems of such a theory may be true without being *interpretative*; the substituend for 'p' in a given correct instance of the "T-sentence"

σ is true in L iff p

need not be equivalent in meaning to σ, and even if it is, there is nothing in the truth theory as such to tell one that that is so.

If a truth theory for a language is to be part of an extensionalist meaning theory for the language, then it must be that someone who knows that truth theory and knows that it meets certain further conditions will be in a position to understand utterances in the language. And these further conditions, for the extensionalist, must not introduce entities as contents of sentences. What form, then, should an extensionalist meaning theory for a particular language take? That is, what sort of correct theory of a language L would be at once suitably extensionalist in its avoidance of meanings and yet such that knowledge of what that theory stated sufficed for enabling one to understand utterances in L? Davidson's well-known answer is this:

[MT]One would have a theory that sufficed for interpreting utterances in L if (1) one had, and knew what was stated by, a correct, extensional, finitely axiomatized theory of truth for L in the style of Tarski, somehow relativized to utterances of sentences; (2) that theory satisfied such-and-such empirical constraints (mostly having to do with the principle of charity); and (3) one knew that (1) and (2).

In other words, "someone is in a position to interpret the utterances of speakers of a language L if he has a certain body of knowledge entailed by a theory of truth for L—a theory that meets specified empirical and formal constraints—and he knows that this knowledge is entailed by such a theory" (Davidson 1976, p. 172). On this view, the meaning theory for a language L would not be the truth theory for L; rather, it would be what one knows as characterized in [MT], namely, that such-and-such a truth theory satisfies such-and-such constraints.

Whatever else a meaning theory for a language L is, it must also be, we are supposing, a compositional truth-theoretic semantics. In light of this, I think it is safe to say that while an extensionalist with respect to compositional semantics might well disagree with Davidson over the nature of the empirical constraints alluded to in (2), he would have to agree with the rest of Davidson's characterization. In other words, we may take the following to be definitive of the extensionalist's answer to the question of the form that a meaning theory for a particular language L must take: it must be a correct, extensional truth theory for L that satisfies conditions (themselves entailing no quantification over meanings) such that knowing the truth theory and knowing that it satisfied those conditions would suffice for interpreting utterances of speakers of L.

There is a curious feature of Davidson's proposal that we should pause to register, although its full import may not be apparent until later. Let M be the correct meaning theory for a natural language L, and let us suppose that M is as Davidson says it would be—that it satisfies the characterization [MT]. (Davidson, for reasons having to do with indeterminacy, would not say that a language *must* have a *uniquely* correct meaning theory; the assumption of uniqueness is merely a useful expedient in the present context.) What is curious is that Davidson evidently does *not*—and certainly *should not*—hold that

(a)   understanding L requires knowing that M is the case;

while he *does* hold that

(b)   what makes M a theory of meaning for L is that knowledge that M is the case *would* suffice for understanding L

and that

(c)   M is entailed by the correct theory of a person's understanding of L.

Davidson has been fairly careful about avoiding a commitment to (a)—see, for example, Davidson 1973b and 1986—and well he should be; for whether or not knowledge of the kind alluded to in [MT] would, if one had it, suffice for understanding a language, it seems very clear that no actual speaker has such propositional knowledge. Consider, in this regard, nine-year-old Paul. You utter the sounds 'It's raining'; he hears your utterance and knows that you said that it was raining; but it is preposterous to suppose that Paul understands your utterance by virtue of knowing that the fact that your utterance has the truth condition it has is entailed by some correct, finitely axiomatized truth theory of English that satisfies the Davidsonian empirical constraints.

That Davidson holds (b) is obvious; and likewise, I think, as regards his holding (c). For Davidson clearly does hold that the reason for thinking that every natural language has a correct meaning theory is that that assumption is needed to explain language understanding—to explain one's ability to interpret utterances in a language.

But if M, the correct meaning theory for L, is needed to explain one's understanding of L, though not in the way that (b), the definition of a meaning theory, suggests, then how is it needed to explain the ability to know what is said by utterances in L? Why, in the absence of an answer to this question, should one even suppose that Davidsonian meaning theories are needed to explain language understanding? The trouble deepens when one further reflects that (a) we do not really have a complete proposal about the nature of meaning theories for particular languages, because we do not really know what a Tarskian truth theory for a *natural* language would look like, nor do we have a very specific proposal about the nature of the empirical constraints alluded to in [MT], and that, consequently, (b) we really do not know if it is true that, had we a Davidsonian meaning theory for a language, knowledge of the theory would suffice for interpreting speakers of the language. Let me repeat, however, that these remarks are not intended as objections, but merely register a certain puzzle, one to which I shall be returning.

It will help later in the chapter if I am a little more specific now about the curious feature in question, and if we notice that it would appear to be an inevitable feature of *any* correct extensionalist meaning theory for a particular language.

Let us say that Φ is a *content-determining feature* of the sentence σ if the knowledge that σ has Φ, together with one's interlinguistically applicable knowledge, suffices for understanding utterances of σ; suffices, that is, for enabling one to know what a speaker says in uttering σ.[2] Intuitively, to know that σ had Φ would be precisely to know what σ meant. Now it follows from Davidson's proposal [MT] that natural-language sentences have content-determining features. What is curious is that whereas, on Davidson's theory [MT], every sentence of a language has a content-determining feature, *no one who understands the language knows, for any sentence σ and its content-determining feature Φ, that σ has Φ.*

Consider the sentence

[ii]   La neige est blanche.

Davidson would hold that [ii] has a content-determining feature—a feature such that knowledge that [ii] had it would suffice for interpreting an utterance of [ii]. For his theory of meaning (together with what we in fact know about the meaning of [ii]) commits him to the following claim:

> It will suffice for a person to interpret literal utterances of [ii] if (refinements aside) he knows (a) that [ii] is true iff snow is white, (b) that that fact is entailed by a correct, finitely axiomatized, extensional, Tarski-style truth theory for the language to which [ii] belongs, and (c) that that truth theory satisfies————empirical constraints.

(Imagine the blank filled by a specification of the empirical constraints forthcoming from Davidson's finished theory.) My point is that, even if this were true (and I doubt, incidentally, that it is), the content-determining feature specified is not one that enters into anyone's propositional knowledge. I hasten to add that I am not denying that Davidsonian content-determining features enter into one's *nonpropositional* knowledge, nor that the possession of such features is in some sense "internally represented" as subdoxastic states; my point is merely that if Φ is the Davidsonian content-determining feature of [ii], then no one knows that [ii] has Φ. In sum, if there are Davidsonian content-determining features, then they are not within the ken of plain folk.

At the same time, I think it is clear that it is preposterous to suppose that Davidson's extensionalist program in semantics is correct except that he has been mistaken about what the content-determining features of utterances are, and that the real content-determining features *are* within the ken of plain folk. In other words, it seems clear that if there are *extensionalist* content-determining features, then they are not within the ken of plain folk.

So much for curious features later to be exploited. The one other preliminary matter I want to touch on is the connection between sententialist theories of propositional attitudes and extensionalist compositional meaning theories. I have in mind a twofold connection.

First, the extensionalist is constrained to be a sententialist with respect to the belief relation. That is, he is constrained to see believing as a relation to a sentence or utterance of a public language, because the alternative to that would be the Fregean position, which sees believing as a relation between a person and a proposition.[3] But one who was a propositionalist with respect to propositional attitudes could not coherently be an extensionalist with respect to compositional semantics.

Second, the sententialist is constrained to be an extensionalist with respect to compositional semantics.[4] The motive for the view that believing is a relation, not to things that *are* contents (propositions of one kind or another), but to things that *have* content (sentences or utterances), is the desire to avoid any ontological commitment to contents; so the sentientialist, who takes believing to be a relation to a linguistic entity, to something that has content, will not want self-defeatingly to account for the having of content of linguistic entities in terms of *their* being related to contents, but will construe their having of content in an extensionalist, truth-theoretic way.

So let us suppose that one is an extensionalist as regards compositional semantics. Because one believes that every natural language has a compositional truth-theoretic semantics, one believes that propositional-attitude verbs are relational predicates; and because one is an extensionalist, one believes that propositional attitudes are not relations to things that are contents, but rather are relations to things that have content—sentences or utterances. It will help to begin with the simplest version of this idea.

5.3 *Believing as a Relation to Sentences*

If the sentientialist theory is to be tenable, it must not imply that only speakers of a natural language can have beliefs; room must be left for chimps, dogs, very young children, and feral human adults. One who holds the classic sentientialist position would take believing to be a relation between a believer and some sentence-type, a relation that obtains by virtue of the meaning or content of the sentence in the language to which it belongs, but not a relation that requires the believer to understand the sentence. This theorist would represent the logical form of

[a]   Henri believes that love is cruel

as

[b] B(Henri, 'love is cruel').

That is, he would represent [a] as saying that Henri stands in the belief relation to the English sentence 'love is cruel'. This would not in any way imply that Henri speaks English; for there are any number of relations that one can stand in to a sentence without understanding it, and the idea now is that the belief relation is one of them. Perhaps, to paraphrase a remark of Davidson's (1975, p. 167), in uttering [a] it is as though one were saying that Henri was in that state of mind we would be in were we to utter 'love is cruel' assertively and sincerely.

If Henri stands in the belief relation to 'love is cruel', then that must be because of certain of that sentence's features and not others. Clearly, consisting of three words would be irrelevant, while being true iff love is cruel would be relevant. For the classic sentientialist, *what* sentence one believes when one has a belief is determined by the meaning, or content, of that sentence. It is because 'love is cruel' means that love is cruel that

Henri stands in the belief relation to it. It is this fact that makes trouble for the classic theory, as we shall now see.

One well-known problem with the sententialist theory in the simple form that would represent [a] as [b] is this: a sentence can have more than one meaning. First, a sequence of marks or sounds can be a sentence of more than one language, with a different meaning in each. Davidson gives the example of the sounds 'Empedokles lēpt', which in German tell us that he loved, and in English what he did from the top of Mt. Etna (1968, p. 98). Second, a sequence of marks or sounds can have more than one meaning and truth condition even within a language, as we can see from the sentence 'visiting relatives can be boring'.

The fact that a sentence may have different meanings both within and between languages is a problem for the classic sententialist theory for the following reason. According to that theory in its unqualified form, the truth conditions of a belief are just those of the sentence believed. Thus the belief ascribed in a belief ascription would, unacceptably, have as many truth conditions as the sentence contained in the 'that'-clause. For example, if there were some language in which 'love is cruel' meant that kangaroos fly, then [a] would ascribe to Henri both a belief that was true iff love is cruel and a belief that was true iff kangaroos fly.

One can imagine two ways of attempting to repair the classic sententialist position in view of the problem of multiplicity of meaning.

1. One might try revising the position by taking believing to be a relation among a believer, a sentence, and *a meaning or interpretation of that sentence*, thus:

[c] $B(x, \sigma, m)$.

This would yield for [a]:

> B(Henri, 'love is cruel', the relevant meaning (or interpretation) of 'love is cruel').

Now this suggestion is incomplete pending some account of what 'm' in [c] is to range over—some account, that is to say, of what sorts of things meanings or interpretations are supposed to be. If meanings are taken to be *Fregean* meanings—things that *are* contents, *propositions* of one kind or another—then there are two problems. First, as we noted in the last section, the traditional motivation for adopting a sententialist theory of belief has been to avoid an ontological commitment to meanings; so this maneuver is simply unavailable to this sort of theorist. Second, and more important, if propositions are taken to be the values of 'm' in [c], then the reference to the sentence becomes wholly otiose, and the theory collapses into a notational variant of the already discredited propositional theory of propositional attitudes. For if believing is a relation to a sentence that obtains by virtue of the meaning of that sentence, then in believing any sentence one is believing every sentence with the same meaning. So if the meaning of a sentence is a proposition, then the three-place theory can enjoy no advantage over the two-place theory that results from merely dropping the former's superfluous middle term.

But if "interpretations" are not contents (i.e., propositions), what can they be? The problem for the sententialist who eschews meanings—that is, the extensionalist as regards compositional semantics—is not that he cannot make sense of a sentence having an interpretation, but that he cannot make sense of this in a way that delivers interpretations *as entities over which he can quantify*. The extensionalist, roughly speaking, interprets a sentence by deriving a "T-sentence" for it from a correct truth theory that meets relevant empirical conditions. But the T-sentence, of the wholly extensional form 'σ is true in L iff p' (wherein 'p' is not a quantifiable variable but simply holds the place of a sentence whose occurrence is extensional), correlates the sentence with no meaning; and the T-sentence cannot itself be construed as the interpretation, as a value of 'm' in [c], for it is a *sentence* and would itself need an interpretation, thereby providing the first step in an infinite regress. So the extensionalist cannot deliver interpretations as entities over which one can quantify; but such entities are precisely what are needed in order to make sense of [c].

2. This second suggestion is not so much a revision of the classic sententialist position as a *reading* of it that would hope to be immune to the problem of multiplicity of meaning. In objecting to the representation of [a] as [b] I relied on the possibility that the sentence 'love is cruel' might also be a sentence of some language in which it means, say, that kangaroos fly. But might one not reject this manner of speaking and offer instead that if the *marks* 'love is cruel' mean that kangaroos fly in language X, as well as meaning what they do in English, then we should say that there are two distinct, nonidentical sentences, both of which are "realized" or "manifested" or "constituted" by those marks? On this construal, [a] would be more illuminatingly represented, not as [b], but as

B(Henri, the English sentence whose graphemic realization is 'love is cruel').

Even this is just a first approximation, as what is required is a notion of *sentence* such that it is impossible for there to be ambiguous sentences; for unless sentences are individuated by their meanings, one has not avoided the problem raised by the possibility of multiple meanings. One trouble with such a very fine-grained understanding of *sentence* is that it is by no means clear that we could find an ontological category of sentences that was distinct from marks and sounds and that individuated sentences by their meanings without again reifying "interpretations" as objects over which we could quantify. In this case we would again have the objection lately leveled against representing the belief relation in the style of [c]. If meanings were entities, we could take a sentence to be an ordered pair of a sequence of sounds or marks and a meaning. But how could we otherwise get the desired individuation of sentences?

Rather than try to answer this question, I want to turn to what I take to be the most promising sententialist theory of propositional attitudes: the theory suggested in Davidson's seminal article "On Saying That" (1968). But whether or not a theory along Davidsonian lines of the logical form of propositional-attitude ascriptions is the most promising, the main problem such a theory will encounter will also prove to be an insuperable problem for any sententialist account of propositional-attitude relations. It will reward us, then, to study Davidson's account of saying that, and the theory of propositional-attitude relations implicit in it.

5.4 Davidson on Saying That

Davidson does not *explicitly* offer what we are in search of, a relational theory of propositional attitudes that tells us what propositional attitudes are relations to. But in his article "On Saying That" he does propose such a relational account of one kind of propositional attitude, that ascribed in sentences of the form 'x said that p'; and a partial account of the logical form of all propositional-attitude ascriptions is offered that would at least greatly constrain answers to the question we have been concerned with. Actually, one problem that I shall raise is about the way Davidson intends his theory of saying-that to generalize to believing and the other propositional attitudes. Consequently, my most perspicuous strategy is first to describe Davidson's theory of saying-that and then to raise problems for it that would challenge the claim that that account provides the basis for a generalization applicable to all propositional attitudes.

The classic sententialist took belief ascriptions to contain (as it were) a two-place predicate 'believes that' and two singular terms, one denoting an alleged believer and the other—the sequence of words following 'that'—denoting itself. Switching from believing to another propositional attitude, this theorist would represent the logical form of

[1]   Galileo said that the earth moves

as

S(Galileo, 'the earth moves').

In other words, 'said' (or 'said that') in [1] expresses a two-place relation that, if [1] is true, relates Galileo to the sentence-type 'the earth moves'.

This relation will obtain by virtue of the meaning of the content sentence 'the earth moves' but is consistent with Galileo's having been a monolingual speaker of Italian.

Davidson, too, is eager to account for the logical form of [1]; he would like, that is, an account that leads us "to see the semantic character of the sentence—its truth or falsity—as owed to how it is composed, by a finite number of applications of some of a finite number of devices that suffice for the language as a whole, out of elements drawn from a finite stock (the vocabulary) that suffices for the language as a whole" (1968, p. 94). For if Davidson could not give such an account, this would call into question his Tarskian program, which requires that there be such an account. This is one connection for Davidson between the theory of meaning and saying-that; another, of course, is that the theory of meaning has as its concern language understanding, and that consists precisely in the ability to know what speakers of a language are saying when they utter sentences of the language. Consequently, an account of saying-that must be part of any complete account of language understanding.

But while Davidson shares the need to account truth-theoretically for the logical form of [1], and while he would applaud the classic sententialist's eschewal of propositions as referents of 'that'-clauses, he would still find fault with that theorist's representation of [1] on the following two counts. First, sharing an objection already made, Davidson would object to taking the relatum of the saying-that relation to be a sentence "both because ... the reference [to a sentence] would then have to be relativized to a language, since a sentence may have different meanings in different languages; but also ... because the same sentence may have different truth values in the same language" (1975, pp. 165–166). Second, Davidson would raise an objection not raised in the last section, one that he would also raise against the Fregean: both the Fregean and the classic sententialist assign to the content sentence in [1], 'the earth moves', a semantic role that is radically different from its normal one. They construe it (qualifications aside) as the larger part of a *singular term*, 'that the earth moves', which refers in [1] to what Galileo said—to a proposition, for the Fregean, to the sentence 'the earth moves' for the classic sententialist. Here, Davidson is well aware, both theorists are motivated by failures of coextensional substitutions in the content sentence to preserve truth value. Even so, Davidson would prefer a theory in which the content sentence had only its old familiar semantic properties. At the same time, Davidson recognizes the need for a relational theory of propositional-attitude verbs to cohere with his Tarskian conception of a compositional semantics.

Thus Davidson wants a theory of [1] that satisfies the following desiderata:

a. 'Said' in [1] is represented as a two-place relational predicate.[5]
b. The things in the range of that relation have truth values but are neither propositions nor sentences.
c. A relatum of that relation *chez* Galileo (i.e., something to which Galileo stands in the saying relation of indirect discourse) is referred to in [1].
d. The content sentence 'the earth moves' has in [1] its normal and familiar semantic properties, its normal sense and reference. It is not part of any singular term; the only reference of 'the earth' is the earth, and the only extension determined for 'the earth moves' is its truth value. Substitutivity *salva veritate* in the content sentence applies as usual.

Davidson's terrifically ingenious solution is well known. What we have in [1] is an instance of parataxis. Semantically speaking, the utterance of [1] is not the utterance of one sentence that contains 'the earth moves' as a part, but rather utterances of two sentences paratactically joined, something best represented as

Galileo said that. The earth moves.

Here 'the earth moves' is seen to occur, not as part of a single sentence that contains the 'said' construction, but as an autonomous utterace with its predictable sense and reference: this utterance is true iff the earth moves. At the same time, the word 'that' in the first utterance occurs as a *demonstrative*, whose referent is the utterance that follows it; and the first utterance is true just in case Galileo stands in the saying relation of indirect discourse to the referent of 'that', i.e., to the utterance in question of 'the earth moves'. And he will stand in that relation, Davidson tells us—not as part of his account of the logical form of [1], but as an intuitive and informal gloss of it— provided that he himself produced an utterance that matches in content the speaker of [1]'s utterance of 'the earth moves'. This explains why it is that, although the occurrence of a content sentence is autonomous, it is typically not *asserted*: the speaker produces it not to express his own opinion but so that he will have produced an utterance that itself has a content that can be exploited to reveal the content of some utterance, no doubt in Italian, of Galileo's.

In this way the above desiderata are achieved.

We achieve (a) because 'said' is in effect represented as

[2] $S(x, u)$,

that is, as a two-place relation between a speaker x and any *actual* utterance u that matches some utterance of x's in content.[6]

We achieve (b) because these utterances have truth values.

We achieve (c) because 'that' in [1] is a singular term that refers to an utterance—viz., the utterance of the sentence following it—to which Galileo stands in the saying-that relation.

And we achieve (d) because the "analysis accounts for the usual failure of substitutivity in attributions of attitude without invoking any non-standard semantics, for the reference of the 'that' changes with any change in the following utterance" (Davidson 1979, p. 119).[7]

Davidson is aware that his theory must be importantly revised in order to account for quantifications into 'that'-clauses; because as his theory now stands, it has no way of making sense of an utterance such as

Galileo said of a certain person that she baked terrific lasagna.

Nor, relatedly, can it account for the ambiguity, induced by possibilities pertaining to Galileo's knowledge or ignorance of who baked terrific lasagna, of

Galileo said that his mother baked terrific lasagna.

The problems raised by these "*de re*" issues are formidable, and I am aware of no very plausible solution available to Davidson. But these familiar problems are not ones that I shall press.

Another problem with Davidson's theory of saying-that with which I shall not be concerned but which I do feel compelled just to mention (partly because, to my amazement, I have never seen it raised before), is this: it is by no means clear what the application of Davidson's theory to *French* would be. For it is essential to at least the initial *plausibility* of Davidson's theory *as applied to English* that the word 'that' does have a use as a free-standing demonstrative; otherwise the suggestion that 'that' in [1] ('Galileo said that the earth moves') is a demonstrative would be worse than bizarre. But now consider the French translation of [1]:

[1'] Galilei a dit que la terre bouge.

The word 'que' in French has no use as a demonstrative. So what could possibly be the application of Davidson's theory to [1']? (To be sure, Davidson could restate his theory in a way that did not entail that 'that' in [1] was a singular term. He would then probably have to say that 'that' was not occurring as a genuine semantical unit but was an orthographic part of the semantically primitive verb 'to say that'. But then there would be no term in [1] that carried the reference to the utterance of 'the earth moves', and one may wonder about the plausibility of the paratactic account without the attendant claim about 'that'.)

At all events, it is a few other problems that I want now to raise for

Davidson's theory of saying-that, and for the extension of it to belief ascriptions.

5.5 Three Problems

I shall now describe three problems for Davidson's theory, each of which seems to require, at best, that the theory be revised in some important way. In each case I shall mention a possible or mandatory revision, but I shall not dwell on them or draw dire conclusions until the end, when the conclusion reached will have application to any sententialist position.

First Problem

Davidson intends his account of the logical form of [1] to be the basis for a general account of the logical form of propositional-attitude ascriptions, and his account of saying-that would be of only marginal interest if this were not the case. How, then, does Davidson intend his theory to be extended to the other attitudes, and to believing in particular?

Consider this utterance:

[3]   Galileo believed that the earth moves.

Davidson has made it clear (in, for example, Davidson 1975) that he intends the analysis of the logical form of [3] to have this much in common with that of [1]: First, the logical form of [3] is that of two utterances paratactically joined, and thus best represented as

Galileo believed that. The earth moves.

Second, as in [1], 'that' in [3] is a demonstrative, its referent the utterance following it of 'the earth moves'. Third, 'believes' is thus a two-place relational predicate, and the range of the belief relation—the values of 'y' in the schema 'x believes y'—includes actual utterances.

But now we come to an important *dissimilarity*, and with it the first problem. For whereas the saying-relation of [1] could plausibly be represented as [2]—that is, as a relation to *actual utterances*—the believing-relation of [3] cannot be correctly represented as a two-place relation,

$B(x, u)$,

which relates a believer x to an *actual utterance* u. The representation of the saying-that relation as [2] is plausible because if

Galileo said something

is true, then there can be no barrier to inferring

$(\exists u) S(\text{Galileo}, u)$,

for there is always Galileo's own utterance to be an utterance to which he stands in the saying-relation as portrayed in [2]. But if

Galileo believed something

is true, then there *is* a barrier to inferring

$(\exists u) B(\text{Galileo}, u)$;

namely, that there may not be any actual utterance that gives the content of Galileo's belief. (Cf. Loar 1976a, p. 148; Leeds 1979, p. 51.) He may never have expressed his belief, and it may be that no one ever produced an utterance that conveys the content of his belief. Believing could be represented as a relation to actual utterances only if one could be assured that for every belief there was some actual utterance that gave the content of that belief; but of course one cannot be so assured.

Well, what things are available to Davidson to be the objects in the range of the belief relation, that is, the values of 'y' in 'x believes y'? There are two moves that might be entertained by way of answering this question. One is still within the bounds of *sententialist* theories of the belief relation, while the other jumps those bounds and regresses to the theory that believing is a relation, not to any sort of *public-language* entity, but to a mental representation, in this case, a belief state-token.

The nonsententialist move seeks to press an analogy with the analysis of the saying-that relation. According to Davidson, an utterance of [1] ('Galileo said that the earth moves') is true provided that some utterance-token of Galileo's had the same content as the speaker of [1]'s utterance of 'the earth moves'. Why not say, then, that an utterance of [3] ('Galileo believed that the earth moves') is true provided that some belief state-token of Galileo's had the same content as the speaker of [3]'s utterance of 'the earth moves'? And if one can say that, then why not say, further, that believing is a relation between a person and a belief state-token? Anything is a *candidate* for being a value of 'y' in 'x believes y' if it has a truth value, and the neural state-tokens that are beliefs have them: if neural state-token n is my present belief that worms do not have noses, then that state, being a belief that worms do not have noses, is true if and only if worms do not have noses. The state n, we have already noted (in section 4.1), is a *mental representation*: since it has the truth condition it has, it represents the state of affairs that worms do not have noses. It may seem a little strange to say that believing is a relation to beliefs, but we can get over that. And if we do say that, then there is no trouble with representing 'Galileo believed something'. That becomes just what we might expect,

$(\exists x) B(\text{Galileo}, x)$,

the value of 'x' that makes this true being any belief state-token Galileo happened to be in.

The preceding chapter may already have discredited the view that believing is a relation to a mental representation; I shall ignore this possibility, however, and raise three problems that might be raised by someone who had not read that chapter.

1. On Davidson's theory of saying-that, [1] first gives way to

Galileo said that. The earth moves.

And then the logical form of the first utterance is represented as

S(Galileo, that).

As a representation of *logical form*, this is satisfying. Among other virtues, the form, thus represented, nicely mirrors the sentence's surface structure; for example, although 'S(Galileo, that)' gets *analyzed* as

$(\exists x)(x$ was an utterance & x was by Galileo & x had the same content as that),

nothing about sameness of content enters into the representation of logical form. From the point of view of logical form, 'says' is a semantical primitive that happens to be roughly explicable in a certain way.

But now let us consider the required treatment of [3] if believing is a relation to belief states. As with [1], [3] first gives way to

Galileo believed that. The earth moves.

But a big difference emerges at the next stage, in the representation of the logical form of 'Galileo believed that'. That cannot be represented as

B(Galileo, that),

for the referent of 'that' is an utterance, and brain states, not utterances, constitute the range of the belief relation on the present hypothesis. The representation of logical form must either be

$(\exists x)(B$(Galileo, x) & x had the same content as that),

at best, or

$(\exists x)(x$ was a belief state & Galileo was in x & B(Galileo, x) & x had the same content as that),

at worst. Either representation would be a very significant departure from the neatness of Davidson's original idea, and a great deal of work would have to be done before it could be made plausible as a representation of logical form.

2. If neural state-token n is a belief that worms do not have noses, then it has content: it has the content ascribed in the 'that'-clause, 'that worms do not have noses'. On most views, 'that'-clauses do not refer to beliefs—that is, to the neural state-tokens that are beliefs—but to entities which have truth values and other content-determining features that *determine* the content of beliefs. Thus, for the propositionalist, n's having its content just is its standing in the relevant belief relation to the proposition that worms do not have noses; and for the sentientialist, n's having its content just is its standing in the relevant belief relation to a certain linguistic entity with the relevant content. For the propositionalist and the sentientialist, then, one needs no *independent* account of the content of beliefs; the theory of belief content *just is* the theory of content for the objects of belief. That one needs no independent account of the content of belief state-tokens is part of the attraction of these views. But on the view being proposed, according to which believing is a relation to belief state-tokens, *one would need an independent account of the content of belief state-tokens.* If my utterance of [3] means that Galileo believed some belief state-token of his that had the same content as my utterance of 'the earth moves', then we are owed some independent account of the content-determining features of that belief state-token that would show this to be true. And what might such an account look like? Davidson seems not to have addressed this question.

3. Moreover, it is not even clear that it could make sense for Davidson to say that a belief b had the same content as an utterance u. For how is the sameness-in-content relation invoked in the representation of the logical form of [3] to be spelled out? We could not without circularity say that b and u had the same content if, for one and the same such-and-such, b was a belief that such-and-such while u was a statement that such-and-such. Evidently, the claim that b and u had the same content would have to mean that there was some content-determining feature Φ such that b had Φ and u had Φ.[8] But for Davidson the content-determining features of utterances are to be unpacked in terms of what gets ascribed in theorems of a Tarskian truth theory for the language to which the utterance belongs, which truth theory satisfies certain formal and empirical constraints. Mental representations, we have already noticed (in 4.1), are cheaply purchased: we have them if brain states are beliefs. But would Davidson want to be committed to the view that brain states are, or involve, sentences of a neural language that enjoys a Tarskian description?

So much for the retrograde nonsententialist answer to the question of what for Davidson might be the values of 'y' in 'x believes y', given that those values cannot be utterance-tokens. *Our* present interest in Davidson, fueled by the theory of content, is in what *sentientialist* theory of the belief relation he may have to offer. And the only remaining sentientialist answer, it would appear, is that believing is a relation to *utterance-kinds*, or possible utterances (I think that for our purposes we can take these as coming to the same thing). Because kinds can be uninstantiated, this revision would not be subject to the difficulty that infected the theory that believing was a relation to utterance-tokens.

But if Davidson is constrained to say that believing is a relation to an utterance-kind, then this will have for him the following problematic features.

1. Davidson's theory of propositional attitudes is driven by his need to find a theory of them that coheres with his account of the form that a meaning theory for a particular language should take. Now the hallmark of his famous Tarskian proposal about the form that a meaning theory should take is that it is *extensional*; not for Davidson is a compositional semantics whose theorems relate sentences to intensions, but rather one that issues in the well-understood extensionality of

'Snow is white' is true iff snow is white.

Now the problem with the only apparent extension of Davidson's account of saying-that to believing is just this: *How is one to square a quantification over utterance-kinds with this extensionalist program?* On the face of it, utterance-kinds are universals; if one has them, one has properties, propositions, and the lot, and no need to worry then about achieving an extensionalist semantics (cf. Leeds 1979, p. 51). (Utterance-kinds cannot be construed as sets, for then all beliefs whose contents had never been expressed would have, unacceptably, the same object, viz., the empty set.)

2. If Davidson is constrained to say that believing is a relation to an utterance-kind, then an utterance-kind, and not an actual utterance, should be represented as the relatum of the belief relation that is referred to in [3], 'Galileo believed that the earth moves'. Davidson, in other words, has misrepresented his position on the logical form of [3] if he is constrained to say that believing is a relation to utterance-kinds. The logical form of 'Galileo believed that' in [3] should not be represented as

B(Galileo, that),

where 'that' refers to the actual utterance of 'the earth moves', but should be represented as, say,

B(Galileo, the utterance-kind to which that belongs).[9]

In still other words, the skit involved in the utterance of [3] should be portrayed thus:

[4]   The earth moves.
        Galileo believed that kind of utterance.

3. Unfortunately, one cannot just say that believing is a relation to an utterance-kind; one has to say what *sort* of utterance-kind. The issue here can be illuminated by noticing the glaring inadequacy of [4]: the utterance of 'the earth moves' will be of *many* kinds. Which one, then, is being referred to in [3]? Presumably, the kinds would have to be individuated by the *contents* of the utterances they subsume. Perhaps, then, a better version of the skit involved in the utterance of [3] would be

> The earth moves.
> Galileo believed the utterance-kind to which an utterance belongs just in case it has the same content as my last utterance.

But even this will not do as it stands. One reason (another comes later) is that 'content' is a term of art in this context, and we really have not been told what is being referred to in [3] as the relatum of the belief relation *chez* Galileo until we have been given an account of what the content-determining features of an utterance are. This is not the tired old objection that Davidson's account of saying-that relies on an unexplicated notion of sameness of content. *That* objection is a bad one; for Davidson's account of the logical form of saying-that sentences relies on no such notion. On Davidson's theory, 'says' of indirect discourse is a *semantically primitive* predicate that relates a person to an actual utterance, and it is further consistent with his theory to hold that the relation expressed is not strictly definable. Talk of "sameness of content" is intended merely as an informal gloss on conceptual connections that the saying-that relation bears to other of our semantic concepts—as " 'an expository and heuristic device': an aid in instructing novices in the use of the saying primitive" (McDowell 1980, p. 231; the inner quotation is from Davidson 1976, p. 177). But the point that I am making is that the role of "content" in Davidson's theory cannot be comfortably trivialized in this way *on the revision being entertained*. On the required revision, 'that' may still be seen as referring to an actual utterance, but now it will no longer enjoy a primary occurrence. Its occurrence will be ensconced in an implicit occurrence of the singular term 'the kind of utterances having the same content as that', and my point is that we will not know the *reference* of that singular term until we know what notion of content is here intended.

But is there really a problem here? Is not the needed sense of 'sameness of content' already available in Davidson's theory of the form that a meaning theory for a particular language should take? We are shortly to see that the answer to this question is no.

Second Problem

The objection here, which I owe to Brian Loar (in conversation), is that Davidson's theory of saying-that is in conflict with a certain correct principle about the function of singular terms in content sentences. Before this principle can be stated, we need the following definition:

> An occurrence of a singular term in a sentence is a *primary* occurrence iff that occurrence is not properly contained within the occurrence of some other singular term.

Thus, the occurrence of 'that car' in

> That car is blue

is primary, whereas in

> George's car is blue

only 'George's car' has a primary occurrence; 'George' has a secondary occurrence.

Now I can state the principle alluded to, which is this:

[P]   If the occurrence of the singular term t in ⌜So-and-so said that ... t ...⌝ is primary and refers to x, then that sentence is true only if so-and-so also referred to x.

Thus, suppose I say,

> Ralph said that she drove that car,

myself referring to a certain woman and a certain car. Then my utterance is true only if Ralph also referred to that woman and that car. The reason for the restriction to primary references is this. Consider my utterance of

> Ralph said that she drove George's car,

where I again refer to a certain woman and a certain car. In order for my last utterance to be true, Ralph must have referred somehow to George's car; but he need not have referred to George, for he need not have referred to the car as George's car. Perhaps the utterance of Ralph's that makes us samesayers is his utterance of 'She drove that car'.

We can see the problem for Davidson in all this if we now consider

[5]   Laplace said that Galileo said that the earth moves.

It follows from Davidson's theory that the second occurrence of 'that' in [5] is the primary occurrence of a singular term whose referent is the utterance following it of 'the earth moves'. Whence we have the following argument in refutation of Davidson:

> 1. [P].
> 2. If Davidson's theory is correct, the second occurrence of 'that' in [5] is a primary occurrence, whose referent is the occurrence in [5] of 'the earth moves'.

3. But [5] can be true even though Laplace did not refer to that utterance.

4. Ergo, Davidson's theory is not correct.

This argument is valid, and the only premise Davidson could conceivably challenge is (1). But how is the strategy of denying [P] to be pursued? Davidson cannot with any degree of plausibility simply claim that the uses of 'that' in question constitute the sole exception to [P]. He must either (a) discredit the principle independently of its present application or else (b) give a *principled* explanation of why the occurrences of 'that' in question constitute an exception to [P]. But I am doubtful that either of these strategies can be pursued successfully. It seems to me that the more promising way out for Davidson would be to revise his theory just enough to bring it in line with [P]. The needed revision turns out to be the one he is already committed to if his paratactic theory is both to accommodate belief ascriptions and to remain a sententialist theory of the belief relation. The idea is to construe 'that' as really having a secondary occurrence in the implicit singular term 'the kind of utterances having the same content as that'. This would plainly square [5] with [P], but it would also, alas, encounter the difficulties we have just finished rehearsing in the first problem.

Third Problem

This, I think, is the really urgent problem. Succinctly put, the objection is as follows: Davidson's representation of

[a]   Sam PAs that flounders snore.

as

[b]   Sam PAs that. Flounders snore.

cannot be right, for (1) one cannot know the *assertion made*, the truth stated, by [a] without knowing *what* Sam PAs, the *content* of his PA; but (2) one can know the assertion made by [b] without knowing what Sam PAs, the content of his PA.

Now (1) seems correct. If in uttering 'Sam said that flounders snore' you assert truly that Sam said that flounders snore, and if I know what truth you asserted in your utterance, then I know that Sam said that flounders snore. And if I know this, then I certainly know the content of Sam's statement. I know that what Sam said is about flounders and snoring; and I know, especially, that what he said is true just in case flounders snore. Davidson, if he acknowledges (2), is evidently constrained to maintain either that I can know the truth you asserted without knowing that Sam said that flounders snore, or that knowing that does not carry with it any knowledge whatever of the content of Sam's statement. What basis can he have for pursuing either of these disjuncts other than the need to be consistent with his theory?

But (2) is just as certainly correct. To see this clearly, let us start with the following dialogue:

> *Pierre:* La neige est blanche.
> *Donald:* Tarski said that.

The relevant point about this is that it is a consequence of Davidson's theory that one can know what Donald asserted without knowing the content of Pierre's utterance, and thus without knowing the content of Tarski's saying. For one can know that some utterance of Tarski's had the same content as Pierre's utterance without knowing the content of either utterance.

With this in mind, let us now consider the Davidsonian representation of

[6]   Sam said that flounders snore,

which, of course, is

[7]   Sam said that. Flounders snore.

Here the only *assertion* made is made by the first utterance, 'Sam said that'. What this asserts, according to Davidson, is that some utterance of Sam's has the same content as the foregoing utterance of 'Flounders snore'. But this, as (2) correctly notes, can be known without knowing the content of either utterance. So, on Davidson's account, one can know the assertion made by [6], namely, the assertion made by the first utterance in [7], without knowing the content of what Sam said. To be sure, one who knows English and hears the whole of [7] will know the content of Sam's statement because he knows the meaning of 'flounders snore'; but that hardly controverts (2). For if *all that one knew* was what was *asserted* by the first utterance of [7], then one would not know what Sam said.

Here is what I take to be another, but non-epistemic, way of making essentially the same objection (to forestall a certain reply, I have changed the example from saying to believing): (1) The sentence

[i]   Sam believes that flounders snore

entails

[ii]   Sam believes something that is true iff flounders snore

in this sense: there is no possible world in which Sam believes that flounders snore but does not believe something that is true iff flounders snore. (2) But [ii] would not be entailed by [i] if Davidson's theory were correct. For if that theory were correct, then [i] would be representable as

Flounders snore.
Sam believes that.

And from this one cannot in any sense infer [ii] without the further, contingent premise

That (i.e., the preceding utterance of 'Flounders snore') is true iff flounders snore.

Is there any way Davidson's theory can be revised to avoid this objection? Perhaps. At least there is a line to be explored, an extension of the revision already seen to be required by the preceding two objections.
On Davidson's original, unrevised theory, [6] got represented as

S(Sam, that),

the referent of 'that' being the utterance in [6] of 'flounders snore'. Then we noticed that if Davidson is to avoid the first two of our objections, he would do better to represent [6] as

[8]   S(Sam, the utterance-kind to which an utterance belongs just in case it has the same content as that),

'that' construed as before, only now having a secondary, rather than a primary, occurrence.
But even [8] will not escape our third objection; for someone could know the assertion made by [8] without knowing the content of the utterance referred to by 'that'. What is needed is to get a specification of the actual content of the content sentence 'flounders snore' into the reference to the utterance-kind.
Recall Mme S's utterance 'Monsieur, votre fille a mordu mon singe encore une fois'. To understand her utterance, we have noted, is to know what she said in it. Suppose that one knows that she did say something in producing her utterance. What *more* would one have to know in order to know what she said and thereby to understand her utterance? Intuitively, one wants to answer: the *content* of her utterance. Earlier, in 5.2, I described the compositional semanticist's thought that there is some feature of Mme S's utterance such that if one knew that the utterance had it, then one would be in a position to interpret Mme S's utterance, that is, to know what she said in producing it. Suppose that utterances have such content-determining features and that Φ is that feature for the utterance of the content sentence 'flounders snore'. This, to repeat, would be to say that if someone were to utter 'Flounders snore' assertively, then a hearer would be in a position to interpret that utterance—to know what the utterer said—if the hearer knew that that utterance had Φ. Then one could entertain avoiding our third objection by revising Davidson's theory in such a

way as to yield the following representation of the skit performed in uttering [6]:

[9]   Sam said the kind of utterances that are Φ, like that.
       Flounders snore.

In short, if Davidson is to have a theory of propositional-attitude ascriptions that avoids the three objections raised, then he will have to find content-determining features of utterances and construe propositional attitudes as relations to *utterance-kinds as individuated by those features*, in the way indicated by [9].

There are, I think, several problems with this entertained way out, but here is the most serious of them: In order for there to be content-determining features that enter into propositional-attitude ascriptions in the way indicated in [9], such features will obviously have to be within the ken of ordinary people; but the only content-determining features that are even prima facie available do not enter into anyone's propositional knowledge.

This objection brings us back to Davidson's theory of the nature of meaning theories for particular languages, and to the curious feature of the theory noted in 5.2: that whereas, on Davidson's theory [MT], every sentence of a language has a content-determining feature, no one who understands the language knows, for any sentence σ and its content-determining feature Φ, that σ has Φ. For suppose that Sam utters, assertively and literally, the sentence

[10]   Flounders snore,

and that Carla knows this. Is there any feature Φ of [10] such that if Carla also knew that [10] had Φ, then she would be able to interpret Sam's utterance—be able, that is, to know that in uttering [10] Sam said that flounders snore? Now Davidson, we know, does hold that there is such a feature. For his theory of meaning commits him to holding that

> It will suffice for Carla to interpret Sam's utterance of [10] if (refinements aside) she knows (a) that [10] is true iff flounders snore, (b) that that fact is entailed by a correct, finitely axiomatized, extensional, Tarski-style truth theory for the language to which [10] belongs, and (c) that that truth theory satisfies————empirical constraints.

(Imagine the blank filled by a specification of the empirical constraints forthcoming from Davidson's finished theory.)

But we have already noticed the main problem with this as regards our present concern. Even if it were true, the content-determining features specified are not ones that enter into anyone's propositional knowledge. As I put it in 5.2, if there are Davidsonian content-determining features, then they are not within the ken of plain folk. This means that we cannot construe propositional attitudes as relations to utterance-kinds as specified by such content-determining features; for that proposal makes sense only if plain people know that these features are features of utterances.

Now the point just made about Davidsonian content-determining features remains true no matter how the blank in (c) is filled: the knowledge required by (b) already secures that whatever content-determining features are determined by a specification of empirical constraints will be beyond the ken of plain folk. This means, it was noticed in 5.2, that if there are any extensionalist content-determining features, then they, too, will be beyond the ken of plain people. If there is *any* extensionalist meaning theory for a language *L* that explicitly states something knowledge of which would suffice for interpreting utterances in *L*, then no one knows what that theory states.

5.6 Some Consequences

I conclude that there can be no correct sentdentialist theory of propositional attitudes for at least this reason. Any such theory would require that the values of '*y*' in

x PAs y

be utterance-kinds individuated by features that are content-determining, within the ken of plain folk, and consonant with the extensionalist account of compositional semantics. But no such features will ever materialize.

Since there can be no correct sentdentialist theory of propositional attitudes, I also conclude that there can be no correct extensionalist account of compositional semantics for natural languages. For in 5.2 we saw that the extensionalist with respect to compositional meaning theories was constrained to be a sentdentialist with respect to propositional attitudes. This conclusion, however, is about to be swallowed by the larger conclusion that there can be no correct account of compositional semantics of any kind.

Earlier chapters argued that there can be no correct nonsententialist account of believing. As this one concludes that there can be no correct sentdentialist account, I further conclude, by elimination, that the relational theory of propositional attitudes is false: nothing is available to constitute the range of values of '*y*'.

I thus conclude that various phenomena that would appear to support the relational theory must not really support it. For example, one would think that if John believes that snow is white and Mary believes that snow is white, then there is something that John and Mary both believe. But if the relational theory is false, then the last conditional is false—either that or the ostensible quantification in its consequent over things believed is not all that, to a Quinean eye, it might appear to be.

I further conclude that no natural language has a correct compositional truth-theoretic semantics; for if they did, then the relational theory of propositional attitudes would be correct.

I further conclude that no natural language has a correct compositional meaning theory; for I cannot see how such a theory could fail to be a truth-theoretic semantics.

So I must also conclude that compositional semantics are not needed to explain language understanding, or anything else.

I cannot pretend, however, that the arguments I have so far given can bear so much weight. Evidently, I have further work cut out for me, material for later chapters.

Another consequence should also by now be apparent: the physicalism that was one of the hypotheses of chapter 1 must be false. If there are true ascriptions of belief, then the truths that those ascriptions state cannot be truths that are also statable by sentences that contain no mentalistic or intentional terms. This is the next topic.

Chapter 6
Ontological Physicalism and Sentential Dualism

6.1 Introduction

Chapter 1 implicitly defined a hypothetical philosopher by the nine hypotheses—some widely held, others less widely held—to which he subscribed:

1. There are semantic facts: words have meaning and reference, and people perform propositional speech acts in producing those words.

2. Every natural language has a correct compositional meaning theory: a finitely statable theory that gives the meanings of the language's primitive vocabulary and specifies compositional mechanisms that then generate meanings for each of the language's infinitely many sentences.

3. Every correct compositional meaning theory for a language L is also a truth-theoretic semantics for L: in addition to generating a meaning for each meaningful sentence of L, the theory also generates a truth condition for each utterance in L that has one.

4. The reason for thinking that (3) is true is that it would not be possible to account for one's ability to understand utterances of indefinitely many novel sentences of a language without the assumption that that language had a compositional truth-theoretic semantics. This evidently requires that such a semantics somehow be adverted to in the explanation of one's language processing, that is, in the explanation of one's ability to go from the perception of sounds to the knowledge of what said in the production of those sounds.

5. There are psychological facts as well as semantic ones: I believe that I am alive, and you desire that you stay alive; we both hope that a nuclear holocaust is averted.

6. The "token-token identity theory" is correct: at least in humans, beliefs and desires are neural states, states of the nervous system.

7. The relational theory of propositional attitudes is correct: believing is a relation to things believed, to values of the objectual variable 'y' in the schema 'x believes y'.

8. Semantic and psychological facts are not irreducibly semantic or psychological: the truths expressed by belief- and meaning-ascribing sentences are also expressible by sentences devoid of semantic or psychological terms.
9. Semantic facts reduce to psychological facts à la the Gricean program IBS.

At this juncture one thing is very clear, if what has gone before is correct: our hypothetical philosopher is in very big trouble.

If the semantic reduced to the psychological in the way required by (9), intention-based semantics, then the content of propositional attitudes would in its turn be explicable without any appeal to the meanings of public-language items. So when IBS was taken in conjunction with (7), the relational theory of propositional attitudes, the task of the IBS theorist was to find objects of belief with non–public-language semantic features that accounted for the content of beliefs. But it was, I trust, clear by the end of chapter 4 that none of the *candidate* belief objects that could make (9) consistent with (7) were the objects of belief; that is to say, IBS cannot be true if the relational theory of propositional attitudes is true. However, we also know that (7), the relational theory, is seriously threatened, and one can imagine an IBS theorist taking momentary solace in this. But such solace must indeed be momentary, for we shall later see that IBS *presupposes* the relational theory of propositional attitudes, and then it will be clear that as IBS cannot be true with or without the relational theory, it cannot be true.

Now the relational theory (7) is certainly false, if the conclusions so far reached are correct. For if believing is a relation to things believed, then those things must surely be either propositions (of one stripe or another), or mental representations, or sentences or utterances of a public language; but, it was argued, believing is not a relation to any of those things.

The falsity of (7) has profound consequences. I have just mentioned the connection with (9), and later in this chapter I shall argue that the falsity of (7) supports my own solution to the mind-body problem. But the most obvious and direct result of the falsity of (7) is that it arguably refutes (3), the hypothesis that natural languages have compositional truth-theoretic semantics. For, as already noted in section 1.3, a compositional truth-theoretic semantics for English would have to treat 'believes' as semantically primitive, and the construal of 'believes' as a relational predicate is arguably the only tenable way this could be done. Consequently, I submit, there can be no cogent denial of the relational theory (7) that does not carry with it the denial of (3), the denial, that is, that English (and every other natural language) has a compositional truth-theoretic semantics. And of course if (3) is false, then so is (4), which presupposes (3). At the same time it is very hard to see how a correct compositional meaning theory for a natural language could avoid being a truth-theoretic semantics. After all, it is evidently a fact about the *meaning* of 'snow is white' that an utterance of it is *true* just in case snow is white. So the falsity of (7), the relational theory of propositional attitudes, strongly threatens the truth of (2), as well as that of (3) and (4), and as well as that of (9).

With so much at stake, one might well feel that what is most in trouble is the claim that (7) is false, and with this I sympathize. Now it happens that the falsity of (7) would *directly* threaten (3), the hypothesis that natural languages have truth-theoretic semantics, and it is the falsity of (3) that would in turn threaten many of the other hypotheses. Thus, rather than speak glibly of the falsity of (7), I should say at this point that we have a tension, a dilemma, and that the case against (7) must be weighed against the case for (3). In this light, we can speak with confidence of the falsity of (7) only after the case for (3)—namely, the language-processing hypothesis (4)—has been refuted. Now I do think that (4) is false and that there is no other good reason for believing (3), and this is a dominant topic of the next two chapters.

The physicalistic hypothesis (8), which is the topic of this chapter, is also threatened—refuted, I should say. For it would appear that if all that has gone before is correct, there can be no reduction of propositional-attitude facts to facts statable in a nonmentalistic, nonintentional idiom. (And if there can be no "physicalistic" reduction of propositional-attitude facts, then there clearly can be none of semantic facts either; so, to keep the discussion as simple as possible, its primary focus will be the irreducibility of belief reports.) Our hypothetical philosopher must be now realize that if it is a fact that he believes that he owns more than two pairs of socks, then that fact is not physicalistically reducible; it is not a fact statable without mentalistic and intentional idioms.

Some will think, and perhaps our philosopher is among them, that the falsity of (8) threatens nearly all of the other hyppotheses. For the philosophers to whom I allude are so repelled by the prospect of there being brute, primitive, irreducibly semantic or psychological facts that they are prepared to deny that there *are* semantic or psychological facts should (8) be false because the requisite reductions are not forthcoming. For these prospective eliminativists the falsity of (8) would carry with it the falsity both of (1), which posits semantic facts, and of (5), which posits psychological facts; and with the possible exception of (7), each of the other hypotheses presupposes the truth of (1) or (5).

So what is our theorist now to do? Is he to be prideful of his consistency and deny that we have beliefs with content and words with meaning, or, even worse, to recant, to renounce the scruples of the natural scientist and "just surface listlessly to the Sargasso Sea of mentalism" (Quine 1975, p. 91)? Neither, I should recommend; but to prepare the way for the resolution of his dilemma, I need to be clearer than I have so far been about *reduction* and *physicalism*.

6.2 Reduction and the Varieties of Physicalism

It will help to begin by distinguishing between the reduction of *extralinguistic* psychological *entities*—substances (believers), states or events (beliefs), or properties (believing that such and such, being a belief that such and such)—and the reduction of psychological *sentences*. When, as regards the former, our concern is with objective, language-independent things, of whatever ontological category, then to say that A's reduce to B's is just to say that A's *are* B's. Reduction here is identity; if, for example, belief properties reduce to functional properties, then every belief property is identical to some functional property. But sometimes talk of reduction has as its topic predicates or the sentences containing them. To say in the context of the mind-body problem that A-sentences reduce to B-sentences is to say that every A-sentence enjoys some suitably strong equivalence relation, typically necessary equivalence, to some B-sentence.

The distinction between entity reduction and sentence reduction is easily elided if one supposes that there are objective, language-independent belief properties, properties such as being a belief that flounders snore. For their reduction would induce the corresponding reduction for belief sentences, and a reduction of belief sentences would virtually assure the identification of belief properties with properties specifiable in a nonmentalistic idiom.

The distinction between entity reduction and sentence reduction becomes of interest when one entertains the possibility that (a) there are no belief properties, but (b) there are true belief-ascribing sentences. Taking this possibility seriously, one cannot glibly identify physicalism with the doctrine that there are no irreducibly mental entities—whether substances, events, or properties. For that would leave open the possibility of a position whose physicalistic credentials may not be immediately evident: namely, the position that affirms (1) that nothing extralinguistic is irreducibly psychological; (2) that there are no belief properties; and (3) that there are true, but irreducible, belief-ascribing sentences.

It will be useful, then, to follow the distinction between entity reduction and sentence reduction with a corresponding distinction between what—if we can divest the term of its emotive connotations—may be called two kinds of physicalism: *Ontological Physicalism*, which holds that there are no extralinguistic, irreducibly psychological entities of any ontological category; and *Sentential Physicalism*, which holds that there are no irreducibly psychological sentences. The two kinds of physicalism will roughly coincide if there are belief properties; but they become interestingly different when, for whatever reason, one contemplates denying that such properties exist. Consequently, one cannot argue merely from the truth of Ontological Physicalism to the truth of Sentential Physicalism. Sentential Dualism—that there are true but irreducible psychological sentences—is consistent with Ontological Physicalism; but they can both be true only if there are no belief properties.

I take it that Sentential Physicalism has already been shown to be false: that is the cumulative conclusion of the chapters before this. Given the falsity of Sentential Physicalism, the course I propose to take between the emptiness of eliminativism and the excesses of dualism is this: to accept Ontological Physicalism *and* Sentential Dualism. *Ontological* Dualism, I shall argue, is indeed insupportable; so if there are belief properties— properties such as being a belief that flounders snore—they are not irreducible. At the same time, the falsity of Sentential Physicalism tells us that if there are belief properties, they *are* irreducible—for the desired reductions are simply not to be had. And the argument that results leaves no choice:

> If there are belief properties, they are not irreducible.
> If there are belief properties, they are irreducible.
> *Therefore*, there are no belief properties.

The existence of belief properties thus denied, the way is open to accept Sentential Dualism in conjunction with Ontological Physicalism. Although there is no extralinguistic entity of any ontological category that is irreducibly psychological, there are sentences which ascribe beliefs that are both true and irreducibly psychological. Since there are true (but irreducible) belief-ascribing sentences, there are believers and (possibly) beliefs; since Ontological Physicalism is true, these psychological entities are not irreducibly psychological: believers are bodies, that is, occupiers of space, and beliefs, in humans at least, are states of the nervous system. Since Sentential Dualism and Ontological Physicalism are both true, there are no belief properties. It remains, of course, to be argued that Sentential Dualism is justified given nominalism with respect to belief properties; for there are evidently such nominalists—Quine, for one—who would hold that, strictly speaking, there are no true belief sentences if Sentential Physicalism is false.

I have, then, two debts to discharge. First, I must justify acceptance of Ontological Physicalism: what, after all, is so terrible about Ontological Dualism? Now the falsity of Sentential Physicalism has, I am supposing, already been established, and it together with Ontological Physicalism entails that there are no belief properties. Given Ontological Physicalism and the falsity of Sentential Physicalism, one must choose between (a) the total elimination of beliefs and believers—that is, the thesis that there are no true belief sentences—and (b) Sentential Dualism. Since I opt for (b), my second debt is to justify acceptance of Sentential Dualism—that is, to show that there is no reason not to believe that there are true belief sentences, given that those sentences are irreducibly psychological and that Ontological Physicalism is true.

There are, however, two other things that I should do before turning to the foregoing two tasks. First, I should clarify what precisely is being denied when I deny the existence of belief properties. For, as I have already intimated in earlier chapters, I certainly have no objection to the *pleonastic* use of 'property' that enables us trivially to move back and forth between 'Ralph believes that flounders snore' and 'Ralph has the property of believing that flounders snore'; nor do I object to the *ostensible* quantification over properties that follows trivially from a predicate's being true of a thing, as we find in 'Ralph and Louise have something in common—they both believe that flounders snore'.

What is at issue as regards the *existence* of belief properties is *Realism* with respect to them. When I deny the existence of belief properties, what I am denying is this metaphysical theory: that there exists the property of believing that flounders snore and that that property is as ontologically and conceptually distinct from the *predicate* 'believes that flounders snore' as Saul Kripke is from the *name* 'Saul Kripke'. According to the Realism that I find objectionable, there is, on the one hand, the objective, abstract, eternal property of believing that flounders snore, and there is, on the other, the predicate 'believes that flounders snore'; and it is by virtue of the latter's standing in a certain contingent relation to the former that it, the predicate, has application to just those things that believe that flounders snore—just as the name 'Saul Kripke' has its semantic properties by virtue of standing in a certain contingent relation to the person Saul Kripke. If there is a sense of 'properties exist' that is merely tantamount to 'there are meaningful predicates'—a sense perhaps explicable in terms of substitutional quantification—then in that sense of 'property' I am happy to be a dualist; for I am, I have declared, a dualist as regards belief predicates. It must be understood in what follows that what I am denying is the existence of the Realist's "nonpleonastic" properties.[1]

And of course the same goes for "facts". In the relevant, nonpleonastic, Realistic, ontologically loaded sense of 'fact', there are belief facts—for example, the fact that Ralph believes that flounders snore—just in case there are, in the same Realistic sense, belief properties (which is why in glossing Ontological Physicalism I did not mention belief facts in addition to belief properties). I have no trouble with the *pleonastic* sense of 'fact' that allows us to move back and forth between 'Ralph believes that flounders snore' and 'It's a fact that Ralph believes that flounders snore'. So now it is clear what I should say to the philosopher who tells us that he cannot stomach the thought of there being irreducibly psychological facts: "It all depends on what you mean by 'fact'. If you mean this in the sense that carries with it an ontological commitment to genuinely language-independent nonpleonastic belief properties, then you are right to be repelled: Ontological Dualism is indeed false. If, however, you mean 'fact' in the pleonastic sense in which it follows that there are belief facts just from there being true belief-ascribing sentences, then your being repelled rests on a mistake, doubtless one induced by the pun on 'fact': for Sentential Dualism is true."

The second preliminary matter is a point of clarification needed to forestall a false impression. In arguing against the existence of non-pleonastic propositional-attitude properties and facts, I do not want in any way to imply that I think that some other sorts of properties and facts— say, physical properties and facts—are genuinely language-independent. In fact, I do not recognize *any* nonpleonastic properties or facts. I favor nominalism across the board, and especially do not think that properties are needed as the semantic values of predicates. The basis for this thorough-going nominalism with respect to properties is discussed in section 8.5. In this chapter I offer arguments against the existence of *belief properties* that are not generalizable to all properties. The case against belief properties may be overdetermined.

I turn now to the argument for Ontological Physicalism, and, with this, the reason for being a nominalist with respect to belief properties.

6.3 Ontological Physicalism

Earlier, in 2.2, I said that there were three mind-body problems: concerning things, state and event tokens, and properties. On the face of it, then, we have mental entities of three ontological categories: minds, mental states, and mental properties. As regards the putative entities of any one of these categories, there are three positions one might take, positions that define one's solution to the mind-body problem generated by the putative entities of that ontological category:

1. One can affirm the existence of the mental entities of that category and maintain that they are irreducibly mental.

2. One can affirm the existence of the mental entities of that category and deny that they are irreducibly mental. In the case of minds, this would be to deny Cartesian Dualism, and to maintain that minds are also occu-piers of space. In the case of mental state (event, process) tokens this would be to maintain that those state (event, process) tokens are identical to phy-

sical state (event, process) tokens. And in the case of mental properties this would be to maintain that mental properties are identical to properties intrinsically specifiable nonmentalistically, such as functional properties.

3. One can deny that there really are any mental entities of the ontological category in question.

Ontological Physicalism holds that position 1 is not correct for any ontological category. To establish this for minds is just to refute Cartesian Dualism, the doctrine that minds are substances having only mental properties and no physical properties whatever. I shall pass over most of the familiar and, to my mind, utterly persuasive considerations against Cartesian Dualism, as I do not really anticipate any serious challenge to them. But I shall begin with an argument that does entail the falsity of Cartesian Dualism; this is an argument to show that mental state (event, process) tokens are identical to physical state (event, process) tokens. The argument —which I suspect is just one articulation of what many think is wrong with a dualism of events—will also function as a useful preliminary to the main argument against the existence of irreducibly mental properties, and that argument, together with another, will complete my case for Ontological Physicalism. To facilitate exposition, my arguments will be about beliefs and belief properties, but with the exception of the last argument in this section they have clear generalizations to all mental states and properties.

Beliefs are physical states
It will be useful to state the argument for this in terms of a particular case, as the pertinent generalization is straightforward. So let us suppose that Ava, about to cross the street, sees that a car is coming and steps back to the curb. We then have the following argument to the conclusion that Ava's coming to believe that a car was coming was identical to some neural event in her.

(1)   There was within Ava an unbroken chain of neural events that began with the stimulation of receptor cells in her eyes by light reflected from the oncoming car and ended with her stepping back, and each of these neural events was a cause of the one following it and thence of her stepping back.

By 'unbroken' I mean more than that the events were temporally and spatially contiguous; it also signifies that the causal laws which subsume these events and explain their causal efficacy do not require, as a cause of Ava's stepping back, the occurrence of any event cotemporal with some event in the chain of neural events but not itself a member of that chain. As these laws are laws of neurophysiology, laws that pertain to the electrochemical properties of the neural events they subsume, this premise implies that there is a sufficient explanation of Ava's stepping back wholly within the language of physical science. Of course, this premise is a bet, as no one can give complete neurophysiological explanations of bodily movements; yet it is a reasonable bet in view of the well-known fact that we are not hollow inside but house billions of neurons sending forth and receiving electrochemical impulses, from receptor cells to effector cells, trillions of times each instant we are alive.

(2)   Ava's coming to believe that a car was coming was a cause of her stepping back.

After all, Ava stepped back *because* she saw that a car was coming; she would not have stepped back had she not believed that a car was coming. Evidently, Ava's stepping back was made to happen by her coming to believe that a car was coming.

(3)   Therefore, either

Ava's coming to believe that a car was coming was *identical to* the simultaneous neural event that was a cause of her stepping back

or else

Ava's stepping back was *causally overdetermined*: there were two causal chains leading to her stepping back, one containing (during the relevant time span) only neural events, the other containing at least one irreducibly mental event—viz., Ava's coming to believe that a car was coming.

Suppose that b, the event of Ava's belief acquisition, occurred at time t. Premise 2 tells us that b was a cause of Ava's stepping back. But premise 1 tells us that a certain neural event n occurred at t and that it was a cause of Ava's stepping back. Now, either $b = n$ or $b \neq n$. If $b = n$, then only one event occurred at t that was a cause of Ava's stepping back, and that event was both a token of some neural event-type and a coming to believe that a car was coming. If, on the other hand, $b \neq n$, then two *distinct* events occurred at t, both of which were causes of Ava's stepping back; and that, by definition, is causal overdetermination.

(4)   But there was no causal overdetermination of the sort entertained in (3).

The difficulty is not with causal overdetermination per se, but with special properties of the sort of causal overdetermination of Ava's stepping back that would obtain if the mental and neural causes were not identical.

a. If this sort of causal overdetermination obtained, then a mental event could *never* cause a bodily movement *except* in a case of causal overdetermination where there was a simultaneous and distinct neural cause of the movement. For one would be driven to the overdetermination hypothesis only if one made the assumption underlying premise 1, that all bodily movements have complete explanations in neurophysical terms. This causal superfluousness is hard to believe in; it is hard to believe that God is such a bad engineer. Certainly this causal superfluousness is not a feature of the kind of causal overdetermination that is unproblematic. If the firing of a gun and a soprano's hitting a high note are simultaneous causes of the shattering of a wine glass, we do not suppose that either cause could only have been causally operative in the presence of a cause of the other type.

b. It is evidently reasonable to suppose that if an event e caused an event e', then there is some "full-fledged causal law" that covers the events and explains their causal relation.[2] And if e and e' are, as cause and effect, subsumable under such a causal law, then one should expect there to be event descriptions F and G such that (i) e satisfies F and e' satisfies G; (ii) an event's satisfying F is *causally* sufficient for that event's causing the occurrence of some event satisfying G; and (iii) the proposition that F-events cause G-events is not "analytic" or "metaphysically" necessary: there is some possible world in which F-events do not cause G-events. Now, to whatever extent this broadly Humean picture of causality is plausible, to that extent it is implausible that there is a causal overdetermination of acts by neural and mental events; for if Ava's belief acquisition is not identical to any neural event, then one should not suppose it to be covered by any causal law. For suppose that Ava stepped back because she saw that a car was coming, and that her coming to believe that a car was coming was not identical to any neural event. If there is *any* "law" that applies to the mental causation of her act, it is surely some belief/desire generalization, some generalization that refines and completes, and otherwise makes respectable, the platitude that if a person desires to avoid a certain result (say, getting run over by a car), believes that she will avoid that result by doing an act of a certain type (say, stepping back to the curb), believes that she is able to perform an act of that type, does not believe that there is any better, or equally good, way of avoiding that result, does not have any stronger and conflicting desire, is able to perform an act of the type in question, and is not prevented from doing so, then, *ceteris paribus*, she will perform an act of that type. What is problematic here is that, first, it is by no means clear that this "generalization" has any true completion, and, second, to the extent that we can fill it out, to that extent it begins to look more and more analytic, more and more expressive of truths constitutive of our propositional-attitude concepts, and thus less and less like a contingent, causal law.[3] Of course, none of this threatens the broadly Humean conception of causation if mental events are neural events; for then the genuine causal law covering both the mental event and the act it causes can be a law of neurophysiology.

c. Suppose that we have an undisputed instance of causal overdetermination, where c_1 and c_2 are the distinct simultaneous causes of their common effect e. Suppose, too, that the broadly Humean conception is correct, and that L_1 is the causal law subsuming c_1 and e, while L_2 is a distinct law subsuming c_2 and e. Then we can certainly rule out this bizarre thought: that L_1 is nomologically superfluous in that there can never be two events c' and e' related by L_1 as cause and effect *unless* there is also some event c'', distinct from c' but simultaneous with it, such that c'' and e' are related by L_2 as cause and effect. One need only reflect on any possible case of causal overdetermination, such as the wine glass example already used, to appreciate the obviousness of this point; the causal economy of our world is plausibly something we should subscribe to as a methodological principle akin to Occam's Razor. Now, however, suppose that the mental/neural causal overdetermination in question does obtain and that causal laws exist to explain these causal sequences, L_m being the law that covers the mental event and the act it causes, L_n the law that covers the neural event and the same act as that also caused by the simultaneous mental event. Then L_m would be nomologically superfluous in the bizarre sense just entertained; that law would never have application unless L_n (or some other neural law) also had application to provide a different causal chain for the act in question. This nomological superfluousness of causal laws is at least as hard to believe in as its consequence, the already disparaged nomological superfluousness of mental causes.

So much for a first pass at some reasons for believing (4); the argument's conclusion now follows ineluctably:

(5)   Therefore, Ava's coming to believe that a car was coming was a neural event—there was one event that was an acquisition of that belief and also a token of some neural event-type.

As regards the generalization of this conclusion to belief *state*-tokens, I shall assume without argument that if Ava's coming to have her present belief state-token is a neural event, then that state-token which is her belief is a neural state-token.[4]

I find this line of argument rather compelling.[5] My one serious reservation is that we have need of it only if we are entitled to a genuine ontology of events, and it is not clear that we are entitled to that. Yet this is not a reservation that I am required to worry about. For if we have no genuine ontological commitment to events (states, processes, and so forth), then they pose no threat to Ontological Physicalism; and if there really are events (in the 'really are' of objectual quantification), then I call on the argument just laid out. So I feel entitled to step around the messy question of the ontological status of events. Besides, none of this prejudices the argument I shall now make against the existence of irreducible belief properties, and it will be expositively convenient if the foregoing argument about event- and state-tokens, and the "token-token materialism" it implies, is taken as my official position on propositional-attitude state-tokens.

There are no irreducible belief properties
So let us assume that belief state-tokens are neural state-tokens; this will simplify, but will not prejudice, the argument to show that if there are genuinely nonpleonastic belief properties, they are not irreducible. This argument may take the form of a *reductio*: we will suppose that there is an objective, language-independent, and *irreducible* property of being a belief that a car is coming and that n, the neural state-token that happens to be Ava's present belief that a car is coming, has that property, and then derive unacceptable consequences from this supposition.

We may begin, then, by supposing that

(1)   Ava is in neural state-token n; n has B, the nonpleonastic property of being a belief that a car is coming; and B is not identical to any property that is intrinsically specifiable in a nonmentalistic, nonintentional idiom.

I have already argued that there is a complete neurophysical explanation of Ava's stepping back, and this (when the existence of properties is not in question) may be taken to imply that

(2)   there is a neurophysiological property P of n's that is the most comprehensive property entering into the neurophysiological explanation of n's being a cause of Ava's stepping back, and that is thus causally necessary and sufficient for n's being a cause of the stepping back.

The property P, in other words, is fully explanatory of that bodily movement of Ava's that was her stepping back.

(3)   But if there is a nonpleonastic property B, then it is also a causally essential property of n's with respect to n's being a cause of Ava's stepping back: had n not had B, n would not have caused Ava's stepping back.

It is not just that Ava's belief caused her to step back; it is also true that that state would not have had that effect had it not been a belief that a car was coming. We are not to suppose that B, like the property of occurring on a Saturday, is a causally irrelevant property of n's.

The problem now is to make good sense of (1), (2), and (3) being true together. In other words, how, given (1), can one make sense of (2) and (3)? The antidualist with respect to B would have no problem in reconciling (2) and (3) being true together: he would claim, roughly speaking, that for some physical property P' contined in P, B was identical either to P' or to some functional property realized by P'. But one who holds the property dualism of (1) does have a problem; for this theorist must evidently explain the joint truth of (1)–(3) in one of the following four ways, none of which, I think, is acceptable. Therefore, one of (1)–(3) cannot be right, and if any must go, it is (1).

The four ways in which the property dualist might try to explain the consistency of (1) with (2) and (3) are as follows.

A. The dualist might deny that the causal efficacy of B can be explained in terms of the causal efficacy of P, and seek to account for the former by the claim that, while there is no causal overdetermination at the level of causes (since, we are assuming, the belief state-token is a neural state-token), there is overdetermination at the level of *causal laws*. That is to say, there is one causal law L containing P and another L' containing B; subsumption under either law is sufficient to explain n's being a cause of the stepping back, and n is covered by both laws by virtue of having P and B. Somewhat more exactly, we might suppose that there are properties of state/event-tokens Q, E, and E' such that (i) Q entails B; (ii) Ava's stepping back has E and E'; (iii) n has Q; and (iv) L says that P-states cause E-events, while L' says that Q-states cause E'-events.

Reply. This sort of overdetermination is in danger of being as difficult to believe in as the one that postulated an overdetermination of actual causes, and for pretty much the same reason: superfluousness with respect to independent application. Because all bodily movements have complete explanations in wholly physical terms, L' would never explain a sequence of events except when that sequence was already explained by an L-style physical law. The qualification 'in danger of' is needed for the following reason. A reasonable version of the unity of science would hold that the laws of no special science have application independently of the laws of physics (think of the way Boyle's law is explained by the underlying laws of nuclear physics). This could be viewed as a kind of acceptable "overdetermination" at the level of causal laws, and it is imaginable that the dualist who proposes (A) would try to claim that his overdetermination was acceptable in the same way. The difficulty is in seeing how he could coherently suggest this, given that the nonpleonastic property B was irreducible and given his denial that its causal efficacy could be explained in terms of P's. Although I do not have a theory of acceptable intertheoretic relations to offer, it does seem clear that the onus is on the proponent of (A) to defeat the assumption that his overdetermination would not fit into the acceptable mold.

Moreover, as I have already argued above, it is unlikely that we would find anything like a reasonable candidate for L'. First, it is doubtful that any correct substituend for 'Q' would present itself; then it is doubtful that any correct belief/desire generalization—which is what L' would surely have to be—would be a full-fledged *causal* law, as opposed to an analytic truth.

B. Who needs to embed the belief property B in a causal law? The dualist might simply claim that it is a brute, primitive, inexplicable metaphysical fact that B is causally essential in the way explained. That is to say, there is no causal law that contains B, but B is nevertheless a causally essential property of n with respect to n's being a cause of the stepping back. Period. B is causally essential to n's having its effect, but that fact is in no way to be explained by B's involvement in any causal law, nor is it to be explained as being in any way inherited from the causal efficacy of P; B is causally necessary and that is that.

Reply. Believe it if you can. The charge of superfluousness—as regards B's being causally essential to n's having its effect—is now even more resounding. In (A) Plato's Heaven was being populated with things whose only apparent job was to do something that was already being done, but at least they superfluously did something. Now it is being suggested that we populate Plato's Heaven with a property that does nothing. B has the second-order property of being causally necessary for n's having its effect, but that second-order property is really idle, as B is not part of some larger property that is necessary *and* sufficient for n's causing Ava's stepping back (and, to rule out the property of being B and P, does not contain a property that is itself causally necessary and sufficient for n's having its effect).

C. The dualist might try going *epiphenomenalist*: n's having P causes n's having B, and there is an end to it. That is all there is to the causal relevance of B: it is wholly inherited from P.

Reply. Talk about your "nomological danglers"—now B does not even do an idle part of a superfluous job! In words that Frank Jackson has put in the mouth of the materialist, belief properties on the epiphenomenalist proposal "are an excrescence. They *do* nothing, they *explain* nothing, they serve merely to soothe the intuitions of dualists, and it is left a total mystery how they fit into the world view of science." Jackson, who favors mental-property epiphenomenalism, protests that the materialist's complaint rests on "an overly optimistic view of the human animal, and its powers" (1982, p. 135).[6] But this is not right. The materialist's point is that it is bad science to suppose that things instantiate properties of a certain kind when one has no coherent account of how or why they came to instantiate them.

Related to the last point is this deeper one. If having P causes having B, then that should be subsumable under some psychophysical, full-fledged causal law. At the least, *some* sort of mechanism ought to explain the causal connection between P and B. But it seems most implausible that there is a full-fledged causal law linking P and B (especially when one reflects on the possibility of B being had by quite different kinds of physical states—those of a constructed information-processing system, for example); and what sort of non-law mechanism could the epiphenomenalist conceivably offer?

D. The dualist might claim, finally, that n's having B *supervenes* on n's having P, where "supervenience" is a primitive metaphysical relation between properties that is distinct from causation and more like some primitive form of entailment. The claim here would be that, although B is in no sense identical to or contained in P, and although there is no formally representable entailment of B by P, nevertheless it is simply a brute, inexplicable metaphysical fact that there is no possible world in which a state has P but not B. As in (C), the causal relevance of B with respect to n's being a cause of Ava's stepping back is not anything that B has intrinsically; but here the causal relevance of B derives entirely from B's standing in the supervenience relation to P. P is the property that really has the causal power, the property contained in the causal law that explains n's being a cause of the movement; and B simply inherits its causal relevance from the fact that it supervenes on P.

Reply. G. E. Moore was a non-naturalist in ethics: he held that moral properties could not be identified with natural properties; and he held, on the positive side, that they were simple, irreducible, unanalyzable, non-natural properties, and that, being non-natural, they were discerned through a special faculty of moral intuition (Moore 1903). Tough-minded physicalist types (including many Logical Positivists) agreed that moral properties could not be reduced to natural properties ('physical or topic-neutral properties', we would say), but had no sympathy at all with Moore's positive thesis, which postulated a realm of non-natural properties and facts. These properties, it was felt, could not be made sense of within a scientific world view; they were obscurantist and produced more problems than they solved. At the same time, philosophers who abhorred Moore's irreducibly non-natural properties knew that he also held this thesis about them: that it was not possible for two things or events to be alike in all physical respects while differing in some moral property (Moore 1942). No one thought that Moore's positive theory of moral properties was in any way mitigated by this further supervenience thesis. How *could* being told that non-natural moral properties stood in the supervenience relation to physical properties make them any more palatable? On the contrary, invoking a special primitive metaphysical relation of supervenience to explain how non-natural moral properties were related to physical properties was just to add mystery to mystery, to cover one obscurantist move with another. I therefore find it more than a little ironic, and puzzling, that supervenience is nowadays being heralded as a way of making non-pleonastic, irreducibly non-natural mental properties cohere with an acceptably naturalistic solution to the mind-body problem. In fact, the supervenience response (D) is hardly any improvement on the epiphenomenalist response (C). It does remove the need to find a causal law linking P and B, but does nothing to remove the "nomological dangler" objection; and the appeal to a special primitive relation of "supervenience," as defined above, is obscurantist in the extreme.[7] Supervenience is just epiphenomenalism without causation.

Anyway, that is why I believe that if there is a genuinely objective, language-independent property of being a belief that a car is coming, that property is not irreducible. Suppositions (1)–(3) are true together only if (A), (B), (C), or (D); but not one of these is true; and if one of (1)–(3) must go, it is (1).

That gives a complete case for Ontological Physicalism (although I am about to add to it). In short, belief state-tokens, assuming they exist, are physical state-tokens; and if there are nonpleonastic belief properties, they are not irreducible.

Perhaps this has the appearance of an impasse. On the one hand we have the argument just presented to show that there cannot be irreducibly mental belief properties; on the other hand it seems impossible to find a correct reduction for those properties. Well, if this is an impasse, the way out of it is staring us in the face: deny that there are belief properties (nonpleonastic belief properties, of course). Indeed, our impasse is an argument for this nominalistic position. For we have good reason to conclude both that

> if there are belief properties, they are not irreducible;

and that

> if there are belief properties, they are irreducible (for there is no correct reduction).

And from this it follows that

> there are no belief properties.

There is in fact another, altogether independent, route to the same conclusion, although stating it will invite questions that are not answered until the next chapter. But it should be stated now because it offers further support for Ontological Physicalism: if there are no belief properties, then, *a fortiori*, there are no irreducible belief properties.

There are no belief properties

Suppose that there were a genuinely objective, language-independent, non-pleonastic property of believing that flounders snore. Then we would be in a position to assert two further things. The first is that the property would surely be the meaning, or "semantic value," of the predicate 'believes that flounders snore'. It would, that is, be essential to understanding the sentence 'Ronald believes that flounders snore' that one was acquainted with the property of believing that flounders snore and knew that the sentence was true just in case Ronald had it; and it would therefore be essential to understanding the predicate 'believes that flounders snore' that one knew that it predicated the property of believing that flounders snore. Let us for convenience put this first proposition thus:

(1)   If there is a language-independent property of believing that flounders snore, then the predicate 'believes that flounders snore' expresses it.

The second thing we may assert is that

(2)   if there is a language-independent property of believing that flounders snore, then it is a *noncomposite* property.

To say that the property is noncomposite is to say that it is not a function, or construction, of any other properties, relations, or things. The property of loving Margaret Thatcher (if there exists such a property) is composite: it is determined by the love relation and Margaret Thatcher. The reason that the property of believing that flounders snore (if it exists) is not also composite has to do with the falsity of the relational theory of believing. For the only way one can tenably take the property expressed by 'believes that flounders snore' to be composite is to take 'believes' as a relational predicate, and thus believing as a relation between believers and things believed; but, I have argued, the relational theory is false.

Now it follows from (1) and (2) that if there is a nonpleonastic property of believing that flounders snore, then 'believes that flounders snore' is *semantically primitive* in the sense, roughly, that one had to learn its meaning as a single unit, all at once, by learning that the predicate expressed the noncomposite property of believing that flounders snore. Because the semantic value of the predicate is noncomposite, one is precluded from taking the predicate to be semantically complex—to have its meaning built up out of the meanings of its parts; for if the property expressed is non-composite, there is nothing to be the meanings of the parts—nothing, in particular, to be the meaning of 'believes'. Semantically, 'believes that flounders snore' would be on a par with 'sleeps'.

Now that would make English unlearnable. For there are infinitely many predicates of the form 'believes that σ', and what applies to 'believes that flounders snore' must also apply, *mutatis mutandis*, to every belief predicate.

One would need an infinite amount of time to learn one by one the meanings of the infinitely many belief predicates. Since English is learnable, we may conclude that there are no language-independent belief properties to be the semantic values of belief predicates.[8]

That concludes my case for Ontological Physicalism. In taking the line that, to whatever extent there are genuinely language-independent mental entities (of the propositional-attitude variety) of any ontological category, they are not irreducibly mental, I have been constrained to take a nominalistic line on the existence of belief properties. This, we have seen, leaves me free to adopt Sentential Dualism, the thesis that there are true, but irreducible, belief-ascribing sentences, and to the defense of that thesis I now turn.

6.4 Sentential Dualism

I believe that some dogs have fleas. That sentence—i.e., that sequence of marks on paper—is true, and therefore has meaning. And yet, that sentence is irreducibly mental and intentional: the truth that it states cannot also be stated by a sentence devoid of mentalistic and intentional idioms. I am therefore committed to Sentential Dualism, the doctrine that there are true but irreducible belief-ascribing sentences. What justifies me in holding Sentential Dualism? That is an easy question to answer: I know in the usual way that I believe that some dogs have fleas, and the first few chapters of this book give my reason for thinking that such truths are not truths statable in other, physicalistic or functionalistic or whatever, terms. So I prefer to ask, What would justify one in denying Sentential Dualism at the cost of denying both that marks and sounds have meaning and truth values and that people have beliefs and other propositional attitudes? (For it is obvious that marks and sounds have no semantic features if the people who produce them have no beliefs or intentions.) In other words, why should one esteem Sentential Physicalism to the point where, should it prove false (as I think it has), one is prepared to be a total eliminativist with respect to the psychological and the semantic and deny that there are any true belief- or meaning-ascribing sentences (actually, any true sentences!)?

No doubt some will balk at this way of putting the question, because they remain unconvinced that Sentential Physicalism is false; they still hope for the elusive reduction, may even think that they have it. Nevertheless, *my* issue must be just this: Is there any reason to think that belief sentences cannot be true, given Ontological Physicalism, nominalism (at least with respect to belief properties), and the falsity of Sentential Physicalism?

My own view is that the good case for physicalism is a case for Ontological Physicalism, and that those good reasons do not extend to Sentential Dualism when the existence of belief properties is denied. But at least one philosopher thinks that the question just asked has an affirmative answer. Quine, whom we know to be a nominalist as regards properties, wrote in *Word and Object* that he was favorable to Brentano's thesis that "there is no breaking out of the intentional vocabulary by explaining its members in other terms," and then remarked:

> One may accept the Brentano thesis either as showing the indispensability of intentional idioms and the importance of an autonomous science of intention, or as showing the baselessness of intentional idioms and the emptiness of a science of intention. My attitude, unlike Brentano's, is the second.... If we are limning the true and ultimate structure of reality, the canonical scheme for us is the austere scheme that knows ... no propositional attitudes but only the physical constitution and behavior of organisms. (1960, p. 221)

I shall consider two lines of argument to show that Sentential Dualism is unjustified even on the assumption that there are no nonpleonastic belief properties.

1. The passage from Quine suggests one objection to Sentential Dualism: if we accept Sentential Dualism, then we shall have to join with Brentano in recognizing "the importance of an autonomous science of intention." I think the implicit idea is that our commonsense psychological and semantic notions are theoretical terms in a commonsense theory of linguistic and nonlinguistic behavior, and that if these notions are irreducible, as Sentential Dualism asserts, then the commonsense theory will be *autonomous*, cut off from physics and the rest of respectable science. But to be isolated in this way from the rest of science is to be *discredited*. (Cf. Wright 1984, p. 767.) And if the commonsense theory is discredited, then its theoretical terms cannot be true of anything, and sentences such as 'I believe that some dogs have fleas' cannot be true.

This is vague. In what disastrous way would the commonsense theory be rendered "autonomous" if its theoretical terms were irreducible? It will help in trying to answer this question to have the Quinean line join forces with a methodological argument that Hartry Field has proposed for Sentential Physicalism.

According to Field, physicalism—"the doctrine that chemical facts, biological facts, psychological facts and semantical facts are all explicable (in principle) in terms of physical facts [construed so as to include functional facts]"—functions as a "high-level empirical hypothesis, a hypothesis that no small number of experiments can force us to give up" (1972, p. 357). It is, Field claims, a hypothesis that we are justified in accepting because assuming it has been a fruitful research program, leading to discoveries (the physical and chemical bases of genetic facts, for example) that would not otherwise have been made.

Amalgamating Quine and Field, we get this argument:

(1)   'Believes', 'desires', 'means', and the like are theoretical terms of a commonsense psychological (or psychosemantical) theory.

(2)   The justification for methodological physicalism (as we may call what Field has in mind) and the nature of the commonsense theory require that, should the theory's theoretical terms ('believes', etc.) prove physicalistically irreducible, then the theory must be deemed false, and its terms true of nothing.

(3)   Therefore, Sentential Dualism must be deemed false: belief sentences cannot be both true and irreducible.

But I do not find this argument persuasive. I doubt both of its premises. As regards (2), I doubt that there is any justified "high-level empirical hypothesis" that requires that theoretical facts be *reducible* to physical facts. A *reduction requirement* would be plausible only if it were plausible that theoretical terms were defined by the theories that introduced them. But it would seem rash to conclude that commonsense psychology cannot be true because, as we saw in section 2.4, it is not rich enough to define our commonsense propositional-attitude notions.

It does seem plausible to me that we should require that any theory be consistent with the assumption that physics is in some sense basic and explains all physical events. This would be enough to motivate research into the chemical foundations of genetics, but it seems far from requiring the reducibility of all theoretical constructs to physical terms. *At the most*, it seems to me, it should be required of a theory that its theoretical terms be physically realized. But *realization* does not imply *reducibility*.

To see the point clearly, consider the following argument (which I *suspect* may be lurking behind Quine's eliminativism):

Commonsense psychology (or psychosemantics) is a theory, and the concepts *belief, desire, meaning*, and so forth are among its theoretical constructs. Now consider the theory schema that results from stating the theory and replacing its intentional terms ('believes', 'means', etc.) with schematic letters. To discover that that schema was not satisfied, was not made true, by nonintentional entities or constructs—say, by neural states or behavioral dispositions—would be to discover that the commonsense theory was false. But the acknowledged irreducibility of the intentional constructs shows that they enjoy no realization by nonintentional entities or constructs, and therefore that the theory is false.

In other words:

(a)   Our intentional idioms—'believes', 'means', 'intends', and so forth—
       are not true of anything if the folk theory that embeds them as
       theoretical constructs fails to be satisfied by our neural and behavioral
       states; that is, if our nervous system is not functionally organized in
       the way that it would have to be in order to *realize* the theoretical
       constructs of folk theory.
(b)   But the *irreducibility* of our intentional idioms proves their *unrealiz-
       ability*.

And then of course it follows that no one believes anything, no sounds
mean anything—although the deducer might hasten to add that that does
not preclude ascriptions of belief and meaning from having a certain *instru-
mental* value.

It should be noticed that this argument to eliminativism is quite different
from the argument that sustains the eliminativism of philosophers like Paul
Churchland (see Churchland 1981). For in their argument the irreducibility
of intentional notions is denied. For them, folk psychology is a functional
theory, and psychological idioms are theoretical terms functionally defined
by the theory. But if a belief state is a functional state, then a person is in
it only if he is in some neural state that has the functional role that defines
the belief; and it is the claim of Churchland and others that as the neu-
rosciences develop, it will become evident that no inner states have those
functional roles, and that therefore folk psychology is false, and that therefore there are no propositional attitudes. So the route to eliminativism that
we are presently considering is very different; it does not argue, with the
eliminativist-functionalist, that belief states are unrealized functional states,
but rather that belief states cannot be realized by physical states because
intentional idioms are irreducibly intentional and mentalistic.

But how does *irreducibility* imply *unrealizability*? In fact, it does not imply
it. For suppose that there really is a folk psychology, a commonsense
psychological theory that is common knowledge among those who have
mastered our intentional concepts. In 2.4 we saw that (i) such a theory
could not *define* its propositional-attitude vocabulary even if (ii) its relevant
Ramsey-sentence were true; that is, even if the theory's psychological
state-types were realized. Since *realizability* does not imply *reducibility*,
irreducibility can hardly imply unrealizability.[9]

So much for premise 2 of the Quine/Field argument. I doubt premise 1
because I doubt that there *is* a folk psychology.

I have a real concern not to get caught up in quibbles about the word
'theory'. I mean essentially two things when I deny that there is a folk
theory. The first is a logical point about definition and realization. Only a
complete, closed sentence can serve as the basis for the theoretical defini-

tion of some term in it. A mere sentence *frame* (such as [P] of 2.4), with the
'. . .' or *'ceteris paribus'* of ellipsis,[10] cannot define any belief property referred to in it, because it simply fails to determine any determinate functional property with which to identify that belief property. What property,
after all, is expressed by '*x* is red and . . .'? Consequently, in the absence of
completions of the commonsense belief/desire *"ceteris paribus"* generlizations
there is nothing to be physicalistically realized: whatever platitudes—or,
better, platitude schemas—might be called a folk theory, they are simply
precluded logically from having "realizations." But, as I argued in 2.4, it is
doubtful that these *ceteris paribus* generalization schemas have true completions. Certainly none are specifiable. The thought that such completions are
to be expected strikes me as being as absurd as the thought that the *ceteris
paribus* generalizations of (what might be called) commonsense physics—
such as, 'If a flying baseball strikes an ordinary house window, then, *ceteris
paribus*, the window will break'—enjoy true completions that elevate them
into seamless laws. The interesting question is why anyone would ever
have expected a completion. The answer, I suspect, is that *commonsense
belief/desire explanations of behavior would not be valid if there were no complete
belief/desire laws.* The culprit is the covering-law model of explanation. (See
Hempel and Oppenheim 1948; Hempel 1965a.) The second thing I mean
when I say that there is no folk theory is that the covering-law model of
commonsense psychological explanation is false.

Al flies to Key West, Bob asks why he went there, and Carla explains
that Al wanted to see his sister who lives there. Let us set up a straw man,
the "very naive covering-law theorist." This theorist is invited to explain
how the truth Carla asserted, the "explanans," that Al wanted to see his
sister who lives in Key West, explains the "explanandum," the fact that Al
went to Key West. The naive theorist responds thus: Carla knows a certain
general psychological law (or laws) and a conjunction of particular facts,
which includes the fact that Al wanted to see his sister; the two together
constitute the complete explanans and entail the fact-to-be-explained, that
Al went to Key West. The naive theorist adds that all of the explanans
except the fact that Al wanted to see his sister was common knowledge
between Bob and Carla; she merely provided the missing piece enabling
him to make the needed inference.

What makes the naive theorist's story naive is, of course, that it is simply
obvious that Carla would not, and need not, know any such explanandum-
entailing explanans. The question now is whether one should seek to refine
the naive story—say, by "probabilizing" the explanation and imposing
requirements of "maximal specificity" (see Hempel 1965a), or perhaps by
postulating subdoxastic representations of complete laws that are not available to consciousness—or reject it altogether. I think that it should be
rejected altogether.

Consider the following law schema:

[L]   If x desires p and believes that p is likely to obtain if x does A and . . . , then x does A.

To the extent that one is attracted to some version of the covering-law model of commonsense psychological explanation, of which Carla's explanation is an instance, to that extent one will feel that [L], or *some* sort of completion of it, must enter into the full story of Carla's explanation. But how? It is obvious that Carla, ordinary person that she is, knows no nonprobabilistic completion of [L]. And I think it is nearly as obvious that she knows no "probabilistic" completion of [L]; especially when I tell you that Carla is a ten-year-old child. Could it be that what Carla believes is not some completion of [L], but that there is some completion of [L]? Surely this stretches credulity to the breaking point. Similarly, to hypothesize at this point the existence of a subdoxastic state which represents the completion that no one knows would be to hypothesize without warrant. We should give up the idea that beliefs involving [L], or subdoxastic states representing completions of it, play any role in folk psychological explanations. No doubt something like [L] is the merest tip of some exceedingly complex information-processing story; but there is no reason to suppose that that is a story that we must be able to tell in order to explain behavior in terms of beliefs and desires. Nor is there any reason to think that the full story is to be told using concepts of belief and desire. They might be concepts that have evolved because of their great utility to our quotidian needs, but whose utility is there exhausted: rigorous scientific theorizing will need other concepts. Rather than conclude that there are no beliefs and desires because those concepts cannot be embedded in theorizing of a certain kind, one would do better to conclude that that is not their point. After all, what I have just said about the concept of belief also applies to virtually every other one of our concepts.

Carla believes, and said, that Al went to Key West *because* he wanted to see his sister. That true assertion functions in the circumstances as an explanation because of the interests and presuppositions Bob had in asking why Al went to Key West, but one may wonder about the analysis of such 'because'-statements. One may also wonder if such statements admit of "analysis." Why should they, when no successful analysis has ever been given of them or any other kind of philosophically interesting statement? This does not mean that there is nothing to be said: if Al went to Key West because he wanted to see his sister, then he would not have gone there if he had not had that desire, unless there had been other causes of his going. I doubt, however, that there is much more to be dragged out of our understanding of 'because'. I especially doubt that knowledge of "because-facts" requires knowledge of lawlike generalizations. The child drops a glass and quickly learns that the glass broke because she dropped it; she may learn this even if she lives in a house with mostly plastic glasses and knows that dropped glasses in her house tend not to break. Where is the lawlike generalization here that sustains the child's knowledge?

Many who are inclined toward a covering-law view of folk psychological explanation would be less inclined if they had an alternative model of explanation. But as Gilbert Harman suggested several years ago, "seeing a person as a nondeterministic automaton helps us to see why the covering-law theory breaks down in [the case of commonsense psychological explanation]" (1973, p. 52). Suppose that we are information processors who think in a neural code. If we further suppose that all formulae tokened as beliefs are fully determined by inputs and other formulae tokened as beliefs, that all formulae tokened as desires are fully determined by inputs and other formulae tokened as beliefs and desires, and that all intentional behavior is fully determined by what formulae are tokened as beliefs and desires (this is oversimplified, of course), then we are supposing that we are deterministic automata. This means that the program that describes our internal processing, the one that defines the abstract automaton we instantiate, "implies that any combination of internal states and input always has a unique result" (Harman 1973, p. 44). If this is what is supposed, then it may be mandatory to think that there are complete belief/desire generalizations. For if Al is a deterministic automaton and it is appropriate to say that he went to Key West because he wanted to see his sister, then it seems likely that a complete description of his beliefs and desires prior to going would instantiate the antecedent of a correct belief/desire generalization. But if Al is a nondeterministic automaton, this would not be implied. When we say that he went to Key West because he wanted to see his sister (and believed that she was there), we are describing mental states of Al's that led to his behavior under a description that shows that his behavior was in the relevant way made possible, though not required, by his antecedent mental states. What is needed to flesh out this suggestion is not a fuller articulation of a "folk theory" but a better understanding of the conceptual roles of our beliefs and desires, including our beliefs about the beliefs and desires and behavior of others.

This brings me to the other line of argument against Sentential Dualism that I shall discuss.

2. In section 6.3 I offered an argument to show that there are no *non-pleonastic* irreducible belief properties, and one may wonder why the same sort of argument could not be used to show that there are no *pleonastic* irreducible belief properties—to show, that is, that belief *predicates* cannot be irreducible and thus that Sentential Dualism is false. It would be easy to state the argument. I have acknowledged the propriety and truth of sen-

tences that ostensibly refer to or quantify over properties—Michele is funny; so (trivially and pleonastically) she has the property of being funny; Jules and Mother Teresa are humble; so (trivially and pleonastically) there is something that they have in common, viz., humility. (What I have denied is that this harmless way of talking, perhaps best made sense of by appeal to substitutional quantification, carries with it an ontological commitment to any extralinguistic entities.) So one could simply run through the earlier argument on pages 150–154 replacing all occurrences of 'nonpleonastic' with 'pleonastic' and end up with an argument that concludes that there are no irreducible pleonastic belief properties. Why would the "pleonastic" version of the argument be any less sound than the "nonpleonastic" version of it?

I believe that it would be less sound; that what is at issue is nothing less than an obnoxious metaphysical dualism of properties versus a benign dualism of conceptual roles for belief and other *predicates*. The irreducibility of belief *predicates* is an innocuous feature of their conceptual roles and implies no insupportable ontological proposition whatever.

To set the stage for seeing this, let us now focus on a slightly altered version of the Ava example (page 150). We may start by contrasting two glosses of the following sentence:

[α]   Ava would not have stepped back had she not had the property of believing that a car was coming.

The *nonpleonastic* gloss is as follows. To explain the truth of [α], we need recourse to the extralinguistic referents of the singular terms in [α]. First, of course, there is Ava, who is entirely independent, conceptually and onto-logically, from her name 'Ava'; to explain the truth of [α], we must first see the name 'Ava' as standing in a certain contingent relation to Ava, a relation by virtue of which the former refers to the latter. Then there is the property of believing that a car is coming. That property is as conceptually and ontologically independent from the singular term 'the property of believing that a car is coming' as Ava is from 'Ava', and all that was just said about Ava and 'Ava' carries over, *mutatis mutandis*, to the belief property and the singular term that happens to refer to it. What makes [α] true is that its wholly language-independent referents stand in the complex counterfactual relation that [α] predicates of them. When we add that the property of believing that a car is coming is not identical to any property specifiable in physical or functional terms, then, we know from the argu-ment lately considered, it is difficult coherently to explain how the irre-ducibly mental property of believing that a car is coming can have the causal power that [α], on the nonpleonastic gloss, ascribes to it.

The *pleonastic* gloss is as follows. We begin not with [α] but with

[a]   Ava stepped back because she believed that a car was coming.

The only *entity* whose existence we require in order to explain the truth of
[a] is Ava. The sentence is true because she satisfies the open sentence '*x*
stepped back because *x* believed that a car was coming'.[11] There simply is
no property that has (second-order) causal properties in need of explanation. But [a] trivially admits of a stylistic, though pleonastic, paraphrase:

> Ava stepped back because she had the property of believing that a car
> was coming.

Because Ava's stepping back was not overdetermined, we further get

[α]   Ava would not have stepped back had she not had the property of
believing that a car was coming.

Only now, on the pleonastic gloss, 'the property of believing that a car was
coming' is not a genuinely referential singular term, and to account for the
truth of [α] we do not need to suppose that there must be any mental
properties having any causal powers.

   None of this, however, answers the charge that an argument can be
launched against Sentential Dualism that parallels the one against the
existence of irreducibly mental belief properties. It merely remainds us that
the charge must be substantiated with respect to [a], and not [α]. But it
might be thought that it can be so substantiated. For the nominalist about
belief properties who champions Sentential Dualism must still show how [a]
can coherently be true together with

[b]   Ava stepped back because she was in such-and-such a neural state.

But are not the options available to the nominalistic Sentential Dualist for
showing this just variants of the disparaged options (A)–(D) (see pages
151–153) available to the dualistic Realist about belief properties?

   As regards (A'), the variant of (A), I should still maintain that there is no
causal overdetermination at the level of causal laws. No psychophysical
causal law contains the predicate 'believes that a car is coming'; the only
causal law applicable to Ava's stepping back contains the very complex
neurophysical predicate that the dummy 'such-and-such' of [b] is going
proxy for.

   Now the Realist's option (B) held that it was simply a brute, primitive,
inexplicable metaphysical fact that the property of being a belief that a car
is coming was causally essential to Ava's belief's being a cause of her
stepping back. The relevant variant (B') would be that it is simply a brute
fact that Ava stepped back because she believed that a car was coming, and
that is that. This is not to be explained in terms of any psychophysical or
psychological causal law, nor in terms of any logical, quasi-logical, or causal

relation to the fact that Ava is in a brain state of the type that enters into the physical explanation of her stepping back, the neural state-type alluded to in [b]. Thus described, (B') may seem as counterintuitive as the Realist's (B); but I shall have more to say about (B') later, embedded in a larger description.

Nor can I accept (C'), the variant of (C). Epiphenomenalism at the level of predicates is no less objectionable than epiphenomenalism at the level of properties. There is, I believe, no sense in which Ava's being in a neural state of the type alluded to in [b] causes her to believe that a car is coming.

What of (D'), the presently relevant variant of the "supervenience" option (D)? Here it may seem that there is a way of showing how the truth of [a] can be explained in terms of the truth of [b] that is more acceptable than the supervenience thesis offered to the Realist about belief properties in (D). The Realist who would take refuge in a supervenience relation between nonidentical properties must construe that relation as a primitive metaphysical relation, and that seemed to be exceptionable on two counts: it seemed highly obscurantist, and it left the supervening property dangling nomologically.

Properties eschewed, we have this mild enough supervenience thesis:

[S]   Given that Ava believes that a car is coming toward her, she also believes this in every possible world that is physically indistinguishable from the actual world.[12]

Now I do not think that this can be *proved*; I especially do not think that, given just a complete physical description of the world, one could ever demonstrate that Ava believed that a car was coming (for that would probably be possible only if one had a reduction of the sort I claim to be impossible). At the same time, [S] seems right to me, at least to the extent that I cannot describe a plausible counterexample to it.

But if [S] is right, then it would not be too difficult to conjure up an argument to show that

Ava would not have stepped back had she not believed that a car was coming toward her,

given that

Ava would not have stepped back had she not been in such-and-such a neural state.

And from here it surely can be just a short step to showing how

[a]   Ava stepped back because she believed that a car was coming

would be true given that

[b]   Ava stepped back because she was in such-and-such a neural state

was true. And would this not show how, consonantly with my Sentential Dualism, [a] can coherently be true together with [b], and thus answer the charge that an argument can be launched against Sentential Dualism that parallels the one against nonpleonastic irreducible belief properties?

I suppose I accept this as far as it goes; but I am unclear how far that is. The task is to 'show how [a] can coherently be true together with [b]', and I fear that, as "making coherent" is an enterprise not easily quantified, some may protest that an uncritical reliance on "supervenience" is as much in need of explanation as that which is being explained in terms of it. With this, I admit, I am in sympathy. If there is a puzzle to be resolved concerning the joint truth of [a], [b], and Sentential Dualism, I should prefer to resolve it without a facile reliance on the supervenience fact [S].

Meanwhile, I have not accepted any of (A')–(D'). Could it be that there really is an argument against Sentential Dualism that mimics the Onto-logical Physicalist's argument to show that there are no irreducibly mental belief properties?

There is first of all this to notice. The potentially mimicked argument concludes that if there are belief properties, they are not irreducible. But this was not then used to show that belief properties are reducible. Rather, it was joined to the even more compelling argument that those alleged properties are not reducible, and the conclusion was duly drawn that there are no belief properties. What is the opposite number of that argument, now that only belief *predicates* are at issue? It can hardly be that there are no belief predicates! But the irreducibility of belief predicates is, I must assume, a fact; the case for it is surely far stronger than any merely a priori argument to show, even in the absence of the ability to specify one, that there must be a reduction. It is further undeniable that if people have beliefs and desires, then they behave as they do *because* they believe and desire the things they do believe and desire. It would therefore seem that if there is any eliminativist argument in the offing that would even remotely parallel the one from 6.3, it must have as its conclusion that no one believes or desires anything at all. We would do better, surely, to find a way of making the joint truth of [a] and [b] palatable against the background of the irreducibility of belief predicates and all that that carries with it. To this I now turn. I begin with a couple of parables, the first of which is, I confess, merely a setup for the second. After this we shall be in a better position to say which of (A')–(D') should be accepted.

6.5 Two Parables

There are two versions of the genesis of dogs, the *credible* version and the *incredible* one. The credible version is as follows.

Some time near the beginning God created two kinds of creatures. The first were four-legged, hairy, barking creatures that we, had we been around then, would have called dogs. Actually, these animals *were* dogs; but I have described their creation as I did to mirror God's intention. For when God created dogs, He was merely implementing an intention whose content was specifiable without using 'dog'. God's intention was simply to create creatures of such-and-such genotypes, of such-and-such phenotypes, and of such-and-such behavioral dispositions. In a sense, God did not then have the concept *dog*; He only had, as it were, fairly complex ways of saying what it was that He was creating. Nevertheless, He created dogs all the same; and while He was at it, He created all the other beasts, too.

Next God created some protohumans. Here it was God's intention to create a certain kind of information-processing system that would survive fairly well in the world He had just finished creating. These information processors processed in a neural machine language, E, the sentences of which we may represent by referring to their synonymous English counterparts (in other words, we may think of the protohumans as thinking—that is, processing—in written English). Inside the head of each protohuman was a large box marked 'B', and a sentence of the *lingua mentis* E was tokened as a belief just in case a token of it occurred in B.[13] The "conceptual role" of an inner formula, we may still say, is that complex counterfactual property of the formula knowledge of which would inform one of the conditions under which the formula would occur in B. The conceptual role of a subsentential expression remains the contribution it makes to the conceptual roles of the infinitely many sentences in which it occurs.

When God first created E, the neural machine language of the proto-humans, He neglected to give it single words for the different varieties of animals. This made for much cumbersome and time-consuming processing, and God quickly saw that He could easily enhance the performance and survival of the protohumans by stocking E with words like 'dog', 'cat', 'wolf'. But God did not introduce 'dog' into E as a *defined* term, eliminable in principle by a merely hulky paraphrase; He gave 'dog' a conceptual role that precluded its reduction to other terms. Given a glimpse of a typical collie, the sentence 'There is a dog' would go straightway into a proto-human's B-box, *unless* the B-box already contained some defeater, such as 'That creature is the mutant offspring of two turtles'. But it was simply not possible to sum up the positive and negative conditions that would put a sentence like 'There is a dog' into the B-box in a way that would yield anything like a reductive analysis of the predicate 'is a dog'. This irreducibility of 'dog' is, then, merely a feature of the word's conceptual role, a feature, we may conjecture, that enhances its information-processing—and hence survival—value.

What if one of these protohumans, the sagest philosopher and scientist among them, were to realize that the foregoing was true of him? It is very difficult to see what he could find in this that would lead him to conclude that there were no dogs. Certainly there would be nothing in the conceptual role of 'dog' that would make his realization of his situation result in the removal of 'There are dogs' from his B-box. He would, especially, not be misled by the irreducibility of the sentence 'There are dogs' into thinking that, in any stronger, nonpleonastic sense of 'fact', the world contained the irreducible fact that there were dogs, a fact not reducible to, but somehow over and above, the fact that there were creatures of a certain appearance, ancestry, demeanor, and genotype.

The *incredible* version of the genesis of dogs is as follows.

When God first created those hairy barking animals that we would call 'dogs', He had not yet created dogs. This is because He had not yet brought into existence the primitive and irreducible *property* of being a dog and seen to it that the barkers instantiated it. On this version of the genesis of dogs, God at some point created Plato's Heaven, a world of objective, language-independent universals, and here was to be found the primitive and irreducible property doghood. Then in constructing four-legged, hairy, barking creatures, God created His first dog only when He saw to it that one of those creatures instantiated doghood. And now the irreducibility of 'dog' in E is explained not by appeal to advantageous features of its conceptual role but by the term's "expressing" the wholly external, primitive, and irreducible property doghood.

I did say that this version was not credible.

Now there are also credible and incredible versions of the genesis of propositional attitudes. The credible version is as follows.

God again created protohumans, information processors processing in E, their neural machine language; only now the story of their creation needs to be elaborated in these further respects. First, in creating the protohumans God's intention was merely to create physical information-processing *machines* of a certain type; the content of God's intention was wholly ascribable without use of any propositional-attitude idioms; in creating the protohumans it was as if He were creating IBM computers. Second, in creating the protohumans God did in fact create physical systems having certain primitive beliefs and desires—a desire to eat, a belief that something edible was in sight. (Think of it this way: had we been there, we would have described the protohumans as having those beliefs and desires.) But, third, the machine language E, as originally created, was a simple and impoverished language in that it contained no propositional-attitude expressions. The protohumans had beliefs and desires but lacked the concepts of belief and desire; hence they had no beliefs about their beliefs and desires. Had we been around, we would have regarded the protohumans much as we might now regard adult, languageless humans raised in the wild, ascribing to them at least some propositional attitudes.

It was at this point in the history of the world that God realized that He could considerably enhance the performance capabilities of His information processors, and thus enhance their capacity to survive and flourish, by enriching E in a certain way. God added to E propositional-attitude expressions; that is to say, He added such terms as 'believes', 'desires', and 'intends' to E and gave them conceptual roles that would, I hazard, lead us to say that the protohumans now had the concepts of belief, desire, and intention. The conceptual roles of these expressions were not equivalent to those of any other expressions in E, and it is difficult to see how the addition of these terms to E could have been advantageous had that not been the case. This in part explains why the sage philosophers among the protohumans came to realize that their propositional-attitude idioms were not reducible to any other idioms (now I am getting ahead of my story).

Anyway, the conceptual roles of 'believes' and 'desires' in E had the following features of interest to us. If a protohuman S had in his B-box sentences of the forms

x desires p

and

x believes that $(p$ if x does $A)$,

and if certain further conditions obtained, then S would also have in B the appropriate substitution-instances of

x will (probably) do A

and

If x does A, then x does A because x desires p and believes that $(p$ if x does $A)$.

The "certain further conditions" was a rather mixed bag, requiring that some further sentences be in B (such as, perhaps, 'x believes that x can do A'), that others *not* be in B (such as 'x believes that $(q$ if x does $A)$ and x desires not-q more than x desires $p)$'), and even that certain conditions obtain that could only be stated in neurophysical terms (for the protohumans were nondeterministic automata, and the movements of inner sentences in and out of S's B-box were not *completely* describable in terms of any flow-chart–specifiable algorithm). In any event, there was no way of recovering from the conceptual roles of 'believes' and 'desires' in E anything close to a lawlike generalization that would take one from what a protohuman believes and desires to what he will do. Still, the beliefs protohumans formed in this way about what other protohumans would do were fairly reliable: chances were, if Adam had in his *B*-box 'Eve will step back', then Eve would step back.

This was no surprise to God; He had arranged it that way. When God originally created protohumans, He created physical mechanisms whose every movement was explicable by full-fledged causal laws couched wholly in physical—that is, for the most part, neurophysical—terms. In this respect protohumans were just like our computers, machines whose every movement is explicable in terms of the physical features of their inner physical states. When God added 'believes' and other terms of its kind to *E*, He simply provided them with conceptual roles that would *mesh* with the underlying physical workings of protohumans in a way that would assure the reliability, in general, of behavioral expectations. The conceptual role of 'believes' was such that there was a *causal link* between, say, Eve's being in a brain state of a type that would cause her to step back and Adam's having in his *B*-box 'Eve believes that a snake is coming toward her' in a way that would lead him to expect that Eve would step back. God was exploiting this causal link to the survival advantage of Adam and his fellow protohumans when He also made the conceptual role of 'believes' such that Adam, upon seeing Eve step back, also had in his *B*-box 'Eve stepped back because she believed that a snake was coming toward her' and 'Eve would not have stepped back had she not believed that a snake was coming toward her'.

Eventually protohuman philosophers and scientists came to realize that the credible version of Genesis described them, and this realization did nothing to preclude the further entry into their *B*-boxes of sentences of the form '*x* believes *p*'. They simply had, we might say, no belief better entrenched than their belief that they had beliefs that, together with their believing the credible version of Genesis, could lead them to conclude that no one believed anything. But *should* they have reached that eliminativist conclusion? I can see no reason why; to me the credible version of the genesis of propositional attitudes and propositional-attitude concepts *removes* what threatens to be an ontological mystery—how [a] and [b] of the last section can be true together—and puts the notion of "supervenience," and its relation to propositional-attitude concepts, in a new, more helpful light. Each step in the credible version of the genesis is evidently in principle acceptable. How, then, could they add up to something unacceptable?

Things are altogether otherwise with the incredible version of the genesis of propositional attitudes and propositional-attitude concepts.

Here God again began by creating information-processing systems whose every movement was wholly explicable in wholly physical terms; again the content of God's intention in creating these machines was specifiable without use of any propositional-attitude idioms (God intended to build a machine that would move in such-and-such ways when it was in

such-and-such neural states, and did not intend, initially, to create something that would behave in such-and-such ways when it had such-and-such
beliefs and desires). This time, however, the protohumans, as first created,
did not have propositional attitudes: they were purely physical devices
with no mental states whatever.

What God next did was create (objective, language-independent)
propositional-attitude *properties*. These properties were not identical to any
physical or functional properties; a universe was forged that was ontologically dualistic at the level of properties. Then God gave the propositional-
attitude properties certain (second-order) *causal* properties. As a result of
this construction, a property such as the property of being a belief that a
snake is coming toward one was such that the possession of that property
by a neural state-token could be causally essential to that state's being a
cause of a protohuman's stepping back. In giving belief properties such
causal powers (powers, by the way, not accounted for by any causal laws)
God was, from an engineering point of view, being irresponsible: belief
properties and their causal powers were utterly superfluous, as every
movement of every protohuman had already been causally accounted for
in nonmental terms. Next, of course, God saw to it that certain neural states
of protohumans had the newly created propositional-attitude properties,
and so it was that protohumans came to have beliefs and desires.

Thus, on the incredible story, Eve stepped back because she believed
that a snake was coming toward her. There was, then, some neural state-
token n of hers that was her belief and a cause of her stepping back. A
complete explanation of that movement was available in wholly physical
terms; in particular, n had neurophysical features that were causally necessary and sufficient for its being a cause of the stepping back. At the same
time, n had the irreducibly mental property of being a belief that a snake
was coming, and it was simply a brute fact, explicable neither by appeal to
any causal law nor by reference to intelligible relations to physical properties, that n would not have caused Eve to step back had n not had the
property of being a belief that a snake was coming. Things were that way
just because God, for reasons or no reasons of His own, had made things
that way.

Finally, as in the credible version, God supplemented E, the protohumans'
machine language, with 'believes', 'desires', and the rest; only now God's
motive in enriching E was to provide E with terms that would have as their
semantic values the newly created propositional-attitude properties, thus
enabling the system of mental representation E to represent abstract entities that it had hitherto been unable to represent.

It is no wonder that the sage philosophers among the protohumans
choked on this version of their genesis.

Let me now try to say what features of the parable are applicable to us and how they help to make coherent the joint truth of [a] ('Ava stepped back because she believed that a car was coming'), [b] ('Ava stepped back because she was in such-and-such neural state'), and Sentential Dualism.

First, there is the conceptual story. It is constitutive of our propositional-attitude concepts that when we believe that a person has certain beliefs and desires, and certain other (not readily articulable) conditions obtain, then we form expectations about what that person will do and about the reasons for which he or she will do it. That is, if one goes from thinking that x has certain beliefs and desires to thinking that x will do A, then when x does A, one also moves to the belief that x did A *because* x had those beliefs and desires. All this is, so to say, just part of what it is to have our propositional-attitude concepts. (Here it is harmless, perhaps helpful, to pretend that we think in English and that in talking about our concepts of belief, etc., I am talking about the conceptual roles of 'believes', etc., in inner English.) It is a fact that we have these concepts; a full explanation of *why* we have them, one may assume, would at some point advert to the survival value that they have for us.

Second, there is the mesh of the conceptual story with our underlying physical reality. When, in paradigm cases, one forms the belief that x had such-and-such beliefs and desires and that because x had them, x did an act of type A, then x will have been in neural states and physical circumstances that fully explain the bodily movements constitutive of x's doing A. This is not anything that one need be aware of; it is not, to be sure, revealed in our propositional-attitude concepts (in the conceptual roles of 'believes', etc.). It is simply a fact about the relation between our cognitive apparatus and the physical world we inhabit that there is the coincidence being remarked on. This coincidence conduces to our survival and well-being, and this fact, presumably, must enter into any complete explanation of it.

Third, and finally, there are [a] and [b]. Now both are true. I know that [b] is true because I know that we are not hollow inside, and know enough about the inner neural story to find it impossible to doubt [b]. And I know [a]. That is, I am prepared to, and do, assert it, and there is nothing to defeat the assertion. If God were looking into my head, He would, of course, explain my asserting [a] as my acting ineluctably, given the contents of my B-box and the conceptual roles that 'believes' and the rest have for me. But that, needless to say, is not how *I* explain my assertion. I explain it by indulging further in the conceptual roles of 'believes', etc., and the present contents of my B-box: I give, that is, my evidence for [a]. Does the "supervenience" hypothesis (D') "explain" [a] in terms of [b]? If one thinks that it does, that is fine with me; for (D'), we have seen, would be acceptable, if acceptable at all, in ways that (D) (the supervenience hypothesis available to the Realist about mental properties) would not be. But I should not mind if one were to reject (D') or fail to find it explanatory. Then I should prefer (B') of the choices earlier offered: it is simply, so to say, a happy coincidence that [a] and [b] are true together. But now we know why it is a *happy* coincidence, and that is more than the Realist about belief properties can say about (B).

6.6 Kripkenstein Meets the Remnants of Meaning

Radical that I am, I hold that people have beliefs and desires, and that they mean things by the noises they utter. Of course I mean snow by 'snow', and so do you. Of course I believe that Harvard University is not in Miami Beach, and so do you. Each of us wants not to be deep-fried in oil.

I also hold that such sentences as those of the last paragraph are irreducible: the truths they state are not statable by sentences devoid of psychological or intentional idioms. In this my Sentential Dualism consists. My Ontological Physicalism consists in my denial that there is anything extralinguistic, of any ontological category, that is irreducibly mental or intentional. I deny, therefore, the metaphysical theory that asserts a Realism of belief properties: there is no abstract, language-independent entity, the property of believing that Harvard University is not in Miami Beach, that stands to the predicate 'believes that Harvard University is not in Miami Beach' as the person Greta Garbo stands to the name 'Greta Garbo'. Since there are no language-independent belief properties, there are of course no language-independent belief facts, either: there is no objective, language-independent entity that is the fact of Quine's believing that Harvard is not in Miami Beach.

None of this is to deny that there are psychological or semantic facts—in the trivial, pleonastic sense of 'fact'. Of course it is a fact that you mean snow by 'snow'; that is to say, you mean snow by 'snow'. And of course it is a fact that Quine believes that Harvard is not in Miami Beach; that is to say, he believes that Harvard is not in Miami Beach.

But what, an inattentive philosopher might still ask, makes it the case that Quine believes that Harvard is not in Miami Beach? Well, what is really being asked here?

If the question concerns the causal explanation of Quine's having this belief, or the reasons that he has for having it, then no doubt there is some plausible story to be told, though I do not see that it is the philosopher's job to tell it.

If the question is an invitation to give a necessary and sufficient condition for believing that Harvard is not in Miami Beach in nonpsychological and nonintentional terms, then it is an invitation to do the impossible.

If the question is an invitation *either* to give a reductive analysis *or else* to aver that Quine's believing that Harvard is not in Miami Beach is a primitive and irreducible mentalistic fact, then again we are being asked a question with a false presupposition. For there is no property expressed by the meaningful predicate 'believes that Harvard is not in Miami Beach', and thus there is no fact corresponding to the true sentence 'Quine believes that Harvard is not in Miami Beach'. To be sure, it is a fact—pleonastically speaking, and thus without "ontological commitment"—that Quine believes what he does about Harvard's location and that the sentence ascribing that belief enjoys no paraphrase untainted by mentalistic idioms; but only a confused Brentano would find comfort in this.

This line has application to a paradox that Saul Kripke has located in the work of Wittgenstein (Kripke 1982), and I hope that the following brief consideration of that paradox will illuminate both it and the line.

"Let me see," Clem murmurs to himself, "68 plus 57, that's ... um, um, ... 125."

"Are you sure you don't mean 5?" his kibitzer friend Philo asks.

"Say what?" a startled Clem responds, confident he could not have been *that* far off.

Philo patiently explains. "I grant that if you are now using 'plus' to mean the addition function, then you gave the right answer: 125 is indeed the value of that function for the arguments 68 and 57. But it was my assumption that you intended to be using 'plus' as you did in the past, including yesterday, when you last used that term, and it seems to me that perhaps in the past, right up to today, you meant quaddition by 'plus'. As is well known, quaddition is just like addition when each of the quadded numbers is less than 57, but when one of them is equal to or greater than 57, well, then their quum is 5. Didn't you used to mean *quus* by 'plus'?"

"That's the dumbest damn thing I ever heard," Clem explodes. "I've *always* meant addition by 'plus'."

"No doubt you're right," Philo agrees, barely able to contain himself. "But then there must have been some *fact* about you in the past, indeed yesterday, some fact about or pertaining to your use of 'plus', that you can cite and that will refute the ridiculous hypothesis that, to conform with your prior intentions, you should've said just now that 68 plus 57 is 5. Pray tell, *what is that fact?*"

At this point Philo considers each of the candidate facts that either he or Clem can think of, and shows that none of those facts about Clem can establish that he meant addition rather than quaddition by 'plus'. He concludes that there can be no fact of the matter as to what Clem meant, and *a fortiori* none as to what he now means.

Usually when we have a philosophical paradox, that paradox can be stated as a set of mutually inconsistent propositions each of which looks, or can be made to look, pretty plausible when viewed on its own. Then one solves the paradox by revealing which of the propositions must be rejected. Can the Kripkensteinian paradox be formulated in such a format? Actually, I think that Kripke's exposition is suggestive of more than one paradox statable in the canonical format, and I turn now to one of them. I do not claim that this is exactly how either Wittgenstein or Kripke would choose to paraphrase the paradox; I only claim that the following formulation is Kripke's rendering of Wittgenstein's paradox as it struck me, as it presented a paradox for me.

[P$_1$]

[1] Yesterday Clem meant addition rather than quaddition by 'plus'.
[2] But there is nothing in Clem's past history that could establish that he meant the one rather than the other; there simply is no fact about Clem that constituted his state of meaning addition rather than quaddition.
[3] But [1] and [2] are incompatible: if nothing in his past history can establish that he meant one rather than the other, then there is no fact of his having meant addition rather than quaddition, and thus it is not the case that he did mean addition rather than quaddition by 'plus'.

The plausibility of [1] and [3] is intuitive and manifest; that of [2] is established by argument. First it is argued that there is no fact that would imply "a reduction of the notions of meaning and intention to something else" (Kripke 1982, p. 41); then it is argued that there is no irreducible, *sui generis* fact. Meaning addition by 'plus' is not "an irreducible experience, with its own special *quale*, known directly to each of us by introspection"; nor is it "simply a primitive state, not to be assimilated to sensations ... or any 'qualitative' states ... but a state of a unique kind of its own," for this move "seems desperate: it leaves the nature of this postulated primitive state—the primitive state of 'meaning addition by "plus"'—completely mysterious. It is not supposed to be an introspectible state, yet we supposedly are aware of it with some fair degree of certainty whenever it occurs" (p. 51).

Presently I shall ask which of these three incompatible propositions must go, but first I want to point out that there was no need to state the paradox in the past tense; the following does every bit as well as [P$_1$]:

[P$_2$]

[1] Clem means addition rather than quaddition by 'plus'.
[2] But there is nothing in Clem's biography that establishes that he means the one rather than the other; there simply is no fact about Clem that constitutes his state of meaning addition rather than quaddition.

[3]   But [1] and [2] are incompatible: if nothing about Clem can establish
       that he means one rather than the other, then there is no fact of his
       meaning addition rather than quaddition, and thus it is not the case
       that he does mean addition rather than quaddition by 'plus'.

And now I submit that to whatever degree $[P_2]$ is a paradox, so is this:

$[P_3]$

[1]   Clem believes that there are lions in Africa.
[2]   But there is nothing in Clem's biography that establishes that he
       believes that there are lions in Africa; there simply is no fact about
       Clem that constitutes his state of believing that there are lions in
       Africa.
[3]   But [1] and [2] are incompatible: if nothing about Clem can establish
       that he believes that there are lions in Africa, then there is no fact of
       his believing that, and thus it is not the case that he does believe it.

For here, too, [1] and [3] are manifestly plausible, and arguments can be
launched for [2] that parallel those of the other two [2]'s to establish that
there is neither a "reducible" nor an "irreducible" fact of Clem's believing
that there are lions in Africa. So I further submit that we should certainly
begin on the assumption that a single solution solves each of these para-
doxes. What, then, is that solution?

I know that many will want a "straight solution"; will want, especially,
to deny each [2] by insisting that there really is some functionalist, quasi-
functionalist, or physicalist reduction of the psychological facts in question.
But, as I have repeatedly emphasized, I have my own reasons, as well as
Kripkenstein's, for thinking that on this score Kripkenstein is dead right: if
there is a fact of the matter here, it is not one statable in a nonmentalistic
idiom. At the same time, I also agree that there is no irreducibly mental fact
of Clem's meaning addition by 'plus' or of his believing that there are lions
in Africa—at least not if we take 'fact' with any degree of ontological
seriousness.

The solution that I favor is simply this: each [2] and each [3] is ambiguous, for 'fact' and equivalent idioms can be read *pleonastically* or *non-
pleonastically*, in an ontologically loaded sense that implies the existence of
genuinely language-independent propositional-attitude properties. On the
pleonastic reading, [3] is true but [2] is false: Clem means addition by 'plus'
and believes that there are lions in Africa, so it is a fact that he means and
believes what he does. On the nonpleonastic, no doubt "intended," reading,
[2] is true but [3] is false. There is indeed no objective, language-independent,
nonpleonastic fact that "establishes," "makes it the case," or "constitutes"
either Clem's meaning addition or his believing there are lions in Africa, for
there is no property that is ontologically and conceptually distinct from,

and expressed by, either the predicate 'means addition by "plus"' or the predicate 'believes that there are lions in Africa'. So [2], on the non-pleonastic reading, is true. But on that reading it is *not* incompatible with [1]: from the inexistence of "Fregean" facts that make it the case that Clem means addition or believes that there are lions in Africa, it just does not follow that he does not mean addition or have his belief about the location of lions. So [3], on the nonpleonastic reading, is false.

Here, to repeat, are the pertinent facts about Clem as regards the solution of the paradox:

[a] Clem means addition by 'plus' and believes that there are lions in Africa. Thus, trivially and pleonastically, it is a fact that he means addition by 'plus' and believes that there are lions in Africa.

[b] The foregoing sentences about what Clem means and believes are not reducible to any sentences devoid of semantic, intentional, or mental terms. Thus, the pleonastic fact that Clem means and believes what he does is not a fact statable in nonmentalistic, nonsemantic, and non-intentional idioms.

[c] There is no nonpleonastic property of meaning addition or of believing that there are lions in Africa; that is, there is no property expressed by the predicate 'means addition' or by the predicate 'believes that there are lions in Africa' that is ontologically and conceptually distinct from those predicates in the way that Greta Garbo is distinct from the name 'Greta Garbo'. Thus, there is no nonpleonastic fact expressed by either of the sentences in question. (And thus the way is open for one to be an Ontological Physicalist.)

Now clearly, if [a]–[c] are true, there can be no question of showing what makes it the case that Clem means addition by 'plus' or believes that there are lions in Africa; the demand to be told what makes those things the case, or constitutes their being the case, is a demand for the impossible. If [a]–[c] are true, then *nothing* establishes, constitutes, or makes it the case that Clem means addition by 'plus' and believes that there are lions in Africa; and yet he means the one and believes the other all the same. That much is surely clear. Once we have given the *evidence* for [a] (which of course we have had at our disposal all along) and the arguments for [b] and [c], there remains nothing to do by way of resolving the paradox except to *defeat* reasons for thinking that [a]–[c] are *not* mutually consistent; and this I have already tried to do.

Possibly one is still not fully satisfied. "Look," one might protest, "suppose that Clem dropped dead yesterday at the age of fifty-four, after fifty years of using the word 'plus', and that we're fortunate enough to have the sound movie of his entire life, together with a complete physical and functional description of him at every moment of his life, and together with a running report of his stream of consciousness. In considering all of this, we formulate two hypotheses, both of which are empirically adequate: (1) Clem meant addition by 'plus' and (2) Clem meant quaddition by 'plus'. Now we're to suppose, even though none of the aforementioned proffered facts can be appealed to as establishing either that he meant addition or that he meant quaddition, that nevertheless he really did mean addition and that we know it. Isn't *that* a puzzle, and has that puzzle been resolved?"

Well, I suppose that is a puzzle, and here is another one just like it. There are two hypotheses that for me are empirically adequate: (i) Most of my sense experiences are perceptions, caused by physical objects that exist independently of me; (ii) there are no physical objects, and all my sense experiences are directly caused in me by God, that Evil Demon. Nevertheless I suppose that there really are physical objects existing independently of me and that I know it.

Chapter 7
Compositional Semantics and Language Understanding

7.1 Introduction

It is a platitude that the meaning of a sentence is determined by the meanings of its component words and the mode of composition of those words in the sentence. Speakers of a natural language have the ability to understand utterances of novel sentences, sentences they are encountering for the first time; and it may seem obvious that one understands the utterance of a novel sentence because one knows the meanings of the words contained in it and, in some sense, knows a rule for determining the meaning of the sentence on the basis of its syntax and the meanings of its words. Since the beginning of analytical philosophy of language—that is, since Frege—it has been more or less taken for granted that natural languages have compositional meaning theories, theories that construct the meanings of complex expressions out of the meanings of their component parts.

Likewise for that other widely held hypothesis, that every correct compositional meaning theory is also a compositional truth-theoretic semantics, where

> a *compositional (truth-theoretic) semantics* for a language L is a finitely statable theory that ascribes properties to, and defines recursive conditions on, the finitely many vocabulary items in L in such a way that for each of the infinitely many sentences of L that can (in principle) be used to make truth-evaluable utterances, there is some condition (or set of conditions) such that the theory entails that an utterance of that sentence is true iff that condition (or a certain member of the set) obtains.

What good reason is there for holding that each natural language has a correct compositional semantics?[1] Perhaps other answers are possible, and in the next chapter this is taken up, but the most often proclaimed answer is given in the fourth of the widely held hypotheses of chapter 1:

[U] It would not be possible to account for a human's ability to understand utterances of indefinitely many novel sentences of a language without the assumption that that language had a compositional semantics.

"The central problem to be explained by a theory of meaning," one writer has recently declared, "is what is often called the *productivity* of language: the fact that competent native speakers have the ability to produce and understand sentences never before encountered, and to do this appropriately" (Hornstein 1984, p. 123). The most commonly expressed reason for supposing natural languages to have compositional semantics is that that hypothesis is needed to solve this "central problem."

I have reason to doubt the widely held hypothesis that every natural language has a correct compositional semantics, and, *ipso facto*, reason to doubt that other widely held hypothesis, [U], which for many provides its motivation. For I have argued that still another widely held hypothesis, the relational theory of propositional attitudes, is false, and the falsity of that theory would seem to be inconsistent with the proposition that natural languages have compositional semantics. This is so because the only feasible way of accommodating propositional-attitude verbs within a compositional semantics is as *relational* predicates that relate, in the case of 'believes', a believer to what he believes.

Consider the sentence

[a]   Odile believes that existence precedes essence.

If English enjoys a compositional semantics (and if we momentarily ignore Davidson's suggestion that [a] is not a genuine semantical unit), then it must be possible to effect a division of [a] into component parts each of which is assigned some semantic value, and to see the truth condition of [a] as determined, jointly, by the syntactic arrangement of those parts in [a] and by the fact that they have those semantic values. Yet this is just a necessary, and rather minimal, condition. A compositional semantics, by definition, is finitely axiomatizable, and this requires that the smallest parts discerned in [a] and assigned semantic values belong to a *finite* list of semantic primitives that suffices for the language as a whole. This further requirement would be violated if, for example, the ultimate semantic division of [a] were to recognize only 'Odile', whose semantic value was taken to be a certain person, and 'believes that existence precedes essence', whose semantic value was taken to be the set of things that believe that existence precedes essence.

It is clear that 'believes' (or 'believes that', a refinement I shall ignore) must be recognized as a semantical unit in [a], and as among the finitely many semantical primitives of English, if English has a compositional semantics. But what sort of semantic value must 'believes' be recognized as having, if English has a compositional semantics? Frege's suggestion, in effect, was that 'believes' was a relational predicate, its semantic value being, then, the belief relation, a relation that holds between a believer and that entity which is what he believes (see Frege 1891, 1892); in the case of [a], that entity which is the semantic value of the semantically complex singular term 'that existence precedes essence'. For Frege, [a] has just the same logical form as 'Odile admires the most famous French existentialist'.

Frege's hypothesis, which has achieved almost universal acceptance among philosophers of language, is to some degree confirmed by familiar facts already remarked on: quantifier expressions and paradigm singular terms can occur as grammatical complements of 'believes', to form predicate expressions such as 'believes something silly', 'believes everything that Jean-Paul says', and 'believes the most profound philosophical doctrine of our day'; and arguments such as the following are evidently valid:

> Odile and Jean-Paul believe that existence precedes essence.
> So, there is something that they both believe.

> Odile believes that existence precedes essence.
> That existence precedes essence is the most profound philosophical doctrine of our day.
> Therefore, Odile believes the most profound philosophical doctrine of our day.

But if one joins Frege in subscribing to the relational account of propositional-attitude verbs, then one owes some account of what 'that'-clauses refer to (or of what the alleged demonstrative 'that' refers to, on Davidson's version of the logical form of belief ascriptions). While philosophers have been quick to join Frege in thinking that propositional attitudes are relations to things believed, desired, feared, and so on, only some have shared his Platonistic view of what those things are. Here, on the question of what the relata of the supposed propositional-attitude relations might be, there has been something less than unanimity. I have argued that each of the possible answers to this question is false, and have duly concluded that the relational theory of propositional attitudes cannot be right. I must therefore deny that the relational construal of 'believes' is required by its accommodation within a compositional semantics, or else deny that natural languages have compositional semantics.

I choose the latter course for two reasons. First, I do think that the relational account of propositional-attitude verbs is the most plausible way of trying to make them square with the assumption that natural languages have compositional semantics. The only other proposed accommodation of which I am aware is that of Hintikka and his followers, which construes expressions such as 'Odile believes that' as logical operators, on analogy with the treatment of modal operators in modal logic (Hintikka 1962, 1969).

But this theory is notoriously problematic, and would not be immune, in any event, to objections of the sort leveled in chapter 3 against the propositional theory of propositional attitudes.[2]

Second, I think that the semantic compositionality thesis is problematic even apart from the falsity of the relational theory of propositional attitudes. Here there are three points to be made.

1. It is not plausible that natural languages have compositional truth-theoretic semantics unless that is seen as following from the stronger claim that natural languages have compositional *meaning theories* that are truth-theoretic. A *mere* truth theory for a language, however correct, would not be a meaning theory; for knowledge of it would not suffice for understanding utterances. (See the discussion and references in section 5.2.) Thus, if I am right, one who advocates that natural languages have compositional semantics must be prepared to address the question of the form that a correct meaning theory for a particular language should take. Most philosophers believe that languages have meaning theories, but no three of them can be made to agree on the nature of those theories (though at least two of them will agree that meaning theories, whatever else they may be, are at least compositional truth-theoretic semantics). I think that the explanation for this disharmony is that, as natural languages do not have "meaning theories," there is no correct account of the form that a correct meaning theory for a particular language must take. I have already argued (in chapter 5) that a natural language could not have a correct extensionalist meaning theory, and it is difficult to see how a language could have a correct intensionalist meaning theory unless the propositionalist theory of propositional attitudes were correct. So my skepticism is practically a consequence of my negative view on the prospects of there being any plausible positive theory of mental content. Anyway, the issue is further pursued in the next chapter.

2. Propositional-attitude verbs are not the only terms that have proved difficult to accommodate in a compositional semantics. Well-known, although perhaps not insoluble, problems attach to other intentional expressions, such as 'is a picture of'; to 'true' and other semantic terms; to adjectives like 'large' and 'toy' (as in 'toy soldier'); to adverbs and some prepositional phrases; to evaluative terms like 'ought' and 'good'; to pronouns and demonstratives; to ordinary-language quantifier expressions ('all', 'every', 'any', 'most'); and to certain constructions containing "connectives," such as 'Russell and Whitehead wrote *Principia Mathematica*'. And the most popular ways of trying to accommodate modal expressions and counterfactual conditionals seem to incur extravagant ontological debts. Also, in the next chapter we shall see that sentences that ostensibly involve reference to properties, such as 'Humility is a virtue', create a serious problem for the nominalistically inclined philosopher who requires such

sentences to have a logical form determined by a correct compositional semantics. Perhaps it would prove rewarding to give up the idea that there was something to do—giving the "semantics" of expressions—for which a compositional semantics was required.

3. Most important, I do not think that the hypothesis that natural languages have compositional semantics is well motivated. I think that there is no decent motivation apart from [U], the commonly accepted rationale, and I think that [U] is false; I do not think that we must suppose that natural languages have compositional semantics in order to account for our mastery of them. I have already given my *objection* to the compositionality thesis: natural languages have compositional semantics only if the relational theory of propositional attitudes is true, but, I have argued, that theory is false. But if no natural language has a compositional semantics, then [U], the commonly accepted rationale for the compositionality theory, must also be false. My main purpose in this chapter is to make an independent case for the falsity of [U], to give some reason for supposing that our ability to comprehend utterances in a public language does not presuppose a compositional semantics for that language.

In the next section I elaborate just a little more the issues involved. In 7.3, to clear the air for a better reason, I dismiss two bad reasons for thinking that the theory of language understanding will not need recourse to a compositional semantics. The correct reason is given in 7.4 and 7.5; the last section of this chapter and all of the next take up issues spawned by the line taken.

7.2 Meaning, Truth, and Understanding

A compositional truth-theoretic semantics for a language L is a finitely axiomatized theory whose theorems ascribe to each potentially statement-making sentence of L the conditions under which an utterance of the sentence would be true. It is widely held that natural languages have correct compositional semantics, but I doubt that this is so, because I doubt that appropriate semantic values (that is, appropriate base axioms) can be assigned to propositional-attitude verbs.

My target now, however, is [U], the hypothesis that is supposed to support the hypothesis that natural languages have correct compositional semantics. What reason is there for thinking that [U] is true? We obviously have the ability to understand utterances of novel sentences, but why should we suppose that that fact requires the languages we speak to have compositional semantics?

Well, one who has mastery of a natural language L has somehow acquired, after a relatively brief period of exposure to utterances of a finite number of sentences in L, the ability to understand indefinitely many sentences of L that he has never before encountered. Now, in encountering a novel but understood sentence, one is being confronted not with novel words but with familiar words put together, via familiar constructions, in a novel way. This in itself has been taken strongly to suggest that there can be no explaining one's mastery of a natural language independently of the specification of compositional mechanisms that generate the meanings of complex expressions out of the meanings of simpler ones.

From the fact that a meaning theory for a language must state compositional mechanisms that reveal the ways in which the meanings of sentences depend upon the meanings of the words composing them, it does not yet follow that the meaning theory must be a truth-condition-entailing componential semantics. That further hypothesis is, however, motivated by the further observation that (a) to understand an utterance is to know what propositional speech acts were performed in it, and (b) one cannot know what speech acts in the assertive mode were performed without knowing their truth conditions: if in uttering 'Someone was burned' a speaker said that someone was swindled, then to understand that utterance one must know that the speaker said that—which requires knowing that what was said, and hence the utterance as well, was true just in case someone was swindled.

In other words, to understand a public language is to have the ability to understand utterances in it; and to understand an utterance in the assertive mode is to know that it is true provided that such-and-such is the case, where what the speaker said in the utterance was precisely that such-and-such was the case. All this, it has evidently been felt, does motivate the assumption that natural languages have compositional semantics.

That quick and easy justification was pretty glib; not really much of a justification of anything. Can one do better?

In section 1.3 I remarked that a theory of a person's language understanding would be a theory of his language *processing*: it would, at the least, be a theory that explains how one can go from an auditory perception of an utterance to knowledge of what was said, with what truth condition, in that utterance. Evidently [U] requires that at some point in the relevant psycholinguistic account of a person's language processing, reference be made to a compositional semantics for the language in question. But what form, exactly, must be taken by a correct compositional semantics that is also a correct meaning theory? And how, exactly, must it be adverted to in the theory of language processing? Satisfactory answers to these questions clearly are not available; the second question, especially, is seldom addressed.[3] Fortunately the argument against [U] need not await detailed attempts to answer these questions, although a structure will be provided that may constrain a little the form that such answers would have to take.

7.3 What the Argument Is Not

What comes later will be better understood if I point out now that in subscribing to the CS theory (as I shall call the theory that every natural language has a correct compositional semantics) the astute CS theorist is *quite correctly* undeterred by (a) a certain potentially misleading way of using the phrase 'theory of language understanding' and (b) a certain fallacious argument to show that understanding a natural language does not presuppose a compositional semantics for that language.

Both (a) and (b) have as their point of departure the topical thesis— with which a CS theorist may be altogether sympathetic—that we think in a "language of thought," perhaps even, suitably interpreted, the same language we speak. (How could the CS theorist be antipathetic? The empirical hypothesis that we are information processors and thus think—i.e., process—in a neural machine language is consistent with any philosophical position that is itself consistent with the thesis that our thoughts have physical realizations.)

Among those who hope to find philosophical relevance to the problem of intentionality in the hypothesis that we think in a language of thought, there is current the view, critically assessed in chapter 4, that a correct theory of content, or meaning, can be given for the inner system of mental representation, and that this theory will have two components: (1) a *conceptual-role* component and (2) a truth-theoretic, *referential semantic* component—that is, a compositional semantics. I have already argued against this two-factor theory of mental content, but let us for the moment waive the objections raised. What is presently of interest about the dichotomous theory is that subscribers to it claim that only the conceptual-role component enters into the theory of understanding Mentalese. They do not try to justify the claim that Mentalese requires a compositional semantics on the grounds that such a semantics is presupposed by a theory of understanding for the language of thought. They do not, in fact, offer any justification for thinking that Mentalese must have a compositional semantics, but simply assume that that will be required to account for the truth-theoretic properties of our thoughts. I shall return to this last point a little later, and shall assume for the moment that the two-factor theory is correct; for the point to be made here is that it affords no objection to [U]. Having made the charitable assumption, let us concentrate on the conceptual-role component of Mentalese meaning, which is what is of immediate relevance.

The conceptual-role component is supposed to assign conceptual roles to expressions of the inner system. The conceptual role of a subsentential expression is the contribution it makes to the conceptual roles of the infinitely many sentences in which it occurs. The conceptual role of an inner sentence, we already know, is a counterfactual property of that sentence, which property is specifiable independently of any semantic properties the sentence might have, and in a way that details the causal or transitional role of that sentence in the formation of perceptual beliefs and in theoretical and practical reasoning. Not only is the conceptual role of a formula specifiable without reference to the formula's truth condition, it also fails to determine it: the neural sentence whose tokening realizes my belief that water [= H_2O] is potable may be exactly the same neural sentence, with exactly the same conceptual role, as the one that realizes my Twin Earth *Doppelgänger's* belief that twater [= XYZ] is potable. (See the discussion and references in section 4.6.)

Now it is natural to equate a conceptual-role theory for the language of thought with a theory of language-of-thought understanding. For to understand a language is to know how to use it, but to "use" a system of mental representation is just for its formulae to have conceptual roles. Thus, two computers from the same assembly line may use, and so understand, the same inner code, even though, as one has been placed on Earth and the other on Twin Earth, sentences that are understood the same way have different truth conditions. Since the conceptual-role theory for Mentalese is independent of any referential semantical theory of Mentalese, the theory of understanding for Mentalese, construed as a conceptual-role theory, does not presuppose a compositional semantics for Mentalese.

To understand a *public* language, on the other hand, is to have the ability to understand utterances in it. And to understand an utterance is to know what propositional speech acts, with what truth conditions, were performed in it. So it ought to be obvious that, from the fact that (1) the theory of understanding for the inner system of mental representation does not presuppose a compositional semantics for that system, it does *not* follow that (2) the theory of understanding for one's public language does not presuppose a compositional semantics for that language.

Suppose we wanted to program a very sophisticated information processor, Louise, so that she could understand spoken utterances in English; so that, for example, on hearing an utterance of 'She was green' Louise could come to know that the utterer said that a certain woman was inexperienced, and in knowing this know that the utterance was true just in case that woman was inexperienced. Relative to this supposition, the question as regards the need for a compositional semantics in the theory of *public*-language understanding may be posed thus: Would we have to program Louise so that she represented, or somehow realized, a compositional semantics for English? It is the (correct) opinion of the astute CS theorist that no answer whatever to this question is forthcoming from the assumption that the theory of understanding for Louise's *lingua mentis*, her neural (or electronic) code, is a conceptual-role, "use" theory that does not presuppose a compositional semantics.

It is sometimes held that a person's language of thought is his natural language; that English speakers think in English, French ones in French. Of course, all that this can plausibly mean is that there is some salient, but unspecified, relation between one's public language and one's system of mental representation which makes this a useful way to talk. But what would make this a useful way to talk? For the inner code to be one's spoken language it is not enough that there be a meaning-preserving mapping from inner formulae onto outer ones that assigns the same syntactic analysis to all correlated pairs of formulae; for such a mapping could obtain between distinct natural languages. But perhaps the "thinking in English" metaphor would be warranted if, in addition to the foregoing requirement, it were also the case that one's acquisition of one's outer, spoken language *causally* accounted for one's acquisition of one's isomorphic internal language.

If one's language of thought is English, in the foregoing sense, then the theory of understanding English *qua language of thought* will be a conceptual-role theory that presupposes no compositional semantics for English. But from this nothing whatever follows about the need for a compositional semantics in the account of one's understanding of spoken English—that is, in the account of one's ability to know what propositional speech acts are performed in spoken utterances. The use of language in *thought* is one thing, its use in *speech* another. These are different phenomena, to be explained by different theories.

Now we are in a position to appreciate why the CS theorist should be deterred neither by (a) a certain potentially misleading way of using the phrase 'theory of language understanding' nor by (b) a certain questionable argument.

As regards (a), the CS theorist is well aware of a recent tendency to promote "use" theories of language understanding that do not presuppose truth-conditional semantics. He knows, for example, that Hilary Putnam (1978) has written that "the theory of language understanding and the theory of reference and truth have much less to do with one another than many philosophers have assumed," following this with the sketch of a conceptual-role account of "language use" from which it is clear that "nothing in this account of 'use' says *anything* about a correspondence between words and things, or sentences and states of affairs" (p. 99). But a theorist can see the wisdom in this without renouncing his belief in [U]: the correctness of a non—truth-conditional, "use" theory of "understanding" *for the role of language in thought* would imply nothing about the need for a compositional semantics in the theory of a person's ability to understand spoken utterances. Perhaps, the CS theorist may concede, it is true that in acquiring English as a first language one is acquiring two capacities—the ability to understand English utterances and the ability to think in English—and perhaps it is true that an account of the latter capacity would make no appeal to a compositional semantics; nonetheless, the question remains open as to whether a compositional semantics will be needed to explain the former capacity, namely, the ability to know what propositional speech acts speakers perform in their utterances.

The argument to which (b) alludes is Gilbert Harman's (1975). He has not been confused by any pun on 'language use', but has been forcefully explicit in denying that a compositional semantics is needed to explain even the public, communicative use of language, *given that one thinks in one's natural language.* His argument evidently has these two premises:

(1)   We would need a compositional semantics for English only if understanding spoken utterances were a matter of *decoding* a message expressed in one language, English, into a distinct language, Mentalese.
(2)   But since we think in English, no such decoding takes place: "words are used to communicate thoughts that would ordinarily be thought in those or similar words" (p. 271).

The CS theorist ought to deny (1), protesting that what should be at issue is not how we represent thoughts but how we manage to ascribe truth-valuational properties to utterances, however we represent those utterances as having those properties. Thus, we may imagine, Ralph utters the sounds 'She beat him'; you have an auditory perception of them and form the correct belief that Ralph said that a certain female completed a certain running race ahead of a certain male, and that, therefore, Ralph's utterance is true just in case that female did finish ahead of that male. Let it be granted that you think in English and thus do not decode messages spoken in English into a distinct Mentalese: how does that show that no compositional semantics is needed to explain the processing that took you from the auditory stimulation to the knowledge that Ralph's utterance was true just in case a certain state of affairs obtained?

I have just been concerned to show that the CS theory is not threatened by consequences of a theory of mental representation that, it happens, I do not accept. It is also important to show that the CS theory is equally unthreatened by views on mental representation that I do accept. In this regard there are two points to be elaborated:

(A)   Even if we think in a language of thought, there is no true theory of intentionality or mental representation per se that implies that the language of thought has a compositional semantics.
(B)   The truth of (A) does not imply that one's public language does not have a compositional semantics.

As will later become apparent, it is important to my overall argument that we be clear about (A), even apart from the present question, its potential threat to the CS theory; and a useful way of getting clear is to contrast my own views on the language of thought with those of the Strong Language of Thought (SLT) theorist, described and criticized in chapter 4, who holds the two-factor theory of mental representation.

1. The SLT theorist holds that the brain is a computer, that we are information processors who process information in an inner neural code.

Whether or not this is true depends to a large extent on how one chooses to interpret the metaphor of a neural code, but I am by no means precluded from agreeing that there is a true and interesting thesis to be discerned here.

2. The SLT theorist holds that there is some computational relation R such that for each belief that one can have, there is some inner formula such that one has that belief just in case one bears R to that formula; in quasi-symbols:

There is some computational (or functional) relation R such that

$(x)(p)(\exists\sigma)(\sigma$ is a formula in x's language of thought & x believes p iff $R(x,\sigma))$.

This, too, I can accept, with one proviso: that, in conformity with my denial of the relational theory of belief, '(p)' be read *substitutionally* rather than objectually.[4] Then the generalization may be established as true for a particular value of 'x' (i.e., a particular person) in something like the following way. Human beliefs, we may suppose, are neural state-tokens, and it may be discovered that there is some functional property of neural state-tokens possession of which is necessary and sufficient for a state's being a belief. (As I made clear in chapter 2, I am *extremely* skeptical of there being a functional property that is likewise definitive of being, say, a belief *that theater tickets are much cheaper in London than they are in New York;* but the arguments against such an unmitigated functionalism do not extend to the much weaker hypothesis that there is a functional (and possibly computational) feature of neural states that is in some sense criterial for being a belief.) Next we discover that the neural states that realize the subject's beliefs have sentential structure: they are tokenings of formulae in a computational neural machine language. Then we discover a salient isomorphism between the subject's inner and outer languages. For example, let 'Nodnol si yggof' be (a graphemic representation of) a well-formed neural sentence.[5] It may be discovered that the subject stands in the belief-securing computational relation to tokens of that sentence when, and only when, he actively believes that London is foggy; that if he stands in that relation to a neural sentence-token containing 'yggof', then he believes that ... foggy ..., and likewise, *mutatis mutandis*, for the other parts; that if he stands in the belief-securing relation to a neural sentence than contains 'Nodnol', then he is disposed sincerely to assert a sentence that contains 'London'; and so on. In other words, we discover a mapping from the subject's public-language sentences onto his Mentalese formulae such that, for any sentence σ, $\ulcorner$believes that $\sigma\urcorner$ is true of him when, and only when, he stands in the belief-determining computational relation to the image of σ under the discovered mapping; this establishes the foregoing indented thesis, given the qualification about substitutional quantification.

This "weak" language-of-thought hypothesis is, of course, an empirical hypothesis and implies nothing of philosophical substance about the content of mental states. If the hypothesis is true, and if μ is the neural sentence that happens to realize your belief that snow is white, then, trivially and uninterestingly, it may be said that in your head μ "means" that snow is white. (Cf. section 4.1.) In a similarly unportentous way, semantic properties may even be assigned to Mentalese words. If a Mentalese expression α is such that you believe that ... London ... whenever you stand in relation R to a sentence containing α, then α may be regarded as referring to London. Yet this by no means implies that there is anything like a "semantics" for the language of thought or that belief content is being explained in terms of the meaning of inner formulae. It especially does not imply that languages of thought have compositional semantics.

3. The SLT theorist does go on to make those further, unimplied claims, and it is here that I disagree. He claims, we know, that the content of mental states derives from and can be analyzed in terms of the semantic features of neural expressions, and that these semantic features, in turn, enjoy a reduction in naturalistic terms. He claims, in particular, that there are naturalistic facts that select, for each neural sentence, some state of affairs as being its truth condition.

I have already argued against this program; my purpose now is merely to contrast my own views. First, of course, I deny that there is any reduction or "explication" of belief content. Sentential Dualism is true, and if Jane believes that metheglin is tastier than mead, then that fact cannot be analyzed in other terms. Likewise if there is some neural state-token n that happens to be her present belief that metheglin is tastier than mead. There is nothing that "makes it the case" that n is a belief that metheglin is tastier than mead; there is no true and nontrivial completion of the schema

n is a belief that metheglin is tastier than mead iff....

Consequently there is no possibility of providing a semantics—any kind of "semantics"—for the language of thought that will reductively explain the contentful features of beliefs. Trivially, I have just remarked, a neural sentence may be said to mean that such-and-such if its tokening would realize the belief that such-and-such; but that neural sentence has no features, semantic or otherwise, that *account* for the content of the belief that its tokening would realize. (Of course, saying this is consistent with saying that a neural sentence could not realize a certain thought unless that sentence had a certain kind of conceptual role and parts of it stood in relevant causal relations to objects outside the head.) Nor, it further follows, is there any need to provide a truth-theoretic semantics for Mentalese to account for the truth-theoretic features of beliefs. It immediately follows from the fact that Jane believes that metheglin is tastier than mead that she has a belief that is true if, and only if, metheglin is tastier than mead. As nothing needs to be attributed to her language of thought to account for Jane's having her belief, nothing needs to be attributed to it to account for her belief's having the truth condition it has.

Given the initial plunge into talk of a language of thought, it is easy for the unwary to slip uncritically into talk of the "semantics" for the language of thought, and to wonder about the nature of the theory that will account for it. What I have been urging, and what follows from the antireductionism for which I have argued, is that we have no reason to suppose that the language of thought has or needs any kind of semantics. It is especially the case, to pare the point down to something that bears directly on present issues, that we have no reason whatever forthcoming from the theory of intentionality to suppose that Mentalese either has or needs a compositional semantics.

The qualification 'forthcoming from the theory of intentionality' brings me to (B). If one's public language has a compositional semantics, then, on certain reasonable assumptions, so will one's language of thought, and vice versa (clearly this is so if one thinks in one's natural language). So, if I were in a position to conclude that there were no correct compositional semantics for languages of thought, then I could draw the same conclusion for natural languages. True, my denial of the relational theory of propositional attitudes gives me equally, and in the same way, a reason for denying that either the outer or the inner language has a compositional semantics. But what is presently to the point is that I have no other reason for concluding that there is no correct compositional semantics for the language of thought; all that follows from my Sentential Dualism is that there is no route to a compositional semantics for Mentalese from considerations that pertain only to the content of mental states, and consequently no route to a compositional semantics for natural languages from the need for one for systems of mental representation. The way is still left open, then, for the CS theorist to argue that considerations of public-language *understanding* prove that natural languages have correct compositional semantics. He is indeed precluded from basing his argument on the need, independently established, for a compositional semantics for Mentalese;

but those who have thought that considerations of public-language understanding have shown that public languages have compositional semantics
have certainly not meant to rely on any special assumptions about the
truth-theoretic content of beliefs. What I want now to argue is that there
are no such considerations—that [U], the commonly accepted basis for the
CS theory, is false.

7.4 A Counterexample

A person S utters a sentence σ. Another person, A, hears S's utterance of σ
and, even though he has never before encountered σ, instantaneously
forms the correct belief that S, in uttering σ, said that such-and-such, and
that, therefore, what S said, and thus his utterance of σ, is true provided
that such-and-such is the case. In the event, A understands, or knows the
meaning of, σ, understands S's utterance of σ, and manifests his understanding of the language to which σ belongs.

It is the claim of the CS theorist that in order correctly to account for
the language-understanding capacity manifested by A in his processing of
S's utterance, we shall at some point need to postulate a compositional
semantics for the language in question. More generally, I think it involves
only a little exaggeration to say that among those who hold the CS theory
for a considered reason, that considered reason is [U], the conviction that
without the assumption of a compositional semantics there could be no
explaining a person's ability to comprehend indefinitely many utterances of
indefinitely many novel sentences.

If I am right to doubt that any natural language has a compositional
semantics, then I must find fault with [U], and that is the burden of
this section. My goal, however, will not be to explain our language-
understanding capacity in a way that does not imply that the languages we
understand have compositional semantics. The explanation of our capacity
to understand natural-language utterances would be an empirical, scientific
undertaking, the business, surely, of cognitive psychology and psycho-
linguistics. My present purpose is merely to provide a *counterexample* to
[U], and thus to show that we might be so constituted that our language
comprehension abilities proceed without access to a compositional semantics
for the language we comprehend. My counterexample to [U] takes the
form of a description of a possible world in which it is the case that
(1) a certain person, Harvey, has the ability to understand utterances of
indefinitely many novel sentences of a certain language E_1, itself containing
infinitely many sentences, and that (2) the explanation of Harvey's ability
does not invoke a compositional semantics for E_1.

Although the example of Harvey's comprehension of E_1 is plausibly a
counterexample to [U], E_1 falls short of being a full-blown natural language,

and this might suggest that it is owing to features of natural languages not shared by E_1 that a compositional semantics will have to be invoked in explaining our ability to understand utterances in such languages. So, as my objective is to undermine the standard motivation for supposing that our natural languages have compositional semantics, I shall (in the next section) incrementally complicate the Harvey example to the point where he represents a possible model of us. In the end I shall also suggest how certain other special features of Harvey, perhaps not shared by us, may be removed without detriment to the main point.

Harvey, in the possible world now to be characterized, is an information processor, and so thinks (i.e., processes) in an inner neural machine language—his *lingua mentis*, so to say—which I shall call 'M'. It is a contingent but nomological fact about Harvey that he has a belief just in case he stands in a certain computational relation to a tokened sentence of M. To make this vivid, we may pretend that there is in Harvey's head a large box marked 'B' and that a sentence of M is tokened as a belief just in case a token of that sentence occurs in B. (For simplicity I suppose that Harvey is limited to finitely many beliefs.) Further, for every belief that Harvey can have, there is a unique sentence of M whose occurrence in B would realize that belief. Consequently, there is just one formula μ such that Harvey believes that snow is white if and only if μ occurs in B. Since sentences of M realize beliefs, they have, *ipso facto*, semantic, or representational, features: it is fair to say, for example, that μ, the formula whose occurrence in B realizes the belief that snow is white, "means" that snow is white; and some component of μ, being the inner counterpart of the public-language word that refers to snow, may be said, trivially, to inherit that word's semantic features and thus to refer to snow. This does not, however, entitle us to suppose that M has a compositional semantics—or any other kind of semantics. We do not need to ascribe semantic properties to expressions in M in order to account for intentional features of beliefs, but rather the opposite: the semantic features of mental representations, such as they are, are inherited from the intentional features of the beliefs that they realize. This, as I have observed, does not mean that M does not have a compositional semantics, but it does mean that there is no argumentative route from a compositional semantics for M to one for the public language E_1.

Anyway, Harvey, qua computer, is endowed with certain *belief-forming mechanisms*. These mechanisms determine the conditions under which a given sentence of M will occur in Harvey's B-box. If we suppose that, roughly speaking, the appearance of a given sentence in B at a time t is determined by sensory stimulations and the contents of B at times immediately preceding t, then the belief-forming mechanisms determine *how* the occurrence of a sentence in *B* is a function of sensory stimulations and other sentences occurring (or not occurring) in *B*. Thus, for every sentence of *M*, the belief-forming mechanisms will determine a very complex counterfactual property that details the way in which the occurrence of that sentence in *B* is determined by sensory stimulations and other sentences in *B*. I shall call this property of an inner sentence, with some trepidation, its *conceptual role* (as before, the conceptual role of a subsentential expression is its contribution to the conceptual roles of the sentences in which it occurs). I call it that because I need a label and find that other writers use 'conceptual role' when they have such a property in mind; my trepidation is due to my not wanting to be a party to various theoretical claims that others make about the counterfactual properties that I am calling 'conceptual roles'. In particular, I am not proposing conceptual roles as part of a theory of mental content (I deny that there is any such correct theory to be proposed).

Harvey's spoken language, and that of the linguistic community to which he belongs, happens to be nonindexical, unambiguous English, which language I call 'E_1'. My task now is precisely this: to make further stipulations that will show that Harvey's ability to process utterances in E_1 does not presuppose a compositional semantics for E_1. If I can do this, then we shall have a counterexample to [U], the hypothesis in question.

Now Carmen utters the sequence of sounds 'Some snow is purple'. Harvey has an auditory perception of Carmen's utterance and immediately knows, notwithstanding the novelty of the sound sequence uttered, that Carmen said that some snow was purple, and, consequently, that her utterance is true just in case some snow is purple. As this transition manifests Harvey's ability to understand utterances of novel sentences of E_1, my task amounts to this: to state general principles, applicable to any utterance in E_1, that (a) will take Harvey from

[1]   his belief that Carmen uttered the sounds 'Some snow is purple'

to

[2]   his belief that Carmen said that some snow was purple, and thus what she said, and so her utterance, is true just in case some snow is purple,

but (b) will not require that Harvey's processing realize, or be in accordance with, a compositional semantics for E_1.

I think it may be useful, before turning to my stipulations about Harvey, to see what the CS theorist would have to say about him. That theorist, subscribing to [U], must claim that in order correctly to account for the transition from [1] to [2], we must suppose that Harvey's internal processing somehow realizes, or represents, a compositional semantics for

E_1. Now the language comprehension process that begins with Harvey's auditory perception and terminates with his belief about what Carmen said is realized by a sequence of tokened occurrences of inner formulae (only some of which are realizations of consciously held beliefs).[6] The CS theorist is evidently constrained to say that some of these formulae represent segments of Carmen's utterance as having certain semantic values, and that, on the basis of this, and in accordance with a certain compositional semantics for E_1, some formula later in the comprehension sequence represents Carmen's entire sound sequence as having a certain semantic value. This representation, the CS theorist will doubtless want to say, interacts with other formulae representing general psychological, or psychosemantical, principles applicable to speakers of any language, and this interaction in turn results in there being in Harvey's B-box a formula that represents Carmen as having said that some snow was purple. The CS theorist may regard it as an empirical question, to be resolved by scientific research, whether the compositional semantics (or grammar, as it used to be called in Cambridge, Mass., when grammars were finitely statable sound-meaning pairings) is itself internally represented, or whether infantile exposure to some utterances in E_1 has resulted in Harvey's simply becoming "hard-wired" so as to process in conformity with a certain compositional semantics, not itself internally represented.[7]

But what are these "semantic values," and what form will the compositional semantics that ascribes them take? I am aware of no answer that will help us to understand Harvey's comprehension process. This makes it difficult (for me) to assess the claim that in order for Harvey to have the language comprehension ability he is stipulated to have, his internal processing must somehow have some sort of access to some sort of compositional semantics for E_1. In proposing, as I shall now do, that Harvey's understanding of E_1 might proceed without access to a compositional semantics for E_1, I am hardly flying the face of an already available explanatory theory of that understanding.

Here, at any rate, is how, without appeal to a compositional semantics, we can account for Harvey's ability to understand utterances in E_1: we can stipulate that certain expressions in the inner code M have conceptual roles that do explain the transition from [1] to [2], and all others like it, but do not presuppose a compositional semantics for E_1. I shall explain.

Let

[3]   Nemrac derettu 'sŭm' 'snō' 'ĭz' 'pûr'pəl',

[4]   Nemrac dias taht emos wons si elprup,

and

[5]   Nemrac's ecnarettu si eurt ffi emos wons si elprup

be (graphemic representations of) the sentences of the inner code M that realize, respectively, Harvey's beliefs that Carmen uttered the sequence of sounds 'some snow is purple', that Carmen said that some snow was purple, and that Carmen's utterance is true iff some snow is purple.

My intention is to show that Harvey is a counterexample to [U] by showing how 'dias taht' and 'eurt' can have conceptual roles that (a) do not presuppose a compositional semantics for E_1 but (b) do explain the transition from the occurrence of [3] in Harvey's B-box to the occurrence there of [4] and [5] (and, of course, explain all of Harvey's other utterance comprehension transitions).

To do this I do not have to specify the entire conceptual roles of 'dias taht' and 'eurt'. I assume that [4] and [5] have whatever conceptual roles are necessitated by virtue of their being formulae whose occurrence in Harvey's B-box would realize the beliefs that Carmen said that some snow was purple and that Carmen's utterance is true iff some snow is purple. But it is clear that there is nothing in the conceptual roles thus necessitated that presupposes a compositional semantics for E_1; for someone who did not understand E_1—say, a monolingual speaker of Serbo-Croatian—could, without knowing the meaning of 'some snow is purple', correctly believe, perhaps by being told, that Carmen, in uttering that sentence, said that some snow was purple, and that, therefore, what she said, and her utterance as well, is true if and only if some snow is purple. Consequently, my question is this: Given that [4] and [5] realize the foregoing beliefs, what stipulations about the conceptual roles of 'dias taht' and 'eurt' would explain the transition in Harvey from [1] to [2], and all other utterance comprehension processes, but would not presuppose a compositional semantics for E_1?

In order to state these conceptual roles, I need first to assume the existence of a certain function. Let 'δ' be a variable over those structural descriptions in M that, like the description ''sŭm' 'snō' 'ĭz' 'pûr'pəl'', refer to sound sequences that are well-formed formulae of E_1, and let 'μ' range over sentences in M, Harvey's internal system of mental representation. Then, I stipulate, there is a recursive function f, issuing in statements of form

$$f(\delta) = \mu,$$

from structural descriptions in M of the kind described to sentences of M, such that

(i) f is definable in terms of formal features of the expressions in its domain and range, without reference to any semantic features of any expressions in either M or E_1; and

(ii)   if the referent of δ can be used to say that p, then $f(\delta)$ would token the belief that p.

(In making this stipulation I am tacitly assuming that each sentence in E_1 is relevantly correlated with just one sentence in M; otherwise the description of the mapping would be slightly more complex. The existence of f, relative to this assumption, would seem to be unproblematic, in the same way that it is unproblematic that there should be a recursive mapping of French sentences onto English sentences that is statable without reference to any semantic features of those sentences but yet maps each French sentence onto its English translation. It should also be clear from the characterization of f that if M has a compositional semantics, then so does E_1, and vice versa. But, to repeat a point recently labored, there is no reason whatever forthcoming from the theory of mental representation or intentionality for supposing M to have a compositional semantics; the only way left open for establishing a compositional semantics for M is by first establishing one for E_1.)

The conceptual role of 'dias taht' is now stipulated to be such that

if the sentence

⌜α derettu δ⌝

is in Harvey's B-box and $f(\delta) = \mu$, then, ceteris paribus, so is the sentence

⌜α dias taht μ⌝

(where 'α' is a variable over singular terms in M). Thus, if

'Nemrac derettu 'sŭm͡ 'snō͡ ˜ĭz͡ 'pûr′pəl''

is in B and, as happens to be the case, $f($"sŭm͡ 'snō͡ ˜ĭz͡ 'pûr′pəl"$) = $ 'emos wons si elprup', then, ceteris paribus, so is

'Nemrac dias taht emos wons si elprup'.

So, in this way, the conceptual role of 'dias taht' automatically guarantees that if Harvey believes that Carmen uttered 'Some snow is purple', and certain further conditions obtain, then he will believe that she said that some snow was purple.

Clearly, it would derogate from the plausibility of the hypothesis that Harvey even begins to approach being a model of us if we supposed him to be so "programmed" that, upon hearing a sentence that in fact meant p, he automatically believed that the utterer said, or meant, that p. Hence the ceteris paribus clause, which, of course, is just a stand-in for a fuller specification of the conceptual role.

There is more than one psychologically feasible way of cashing out the ceteris paribus clause consistently with my other stipulations, and without smuggling in a compositional semantics for E_1. However, I will stipulate

Harvey to satisfy a style of completion to which I am particularly drawn, as I think that it, or a variant of it, is one that may well have application to us.

I have in mind an analogy between utterance comprehension processes and a possible view of perceptual processes. Given a glimpse of a typical collie, I will believe off the bat that the creature is a dog. At the same time, I do not regard the creature's doggy appearance as being a sufficient condition for its being a dog, as I would disbelieve it to be a dog were I to become convinced that the creature was the bizarre mutant offspring of two turtles. In view of this, one *might* suppose that the transition from the initial visual stimulus, the sight of the creature, to the belief that it was a dog involved an inference to the best explanation, one that invoked a belief that possession of a doggy appearance was some high degree of evidence that its possessor was conspecific with some sample of creatures that was somehow determinative of the species *dog*.

I believe that this "inference to the best explanation" view is implausible, however; it is not even clear what it would come to when doctored so as not to be refuted by a child's belief formations. I think that a closer approximation to the truth would eschew inference and see me "programmed" so as to believe straightway, upon seeing the creature with a doggy appearance, that it is a dog, *unless* I already possess some *defeating* belief, such as the belief that the creature's parents are turtles.

I suggest, then, that we think of the further specification of the conceptual role of 'dias taht', left open by the *ceteris paribus* clause, as being such that, upon hearing Carmen utter 'Some snow is purple', Harvey will straightway come to believe that she said that some snow was purple, unless Harvey's B-box already contains some defeating sentence, such as one that realizes the belief that it is mutually obvious to him and Carmen that she does not believe that some snow is purple. But I will make no (foolish) attempt to delimit the class of potential defeaters, and so must leave the characterization of the *ceteris paribus* clause in the present sketchy state. (Cf. Bach 1984.)

Faced now with the prospect of having to write out the conceptual role of 'eurt' in backwards English, I realize that it is time to depart from this tiresome convention and to suppose, merely for intelligibility of exposition, that Harvey thinks in "the same language" he speaks, and thus that M is E_1. (We may pretend that Harvey's B-box contains a very large blackboard, and that a sentence of E_1 occurs in B just in case a token of it is written on the blackboard.) The conceptual role of 'said that' in M ($= E_1$), now to replace that of 'dias taht', may be stated thus (where 'σ' ranges over sentences of inner and outer E_1, and '$\bar{\sigma}$' is a structural description of the sentence σ):

If the sentence

⌜α uttered $\bar{\sigma}$⌝

is in Harvey's B-box, then, *ceteris paribus*, so is

⌜α said that σ⌝.

Then the example already used comes out as follows:

If

'Carmen uttered 'Some snow is purple''

is in B, then, *ceteris paribus*, so is

'Carmen said that some snow is purple'.

(I was reluctant to begin with this simplification, for fear that the reader might worry that, in the stipulation that Harvey thought and communicated in E_1, semantic assumptions were being entailed that might imply the existence of a compositional semantics for E_1. But there should not be any anxiety on this score now, given that we know how to translate into the tiresome but more explicit convention. Notice that the earlier function f has implicitly been replaced by a purely disquotational function, which maps the quotation description of each sentence of E_1 onto its referent, that very sentence of which it is a quotation description.)

This brings me to the *conceptual role of 'true' in M*, which I stipulate to be such that

if

⌜α said that σ⌝

is in B, then so is

⌜What α said (viz., that σ), and so α's utterance, is true iff σ⌝.

Consequently, having arrived at the belief that Carmen said that some snow was purple, Harvey automatically believes as well that what she said and her utterance are true just in case some snow is purple.

So much for Harvey's mastery of his public language E_1. Harvey, I submit, is plausibly a counterexample to [U], one evident motivation for supposing that natural languages have compositional semantics. We have provided enough of a description of the possible world in which Harvey resides to make plausible the claim that (a) by virtue of the conceptual roles of certain semantic expressions in his inner code, Harvey has the ability to under- stand utterances of indefinitely many novel sentences of E_1, and (b) the account of Harvey's processing of spoken utterances does not require that

E_1 have a compositional semantics. And if Harvey constitutes a counterexample to [U], then, if there is a good reason to think that natural languages have compositional semantics, it cannot be that it is inconceivable how we could explain a person's finitely based ability to know the meanings of—that is, to understand utterances of—the sentences of his language without assuming that his language has a compositional semantics. Despite the artificial simplicity of E_1, the issue with the CS theorist is squarely joined over it.

7.5 The Counterexample Extended

The usual motivation for compositionality has been *just* the ability to understand novel utterances, an ability already present in Harvey's understanding of E_1. Yet one might now wonder if the need for a compositional semantics does not arise in the need to accommodate one or another of those features that separate E_1 from English: indexicality and ambiguity. It might especially be thought that a need for a compositional semantics will enter with indexicals, in the need to explain how, from a speaker's utterance of 'He's retired', one can know that what was said was that Nixon was retired. Let us turn, then, to E_2, which is E_1 supplemented with indexicals, that is, singular terms whose reference is context dependent. My strategy, as before, is to stipulate conceptual roles for expressions in M (now, for convenience, taken to be written, unambiguous English) that account for Harvey's ability to understand utterances in E_2 but do not presuppose a compositional semantics for E_2.

I first stipulate that M contains the predicate

x's utterance of y refers to z [= Ref(x, y, z)].

No doubt this predicate has a complex conceptual role in M, one that links it with predicates ascribing communicative intentions to the utterer; but that is not anything that needs now to be specified; we may take it for granted that the conceptual role of 'Ref' permits its application in comprehension processes involving utterances containing indexicals. It remains to be shown that the role of this predicate can cohere with a noncompositional account of understanding.

The revised conceptual role for 'says that' is as follows (where each t_i is an indexical of E_2, each α and each β_i is an internal singular term, and '$\Sigma(t_1, \ldots, t_n)$' is a structural description of the sentence Σ in which occur the indexicals $t_1, \ldots, t_n$):

If the sentences

$\ulcorner \alpha$ uttered $\overline{\Sigma(t_1, \ldots, t_n)} \urcorner$

and

$\ulcorner Ref(\alpha, \overline{f_1}, \beta_1)$ and ... and $Ref(\alpha, \overline{f_n}, \beta_n)\urcorner$

are in Harvey's B-box, then, *ceteris paribus*, so is

$\ulcorner \alpha$ said that $\Sigma(\beta_1, \ldots, \beta_n)\urcorner$.

The conceptual role for 'true' remains the same. Thus, if

'Ralph uttered 'He is retired''

and

'Ralph's utterance of 'he' refers to Nixon'

are in B, then, *ceteris paribus*, so are

'Ralph said that Nixon is retired'

and

'What Ralph said, as well as his utterance, is true iff Nixon is retired'.

Likewise, if

'Ralph uttered 'She believes that he gave it to her''

and

'Ref(Ralph, 'she', Sally) and Ref(Ralph, 'he', George) and Ref(Ralph, 'it', the Hope diamond) and Ref(Ralph, 'her', Liz)'

are in B, then, *ceteris paribus*, so are

'Ralph said that Sally believes that George gave the Hope diamond to Liz'

and, of course,

'What Ralph said [etc.] is true iff Sally believes [etc.]'.

There is a weak sort of compositionality now implicated in the conceptual role of 'says that' in M, since we are taking account of some aspects of an utterance's internal structure. But, of course, no compositional semantics is being relied on, because each n-ary predicate of E_2, however complex, is being treated noncompositionally, *as if* it were primitive. The upshot is that by making stipulations about the conceptual roles of 'says that' and 'true' in M, we can explain, without recourse to a compositional semantics for E_2, Harvey's ability to understand indefinitely many utterances of indefinitely many novel sentences in his public, indexical language. Indexicality, then, does not carry with it the need for a compositional semantics.[8]

I turn now to E_3, which is full-blown English, and to Harvey's ability to comprehend utterances of ambiguous sentences. To keep the discussion simple, however, I shall ignore indexicality, thus in effect showing how ambiguity can be added, without incorporation of a compositional semantis, to E_1.

Let us suppose that M—English qua language of thought—has the predicate 'means the same as', whose conceptual role permits Harvey to have in his B-box sentences such as

[a]   'Cape' (in one use) means the same as 'short sleeveless cloak' and (in another use) 'promontory of land'

and

[b]   'Henry bought a cape' (in one use) means the same as 'Henry bought a short sleeveless cloak' and (in another use) 'Henry bought a promontory of land'.

The occurrence of [b] in B is of course dependent on the occurrence of [a] in B, but to explain this we need only to stipulate that the conceptual role of 'means the same as' requires Harvey to have in B the sentence

If e means the same as e', then $\ulcorner \ldots e \ldots \urcorner$ means the same as $\ulcorner \ldots e' \ldots \urcorner$.

There is nothing in the conceptual role of 'means the same as', as it occurs in Harvey's head, that requires a compositional semantics for E_3. To accommodate Harvey's ability to understand utterances of ambiguous sentences, we may revise the conceptual role of 'says that' thus (where 'σ' ranges over sentences of the outer E_3, and 'μ' over sentences of M, inner E_2; it may be assumed that the language of thought is ambiguity-free):

If the sentences

$\ulcorner \alpha$ uttered $\bar{\sigma} \urcorner$

and

$\ulcorner \bar{\sigma}$ (in one use) means the same as $\overline{\mu_1}$ and (in another use) $\overline{\mu_2} \urcorner$

and

———

are in Harvey's B-box, then, *ceteris paribus*, so is

$\ulcorner \alpha$ said that $\mu_1 \urcorner$.

The task of filling in the missing Mentalese sentence is analogous to the task of specifying the *ceteris paribus* clause: suggestions here are perforce speculations on empirical issues, ideally to be resolved by some future cognitive psychology. Still, as a first approximation, or gesture, toward the *sort* of filling we might expect, we may stipulate that, in Harvey's head at least, the lacuna is to be filled by this sentence of M:

⌜It is more probable that α believes that μ_1 than that α believes that μ_2⌝.[9]

Then we know that if Harvey has in B the sentences

'Ralph uttered 'Henry bought a cape'',

and

''Henry bought a cape' (in one use) means the same as '... short sleeveless cloak' and (in another use) '... promontory of land''

and

'It is more probable that Ralph believes that Henry bought a short sleeveless cloak than that he believes that Henry bought a promontory of land',

then, *ceteris paribus*, he also has in B the sentence

'Ralph said that Henry bought a short sleeveless cloak'.

Harvey is now plausibly a counterexample to the claim that there could be no correct account of a person's ability to understand natural-language utterances that did not assume that natural languages have compositional semantics. But there is still something that we can do that Harvey has not yet been equipped to do, and that bears on the nature of radical interpretation.

Not enough has been stipulated about M to show that Harvey, on hearing Pierre utter 'La neige est blanche', can figure out that Pierre said that snow was white, or that Mrs. Malaprop, in uttering 'Regular exercise is enervating' said that regular exercise was energizing. Let me then simply stipulate that M contains the predicate

x_1 means for x_2 what x_3 means for x_4,

whose conceptual role is such that (where 'σ' is a variable over all sound or mark sequences)

if

⌜α uttered $\bar{\sigma}$⌝

and

⌜$\bar{\sigma}$ means for α what $\bar{\sigma}'$ means for me⌝

are in B, then, *ceteris paribus*, so is

⌜α said that σ'⌝.

The implicit point about radical interpretation is as follows. In radical interpretation we seek explicit propositional knowledge that will enable us to understand utterances in the native's language J. Since J contains infinitely many sentences, the knowledge sought must be expressible in a finitely stable theory of J. It might be thought that this theory could be a correct *translation manual* from J into the interpreter's public language. Surely, one can understand utterances in J if one can translate J sentences into one's own. But Davidsonians have been scornful of translational theories of radical interpretation. For one could know a procedure for translating one language into another without knowing what the sentences of either language meant. When one translates into one's own language, it is clear, one relies on one's *prior knowledge* of what the sentences of the translating language mean; "but this is knowledge of precisely the kind that was to be accounted for in the first place" (Evans and McDowell 1976, introduction, p. ix). Consequently, it is felt, the translational approach to interpretation "serves only to enable us to conceal from ourselves our utter incapacity to do what we ought to be doing. What we ought to be doing is stating [not a translation manual, which can be known without knowing what the sentences of either the translated or the translating language mean, but] something such that, if someone knew it, he would be able to speak and understand the language" (p. ix). Thus, for the Davidsonian, the explicit knowledge needed in radical interpretation is knowledge of a "meaning theory," a finitely stable theory that "explicitly states something knowledge of which would suffice for interpreting utterances of speakers" of J (Davidson 1976, p. 33). Pretty clearly, if this is correct, then every natural language has a compositional semantics.

The mistake in this line of reasoning is in the presupposition that a meaning theory is needed to account for one's understanding of one's own language. It is true that in radical interpretation one seeks a finitely stable theory explicit knowledge of which will enable one to interpret utterances in J. But for Harvey the only finitely stable theory needed is a *translation manual* from J into Harvey's public language; as no compositional semantics is needed to explain Harvey's understanding of his own public language, no compositional semantics, no "meaning theory," is needed for J.

In this chapter I have tried to show, not that natural languages do not have compositional semantics, but only that the assumption that they do is not *required* to explain one's ability to understand natural-language utterances. I have tried to describe a possible world in which a person's ability to understand utterances in a natural language does not presuppose a compositional semantics for that language. While I recognize that my sketch has been too incomplete to prove the point, I hope that it has not been too incomplete to make it plausible.

Now the person in my possible world is a human computer; he thinks in a neural machine language, a language of thought, and I accounted for his ability to comprehend utterances in his public language by stipulating conceptual roles for expressions in his inner code. Yet the language-of-thought assumption, which I do not dismiss as having no application to us, has been merely a heuristic, and the story need not have been told in terms of conceptual roles of inner formulae, but could have been couched, with only minor adjustments, in terms of the functional, or causal, properties of the neural states that realize our beliefs. In effect, what I have tried to show is that there could be a correct *psychological model* of a person's language processing that does not presuppose a compositional semantics for the mastered language. My psychological model utilized the hypothesis of a language of thought, but I think it is clear that the same effect could have been gained by a less committed account of the structure of the internal states to which the psychological theory implicitly ascribes causal and transitional relations.

7.6 In Other Words

The argument *chez* Harvey has been sufficiently complex to warrant a brief overview of it, with an eye out for those places where the CS theorist might hope to discern a need for a compositional semantics.

Harvey understands the public language E; that is, he is able, on hearing utterances in E, even of what for him are novel sentences, to know what was said in those utterances. I took E to be English, but that was merely an expedient and may now be ignored. The claim I was concerned with was not that E enjoyed a correct compositional semantics, but rather that the hypothesis that it did was necessary to account for Harvey's ability to understand utterances in E. I assumed that one could show that the hypothesis of a compositional semantics for E was not thus required if one could state general principles governing Harvey's language processing that did not presuppose a compositional semantics for E but did show how Harvey could go from an auditory perception of the utterance of an arbitrary sentence of E to a belief, which was in fact correct, about what was said, with what truth condition, in that utterance.

Now it may be that in order to show that Harvey's beliefs were *correct*, one would need to have recourse to a compositional semantics for E, but I do not think that that possibility should cast doubt on the assumption about what it would take to show that invoking a compositional semantics is not necessary to account for Harvey's language *understanding*. I want to leave room for the claim, to be entertained in the next chapter, that although a compositional semantics is not needed to explain language understanding, it is needed to account for the platitude that the semantic features of a complex expression depend in a rule-governed way on those of its parts. Perhaps, then, it will be useful to look at the question about language understanding in the following way.

Assume that E has a correct compositional semantics, and that I am set the task of constructing an information processor that, when placed in the E-speaking environment, can form correct beliefs about what speakers of E are saying. Will I, in the construction of this machine, have to take account of the fact that E has a compositional semantics? I take it that those who have urged [U] would answer this affirmatively; otherwise, I would have no idea what could be meant by the claim that *the reason* for thinking that natural languages have correct compositional semantics is that that hypothesis is needed to explain a person's ability to comprehend utterances of novel sentences.

Now the description I have already given of Harvey may be viewed as an attempt to show how he could be built according to principles that did give him the right beliefs but did not presuppose a compositional semantics for E. I first stipulated, in effect, that Harvey processes in a formal, neural machine language M and that for some computational relation R,

[R] $(\Pi P)(\exists \sigma)$ (Harvey believes that P iff R(Harvey, σ)).

('(ΠP)', it may be recalled, is the universal substitutional quantifier.)

Might it be protested that, right at this point, a move was made that tacitly presupposed, or required, a compositional semantics for M that would—indirectly, via the acknowledged connection between M and E— impose one as well on E?

The argument that a compositional semantics is needed for M could hardly devolve from the connection with E together with the assumption that a compositional semantics is needed for E; in our context of inquiry, that would just be to beg the very question at issue. So, if there is a reason for thinking M needs a compositional semantics, then that reason cannot have anything to do with understanding public-language utterances. But if there is such a reason, one that has nothing to do with public-language understanding, and if *that* is what secures the need of a compositional semantics for E, then no responsible theorist should on this basis claim that we must assume that a compositional semantics is needed for E *in order to account for Harvey's ability to understand utterances in E.* The claim should rather be (1) that Mentalese requires a compositional semantics for reasons that have nothing to do with understanding spoken utterances and (2) that there is an argument from (1) to the possession of a compositional semantics for one's spoken, public language. In any case, the question is academic;

for I have already argued against the only presently relevant argument for (1)—the SLT theorist's claim that a referential semantics for M is needed to account for the truth-theoretic content of beliefs.[10] No such reductive account of intentionality is either needed or possible. But how could I then *construct* Harvey so that he satisfied [R]? Well, perhaps in this way. I *discover* that [R] (actually, what results from [R] when we replace 'Harvey' with a free variable) is true of some typical speaker of E, and I then contrive to give Harvey's neural expressions the same conceptual roles as those of the typical speaker's. I certainly do not need any compositional semantics for M to discover that [R] is true of someone, and it commits me to no reductive thesis whatever if I suppose that two functionally equivalent creatures in the same environment will have the same beliefs.

So let us assume [R], and notice that this is tantamount to assuming a translation manual from M into that fragment of English that comprises the class of substituends for 'p' in [R]; for if Harvey's standing in relation R to a token of a given formula μ of M was what realized for him the belief that snow is white, then we found it harmlessly useful to say that μ "meant" that snow was white. The next and final step (focusing just on E_1) was to assign conceptual roles to the inner correlates of 'says that' and 'true' that took Harvey from beliefs about what sentences of E were uttered to beliefs about what was said, with what truth conditions, in those utterances, but that did not presuppose a compositional semantics for E. It is here, I believe, that the real issue with the [U]-theorist is joined. For that theorist, if his position is to be coherent, must (in the way adumbrated 7.4) be construed as saying that formulae of M that ascribe semantic values to E expressions in accordance with a compositional semantics for E must enter into the processing that is realized in Harvey when he moves from a belief about what sentence was uttered to a belief about what propositional speech act, with what truth condition, was performed in the utterance. The whole point of the conceptual-role story that I gave for 'dias taht' and 'eurt' was to show that such compositional-semantics-involving inner representations need not be implicated in Harvey's language processing. But, it must be confessed, my sketch was no more than that.

7.7 Aspects of Semantic Compositionality

The situation is this. I have, as I had at the beginning of this chapter, a good reason for denying that natural languages have compositional semantics: the thesis that they have them implies the relational theory of propositional attitudes, and there is good reason to think that that theory is false. And I now have some reason for thinking that there is no very good reason for thinking that natural languages have compositional semantics: [U], the most commonly cited reason for thinking that they have them, seems not to be well supported. But the theses with which we have been concerned are intricately connected with many other theses; so, many questions remain. I turn now to one of them, leaving a connected body of others for the next chapter.

I have denied that natural languages have compositional semantics, but I certainly do not wish to deny all aspects of semantic compositionality. I especially do not wish to deny that natural languages contain truth-affecting iterative devices. I should not, for example, wish to deny that

[&] ⌜σ and σ′⌝ is true iff σ is true and σ′ is true.

But my recognition of [&] is perfectly consistent with my reason for denying that English has a correct compositional semantics. For a compositional semantics requires that there be a nonlogical base axiom for each simple nonlogical term of the language, and this is what I deny is possible. I deny, in particular, that propositional-attitude verbs can in this (or any other) way be accommodated within a compositional semantics. A compositional semantics needs two parts: a finite list of semantic primitives and a finite list of recursive rules. Obviously, in denying that the first is possible (in the sense required by the CS theory) I am not denying that the second is possible.

Yet this is not the end of the matter. For in my story of Harvey's ability to understand spoken English I made no appeal to semantic facts such as [&]. What, then, is their status? Does [&] give part of the "meaning" of 'and'? Is knowledge of [&] necessary for mastery of 'and'? Must truths such as [&] figure into a complete account of language understanding?

There is, I think, no very *interesting* sense in which [&] gives part of the meaning of 'and'; for I deny that [&], or anything like it, enters into any sort of theory that in any sense gives the meaning of the sentences that contain 'and'. There simply is no constructive account of sentence meaning. But this, though I graze it again presently, is a point that I develop more fully in the next chapter.

Nor must one who understands English know that [&], or have that truth internally represented. How could it be otherwise? Surely a child may understand 'and' even before he has the concept of a sentence's being true. This is not to deny that, supposing Harvey to think in English, inner 'and' will have a conceptual role that to *some* extent mirrors logical platitudes. For example, we should expect (*ceteris paribus*) σ and σ′ to be in Harvey's B-box whenever ⌜σ and σ′⌝ is in there, and we should expect (*ceteris paribus*) ⌜σ and σ′⌝ to be in B whenever σ and σ′ are also in there. But although this sort of fact is crucial to our translating a neural word as 'and', it does not of itself find theoretical employment for the semantic fact [&]. In fact, though I may be wrong about this (and nothing that I really care about depends on my being right about it), it seems to me that [&] will not enter into the account of Harvey's ability to understand spoken English.

I believe that the import of [&] is explained, and exhausted, by the following two facts. First, what *is* crucial to understanding 'and' is having the ability to know, when a speaker utters a sentence of the form 'σ and σ''', that what he said was that P and Q, for appropriate substitution-instances of 'P' and 'Q'. To understand a literal and assertive utterance of 'Roses are red and violets are blue' is to know that the speaker said that roses are red and violets are blue. Second, it is a *language-independent* truth that every substitution-instance of the following schema is true:

It is true that P and Q iff it is true that P and it is true that Q.

The fact that

it is true that roses are red and violets are blue iff it is true that roses are red and it is true that violets are blue

is not a semantic fact; it is not about words in any language.

In saying that the import of [&] is exhausted by these two facts, I have in mind a contrast with what a CS theorist would say about [&]. This can be brought out if one ignores indexicality and considers a Fregean propositionalist, a CS theorist who thinks that the meaning of the *sentence* 'Roses are red and violets are blue' is the *proposition* that roses are red and violets are blue. This theorist will agree that it is a wholly language-independent truth that this proposition is true just in case the proposition that roses are red and the proposition that violets are blue are both true. But he will think that in order to account for the fact that the sentence means the proposition, we must see 'and' as standing for a certain propositional function, one that determines the familiar truth function. I, on the other hand, think that no such "meaning" or "semantic value" needs to be assigned to 'and' to account for the fact that speakers can say what they do in uttering sentences formed with its help. Here I touch on issues that I am about to discuss more fully.

Chapter 8

Compositional Semantics, Meaning Theories, and Ontology

8.1 Introduction

Natural languages, I have argued, do not have compositional truth-theoretic semantics, and in the last chapter I tried to show that the assumption that they have them is not needed to explain language understanding. Further questions of course remain, and among them are these:

Let it be granted that I have shown that a compositional semantics is not needed to explain language understanding. Might it not be needed for some other reason—perhaps just to explain the platitude that the meaning of a sentence is determined by its syntax and the meanings of its component words?

A meaning theory for a particular language is a finitely stable theory that assigns properties to the words and the modes of syntactic construction of the language in a way that will determine the meaning of each expression in the language. Is there any reason to think that natural languages have meaning theories that are *not* compositional truth-theoretic semantics?

Crucial to my case against semantic compositionality is my claim that 'that'-clauses are not referring expression and that 'y' in the schema 'x believes y' is not an objectual variable. But then how am I to account for the apparent validity of the following inference, and related phenomena?

> Odile believes everything that Jean-Paul says.
> Jean-Paul says that existence precedes essence.
> So, Odile believes that existence precedes essence.

Similar phenomena threaten my nominalism with respect to propositional-attitude properties. For how is one to account for the truth of

> Believing in God is a virtue

or the validity of

Odile and Jean-Paul believe that existence precedes essence.
So, there's some attribute that they have in common—viz., believing
that existence precedes essence.

if no real properties are expressed by predicates of the form 'believes that
such-and-such'? An interesting point will emerge as I answer these questions: namely, that just as the denial of the relational theory of propositional
attitudes is plausible only if natural languages do not have compositional
semantics, so, too, and for just the same reason, the plausibility of nominalism with respect to any class of properties requires natural languages
not to have compositional semantics.

8.2 Compositional Semantics apart from Language Understanding

Frege held that the sense, or meaning, of a complex expression is a function
of the senses of its component parts and that the reference of a complex
expression, which includes the truth value of a sentence, is a function of the
references of its component parts. And he held, of course, that sense determines reference. If we take Frege, as I think we should, as assuming that all
senses are determined from a finite stock of them, then he held that each
language has a correct meaning theory and that each such meaning theory
is a compositional truth-theoretic semantics. Frege thought that these semantic principles were needed to explain one's ability to grasp the thought
expressed by a novel sentence (see chapter 1, note 4; Dummett 1973,
passim); but one can imagine a Fregean, if not Frege, arriving at these
principles by a route that prescinds altogether from considerations that
pertain, at least directly, to language understanding. A theorist may think
that the hypothesis that natural languages have compositional semantics is
simply the best way to account for the platitude that the semantic features
of sentences depend on the semantic features of their parts. Might he not
think this even if he concedes the argument from Harvey? Might it not be
that, first, a compositional semantics is needed to explain the platitude that
the meaning of a sentence is determined by its syntax and the meanings of
its words but that, second, it is not needed to explain a person's ability
to understand sentences? Is there, in short, any reason apart from language
understanding to think that each natural language must have a correct
compositional semantics?

   The meaning of a sentence is determined by its syntax and the meanings of its
words. Let us call this the Platitude, and agree that if a compositional semantics is not needed to explain the Platitude—to explain the way in which
the semantic features of a complex expression depend upon those of its
parts—then there is no reason to believe that each natural language must
have a correct compositional semantics.

Now the Platitude is just that, a platitude. After all, sentences have meaning, and so do words, and the meaning of a word is, in one perfectly good sense, its contribution to the meanings of the sentences in which it occurs. So the Platitude needs to be explained, and the short way with the questions just raised is to show that the hypothesis that natural languages have correct compositional semantics is not needed to explain the Platitude. An even shorter way—and it will be my way—is to show that if the argument of chapter 7 is correct, and we do not need compositional semantics to explain language understanding, then we do not need it to explain the Platitude. One ought to suspect as much. For we did not need a compositional semantics to account for Harvey's understanding of E, and it follows directly from our description of him that his understanding of any sentence of E—that is, how he processes an utterance of it—is determined by its words and syntax.

We may accept the Platitude, but it requires interpretation; if we are to explain it, we must be clear what it comes to. And in this regard it is important to remember how much 'meaning' is a philosopher's term of art, and how the term is actually used in plain speech.

Often talk of "meaning" takes place in the context of translation: we want to know, say, what the French word 'bosquet' means, and our question is answered when we learn that its English translation is 'grove'. It is not irrelevant to notice that, in the context of translation, it is easy to explain the Platitude in a way that does not require us to suppose that natural languages have compositional semantics. For translation of a foreign-language sentence into English is completely determined by the translation of the sentence's words and syntax into English, and there is nothing in translation per se that forces us to suppose that languages have compositional semantics.

Often talk of "meaning" is concerned with definition: we want to know, say, what 'trencherman' means, and our question is answered when we learn that its dictionary entry is 'hearty eater'.

In these two sorts of cases the question may take the form either of 'What is the meaning of x?' or of 'What does x mean?', but in each case the answer is given by mentioning, rather than using, an expression. This does not suggest that meanings are expressions, but rather that talk of what an expression means is often to be understood as being about sameness of meaning. One may even wonder whether there is any use for the form 'x means ...' when something other than sameness of meaning is at issue. How, for example, could one complete any of the following in a way that was correct but was not to be cashed out in terms of sameness of meaning?

'Of' means ....
'Dog' means ....
'She gave it to him' means ....

Now nonphilosophers talk very comfortably of *knowing the meaning* of an expression, and it is again a platitude that one's knowledge of the meaning of a sentence is determined by one's knowledge of the meanings of its words and syntactic construction—nearly the same platitude, I should think, as the Platitude. In view of this, it is encouraging to notice that a compositional semantics is not needed to explain how one's knowledge of the meaning of a complex expression is determined by one's knowledge of the meanings of its parts and mode of construction.

To know the meaning of an expression, in the sense of the vernacular, is not to have propositional knowledge concerning the expression—it is not to know that such-and-such is true of the expression, still less to know that the expression means such-and-such. To know the meaning of an expression is to *understand* it, and this means having a certain processing ability with respect to the expression. To understand an expression is to have the ability to understand utterances of sentences containing it (to know what was said in those utterances), and it follows directly from our description of Harvey that his understanding of a complex expression is determined by his understanding of its parts and syntax. But to account for Harvey's ability to understand spoken utterances we did not have to ascribe a compositional semantics to his spoken language.

I said that to understand an expression is to have the ability to understand utterances of sentences containing it. Put that way, many qualifications are needed. To understand an expression, one must be able to understand utterances of sentences containing it, but not all such utterances: a given sentence may contain other words that one does not understand, or it may be too long or too convoluted for one to process. However, I hope it is intuitively clear that the qualification does not defeat the point that a compositional semantics is not needed here.

Anyway, the point about knowledge of meaning, though on the right track, is still ancillary to our need to explain the Platitude without assuming that natural languages have compositional semantics. To explain the Platitude we want to assign some property to each sentence that may in some sense be regarded as determinative of its meaning, and then to assign properties to each of the sentence's "semantically relevant" parts that are determinative of the property assigned to the sentence. But we are having trouble finding this meaning-determinative property of sentences: there seems not to be *any* way of completing 'The sentence "She gave it to him" means . . .'!

Let us say that a "complete sentence" is a sentence that cannot occur as part of another sentence: 'Snow is white.' is a complete sentence; 'snow is white' is not. And let us say that the *saying potential* of a complete sentence in a population P is all that could be said by an utterance of it in P, in a sense of 'could' that abstracts from the fact that perhaps nothing could be said by the sentence owing to its content ('I do not exist.'), its length, or its convolutedness. The saying potential of a complete sentence is a property of it that is suitably determinative of its meaning.

Let us further say that the saying potential of an expression (word, phrase, or sentence) or syntactic construction is the contribution it makes to the saying potentials of the infinitely many complete sentences that contain it. If, as one is wont to say, the meaning of an expression is its contribution to the meanings of the sentences in which it occurs, then we should not hesitate to see the saying potential of an expression as being suitably determinative of its meaning.

Clearly, the saying potential of a complex expression is determined by its syntax and the saying potentials of its component parts. Our question is whether we can account for this without supposing natural languages to have compositional semantics.

But surely we can. What we may call the *processing role* of an expression in a population is a property of the expression that is determinative of its saying potential in the population. We may think first of the processing role of an expression in a person, for a population is just a sum of persons. There are two aspects to the processing role of an expression in a person. The first has to do with the person's capacity to use the expression to say something, and the second with his capacity to understand utterances of sentences containing the expression. In sections 7.4 and 7.5 I described Harvey's ability to understand utterances in E, his ability to go from the belief that a certain sentence was uttered to a belief about what was said in, that utterance, and therewith I described the understanding aspect of the processing role each expression of E has in Harvey. It is easier to make armchair speculations about the processing involved in language under-standing than about the processing involved in speech production; but I shall assume that this much is reasonably clear: if (as I tried to show) no compositional semantics is needed to explain Harvey's ability to under-stand utterances in E, then (as I did not try to show) none will be needed to explain his ability to say things in E. If we can explain without pre-supposing a compositional semantics the journey of an utterance of a sentence from its auditory perception to a representation in the belief-box of what was said in the utterance, then we can tell what is relevantly the same sort of story about the journey that begins with beliefs and intentions and ends with the utterance of the sentence. And it may be a crucial part of the story that the utterance of the sentence was caused by the belief and intention that, in uttering the sentence, the speaker would be saying such-and-such. Suppose now that the processing role of a sentence σ for Harvey was such that upon hearing an utterance of σ, he would conclude (*ceteris paribus*) that the speaker said it was raining, and that if he, Harvey, were to utter σ it would (*ceteris paribus*) also be with the intention to be, and the belief that he was, saying that it was raining. This would fix the saying potential of σ in Harvey's idiolect (as that by the utterance of which one could say that it was raining), and if the processing role prevailed throughout Harvey's linguistic community, then the processing role of σ in that population would fix the saying potential of σ in it.

Each language has a finite basis, in this sense: there will be a finite number of words and structures in the language whose processing roles determine the processing role of each expression in the language. Since processing role determines saying potential, we could repeat the last point with 'saying potential' substituted for 'processing role'. As the case of Harvey virtually shows, the fact that the expressions of a language have processing roles does not presuppose that the language has a compositional semantics. ("Virtually" because we only glossed the aspect of processing roles involved in Harvey's capacity to understand utterances.) I conclude, therefore, that we do not need to assume that natural languages have compositional semantics in order to explain the Platitude.

Perhaps I might bring this conclusion to bear on my reason for denying that natural languages have compositional semantics in the following way. The sentence 'Michael believes that his car was stolen' has a saying potential among speakers of English: it can be used to say that (a certain) Michael believes that his car was stolen, and the people to whom that is said have the capacity to know that that was said. So the sentence has meaning. The verb 'believes', as it functions in the sentence, also has meaning; for it has a processing role and, *ipso facto*, a saying potential, and the saying potential of the sentence is partly determined by it. Indeed, the verb 'believes' is plausibly a semantic primitive, in that its saying potential is not determined by that of any of its parts. But it is not a semantic primitive in any sense appropriate to a compositional semantics, for no base axiom, no satisfaction clause, can be written for 'believes' that could take its place in a true truth theory for English. This does not, we have seen, prevent an utterance of 'Michael believes that his car was stolen' from being true just in case Michael believes that his car was stolen. For lack of a compositional semantics does not prevent a speaker from saying, in uttering the sentence, that Michael believes that his car was stolen; and if that is said, then what is said, and so the utterance, is true if and only if Michael believes that his car was stolen. That 'believes' has a saying potential means that it makes its contribution to the meaning and hence the truth conditions of a class of sentences; but from this it does not follow that 'believes' expresses or denotes anything, or has specifiable satisfaction conditions.

The concern of this section has been the question of whether there is a reason for supposing natural languages to have compositional semantics that is independent of a concern with language understanding. It seemed plausible that this should focus on the platitude that the meaning of a complex expression is determined by its syntax and the meanings of its component parts, and I tried to show how one could account for that platitude without presupposing a compositional semantics. I now want to consider two further questions that the preceding discussion may have generated in the mind of the reader. I think that the answers to both questions are implicit in the position as already developed, but I hope that clarity may be served by making them explicit (even at the risk of redundancy).

Scott Soames (1987, in press) would agree that a compositional semantics is not needed to explain language understanding; in his terms, "one should not look to semantics for an account of semantic competence." But he does think that natural languages have compositional semantics, and he continues:

> Instead, one should look to [compositional semantics] for an explication of the representational character of language. The central semantic fact about language is that it is used to represent the world. Sentences do this by systematically encoding information that characterizes the world as being one way or another. [Compositional] semantics is the study of this information, and the principles by which it is encoded.

Perhaps this challenge is not really different from the one that I have been dealing with; but it puts it in a different light, and invites a somewhat different response. So the first question I have in mind is, What exactly is my response to this reason for thinking that natural languages must have compositional semantics? Before trying to answer this I will ask the second question; for the two can be answered together.

I have argued that the saying potentials of the finitely many words and expression-forming operations of a language fix the saying potential of each complex expression of the language, but that this does not presuppose that the language has a compositional semantics. Maybe this caused a "How's that go again?" response, a feeling of paradox. For, on the one hand, the story *chez* Harvey did not seem to presuppose a compositional semantics for his spoken language E (that was the point of the story), and it does follow from the story that the saying potential of each sentence of E is determined by those of its parts and syntax. On the other hand, it may seem that if finitely many saying potentials determine those of every expression of the language, then a finite theory ought to be statable whose theorems ascribe a saying potential to each sentence of the language, a statement of what that sentence can (in principle) be used to say. But if this is so, how could that theory fail to be a compositional semantics in the sense in which I have used that label?

For both questions it all comes down to the semantics, or lack of one, for the language of thought—if I may be allowed to maintain that heuristic. The crucial point about Harvey's neural machine language M was that we did not have to ascribe a compositional semantics to it in order to suppose that, for each sentence of M, its occurrence in Harvey's B-box would realize some particular belief; that is,

$(\mu)(\Sigma P)$ (if μ is a sentence of M and in Harvey's B-box, then Harvey believes that P).

We could discover this via a mapping of formulae of M onto English content sentences (i.e., those that occur in 'that'-clauses)—in effect, a translation from M into English—together with the understanding we already have of English. But none of this would yield a finite theory that, for each formula μ of M, delivers a theorem like

If μ is in Harvey's B-box, then Harvey believes that some snow is purple.

It is simply not possible, I claim, to ascribe *in a finite theory* properties to the expressions and expression-forming operations of M that will entail such theorems. And yet, in a perfectly intuitive sense the expressions of M have "meaning." We may say that the sentence 'Nemrac seveileb taht emos wons si elprup' means that Carmen believes that some snow is purple, because its occurrence in Harvey's B-box would realize the belief that Carmen believes that some snow is purple. And we should be happy to ascribe meaning to 'seveileb', for it helps to determine the belief that would be realized by the occurrence in B of any sentence of M which contains that term: if $\ulcorner \ldots$ seveileb $\ldots \urcorner$ is in the B-box, then Harvey believes that ... believes .... That is to say, what belief is realized in Harvey when a sentence μ occurs in B is determined by μ's words and syntax. So, if the meaning of an expression is its contribution to the meanings of the sentences in which it occurs, then the expressions of M have meaning. But, while "the contribution that word w makes to the meanings of the sentences of M in which it occurs" is, I suppose, a property of it (pleonastically speaking, of course), it is not a property that can be ascribed in a finite theory: we could only state the property by assigning to each sentence of M that contains w the particular belief with which it is correlated, and that is not something that can be done in a finite way.

Now the formulae of M are mental *representations*: they represent external states of affairs. Sentences of E, Harvey's spoken language, get their representational character via their liaisons with mental representations. Consequently, if, as I have argued, there is no good reason forthcoming from the theory of intentionality to think that a compositional semantics is needed for Mentalese, then Soames is wrong, and none is needed to account for how our sentences represent external states of affairs. This point was already contained in the point as applied to saying potentials; for the representational character of a natural-language sentence is not to be distinguished from its saying potential.

And we also answer the second question (if there was ever really a legitimate question there). For what was just said about the meaning of subsentential expressions in M applies, *mutatis mutandis*, to the saying potentials of subsentential expressions in E, and this could not be otherwise, as the saying potential of an E word is determined by the "meaning" of its Mentalese correlate in the *lingua mentis* M.

8.3 On the Tenability of Meaning Theories without Compositional Truth-Theoretic Semantics

Suppose it to be granted that natural languages do not have compositional truth-theoretic semantics. Might natural languages nevertheless have meaning theories that are not compositional truth-theoretic semantics?

The question, unfortunately, inherits the vagueness of our informal characterization of what a meaning theory for a particular language is supposed to be—namely, a finitely stable theory of the language that "gives the meaning" of each complex expression in it on the basis of assignments of "meaning" to its simple expressions and syntactic constructions. We would be defining the issue too narrowly to capture all that was potentially of interest if we so understood the notion of a meaning theory that the statement of one in English had to employ the word 'meaning'. What we do want to insist on, however, if we are to understand anything by 'meaning theory', is a theory that, from a finite basis, ascribes a property to each sentence of the language that fixes its meaning in the language, and I can think of no better way of capturing this requirement than Davidson's definition of a meaning theory for a particular language as a finitely stable theory that "explicitly states something knowledge of which would suffice for interpreting utterances of speakers of the language to which it applies" (1976, p. 171).

Actually, there are two questions we should ask now. First, is there any good reason to suppose that each natural language must have a correct meaning theory? And second, is there any good reason to suppose that *no* natural language has a correct meaning theory? I think that the answer to the first question must be no, if the arguments *chez* Harvey about the need for compositional truth-theoretic semantics are correct. For the upshot of that discussion was that we have no compelling reason at all—neither from the theory of intentionality nor from the theory of language understanding nor from the need to account for the Platitude—to think that M enjoys a finitely stable theory that entails, for each sentence of M, a true statement reporting exactly what belief Harvey would have if that sentence were in his *B*-box; a truth, that is, such as

If μ were in B, then Harvey would believe that some snow is purple.

But without a reason to suppose that M enjoys such a finite meaning theory, there is none to suppose that there is a finitely statable theory of Harvey's public language E that issues in theorems ascribing to each sentence of E its saying potential. But then how could a theory of E be a meaning theory for E in Davidson's sense if knowledge of what the theory stated did not apprise us of the saying potential of each of its sentences? So I am inclined to suppose that the first question must be answered negatively.

Matters are less clear as regards the second question. My objection to the hypothesis that each natural language has a correct compositional semantics was that it implies a falsehood, namely, the relational theory of propositional attitudes. But I have no general argument—apart from the remark, tendentious in this context, that it is hard to see how a meaning theory could fail to be a compositional (truth-theoretic) semantics—to show that the only tenable way of treating propositional-attitude verbs in a meaning theory (as opposed to a compositional semantics) is as relational predicates true of a person and what she believes, desires, intends, and so forth. It is difficult to speculate about the sort of base clause 'believes' would require in a meaning theory that was not a truth-theoretic semantics, without first having some idea of what such a meaning theory would look like.

What possible theories, then, are brought to mind by our question about the possibility of non–truth-theoretic meaning theories for our spoken and written languages?

"Conceptual-role semantics" may be mentioned, but I shall take this answer, which does not even make sense in application to a natural language unless we think in it, as having already been refuted: see chapter 4, especially section 4.6.

Hintikka's game-theoretical semantics (see, for example, Hintikka 1982 and its bibliography) should probably *not* be mentioned in this context, for although it is of considerable interest it seems not to be a genuine alternative to more conventional theories; as Christopher Peacocke (1978) has shown, game-theoretic rules generate corresponding truth- and model-theoretic axioms.

Then there is Michael Dummett's brief that a meaning theory for a particular language should be given not in terms of truth conditions but in terms of verification conditions. This influential idea is worth considering in connection with the present question, whether one could devise for a language a correct meaning theory that was not a truth-theoretic semantics.

8.4 Meaning Theories without Compositional Truth-Theoretic Semantics: Anti-Realism and Verificationist Semantics

Dummett agrees with Davidson that

> the best method of formulating the philosophical problems surrounding the concept of meaning and related notions is by asking what form that should be taken by what is called 'a theory of meaning' for any one entire language; that is, a detailed specification of the meanings of all the words and sentence-forming operations of the language, yielding a specification of the meaning of every expression and sentence of the language. (Dummett 1975, p. 97)

Even more, Dummett thinks that it is obvious that natural languages have compositional meaning theories; for, in considering what Wittgenstein's stance on the issue may have been, he has also written:

> The idea—if it *is* Wittgenstein's idea—that no systematic theory of meaning is possible is not merely one which is, at the present stage of enquiry, defeatist, but one that runs counter to obvious facts. The fact that anyone who has a mastery of any given language is able to understand an infinity of sentences of that language, an infinity which is, of course, principally composed of sentences which he has never heard before, is one emphasised not only by the modern school of linguists, headed by Chomsky, but by Wittgenstein himself; and this fact can hardly be explained otherwise than by supposing that each speaker has an implicit grasp of a number of general principles governing the use in sentences of words of the language. If, then, there exist such general principles of which every speaker has an implicit grasp, and which serve to confer on the words of the language their various meanings, it is hard to see how there can be any theoretical obstacle to making those principles explicit; and an explicit statement of those principles an implicit grasp of which constitutes the mastery of the language would be, precisely, a complete theory of meaning for the language. (1978, p. 451)

But while Dummett agrees with Davidson that every language has a correct meaning theory, he does not agree with Davidson that the core of a meaning theory will be a theory of *truth* for the language. For Dummett a meaning theory of a particular language will be built, not around a recursive specification of the truth conditions of the sentences of the language, but around a recursive specification of their *verification conditions*.

It does not obviously follow, however, that a meaning theory of this form will not also be a compositional truth-theoretic semantics in my relaxed sense. For the theory, in determining verification conditions, may also be determining truth conditions in whatever sense the verificationist thinks utterances can have them (cf. Dummett 1978, preface). At the same time, it is not clear that a verificationist semantics would be truth-theoretic in any sense, in part because it is not yet sufficiently clear what a verificationist semantics would look like. At any rate, I must confess to having had a standard truth theory (one that assigns sets of *n*-tuples as extensions of predicates) in mind when I objected that the relational theory of propositional attitudes was false, but that it would be true if natural languages had compositional truth-theoretic semantics. Maybe this is not such a good objection when truth is explained in terms of verification. So the matter is worth looking into; and anyway, we were bound to consider Dummett's views on meaning at some point or other.

Can we, then, discern in Dummett's writings the form of a meaning theory for a particular language to which the falsity of the relational theory of propositional attitudes would not be an objection? Even better, does Dummett have any viable suggestion about the form that a meaning theory for a particular language should take? For if he does, and if it should require the relational theory of propositional attitudes, then we would have in any event to weigh the considerations in favor of verificationist semantics against the case against the relational theory.

We cannot properly understand Dummett's positive speculations about semantics without some understanding of the anti-realism that lies behind them.

Realism with respect to a realm of facts holds that sentences that state those facts may be true even though we are not able to put ourselves in a situation in which we are capable of recognizing that they are true. Such a sentence has, in other words, a "recognition-transcendent" truth condition: a truth condition that transcends our capacity to recognize that it obtains, if it obtains (or that it does not obtain, if it does not obtain). Realism, then, is "a metaphysical assumption—an assumption of the existence of an objective reality independent of our knowledge" (Dummett 1978, p. 121).

Realism is the philosophy of common sense. An argument is needed to get someone not to suppose that 'Thales did not begin to walk until he was thirteen months old' or 'A delicatessen will never be built on the present location of the White House' may be true even though there is nothing he can do now to discover whether or not either of these sentences is true.

Realism, Brian Loar (1987, in press) points out, is also a consequence of the science we accept. It is a consequence of our scientific view of the nature of the world and our capacities for gaining information about it. For our ability to verify statements about physical objects is dependent on quite contingent facts about us and our relation to physical objects (facts, for example, about the way receptor cells in our eyes react to light and about the atmosphere through which light travels); and it is a consequence of our theories that a change in these contingent facts would not affect the facts that we are now able to recognize only because of these contingencies; and this allows us to affirm that things may be thus-and-so even though we are not capable of recognizing that they are that way, which is realism. In Loar's words, "for the relevant range of statements s, the verifiability of s ... is dependent on natural contingencies in such a way that it is a natural or scientific possibility that s be true even if not verifiable."

With so much to be said for realism, why does Dummett deny it? I must confess I have not been able to find the full answer to this question; but something like the following seems to be part of it. (1) The truth in the slogan that meaning is use requires that one's knowledge of the meaning of a sentence be capable of being fully manifested in actual linguistic practice. (2) Now the realist is one who claims, or is constrained to claim, that to know the meaning of a declarative sentence is sometimes to know that the sentence is true just in case a certain condition obtains, where that truth condition is recognition-transcendent. (3) This may be, but then it follows that knowledge of truth conditions, when that is what knowledge of meaning consists in, must be capable of being fully manifested in actual linguistic practice. (4) And it is here that the realist confronts a problem; for it would appear that the only way one's knowledge of a sentence's truth condition could be thus manifested would be in one's displayed re-cognition that the condition obtained (displayed, perhaps, by one's saying, "The sentence is true," in circumstances in which one recognizes that the condition obtains) or that it did not obtain. (5) Therefore, it would appear that realism is false: the realist, by definition, is committed to our having knowledge of recognition-transcendent truth conditions, and to our *under-standing* of certain sentences as consisting in such knowledge; but this evidently means that the knowledge cannot be fully manifested in actual linguistic behavior, which means that it cannot be that in which knowledge of meaning—i.e., sentence understanding—consists.

Despite the validity of this argument, there are problems with each of its three premises.

Premise 2 is in the best shape, but it is hardly obvious. Realism is true provided that there is some sentence σ and some condition C such that (i) C is recognition-transcendent and (ii) σ is true iff C obtains. Acceptance of the right-hand side of that definition is what makes one a realist, and it says nothing about meaning or language understanding. So why must a realist hold that one's understanding of any sentence *consists in* one's knowledge of truth conditions? Why must a realist hold any particular theory of meaning? (Cf. Devitt 1984.)

I must confess to being very sympathetic to this response. As is perhaps becoming apparent, I do not think that there is *any* correct and nontrivial account of what understanding a sentence "consists in"; and at the same time, I am a realist, for I think that it may well be that Thales did not begin to walk until he was thirteen months old, even though I have no way of putting myself in a position to verify that. Nevertheless, there is something to be said on behalf of premise 2. For it is arguable that if one understands the sentence 'Thales did not begin to walk until he was thirteen months old', then one knows that if that sentence can be used to say anything, then it can be used to say that Thales did not begin to walk until he was thirteen months old. But then, trivially, one knows that what would be said by an utterance of the sentence is true just in case Thales did not begin to walk until he was thirteen months old. Whether this is enough for Dummett's purposes is another matter, one that depends on the way to interpret premises 1 and 4 and, once interpreted, the argument for them. But here we are in darker waters.

Premises 1 and 4 are hardly self-contained. A philosopher coming to them without special instruction in Dummett's writings would have little idea of what to make of them, and the little idea he would have would probably be wrong. Certainly questions would arise. How, precisely, is the manifestation demand to be construed, and what argument is there for it? What exactly is it to "recognize" that a condition obtains and to "display" that recognition? And, once these questions are answered, why is displayed recognition of the obtaining of a truth condition the only way that the manifestation demand can be met? It is not absurd to suppose that sentence understanding is a practical skill, and thus something that is manifestable (as being able to speak Italian is manifestable by one's actually conversing in Italian, or being able to water-ski by one's actually water-skiing). But then, the uninitiated philosopher may wonder, why could one not manifest one's understanding of the sentence about Thales by using it to assert that he did not begin to walk until he was thirteen months old, or by interpreting an utterance of the sentence as such an assertion, when it was? For what skill could the understanding of a sentence be if not the skill of being able to use the sentence to say what it says, and to know what others are saying when they use it? And why is it necessary that one's recognition of the obtaining of a truth condition be capable of being *displayed*? One would think that mere recognition that the sentence's truth condition obtained would suffice for manifesting one's knowledge that the sentence had that truth condition.

It is clear, in reading Dummett, that he believes that there is a correct general theory of meaning that (a) conveys what he means by his require-ment that understanding be "capable of being fully manifested in actual linguistic practice," (b) provides a good reason for the imposition of that requirement, and (c) motivates, without begging the question, the claim that, as regards knowledge of truth conditions, the manifestation condition could only be met by the behavior alluded to in (4). But I am unable to piece together that theory—especially to piece it together such that it does not imply a version of behaviorism that is utterly implausible.

What one mostly needs to understand is Dummett's understanding of the sense in which meaning is determined by "use," and how this leads to the view that knowledge of truth conditions is a specific recognitional capacity: "the ability to recognise, if appropriately placed, circumstances which do, or do not, fulfil the truth-conditions of a sentence and to be prepared accordingly to assent to, or withhold assent to, its assertion" (Wright 1976, p. 224). As regards the slogan that meaning is use, this much is clear: for Dummett, "the sense of a word is uniquely determined by the observable features of its linguistic employment . . .; it follows that a grasp of its sense is fully manifested by the manner in which the speaker employs it" (Dummett 1976, p. 135), and is something that is "directly displayed by our linguistic practice" (Dummett 1978, p. iii). But what is one to make of "observable features of linguistic employment," and what counts as one's understanding of a word being "directly displayed in linguistic practice"? Does Dummett suppose that a description of word use in purely behavioral, nonsemantic and nonpsychological terms could suffice to entail that a particular word had a certain meaning, and that knowledge of that barren description could convey the word's sense? But surely Dummett cannot hold something so manifestly implausible. And yet, he does seem to hold that there could be some description of the actual linguistic behavior of a population of speakers that did "not invoke psychological or semantic concepts, but [was] couched entirely in terms of what [was] open to out-ward view" (Dummett 1978, p. 446), which description not only entailed correct ascriptions of meaning to the expressions of the language, but was also such that knowledge of the description was adequate to provide an understanding of the language—even to creatures who did not possess our semantic and psychological concepts.[2] Even Dummett's colleague John McDowell understands him thus: according to Dummett, according to McDowell (1981, p. 237), it must be possible to give a description of our linguistic practice that would convey its point and significance to a cosmic exile; that is, to an intelligent Martian who could not be supposed to share, prior to his possession of the description, our semantic and psychological concepts. And McDowell takes it to be an objection to Dummett's position that " 'intentional' (content-specifying) discourse is not reducible to 'non-intentional' discourse." (p. 238).

Let us waive the question of why anyone should attach the slightest degree of credibility to that sort of behaviorism, and ask instead how it is supposed to lead to premise 4, or, more generally, to the view that sentence understanding consists in "knowing what recognisable circumstances determine [a sentence] as true or false" (Dummett 1978, p. 23). How, that is, does one get from *behaviorism* to *anti-realism*? Actually there are two puzzles here. First: In glossing sentence understanding as something that is capable of being manifested in a certain kind of *recognition*, Dummett is helping himself to full-blooded psychological notions: recognition is a form of knowledge, which in turn entails belief. What sort of description in nonpsychological terms will entail, let alone convey, that a person is now "recognizing" that such-and-such condition obtains? Second, even if we suppose that behaviorism is true and that, therefore, one's understanding of a sentence must be something that is capturable in a statement couched wholly in behavioristically acceptable, nonpsychological, and nonsemantic terms, how does one reach the further conclusion that that purified statement must ascribe a capacity that could only be manifested in the "displayed recognition" that a certain condition obtained which determined the sentence as true or as false?

Lest I be accused of the sin, of the type most often committed by readers of Wittgenstein, of naively ascribing a "crude behaviorism" to Dummett, let me hasten to add that I am not ascribing anything to him. I am simply wondering what Dummett's position is. I am wondering what reasons he is supposed to be giving us for thinking that the premises of the above argument are true.

None of this is to question the meaningfulness of Dummett's claim that one's understanding of a declarative sentence consists in the recognitional capacity already described. What is difficult is to find a cogent argument for that position and, *a fortiori*, against realism. When one reads Dummett one has the impression that he is *arriving* at his anti-realism and verificationist theory of meaning from a theory about the way in which meaning is determined by use that is open to outward view and describable in nonsemantic and nonpsychological terms; it is that theory and that argument that is so difficult (for me) to discern.

But Dummett does think that natural languages have meaning theories; and, as he is inclined to think that the meaning of a declarative sentence is the method of its verification, he is also inclined to suppose that the core of a meaning theory for a particular language will be a recursive specification of the verification conditions of the language's declarative sentences.[3] While Dummett acknowledges that "no serious attempt has ever been made to work out such a theory" (1976, p. 68), he does provide some answers to some questions that would naturally arise in response to the suggestion, stated baldly, that a meaning theory should take the form of a recursive specification of verification conditions.

1. "Whether or not someone's knowledge that a given state of affairs obtains can be taken by him as verifying a statement may depend on

his extralinguistic knowledge and may in no sense derive from his mere understanding of the statement. Jones's seeing a certain numeral on the odometer of her car may verify for her the statement that her husband has again been unfaithful; but that requires background information that is irrelevant to an understanding of the statement. How, then, can a *meaning* theory be a theory of verification conditions?" Dummett of course does not suppose that a meaning theory will specify verification conditions that depend, for their being verification conditions, on contingencies that are irrelevant to language understanding. But he does suppose that understanding a declarative sentence consists in a "canonical method of establishing the truth of the sentence" which he calls its "direct verification" (1976, p. 132). Thus the Dummettian hypothesis concerning the form that a meaning theory should take is more accurately put by saying that it will have as its core a recursive specification of each sentence's *direct* verification conditions. In the supposition that sentences *have* direct verification conditions—conditions that one could know to be *verification* conditions for a given sentence just by understanding that sentence—Dummett is knowingly espousing a doctrine that many philosophers, influenced by Quine, would want to deny (see, for example, Quine 1953b).

2. "Surely there are meaningful sentences for which there are no recognizable conditions that would, should they obtain, *establish* the sentence as true or as false. In what sense can such sentences have 'verification' conditions?" Dummett, in his informal glosses of anti-realist semantics, is wont to characterize it in terms of *conclusive* verifiability. The following is typical:

> A verificationist account takes as central to the theory of meaning the ... notion of that by which we can recognise a sentence to be conclusively shown to be true or to be conclusively shown to be false: we know the meaning of a sentence when we are able to recognise it as conclusively verified or as conclusively falsified whenever one or the other of these conditions obtains. (1978, p. 379)

At the same time, Dummett is aware of the problem with this characterization:

> [I]t is misleading to concentrate too heavily ... on a form of anti-realist theory of meaning in which the meaning of a statement is given in terms of what conclusively verifies it; often such conclusive verification is not to be had. (1978, p. xxxviii)

Dummett thus acknowledges that the "verification" conditions constitutive of the meaning of many statements will be defeasible, and in this connection cites with approval the Wittgensteinian idea that understanding

'John is in pain' involves "knowing that pain-behaviour, or the presence of an ordinarily painful stimulus, is normally a sufficient ground for an ascription of pain, but one that can be rebutted" (Dummett 1978, p. xxxv). For such statements, then, the meaning theory would have to assign to them both the defeasible criteria and their defeasibility conditions. Most empirical judgments (such as 'That's a dog') must fall into this class.

3. "We know what sorts of semantic values have to be assigned to the nonlogical constants of a language in the base clauses of a truth-conditional semantics. But what will these assignments be like in a verificationist semantics?" Dummett has suggested that a verificationist semantics will assign to each one-place predicate "an effective means of recognizing, for any given object, a conclusive demonstration that the predicate applies to that object" (1976, p. 127), it being implicit that this would apply, *mutatis mutandis*, to predicates of any degree; and he has made analogous suggestions about the meanings of singular terms (see, for example, 1973, passim). The stricture about conclusive demonstration would, however, have to be modified in accordance with the concession of the preceding paragraph.

Although many more questions would have to be answered to bring the Dummettian proposal into the full light of day, enough has already been said to enable one to object to it.

Two questions must be answered affirmatively if natural languages have correct meaning theories that are recursive specifications of "direct verification conditions." Is there for each meaningful declarative sentence of a language a direct verification condition such that one would understand the sentence if one knew that the condition was a direct verification condition for the sentence? (I.e., is to know the sense of a sentence to know the method of "directly" verifying it?) If there is, are these direct verification conditions specifiable in a finite, and thus recursive, theory of the language? Since this second question does not really arise unless an affirmative answer to the first is presupposed, I shall turn directly to why I am doubtful that that can be presupposed. Are there, then, meaningful declarative sentences for which there do *not* seem to be direct verification conditions knowledge of which would suffice for an understanding of those sentences? I think the following sentences are reasonable candidates:

[a]   Thales did not begin to walk until he was thirteen months old.

[b]   Betty believes that Australians drink too much.

[c]   Uranium-235 releases an average of 2.5 neutrons per fission.

[d]   That ring is gold.

[e]   Fido is a dog.

a. What could [a]'s direct verification condition possibly be? In order for a condition to be a "direct verification condition" we must be capable of recognizing whether or not it obtains, and Dummett thinks that sentences about the past provide a difficulty for the realist precisely because we cannot assume that for such a sentence or its negation a direct verification condition obtains. But his verificationist theory of meaning requires him to suppose that [a] has a direct verification condition: a condition which *might* obtain, and which is such that if we recognized that it obtained, then we would also know, just from our understanding of [a], that the condition verified it to some degree. Suppose we discovered some written work from the time of Thales that said, perhaps among other things, that Thales did not begin to walk until he was thirteen months old, and suppose we decided that the document provided some degree of evidence for the truth of [a]. How could it plausibly be said that one's mere understanding of [a] equipped one to recognize that the existence of such a document would to any degree verify the statement about Thales? Surely an appreciation of the potential evidential value of ancient documents requires knowledge that goes beyond what is required for an understanding of sentences about when people began to walk. Now we often verify or falsify statements about the past by consulting the present memories of ourselves or others. Could this be the meaning-constituting method of verification we apply to [a] only to find that it yields neither a verification nor a falsification? That might make sense if we knew what to count as recognizing a memory as a memory of Thales. Knowing the meaning of [a] is supposed to consist in one's having a canonical method of verifying it; but it is by no means clear that we have any such method at all.

b. Sentences that ascribe beliefs, such as [b] ('Betty believes that Australians drink too much'), may be in the same boat. Certainly we are often capable of verifying such sentences; but what is at issue is whether we can assign to [b], and to every other sentence like it, a finite set of conditions whose members

1. are recognizable (i.e., can be recognized to obtain whenever they do obtain);
2. include conditions that are verification conditions for [b], and recognizable as such just from an understanding of [b];
3. include whatever annulling conditions the direct verifications have, should they be defeasible, where the annulling conditions are recognizable as such just from an understanding of [b];
4. are such that it suffices for understanding [b] to know the conditions satisfying (2) and (3), and to know that they satisfy them.

How might we know that Betty believes that Australians drink too much? Well, we may have heard her assert that they do; or we may have inferred her belief from other beliefs that we know her to have; or we may have inferred it from her behavior together with various beliefs and desires that we know her to have. Always our evidence for the truth of [b] seems to include facts about Betty's other propositional attitudes; it seems unlikely that our evidence could consist *solely* of facts statable in nonpsychological terms. Yet the requirement of recognizability, (1), excludes conditions about propositional attitudes from the set of conditions assigned to [b] by the correct verificationist meaning theory for English— unless it may be assumed that propositional-attitude facts are reducible to facts that are statable in nonpsychological, patently recognizable terms. For it is essential to Dummett's anti-realism and his verificationist alternative to truth-conditional semantics that verification conditions be conditions that we are capable of recognizing as obtaining whenever they do obtain. This explains why the canonical verification condition for [b] could not be a condition that was only statable thus: it is the condition that Betty believes that Australians drink too much. Of the conditions that enter into the verification of belief attributions, the only ones that have any claim to satisfying the recognizability requirement are those that pertain only to outwardly observable behavior, nonpsychologically described. But now we must ask, How plausible is it to suppose that conditions 1–4 could be satisfied by conditions that were statable in behavioral but nonpsychological terms?

There is a further problem with the accommodation of [b] in compositional verificationist semantics: the latter, like compositional truth-theoretic semantics, seems to require the relational theory of propositional attitudes, and that theory, I have argued, is false. That 'believes' must be treated as a relational predicate true of believers and what they believe seems inescapable if Dummett has given the correct account of how predicates would be treated in the base clauses of a verificationist meaning theory. For according to Dummett, one first determines a predicate as being, for some n, an n-place predicate, and then sees its base clause as specifying for it a procedure for recognizing whether the predicate applies to any given n-tuple of objects. Since meaning theories are finite, they cannot recognize an infinity of semantically primitive one-place belief predicates ('believes that flounders snore', 'believes that Australians drink too much', and the like), but must, refinements aside, treat 'believes' as a semantically primitive two-place predicate with application to believers and the things they believe—whatever those things might be.

c. Dummett, to the best of my knowledge, gives no idea of what he thinks the verificationist should say about theoretical statements such as [c] ('Uranium-235 releases an average of 2.5 neutrons per fission'), and I find it difficult to see what the verificationist *could* say. In order for a verification condition for [c] to satisfy the recognizability requirement, it would have to be statable in terms of nontheoretical, manifestly observable conditions, and the puzzle is how a grasp of such conditions could ever yield an understanding of [c]. This puzzle persists even if one supposes—what may not even be very plausible—that theoretical terms are definable à la the methods of Ramsey (1929) and Lewis (1970a) in terms of directly observational concepts. For although such a definition yields a reduction of the theoretical to the nontheoretical, it does not of itself determine a direct verification condition for each sentence involving a theoretical term. It looks as if a direct verification for [c] would somehow have to summarize, at the least, all of the evidence for the presently reigning theory of nuclear physics that is statable in terms of conditions that we are guaranteed to recognize as obtaining whenever they do obtain; conditions, evidently, statable in wholly "observational" terms. Even if this could be done, let alone done by assignments to terms like 'neutron' and 'fission' in a finitely axiomatized theory, it seems incredible that we could ever come to understand [c] on such a paltry basis; as incredible, surely, as the analogous thought, just considered, that our understanding of propositional-attitude sentences could consist wholly in a knowledge of the behavioral evidence for them. One might as well suppose that one could arrive at the correct physics just by being given an inventory of all actual and possible evidence stated in nontheoretical, observational terms.

d. One trouble with [d] ('That ring is gold') is that most people who understand it have nothing that even begins to approximate to being "an effective means of recognizing, for any given object, a conclusive demonstration that ['gold'] applies to that object" (Dummett 1976, p. 127). Many people who understand [d] do not even know that gold is a metal, and they have no idea that the criterion for being gold is being a metal that has atomic number 79. When these people believe that a thing is gold, they are making an inference from its color, nature, and price (it is an expensive yellow ring), or they are relying on the authority of others whom they suppose capable of determining if a substance is gold. What, then, might be the direct verification condition for [d]? Apropos of this Dummett has written:

> The division of linguistic labour is a fact of which notice must be taken in any account of language as a social phenomenon. The meaning of the word 'gold' ... is fully conveyed neither by a description of the criteria employed by the experts nor by a description of those used by ordinary speakers; it involves both, and a grasp of the relationship between them. (1978, p. 427)

Thus the direct verification condition for [d]—the condition assigned to it by the correct compositional verificationist semantics for English—must somehow capture the fact that the "experts'" criterion for gold is being a metal that has atomic number 79, as well as the reliance of nonspecialists on the authority of those who are able to wield the technical criterion. But a direct verification condition must pass the recognizability test—one (in this case the expert) must be capable of recognizing that it obtains if it does obtain—and this throws us back onto the problem raised by [c]: Can we really be assured of a direct verification condition for 'That has atomic number 79', a condition capable of being recognized whenever it obtains, and such that knowledge that it is the direct verification condition for the theoretical sentence 'That has atomic number 79' will suffice for under-standing the sentence?

e. When we verify a sentence like [e]—when, that is, we come to believe that a thing is a dog—we do so on the basis of the thing's observable features, the way it looks and moves. But these observational conditions are doubly defeasible, as they provide neither a necessary nor a sufficient condition for a thing's being a dog (see section 3.3). If the direct verification condition for [e] includes these defeasible conditions, then it must also include the conditions that would defeat them; and these defeating con-ditions must be ones that we are capable of recognizing whenever they obtain. But I doubt that such defeating conditions can be specified. One problem is that it is not clear that there is any closed list of defeating conditions; but let us waive that, to the advantage of the verificationist, and assume that the criterion for being a dog is belonging to that biological natural kind to which all and only dogs in fact belong (assuming also, of course, that there is such a natural kind). Then it may seem that [e] inherits the problems of [d], since a final determination of whether a thing is a dog depends on knowledge beyond the ken of nearly everyone. But the situation is actually worse; for in the case of biological natural kinds such as *Canis familiaris* even the "experts" seem not to have any way of de-termining decisively whether a thing is a dog, as *they* have no way of identifying the biological species other than as the species of those things which they judge to be dogs by the same criteria everyone else uses. So one wonders what the direct verification condition for [e] could possibly look like.

I think we may reach a general statement of why the prospects of a verificationist semantics do not look good. Consider any concept, the concept of an apple, for example, and consider all the things that are true of it: its role in deductive and inductive and practical reasoning; its rela-tions to other concepts; its defining conditions, if any; and all that may be regarded as potential evidence for the truth of beliefs involving it. Now subtract everything but the potential evidence. Next subtract from the potential evidential conditions all those that are not statable in an obser-vational vocabulary that would secure that the evidential conditions could not possibly obtain without its being possible to recognize that they obtain. Now subtract from that class all the conditions whose evidential status depends on knowledge that is not secured merely by possession of the concept in question (the evidence must be "direct"). Is there a class of conditions that remains? It is hardly certain that there is; but let us suppose that there is and ask this next question. Will a grasp of the remaining conditions, together with the knowledge that they were arrived at in the foregoing way from *some* concept, suffice for a grasp of that concept? Surely not; the identity conditions for the concept will not be the same as those for the class of evidential conditions arrived at unless the concept reduces, in the ways of phenomenalism or behaviorism, to the evidence for it, which will certainly not in general be the case. This means that the "direct verification conditions" for a sentence (if it even has any) cannot capture its *content*; they cannot convey the content of the belief one would have if one accepted the sentence as true because they cannot convey the concepts determinative of that belief. And if a sentence's direct verification conditions cannot yield its content, then a theory that specifies for each sentence of a language its direct verification conditions will fall far short of being a meaning theory of the language, a theory that "explicitly states something knowledge of which would suffice for interpreting utterances of speakers of the language to which it applies" (Davidson 1976, p. 171).

The question that provoked all this was whether there is any good reason for or against supposing natural languages to have compositional meaning theories that are not compositional truth-theoretic semantics. Immediately after raising it I said that there seemed not to be any good reason for thinking that natural languages must have correct meaning theories, but the question arose whether there is any positive reason, as there is against compositional truth-theoretic semantics, for supposing that there cannot be correct meaning theories. It is, I acknowledged, hard to see how there could be such meaning theories. For if knowledge of a theory really sufficed to enable one to understand utterances in the language that the theory was about, then knowledge of the theory would enable one to know the saying potential of the sentences of the language. But knowing this, for declarative sentences, would be tantamount to knowing the truth conditions of utterances that could have them; and how could such a theory fail to be, in the sense stipulated, a compositional semantics? Still, I asked what a meaning theory that was not a compositional semantics would look like. Really the only candidate to present itself was the Dummettian proposal, with which I have lately dealt. Of course I must leave open whether there might not be forthcoming a plausible proposal for the form of a meaning theory according to which such a theory would clearly not be truth-theoretic and would clearly not be threatened by the falsity of the relational theory of propositional attitudes. At the same time, one cannot help feeling that if natural languages have correct meaning theories of any sort, then there ought to be some good reason for supposing that that is so—and what might that reason be?

8.5 *What There Is, Substitutional Quantification, and Compositional Semantics*

It has already been observed how my denial of the CS theory relates in a crucial way to my denial of the relational theory of propositional attitudes: my anti-relationalism is highly implausible if natural languages have compositional truth-theoretic semantics. The same is true, as will now be shown, of my denial of Platonic Realism: it, too, turns out to be plausible only if natural languages do not have compositional semantics. (Actually, I have officially argued against Platonic Realism only as regards propositional-attitude properties, but this restraint will be ignored in the ensuing discussion.) The elaboration and defense of this will solve a still outstanding question: how denying the relational theory is consistent with the validity of 'So-and-so believes that such-and-such; so, there is something that so-and-so believes'.

Let us begin with the issue of Platonic Realism, and the following caricature of that position. As regards the sentence

[a]   Mother Teresa is humble,

the Realist says, we must recognize four distinct entities. First, there is Mother Teresa; this selfless woman is an objective, language-independent entity. Her existence in no way depends on language, let alone on there being a term that refers to her, and one may have knowledge of her that is prior to one's knowledge that 'Mother Teresa', or any other singular term, refers to her. Second, and on the linguistic side, we have the singular term 'Mother Teresa'. This entity refers to Mother Teresa; that is,

Refers('Mother Teresa', Mother Teresa),

which canonical representation makes explicit that in the fact that the name refers to the bearer we have a fact that involves two distinct entities and a certain relation between them. In order to understand [a] and know the truth that it expresses, one must be acquainted with the singular term 'Mother Teresa' and with the person Mother Teresa, and know that the first refers to the second. The sequence of marks 'Mother Teresa' has its meaning in the fact that it refers to Mother Teresa, and an understanding of the term, and of the sentences in which it occurs, demands that one know of the sequence and of the person that the first stands in the contingent reference relation to the second.

The third and fourth entities are humility, the property of being humble, and the adjective 'humble', and much of what was said about the first two entities may, the Realist claims, also be said about these second two. Like Mother Teresa, humility is objective and language-independent; humility, though, is unlike the woman in not occupying space, in having no beginning or end in time, in existing in all possible worlds, and in being instantiated by Mother Teresa and other "particulars." And as with one's epistemic contact with Mother Teresa, one may have acquaintance with the property of being humble that is language-independent, that is independent of one's knowing any term that expresses the property. This possibility of prior acquaintance is as essential to the understanding of the term 'humble' as it was to the understanding of the term 'Mother Teresa'. For the predicate expresses the property; that is,

Expresses('humble', the property of being humble),

which canonical representation, like the one before, reveals that the fact which it conveys contains two distinct things joined by a relation; and it is in this fact precisely that the meaning of 'humble' consists. It is in one's knowledge that the term expresses the property that one's understanding of the term consists; without this knowledge one could not understand sentences, such as [a], in which 'humble' occurs. Just as the meaning of 'Mother Teresa' consists in its referring to the language-independent entity Mother Teresa, so the meaning of 'humble' consists in its expressing the language-independent entity humility, the property of being humble.

For the Realist, then, one understands [a] when one sees it as saying, of Mother Teresa and humility, that the first instantiates the second, and in this respect its semantic structure is better revealed by its more explicit paraphrase,

[b]   Mother Teresa has the property of being humble,

in which the second singular term enjys just the same semantic status as the first.

The sensible Nominalist simply denies all this.[4] There is no entity, "the property of being humble," related to 'humble' in anything like the way that Mother Teresa is related to 'Mother Teresa'. Understanding [a] does require awareness of the woman Mother Teresa: to understand an utterance of [a] one would have to know that the speaker was talking about her. But there is no other thing awareness of which is required to understand [a]. There is not to be found among the things that *really exist* anything that may correctly be called "the property of being humble'.

Yet the sensible Nominalist should be wary of saying straightway that there is no property of being humble; let us see why.

He should agree with the Platonic Realist that [b] is a trivial, pleonastic paraphrase of [a]. His *disagreement* comes at the Realist's claim that 'the property of being humble' in [b] is *referential*; that ostensible singular term refers to nothing. The "logical form" of [b] is not

   Fab,

with '*F*' = '*x* has *y*', '*a*' standing for Mother Teresa, and '*b*' for humility. Since [b] is a trivial, pleonastic paraphrase of [a], it has that sentence's logical form,

   Fa,

with '*F*' = '*x* is humble' and '*a*' as before; [a] carries no "ontological commitment" to anything other than a certain woman. At the same time, the sensible Nominalist should acknowledge the validity of the inference from [a], via [b], to

[c]   There is something that Mother Teresa has (viz., humility).

(We have, after all, no compunction in moving from

   Al is humble and Betty is humble

to

   There is some attribute that Al and Betty have in common (viz., humility).)

   But how can [c] follow from [b] if the occurrence of 'the property of being humble' in [b] is nonreferential? The answer, of course, is that the existential quantification in [c] is a *substitutional* quantification:[5] [c] is true because a substitution-instance of 'Mother Teresa has *X*'—namely, [b]—is true; since [b] carries no ontological commitment to properties, neither does [c], for the ontological commitments of an existential substitutional generalization are only those of the true substitution-instances of its quantified open sentence.

   Quine, in "On What There Is," wrote, "One may admit that there are red houses, roses, and sunsets, but deny, *except as a popular and misleading manner of speaking,* that they have anything in common" (1953a, p. 10; my emphasis). The "popular and misleading [to whom?] manner of speaking" in which one can say truly that there is something (viz., the color red) that red houses, roses, and sunsets have in common is the 'there is' of substitutional quantification. It is the same 'there is' to be found in 'There was lasciviousness in his grin' and 'There's a good chance that you'll win'; it is the quantifier that allows 'There are many things that don't exist—the Loch Ness Monster, God, Sherlock Holmes' (Lycan 1979). Throughout this book, and throughout the work of most non-Platonistic philosophers, there are ostensible quantifications over properties; in a well-known article Quine wrote that 'is valid' "is a verb attachable to a name of a statement and expressing an attribute of the statement named" (1966, p. 164). But no experienced reader thought that Quine was there committing himself to the existence of attributes. Nor will it do to say that he did not really mean what he wrote; for a *truth* was conveyed. These "ostensible" quantifications over properties provide no real problem because they are not taken as quantifications *over* anything; they are implicitly read, as they are supposed to be, substitutionally.[6] As Quine also wrote, "the idiomatic use of 'there is' in ordinary language knows no bounds comparable to those that might reasonably be adhered to in scientific discourse painstakingly formulated in quantificational terms" (1953c, p. 106). It is understandable, then, that Quine's criterion of ontological commitment is *not*

Theory T is ontologically committed to Fs if T implies 'There are Fs',

but rather

T is ontologically committed to Fs if the correct translation of T into Predicate Logic entails '$(\exists x)Fx$', where '$\exists$' is the existential *objectual* quantifier.

(Cf. Gottlieb 1980.)

Nevertheless, substitutional quantification is no ontological panacea, and a problem confronts the Nominalist who thinks that English has a correct compositional semantics, but who recognizes the following sentences as being the truisms they surely are:

[d]   Humility is a virtue.

[e]   Red resembles orange more than it resembles blue.

Now recognition of the truth of [b] seems not to threaten the Nominalist who subscribes to the CS theory; for he can in his semantics provide for a transformation of [b] into its clearly unthreatening paraphrase [a]. The trouble with [d] and [e], as David Armstrong has rightly emphasized (1978, chap. 6), is that they do not enjoy nominalistically unproblematic paraphrases: [d] does not mean that anyone who is humble is virtuous, and [e] does not mean that red things resemble orange things more than they resemble blue things. It would certainly appear that the only coherent way of having a finitely axiomatized truth theory for English that was consonant with the truth and nonparaphrasability of [d] and [e] would be for that theory to have base axioms that respectively assign as semantic values to the singular terms 'humility', 'red', 'orange', and 'blue' the properties humility, redness, orangeness, and blueness. But [d] and [e] *are* both true and nonparaphrasable, and 'humility', 'red', etc., refer to nothing. The correct response, then, is one to which I am already committed: deny that English has a correct compositional semantics, and therewith deny the need to provide references for the *grammatical* singular terms in [d] and [e].

'Humility' in [d] is no more a referential singular term than 'the property of being humble' is in [b]. Understanding an utterance of [d] is not a matter of being acquainted with the abstract entity that is the referent of 'humility' and knowing that the speaker said of it that it is a virtue.

But what, then, is the "logical form" of [d]? How is it to be rendered in the canonical notation of Predicate Logic? The trouble with these questions is that, as they would ordinarily be intended, they tacitly presuppose that English has a correct compositional semantics. When philosophers ask about the logical form of a sentence, they are usually supposing that each of its semantically relevant parts has a semantical value that helps to determine the sentence's truth value; but this is just what is being denied in the denial that natural languages have compositional semantics. As regards the "translation" of [d] into the Predicate Calculus, I am afraid that the best we can do is 'P'; but it would be a mistake to think that we must be able to do better—the mistake, in essence, of supposing natural languages to have compositional semantics. This is not to deny that these statements have "logical form" in the sense that they enter into inferences by virtue, in part, of their grammatical forms. But it is to deny that these inferences can be accounted for by a model-theoretic treatment that requires a compositional semantics for the sentences in question.

In section 1.3, and again in 7.1, it was noticed that the relational theory of belief was to some degree confirmed (and thus my anti-relationalism to some degree threatened) by familiar grammatical and logical phenomena; by, for example, the validity of

[1]   Odile and Jean-Paul believe that existence precedes essence.
       So, there is something that they both believe.

and

[2]   Odile believes that existence precedes essence.
       That existence precedes essence is the most profound philosophical doctrine of our day.
       Therefore, Odile believes the most profound philosophical doctrine of our day.

But the discussion of Platonic Realism shows how substitutional quantification together with the denial of the CS theory may be used to reveal the consistency of the prima facie problematic phenomena with the denial of the relational theory of propositional attitudes.

'That'-clauses, the bane of those who hope to account for the logical form of belief sentences in conformity with truth-theoretic semantics, are *grammatical* singular terms. This is surely dictated by the second premise in [2], and by sentences such as

[3]   That Ronald Reagan dyes his hair is a vile rumor.

But although 'that'-clauses are singular subject expressions, they are *non-referential*. In this respect they are like singular terms that ostensibly refer to properties. What I want to say about [3] is just what I said about 'Humility is a virtue'. In neither case must recognition of the truth of the sentence force us to find a referent for its grammatical subject expression, although it would if English had a correct compositional semantics; in neither case can translation into the Predicate Calculus do any better than 'P'. All this, of course, is already contained in my denial of the relational theory of 'believes'; that is, in my refusal to represent the logical form of

Odile believes that existence precedes essence

as

B(Odile, that existence precedes essence).

Since 'that'-clauses are not referential singular terms, the quantifier in the conclusion of [1] cannot be an objectual quantifier. But that is all right; it can be a substitutional quantifier.[7]

Since 'that'-clauses are not referential singular terms, neither are the singular terms that we may be assured of substituting *salva veritate* for them. If Teddy Kennedy's worst lie is that Ronald Reagan dyes his hair, then we may use this in conjunction with [3] to derive

Teddy Kennedy's worst lie is a vile rumor,

and what we should say about this sentence is just what we should say about [3] and about [d], 'Humility is a virtue'. This point, too, was already implicit in the just-concluded discussion of Platonic Realism; for if humility is Mother Teresa's most commendable attribute, then we may conclude that

Mother Teresa's most commendable attribute is a virtue

and say about it what we said about [d]. So [2] poses a threat to no position of mine.

Chapter 9
Intention-Based Semantics and the Analysis of Meaning

9.1 Introduction

I hold that there are semantic facts (some marks and sounds have meaning, reference, truth value, and so on) and that there are psychological facts (some creatures have beliefs, desires, intentions, and so on). Less confidently, I still hold that conscious mental states are states of the central nervous system; but little else remains of the nine hypotheses that defined the hypothetical philosopher of chapter 1. Yet, curiously, Intention-Based Semantics, which in a way began this whole discussion, still stands, unrefuted by anything that has so far been said.

True, those who propounded the doctrine thought of the ostensible "propositional" variables that occurred in their definitions (the 'p' in 'S meant that p', for example) as genuine objectual variables, and with the falsity of the relational theory of propositional attitudes that is no longer tenable. But what that is essential to IBS would go if those variables were construed substitutionally?

True, some who were initially drawn to IBS were drawn to it for a reason that, with the ascendancy of Sentential Dualism, can no longer apply—namely, its potential usefulness to the physicalism espoused in the eighth of the original nine hypotheses: a reduction of semantic and psychological facts to physical (or topic-neutral) facts seemed implausible unless there were first a reduction of the semantic to the psychological. But the failure of the eighth hypothesis, Sentential Physicalism, does not imply that semantic concepts cannot be defined in terms of propositional-attitude concepts, and no explication of propositional attitudes has been defended that would find a reliance of belief content on public-language semantic features. And it may seem that, quite independently of any concerns emanating from the mind-body problem, one should expect some sort of explication of the semantic. For consider these two sequences of marks on paper:

snow is white

ℐ ℳ ℭ𝒩.

Qua sequences of marks, there is no relevant difference between them—and yet the first is a sentence of a natural language, it has meaning and a truth value, while none of this is true of the second sequence. This observation is bound to invite the question, What is the relevant difference between these two sequences such that the first, but not the second, has these semantic features? One who asks this question expects to be told what *makes it the case* that the sequence of marks 'snow is white' has, among certain people, such-and-such semantic features. And IBS stands ready to tell him, and in terms that must seem, initially at least, along the right track: in terms of the *use*, intentionally but nonsemantically described, that people make of marks and sounds in behavior we regard as communicative.

IBS stands ready to tell, but when it comes actually to telling in what the semantic features of linguistic items consist, it has, alas, not enough to say; it gets stymied. In later sections of this chapter I shall suggest that this failure of IBS to account for the meanings of linguistic expressions—and, indeed, the failure in this area of any sort of "analysis" of our semantic concepts—was inevitable given a conclusion already reached: that natural languages do not have compositional, finitely statable meaning theories. I shall also speculate about the misguided impulse toward reductive analysis.

When we reach the end of this chapter we shall have reached the end of the critical part of this book. The patient reader who has followed me to that point will be eager to know my positive theory of meaning and intentionality, the theories that I propose to take the place of those against which I have argued. That will be the topic of the final chapter.

9.2 Speaker-Meaning and the Structure of IBS

Intention-Based Semantics is that program in the theory of meaning which was implicitly defined in H. P. Grice's famous article "Meaning" (1957). Its hallmark is that it seeks to define all public-language semantic notions in terms of propositional-attitude concepts that themselves presuppose nothing about meaning in a public language. If the program is correct, then

(1) *speaker-meaning*—essentially, a person's meaning that such-and-such is the case or that so-and-so is to do such-and-such—is noncircularly definable as a certain kind of behavior done with the intention of activating belief or action in another;

and

(2) *expression-meaning*—essentially, the semantic features of natural-language expressions—is noncircularly definable as certain kinds of correlations between marks and sounds and types of acts of speaker-meaning.

The definitions will be noncircular in that the terms in which meaning is explicated will themselves presuppose nothing about the concepts being defined in terms of them. The result of these definitions will be that all questions about the meaning of marks and sounds will have been reduced to questions about the content of propositional attitudes: a sequence of sounds will mean that snow is white in a given population *by virtue of* its being related in a certain way by the practices of that population to certain types of propositional attitudes the content of which is that snow is white.

The account of declarative speaker-meaning originally proposed by Grice may be reconstructed thus:

[S]   S means that *p* in uttering *x* iff, for some person *A* and feature Φ, S intends
   (1) *A* to recognize that *x* has Φ;
   (2) *A* to think, at least partly on the basis of thinking that *x* has Φ, that *S* uttered *x* intending *A* to think that *p*;
   (3) *A* to think, at least partly on the basis of thinking that *S* uttered *x* intending *A* to think that *p*, that *p*.[1]

For example, Sally, facing Adam, utters the sounds 'It's snowing'. Adam recognizes that the sound sequence has this feature: it is a conventional device among speakers of English for meaning that it is snowing. From this, together with other of his beliefs, he (unconsciously and instantaneously) infers that Sally produced those sounds in order to inform him that it was snowing. From this, together with other of his beliefs, he (unconsciously and instantaneously) infers that Sally must believe that it is snowing, and that her belief must have been caused in a certain way (by looking out the window, for instance). From this, together with other of his beliefs, he (unconsciously and instaneously) infers that it is snowing. Since Adam reacted in just the way that Sally, in uttering 'It's snowing', intended him to react, she meant, by the conditions of [S], that it was snowing. It is not to be supposed, of course, that Sally had such complex intentions consciously in mind when she spoke; rather, they are supposed to be tacit expectations that she had in speaking and that explain her speech act. (See Schiffer 1982; Loar 1981, chap. 10.)

It is worth pausing over the feature Φ, which is intended to play the key evidential role in the audience's recognition of the speaker's intention; for it is here, as we shall presently see, that the account of expression-meaning connects with that of speaker-meaning. In Gricean communication the speaker *S* acts with the intention of bringing about a state of affairs that will be for the audience *A* *evidence* that *S* acted with the intention of informing *A* that *p*. *S* looks, so to say, for some feature Φ of something utterable *x*, such that, were she to utter *x*, the fact that *x* has Φ would in the circumstances be taken by *A* to be evidence that *S* uttered *x* intending to get *A* to believe that *p*. If *S* wants to inform *A* that it is snowing, she most likely will not be able to do so by uttering 'blah blah schnickkelflicker'; for that sequence of sounds has no feature that would make an utterance of it evidence that the utterer uttered it with the intention of producing in some present person the belief that it was snowing. But the sentence 'It's snowing' does have such a feature. Now what feature of that sentence—that sequence of sounds—would for certain people make an utterance of it in appropriate circumstances very good evidence that the speaker uttered it with the intention of communicating that it was snowing? Well, one wants to say, its *meaning*, and with this the IBS theorist agrees. But he also wants to say that the sentence has some feature that correlates it with the act of meaning that it is snowing (as defined by the theorist); that this feature is specifiable in wholly nonsemantic and (mostly) psychological terms; that it is this feature that makes an utterance of anything having it (such as the sound sequence 'It's snowing') the best possible evidence that the speaker wants to communicate that it is snowing; and that it is precisely this feature that constitutes the meaning of the sentence 'It's snowing'.

In fact, we may simply take it as definitive of IBS that, for every sentence σ of every natural language *L*, there is some feature Φ, constitutive of the meaning of σ in *L*, such that

(a)   Φ has a specification in wholly psychological terms, which include, in particular, those propositional attitudes deemed by the IBS theorist to be constitutive of speaker-meaning;

(b)   by virtue of having Φ, σ is an especially efficacious device among speakers of *L* for performing acts of speaker-meaning of a certain type;

(c)   σ's having Φ entails that σ has whatever meaning σ happens to have in *L*.

The picture we then get with regard to language understanding is this: a speaker utters a (perhaps novel) sentence σ; an audience hears the utterance and somehow forms the belief that σ has Φ, for some Φ satisfying (a)–(c); from his belief that σ has Φ, together with certain other beliefs, the audience concludes that the speaker, in uttering σ, meant that such-and-such.

That, then, is the mold into which the IBS theorist must pour his account of expression-meaning. And it is its account of expression-meaning, its account of the semantic properties of linguistic items, that must test the program of IBS. But before turning to that we must finish our discussion of speaker-meaning; for it is this notion that is for the IBS theorist foundational in the theory of meaning.

When IBS was conjoined with the relational theory of propositional attitudes, one was forced to construe '*p*' in [S] as an objectual variable, and to consider IBS incomplete until it could deliver an account of the values of that variable which showed that their intentionality-determining features were not the very public-language semantic features that IBS sought to reduce to propositional attitudes. Under that constraint IBS was frustrated. But now, having rejected the relational theory, one is free to read 'p' in [S] as a substitutional variable.

Even so, one cannot rest content with Grice's [S], for the following reasons.[2]

i. [S] fails to provide a sufficient condition for meaning that p. A, thinking she is unobserved by S, sees S applying lipstick to her husband Harold's shirt, and reasons thus: "S is manufacturing evidence that Harold has been unfaithful. S intends me to see the lipstick stains and to infer that they got there as a result of Harold's close encounter with a lipstick-wearing female. But dear old S wouldn't try to deceive me in this way if he didn't know that Harold had been unfaithful. So Harold must have been unfaithful." Since that is exactly how S intends A to reason, he satisfies the conditions of [S] for meaning that Harold has been unfaithful. Yet S, in manufacturing the evidence, does not *mean* that Harold has been unfaithful.[3] Now one cannot gain a set of jointly sufficient conditions merely by adding a further condition requiring S to have the further intention that A recognize S's intention to get A to recognize S's intention to get A to think that p. For with respect to any such addition a further Strawson-type counterexample is constructible. This suggests that for S to mean something, all of his meaning-constitutive intentions must in some appropriate sense be entirely out in the open. To accommodate this, I suggested in my book *Meaning* (1972, pp. 30–42) that not only must S intend (1)–(3), he must also intend it to be *mutual knowledge** between him and A that he uttered x with those intentions, where 'x and y mutually know* that p' was stipulatively defined as the infinite continuation of the sequence 'x knows that p; y knows that p; x knows that y knows that p; ....'[4] But there were two problems with this proposed emendation.

First, mutual knowledge* could not be attached in exactly the way I just indicated; for that would still fail to provide a set of jointly sufficient conditions. It would leave open the possibility of a counterexample in which S utters x with intentions (1)–(3) and with the intention that it should be mutual knowledge* between him and A that S uttered x with intentions (1)–(3), but S has the further intention that A should mistakenly think that S did not intend it to be mutual knowledge* that S uttered x with intentions (1)–(3). So it looked as if the only way one could rule out the counterexamples that led to the invention of mutual knowledge* was to secure that the defining conditions for speaker-meaning were such that they could not obtain without it being mutually known* by S and A that they obtained. I tried in *Meaning* to construct a definition that had that feature (see pp. 39–42, and especially p. 41, point 3), but Gilbert Harman

(1974) noticed that I might not have been successful. To the best of my knowledge no one has devised a set of Gricean conditions that do clearly provide a sufficient condition for speaker-meaning.

The second problem with mutual knowledge* is that it is not unreasonable to doubt that any two people ever have it. Of course you know that you did not swim across the Atlantic Ocean yesterday afternoon, and of course you know many other things that never entered your head; and in *Meaning*, after noticing that, I tried to assimilate mutual knowledge* to the "harmless" regress generated by the proposition that if one knows something, then one knows that one knows it, and I tried to provide a finite basis for generating mutual knowledge* (pp. 34–36). Nevertheless, as most commentators would agree, mutual knowledge* is from the point of view of psychological reality at best problematic. At the same time, *something* like it is needed in order to get a revision of [S] that yields a sufficient condition, and several commentators have suggested ways of getting more psychologically plausible versions of mutual knowledge (see, for example, Bennett 1976; Loar 1981; Kemmerling 1986; the essays in Smith 1982). Yet most, if not all, of these proposals have their own problems as regards "psychological reality." (For example, suggestions that S be required *not* to have any intention belonging to a certain recursively specifiable sequence of intentions would seem to make it impossible for any ordinary person ever to know that anyone ever meant anything.) And although many have offered redefinitions of mutual knowledge, no one, to my knowledge, has encapsulated that redefined notion in a revised version of [S]. So it remains unclear that the IBS theorist has any way of stating sufficient conditions for speaker-meaning, let alone sufficient conditions that might actually be realized.

ii. Here is another, but quite different, reason why [S] fails to provide a sufficient condition for meaning that *p*: a person may satisfy the conditions of [S] when he merely means that *A* is to make it the case that *A* believes that *p*. Suppose, for example, that S entreats *A* to bring it about that he, *A*, believes that God exists. This will be a case in which S utters something intending to get *A* to believe that God exists by means of *A*'s recognition of S's intention to get *A* to believe that God exists, but it will not be a case in which S means that God exists; if anything, it will be a case in which S means that *A* is to make it the case that he believes that God exists. In *Meaning* I suggested that in an adequate account of declarative speaker-meaning the speaker must intend the audience to have what I called a "truth-supporting" (as opposed to a pragmatic or prudential) reason for his belief that *p*, but this now strikes me as an especially absurd instance of the superintellectualist conception of mind implicit in the whole IBS approach. I doubt that ordinary speakers can be relied on to have sophisticated beliefs about the sorts of grounds they intend others to have for their beliefs. Also it now seems to me possible that there should be acceptable cases of meaning where the audience is not intended to have any reasons for the belief that the speaker intends to activate by his utterance. The need to see most justified beliefs as based on reasons is another result of overly intellectualist tendencies in epistemology and the philosophy of mind.

iii. That part of condition 3 that requires S to intend A to think that p *on the basis of A's recognition of S's intention to get A to think that p,* while plausibly a necessary condition for *telling* A that p, is not a necessary condition for *meaning* that p. I hope that you will believe all that I say in this book, but I have no hope that you will believe it because I want you to! In *Meaning* I proposed that the "recognition of intention" condition for the production of the intended belief be replaced with a condition that merely required that S's utterance x be related in a certain way to the belief that p.

iv. Nor is it necessary that S intend to *produce* in A the belief that p. There are many instances in which a person means something but only intends to *activate* a belief that the audience in some sense already has (as when one person reminds another of something). So [S] must be revised to accommodate this too.

v. Also as regards their necessity, the conditions of [S] must be relaxed to allow for cases in which the speaker does not have any particular audience in mind, and cases where his expectation of success is not so great as to allow one to speak of *intentions* to produce responses in an audience.

vi. Then there are many prima facie counterexamples where someone means that p but has no intention whatever of activating in his audience the belief that p; may not even have any audience-directed intention. To the first sort belong all the times we say that p when we know our audience already has in mind the activated belief that p, or when we know that there is no chance whatever of our being believed, but say what we say anyway. To the second sort belongs all the stuff we scribble when we do philosophy on paper, stuff that we have no intention of showing to anyone or of later consulting ourselves; we just want to clarify our thoughts in the act of writing. IBS theorists are well aware of these cases and try to deal with them. It seems clear, however, that there is no hope of achieving a neat set of conditions that will accommodate all cases that we should intuitively classify as acts of speaker-meaning, and the theorist's strategy has been to try to explain these "attenuated" cases of speaker-meaning in terms of the theorist's chosen paradigm (see Grice 1969; Schiffer 1972, pp. 68–80). It is important that these cases really be parasitic on the primary case captured in the theorist's definition if it is to be correct that it is just that defined notion that is essential to the account of expression-meaning. And it is important that the problematic cases of speaker-meaning at least be shown to be reducible to some species of behavior the specification of which does not presuppose anything semantic; for otherwise the program will have failed to reduce all public-language semantic facts to psychological facts.

Can a correct IBS account of speaker-meaning be achieved? It has not yet been achieved, and while I do not know how to construct an a priori proof that none can be achieved, I can think of some reasons for being doubtful. First, and foremost, there is the dismal history of attempts to provide reductive analyses of philosophically interesting concepts. Philosophers have been at this game for a couple of thousand years, but it has so far produced not one clear victory, and this suggests that the enterprise of seeking reductive analyses conflicts with some basic truth about the nature of our concepts and conceptual organization. I speculate a little more on this in section 9.5. A second reason is this. In a paradigm case of speaker-meaning our inclination to say that the speaker meant that p is dependent on the speaker's willingness to describe himself as intending to say (or even mean)[5] that p. Now it seems pretty clear that, even if an IBS account of saying were correct, no statement of the extremely complex IBS conditions could replace 'say' in a true statement of the form 'I intended to say that p' without having the result be an obvious falsehood. We have in the case of IBS analyses the Paradox of Analysis with a vengeance: the IBS theorist may be saying what meaning is, but he can hardly be unpacking anyone's *concept* of meaning—no IBS analysans can replace its analysandum *salve veritate* in a propositional-attitude 'that'-clause.

Now let me hasten to say that this is in itself no objection to IBS; for that program purports only to analyze 'S means that p', and not 'x believes that S means that p'. At the same time, the point being emphasized may be perceived as something like an obstacle to the reductivist endeavor. For consider again Sally's utterance of 'It's snowing'. In producing those sounds she intended to be saying that it was snowing, perhaps to mean that it was snowing, and she intended to tell Adam that it was snowing; the *content* of these intentions, we have just been noticing, is irreducibly semantic. The question, then, is this: Can we in a case such as Sally's subtract all of her irreducibly semantic intentions (as we may call them) and expect to be left with enough other intentions to entail the satisfaction of her irreducibly semantic ones? Of course the IBS theorist will claim that his hypothesis implies that we can; but my hunch is that once we take away Sally's intention to be saying that it is snowing, we shall have taken away precisely her contribution to what makes her utterance an act of saying (and thus of meaning) that it is snowing.

In any event, none of this, I think, matters. For let us pretend that the IBS theorist has delivered a correct definition of speaker-meaning. Then this definition will be of questionable interest if it cannot provide the basis for an account of that which most interests philosophers of language—the semantic features of natural-language expressions. The program of IBS calls not merely for a reductive account of speaker-meaning but for a general reduction of the semantic to the psychological. It promises a reductive account of speaker-meaning *that will provide the basis for a reductive account of expression-meaning.*

IBS theorists have had quite a lot to say about the correct analysis of speaker-meaning, but surprisingly little to say about the correct analysis of expression-meaning. This, we shall now see, is not without an explanation. But it does mean that our exposition of the IBS program must be more tentative, drawing less on what has been done in it and more on what it is most plausible to expect from it.

9.3 Expression-Meaning

Since the IBS account of expression-meaning is to be given in terms of its account of speaker-meaning, we need to pretend that we have some such account to work with. For this purpose we may take the account of speaker-meaning to be [S] supplemented thus: S also intends his meaning-constitutive intentions to be mutual knowledge between him and his audience A. That is, if S means that p in uttering x and S's intentions are satisfied, then it is mutual knowledge between S and A that S meant that p in uttering x.[6] "Mutual knowledge" need not be thought of as mutual knowledge*, but only as a dummy for whatever condition secures that, in the needed sense, S intends his meaning-constitutive intentions to be out in the open; we should, however, expect that if two people mutually know that p, then each knows that p and each knows that the other knows that p.

If S is to mean that p in uttering x, then he must expect there to be some feature Φ of x such that mutual knowledge between S and A that S's utterance x has Φ would constitute, in the circumstances, evidence for A that in uttering x S meant that p. Φ need not be a feature that implies that x has meaning; perhaps S utters the sound 'grrr', intending A to recognize that 'grrr' resembles the sound dogs make when they are angry and to infer from that (together with other of his beliefs) that S, in uttering 'grrr', meant that he was angry (see Schiffer 1972, chap. 5). But it is the leading idea of the IBS account of expression-meaning that if x means p in a population to which S and A belong, then x has some feature Φ that (i) relates x in an especially direct and salient way to the act of meaning that p, (ii) makes x suitable as a device for a speaker's meaning that p (i.e., the feature permits an utterance of x to be taken as evidence that the speaker, in uttering x, meant that p), (iii) has a specification in nonsemantic terms, and (iv) accounts for x's meaning p in the relevant population.

It is useful for working into this strategy to begin not with natural-language sentences but with *noncomposite* whole-utterance-types. These are simple signals—an air-raid siren, for instance, or a prearranged gesture that means that the princess is about to enter the palace—that have sentence-like meaning, but whose meanings are in no sense determined by the meanings of any of their constituent parts (see Grice 1968; Lewis 1969; Schiffer 1972, especially chap. 5).

Suppose that it is mutual knowledge in a prelinguistic but precocious community G that 'grrr' resembles the sound dogs make when they are angry.[7] Then in certain highly constrained circumstances it may be possible for one member of G to communicate to another that he is angry by uttering 'grrr' and relying on the tenuous associative connection that the resemblance to dogs forges with the act of meaning that one is angry. But now suppose that 'grrr' has the following feature: it is the sound by whose utterance some members of G have meant that they were angry. As a result of its being mutual knowledge in G that 'grrr' has *this* feature, we should expect, *ceteris paribus*, a member of G to be able to mean that he is angry by uttering 'grrr' in virtually any circumstances in which it is not already precluded that he should mean that he is angry (e.g., because it is already mutual knowledge that he is angry, or that he is not angry, or that no one cares whether or not he is angry). Suppose that 'grrr' has that feature. Then an utterance of 'grrr' constitutes very good evidence that the utterer means that he is angry. Consequently it may come to be the case that members of G always utter 'grrr' when they want to mean that they are angry. Consequently 'grrr' will now be mutually known to have a new feature—viz., it is what members of G utter whenever they mean that they are angry—that makes it an even more reliable device in G for meaning that one is angry. Now we are on our way to a neat self-perpetuating regularity: 'grrr' has the feature of being that by the utterance of which members of G mean that they are angry; because it has that feature, an utterance of 'grrr' can, in a wide range of circumstances, constitute very good evidence that the utterer means that he is angry; because 'grrr' is such a reliable device in G for meaning that one is angry, members of G will continue to use it to communicate that they are angry; and because of this continued use it will continue to have that feature which spawns the use; and so on until something interrupts the cycle.

A self-perpetuating regularity of this sort would be a *convention*, and one of the attractive features of IBS is the way it so nicely meshes with, and exploits, a notion of convention itself defined in wholly psychological and nonsemantic terms (see Lewis 1969, 1975; Schiffer 1972, chap. 5). Now while it seems reasonable to suppose that

> x means p in G *if* there is a convention in G not to mean that p unless one means that p by uttering x, or a convention in G not to utter x unless one means thereby that p,

neither sort of convention can constitute a necessary condition for x's being a noncomposite whole-utterance-type that means p in G. For there may be something else y in G that also means p, so that members of G have the choice of uttering x or y when they want to communicate that p; or x may also have some meaning other than p, or have some established use in G apart from its use in communication.

But the following, from an IBS perspective, may seem on the right track:

> x is a noncomposite whole-utterance-type that means p in G iff (1) it is mutual knowledge in G that there is a practice in G of uttering x and meaning thereby that p, and (2) that practice is precisely the feature of x which members of G exploit (in the way already indicated in the account of speaker-meaning) when, in uttering x, they mean that p.

The notion of a practice is what is wanted here, because there can be a practice of A-ing by B-ing even though there is also a practice of A-ing by C-ing, and even though there is a practice of B-ing that is unconnected with A-ing (cf. Grice 1968).

Let us postpone facing the difficulties of this account of the meaning of simple signals and go directly to what it suggests as regards meaning in a natural language.

The paradigm of a whole-utterance-type is a sentence of a natural language, and most (so to say) of them have never been uttered; so when it comes to sentences, we cannot account for for x's meaning p in G in terms of what members of G do mean in uttering x. It may seem that the IBS theorist should now want to say something along the lines of the following:

> x means p in G iff it is mutual knowledge in G that there are communicative practices pertaining to x or to "constituents" of x such that a member of G utters x in conformity with those practices just in case in uttering x he means that p.

This may be on the right track, but we can be assured of that only after being told what sorts of practices would account for the meanings of sentences. One needs only to try it for some very simple language to become convinced of the hopelessness of stating for each primitive vocabulary item and syntactical construction of the language a separate practice that will yield a finite set of practices that together will determine the meaning of each of the infinitely many sentences of the language. The difficulty will emerge in the need to refer without circularity to each of the other practices in stating the practice for any given word or construction. What is evidently wanted is a single practice that pertains to the language as a whole, and David Lewis (1975) showed the IBS theorist the way to get it.[8] In looking at the IBS development of the Lewisian strategy we should momentarily ignore the fact that, in its tacit acceptance of the propositional theory of propositional attitudes, it already conflicts with results that I claim to have reached.

I shall stipulatively define the notion of *a language* in a way that pre-scinds entirely from linguistic *behavior* but does allow me to ask what makes a language, as stipulatively defined, an *actual language of a given population*; for, as *x* can mean something only by meaning something among certain people, it is the latter notion that is the ultimate concern. Thus, I shall say that a *language* is any function from finite strings of (types of) marks or sounds to propositions. If the function L is a language and σ is in its domain of arguments, then σ may be called a sentence of L and the proposition p such that $L(\sigma) = p$ may be called the meaning of σ in L.

What the IBS theorist now wants to define is a relation R that holds between L and a population G such that if $R(L, G)$ and σ is a sentence of L, then the meaning of σ in G is the meaning of σ in L (i.e., the proposition $L(\sigma)$). This achieved, we may say that L is a language used in G, or an actual language of G. The theorist must define the actual-language relation in terms of his already reduced notion of speaker-meaning and in a way that does not presuppose any of the public-language semantic notions he wants to define in terms of it.

Perhaps he will think first of something like this:

> L is a language of G iff there prevails in G the convention not to utter any sentence σ of L unless, for some p, $L(\sigma) = p$ and one means in uttering σ that p.

But this gives way to an objection similar to one raised in the discussion of the meanings of simple signals: σ may have more than one meaning in G, or a use apart from communicative behavior; moreover, one who uses σ metaphorically, or in any other nonliteral way, need not be violating any sort of convention.

It is better, then, for the theorist to say something along the following lines.

First, as a preliminary definition, we may say that

> there is a practice in G of meaning in L iff often when a member of G means that p, for arbitrary p, he does so by uttering some (perhaps novel) sentence that means p in L.

Then, for the target definition, we get

[L] L is a language of G iff (1) it is mutual knowledge in G that there is a practice in G of meaning in L; and (2) when, for any σ and p such that $L(\sigma) = p$, a member of G, S, utters σ and means thereby that p, S intends it to be mutual knowledge between him and his audience that

$(L(\sigma) = p$ & there is a practice in G of meaning in L) and intends that mutual knowledge to be the basis (in part) of their mutual knowledge that S, in uttering σ, means that p.

In other words, there is a communicative practice in G involving L that has the following consequence for meaning and language understanding. Often when a speaker wants to communicate something, he will utter some string of sounds σ such that $L(\sigma)$ is the proposition he wants to communicate. When he utters σ (perhaps for the first time ever) in order to mean that p, he intends σ to have a certain feature that makes it possible for him to mean that p in uttering σ: namely, that it is mutual knowledge between him and his audience that there is in G a practice of meaning in L and $L(\sigma) = p$.

Doubtless a bit of ingenuity could reveal that even though the IBS theorist helps himself in [L] to everything but the kitchen sink, it still fails to provide even a sufficient condition. Yet the more pressing question is whether [L], or anything like it, can provide a necessary condition for a sentence's having the meaning it has in the actual language of a given population. More pressing still is the question of how on the present approach one is to account for the meanings of subsentential expressions.

The even more pressing question arises because L is simply a function from sentences to propositions, a set containing infinitely many ordered pairs of strings of marks or sounds and propositions; in no sense does it *construct* sentence meaning. How, then, is IBS to account for the meanings of words and syntactical constructions so as to provide a complete account of expression-meaning? The obvious thought is this: the function L will be recursively specifiable—it will have, that is, what Lewis has called a *grammar*;[9] and it will be the fact that this grammar stands in a certain relation to speakers of L that somehow determines the meanings of L's subsentential expressions.

If the function L is recursively specifiable, then it will be possible to discern a finite vocabulary for L, to correlate each vocabulary item with a propositional determinant (a property, relation, particular, or the like), and to specify a finite number of combining operations that derive the meaning of each sentence of L out of the assignments of propositional determinants to vocabulary items contained in it. An ordered pair whose first member is a set of such correlations and whose second member is a set of such combining operations may be called a *grammar for L*. Just as I earlier stipulated that the proposition $L(\sigma)$ shall be called the meaning of σ in L, so I may now say that, if w is a vocabulary item in a grammar Γ, then *the meaning of w in Γ* is the propositional determinant that Γ correlates with w. A grammar for L determines the meaning of each sentence in L, and in determining these sentence/proposition pairings it will also determine infinitely many pairings of sequences of vocabulary items with further propositional determinants. These derived subsentential sequences may be called *phrases of Γ*, and the propositional determinants thus correlated with them their *meanings in Γ*; since Γ determines L, sentences of L may also be called sentences of Γ, their meanings in L also called their meanings in Γ.

A grammar determines a language, but not necessarily vice versa: there may be distinct grammars for L. If Γ and Γ' are grammars of L, then they will, by definition, both determine L; but they may do so in different ways: they may segment sentence components differently (they may have different vocabularies), or they may recognize the same vocabulary but assign its members different propositional determinants (for depending on one's view of propositions it may be possible for the same proposition to be determined by different sequences of propositional determinants). This suggests that if L is an actual language of a population G, then that is so because there is some particular grammar of L that is in some appropriate sense "used" in G. And it further suggests that if Γ is the grammar of L used in G, then Γ determines the *expressions* of L qua language of G, and that an expression e of Γ (and thus of L qua language of G) means m in G just in case e means m in Γ.

What, then, should the IBS theorist take to be the relation between a grammar and a population such that, should a grammar and a population be related in that way, then the meaning that any expression has in the grammar will be a meaning it has in the population? The clue is provided by [L]. For if L is the actual language of G, then members of G will be able to understand arbitrary utterances in L: S will utter the novel sentence σ, and, if L(σ) = p, then A will infer that S meant that p. But how is A able to have such knowledge of the function L? L, after all, is just a set of infinitely many ordered pairs of strings of marks or sounds (the sentences of L) and propositions (their meanings in L). The IBS theorist must stand ready to explain—or at any rate to throw some light on—how speakers of L can correlate the sentences of L with their meanings in L, and it is here that we should expect the notion of a grammar of L to play its explanatory role. If L is used in G, then some grammar Γ of L explains the ability of members of G to correlate the sentences of L with their meanings in L; this is what makes Γ stand in the distinguished relation to G that I, on behalf of the IBS theorist, am trying to explicate.

Adapting an idea of Brian Loar's (cf. 1976a; 1981, section 10.4), I can say,

> Γ *grounds* the use of L in G iff L is a language that is used in G and Γ is that grammar of L which enters into the correct psycholinguistic theory of G's understanding of L.

If L is used in G, then members of G *understand* L; that is, they have the ability to know, upon hearing the utterance of any one of indefinitely many novel sentences of L, what the speaker meant in uttering that sentence.

When a member of G, S, utters a sentence σ of L and means thereby that p, then, if he is speaking literally, he intends it to be mutual knowledge between him and his audience, A, that L is used in G and that $L(\sigma) = p$ and—at least partly as a result of these facts—that in uttering σ S meant that p. A psycholinguistic theory of G's understanding of L would explain the processing that takes A from his auditory perception of S's utterance of σ to his belief that, in uttering σ, S meant that p. Since, by hypothesis, L is (in the sense defined) used in G, A at some point in this processing forms the belief that $L(\sigma) = p$; a psycholinguistic theory of the processing must explain how this is possible, and it is here that Γ will enter in, if Γ grounds the use of L in G. But the definition of the grounding relation leaves open exactly how Γ will enter into the theory of language processing, and it would be unreasonable to expect more than that. Still, the IBS theorist who has gone this far will not want to say that members of G have propositional knowledge of some compositional semantics that formulates Γ as a theory of L, but will doubtless suppose that Γ enjoys some sort of Chomskian internal realization, or at least that members of G are in some sense neurally structured to process utterances in L in conformity with Γ. In his processing of S's utterance of the sentence σ, A will, the idea must go, be in states that segment σ in accordance with Γ and assign to those segments the meanings they have in Γ. In this way A will arrive at his conscious correlation of σ with p, its meaning in Γ, L, and G.

In this way also we arrive at the IBS theorist's final account of expression-meaning—final, that is, relative to the assumption of the propositional theory of propositional attitudes and the need to make further adjustments to accommodate indexicality, ambiguity, moods other than the indicative, and speech acts other than speaker-meaning:

> e means m in G iff e means m in some grammar that grounds a language that is used in G.

(Recall that every sentence of L is also a sentence of every grammar of L; so 'e' ranges over all expressions—words, phrases, and sentences.)

9.4 Troubles with the IBS Account of Expression-Meaning

I have adumbrated *an* IBS account of expression-meaning. It is as complete and as plausible and as squarely in conformity with the essence of the program as any account I have ever seen. It is not, however, *the* IBS theory, for none such exists; and it is possible that some future IBS theorist will succeed in devising a theory of expression-meaning that will avoid the objections I am about to raise against the adumbrated theory.

It will be useful to divide these into two sorts: objections implied by my denial of semantic compositionality and the relational theory of propositional attitudes, and objections that might be raised even by someone who accepted those two hypotheses. I shall present them in that order.

I must deny the theory of the last section on two counts: in its treatment of '*p*' as an objectual variable ranging over propositions (of some sort or other), it presupposes the relational theory of propositional attitudes, and in its appeal to "grammars" it presupposes that natural languages have compositional semantics. My arguments have been made, and although the development of his theory attributed to the IBS theorist conflicts with the conclusions of those arguments, there is nothing in IBS that constitutes an *objection* to them. My question, then, must be this: Can the IBS account of expression-meaning be formulated in a way that does not presuppose either the relational theory of propositional attitudes or semantic compositionality?

As regards the relational theory, we cannot simply decide to read the relevant occurrences of '*p*' as occurrences of a substitutionally quantified variable; for L is a *function*, and that requires that '*p*' in the schema '$L(\sigma) = p$' have *a* reading on which '*p*' is an objectually quantified variable. Besides, the really urgent question is whether the IBS theory can be formulated without a reliance on compositional semantics; for if it cannot be, there is no point in seeing whether it can do without the relational theory.

I am not able to see how IBS can do without compositional semantics.[10] The whole point of the program is to see each sentence as possessing some property that makes an utterance of the sentence potential evidence that the speaker, in uttering it, meant that such-and-such. That evidential basis was spelled out with respect to a practice that obtained with respect to the language, and it had to be, because there cannot be communicative practices for each of a language's infinitely many sentences. This in turn required speakers of L to have propositional knowledge about L, for '*L*' in 'knows that … *L* …' (as it occurs, say, in [L]) is a singular term that refers to the function L. But L is just a set of infinitely many ordered pairs, and I cannot imagine how one could have knowledge of such a thing in a way that would enable one to correlate each sentence in the domain of L with the proposition that L assigns to it, unless one had knowledge of the function in a way that afforded a recursive specification of it, a finite way of generating it. But if one has a recursive way of specifying L, then one will have a compositional semantics for L. Besides, and of course relatedly, IBS is committed to reducing the semantic features of subsentential expressions to features that are intrinsically specifiable nonsemantically and are defined in terms of speaker-meaning. This enterprise, too, would *seem* to require a finite way of assigning to each expression of a language that psychological property that is constitutive of its meaning in the language—which would again imply that the language enjoys a compositional semantics.

It may be, however, that the presupposition that languages have com-positional semantics—which is shared by all developments of IBS and which seems inevitable to me, given the definition of the program—simply boils down to a lack of ingenuity. It has not been *proved* that no IBS account of expression-meaning can be given which does not presuppose that natural languages have finite meaning theories. But there may not be much point in pursuing such an account, once we have seen the other problems with the IBS account of expression-meaning—problems not un-related to those just discussed. So let us turn to objections that might spring from the lips of one who is at ease with compositional semantics and the relational theory of propositional attitudes.

[L] has this consequence: when S, speaking literally, utters a sentence σ of a language L and means thereby that p, then he intends his audience A to know, for some group G to which S and A belong, that there is in G a practice of meaning in L and that $L(\sigma) = p$, and to infer (in part therefrom) that S, in uttering σ, meant that p. On the face of it, this is for the following reasons quite absurd.

First, the definition of speaker-meaning does not of itself imply that 'means that' in sentences of the form 'x believes that y means that p' can be replaced *salva veritate* by a specification of those complex intentions that comprise the IBS analysis—which is good, because it is obvious that it cannot be. I think it is almost as obvious that ordinary people do not believe that there are practices to utter things intending ..., where this is to be completed in the way provided by the IBS account of speaker-meaning. Yet that is precisely what is required by the IBS account of expression-meaning; for the expression 'S means that p' as it occurs in the nested definitions of the last section (and thus in the last paragraph) is *an abbreviation for the theorist's definiens in his definition of 'S means that p'*. The use of 'S means that p' within 'that'-clauses in the definitions of 9.3 is therefore very misleading; if one were now to rewrite those definitions using the definitional expansion of 'means that', one would have serious doubts as to whether ordinary people had the beliefs needed to realize those definitions.[11]

Even worse, it looks as though the IBS account of expression-meaning in effect commits the theorist to claiming that his analysis of speaker-meaning and, in terms of that, his analyses of the other kinds of illocutionary acts really do provide *conceptual* analyses. For this much is surely more clearly true than anything IBS has to offer: to understand a language is to have the ability to know what speakers are *saying*, and thus (some of what they are) *meaning*, when they utter sentences of the language. A correct theory of language processing will see hearers going from auditory perceptions to beliefs about what was said (meant, told, requested) in them. But *that is not entailed by the IBS account of expression-meaning, unless the contents of those beliefs really are given by the IBS analyses.* Language understanding, as conceived by IBS, is an inferential process that ends in a belief to the effect that the speaker produced his utterance with that complex of intentions constitutive, by the theorist's lights, of speaker-meaning. So either these beliefs are taken to entail beliefs about what the speaker said (meant, etc.), or else the account will be wrong. But if the entailment obtains, then that cannot coherently be because believing that *S* had the IBS intentions entails having the *distinct* belief that *S* said (or meant) that such-and-such; it must rather be because the two beliefs are not distinct. Yet it is that hypothesis that is so manifestly implausible.

If I say that 'meant that' in the definitions of the last section is intended to abbreviate the IBS definitional expansion, then that is that; they are, after all, my definitions. But why not read the definitions without that assumption? Because then those definitions will not be defining expression-meaning in terms of the reduced notion of *speaker-meaning*, which is what the whole enterprise of IBS is supposed to be about, but will be defining it in terms of an unanalyzed *concept* of speaker-meaning. The IBS reduction of speaker-meaning would be idle as regards the analysis of expression-meaning; gone would be the claim of a reduction of the semantic to the psychological.

The epistemological woes rehearsed above are mild compared to the ones next to be confronted. [L] requires an ordinary speaker of a language *L* to know that there is a practice of meaning in *L*—to know *that often when a member of G means something, there is some σ and some p such that* $L(\sigma) = p$ *and the speaker means that p in uttering σ*; and it requires that it be mutual knowledge between a speaker and his audience that $L(\sigma) = p$ *whenever σ means p in L and the speaker means that p in uttering σ*. Let *E* be the function that maps each English sentence onto the proposition it expresses (and ignore the fact that there is no such function!), and consider

[E]   *E*('snow is white') = the proposition that snow is white.

In what sense does Clem, who knows as much about set theory as most people know about quantum mechanics, know the proposition that [E] expresses? Plainly there is no sense, strictly speaking, in which Clem knows the truth [E] expresses. If we are to make sense of [L] and the definitions that presuppose it, we must find a way of reading occurrences of '$L(\sigma) = p$' in the 'that'-clauses of those definitions that does not make it obvious that the definitions are never realized.

David Lewis (1975) proposed an account of the actual-language relation which has this consequence: *L* is a language of *G* only if it is mutual knowledge in *G* that members of *G* "try never to utter any sentences of *L* that are not true in *L*" (p. 167)—i.e., try never to utter any sentence σ of *L* unless, for some *p*, $L(\sigma) = p$ and *p* is true. Then, faced with an objection like the one I just raised, Lewis responds:

The common man need not have any concept of L in order to expect his fellows to be truthful ... in L. He need only have suitable particular expectations about how they might act ... in various situations. He can tell whether any actual or hypothetical particular action ... on their part is compatible with his expectations. He expects them to conform to a regularity of truthfulness ... in L if any particular activity ... that would fit his expectations would fall under what *we*—but not *he*—could describe as conformity to that regularity.

It may well be that his elaborate, infinite system of potential particular expectations can only be explained on the hypothesis that he has some unconscious mental entity somehow analogous to a general concept of L—say, an internally represented grammar. But it does not matter whether this is so or not. We are concerned only to say what system of expectations a normal member of a language-using population must have. (p. 180–181)

But the trouble with this reply is that it is not exactly clear how it addresses itself to the objection. If the common man must know *that members of his linguistic community try never to utter any sentence σ of L unless, for some p, $L(\sigma) = p$ and p is true*, then he must know, of the function L, that members of the group try never to utter anything in the domain of arguments of that function unless the value of the function for that argument is true. And if he must have knowledge *of* L (for 'L' here is an objectual variable bound from outside this intentional context), then he must indeed have some "concept," or "mode of presentation," of L. If Lewis has a reply to the objection, then he must have a way of restating the knowledge being required of the common man that does not invite the objection that common people tend not to know any set theory. What, then, is this nontendentious way of ascribing the knowledge in question? We need not cavil about its exactly amounting to a reading of the italicized 'that'-clause immediately above if we can use that nonobjectionable knowledge to achieve a correct IBS account of expression-meaning.

Lewis seems to want to ascribe the following knowledge:

> For all σ, p, if $L(\sigma) = p$, then it is mutual knowledge in G that members of G will try not to utter σ unless p is true.

I shall not comment on whether or not this is adequate for Lewis's purposes; it is enough for us to see that it cannot be used to help the IBS theorist.

The idea is to try to reformulate the IBS definitions getting all references to L *outside* of 'that'-clauses; the only knowledge that we are to require of an ordinary person is knowledge of particular sentences (i.e., strings of marks or sounds) and propositions. But it is by no means clear how one would go about trying to restate [L] in conformity with this strategy, and it is worth spelling out why. The essence of the IBS program for explicating sentence-meaning is, we have noted, to assign to each sentence of a language some property that is both constitutive of its meaning and, roughly speaking, such as to make an utterance of the sentence prima facie evidence that the speaker meant that such-and-such. In the case of a simple signal, a noncomposite whole-utterance-type x that means p in G, the theorist can say that the meaning-determining feature of x is that there is a practice in G of uttering x and meaning thereby that p. But nothing like this can be said as regards a sentence, a *composite* whole-utterance-type that means p in G, for it may mean p in G even if it has never been uttered, or indeed never *could* be uttered (perhaps because it is too long or convoluted to be processed). For just this reason I made the practice pertain not to the sentence but to the language to which the sentence belongs: the relevant evidential feature of an L sentence σ that means p in a group G became the conjunctive feature that *there is in G a practice of meaning in L and $L(\sigma) = p$.* Now in saying that this feature is an *evidential* feature, I mean that one knows what is meant by an utterance of σ by virtue of *knowing that σ has that feature.* There simply is no way of restating the strategy embodied in [L] without requiring knowledge of the language, as well as of its sentences and meanings. [L] really does require the knowledge that it seems to require; the IBS theorist must find some way of showing that the requirement of *that* knowledge is not as absurd as it seems to be, or he must find an alternative account of sentence-meaning that does not require knowledge that no one has.[12]

In either case the IBS theorist is challenged to say what the potentially evidential, meaning-constitutive features of natural-language sentences are in a way that makes it reasonable, or at least not ridiculous, to suppose that plain people can know that sentences have those features. If in their understanding of natural languages ordinary people exercise propositional knowledge that they really have, then it ought to be possible to ascribe that knowledge in a wholly nontendentious way. I cannot see how to do this, and I doubt, for reasons that I will later come to, that anyone can. At one time (see Schiffer 1982, p. 122), in order to avoid the problems that I have been discussing, I suggested that

> L is a language of G iff for all σ, p, if $L(\sigma) = p$, then σ is a *conventional device* in G for meaning that p,

where

> σ is a conventional device in G for meaning that p iff

> (a)   it is practicable for a member of G to mean that p by uttering σ, if it is possible for him to mean that p,

and this just by virtue of its being the case that

(b)   it is mutual knowledge in G that (a).

The idea expressed in (a) is this. Consider the sentence

[*]   Ronald Reagan was born without a nose.

Chances are it may never be possible for any member of our linguistic population to mean that Ronald Reagan was born without a nose; but *if* there should be circumstances in which someone could mean that, then, (a) implies, it would be practicable to mean that by uttering the sentence [*]. But then, the IBS theorist contends, [*] must have some feature that would make an utterance of it evidence that the speaker meant that Reagan was born without a nose. That feature, (b) implies, is that it is mutual knowledge in G that [*] is one way for someone to mean that Reagan was born without a nose, if there is any way for him to mean that.

Unfortunately, this approach, although it avoids some of the pitfalls of [L], has problems of its own. First, there are clear counterexamples to (a). It may be possible for someone to mean that he cannot write a sentence that contains more than three words, but it is not possible for him to mean this by *writing* the sentence 'I cannot write a sentence that contains more than three words'; yet that sequence of mark types has the meaning we take it to have. Second, the definition, via the mutual-knowledge condition (which is needed to forestall other counterexamples), in effect requires speakers of L to know the meaning of each sentence of L, for they must know for each sentence what proposition it might be used to communicate. Yet there are meaningful sentences of each natural language for which speakers of the language do not have such knowledge, owing to the sentences' length or convolutedness.[13]

9.5 The Analysis of Meaning

I have exhausted my wits. I can see no way of devising an IBS account of expression-meaning that does not presuppose the relational theory of propositional attitudes and the hypothesis that natural languages have compositional meaning theories, and that moves me. Less parochially, I cannot see how to devise an IBS account of expression-meaning that does not require us to have knowledge that we seem not to have. And I think I know where things went wrong. It is in the idea that language understanding is a certain sort of *inferential* process; it is in the following picture of successful communication.

S utters the sounds 'Some snow is purple'. A hears those sounds, forms the belief that they mean that some snow is purple, and from this, along with other of his beliefs, infers that S said, and meant, that some snow was purple. The meaning of a sentence, on this picture, is that feature of a sentence recognition of which enables one to know what would be communicated by an utterance of the sentence. Then the IBS theorist steps in. He buys this picture and encapsulates it in his account of speaker-meaning. But he cannot rest content with describing the evidential feature of a sentence as its having such-and-such *meaning*; he must, for his reductive purposes, redescribe the feature in nonsemantic terms. His search for this redescription, however, has been unsuccessful.

My inclination is to think that this inferential model is wrong. Understanding the utterance of a sentence is indeed knowing what the speaker said in it, but when we understand the utterance of a sentence we do not first come to the belief that it means such-and-such and then have that as our basis for thinking that the utterer was saying such-and-such. Rather, like Harvey of chapter 7, we hear the utterance and, owing to the way we are functionally organized, come to a belief about what was said in the utterance without first having somehow to represent the sentence uttered as having some feature that is constitutive of its meaning.

Here is something of an argument against the feature-based inferential model. S utters 'She gave it to him', and this causes A to believe that S, in uttering those sounds, said that Ava gave Ben his Rolls Royce. If the inferential model is correct, then there must be some feature Φ of the sentence that is both determinative of its meaning and such that A believes that the sentence has Φ, and uses that belief to infer what S means. But what could this Φ be? We already have good reason to think that it is not describable in nonsemantic terms, and what is now more to the point is that there seems not to be any relevant feature that is describable in *semantic terms*. This is not to deny, absurdly, that 'She gave it to him' has meaning, but rather to repeat a point made in section 7.2, namely, that there does not seem to be any way correctly to complete the schema

'She gave it to him' means . . . .

But then A cannot infer what was said from his belief that 'She gave it to him' means . . . . There seems, in short, not to be any feature of the sentence that satisfies the sort of inferential model on which IBS is founded. (And notice that we cannot avoid the problem by going unconscious; for if some subdoxastic, unconscious state of A's ascribes to the sentence a meaning-determining feature Φ, then it must be *possible* for one consciously to believe that the sentence has Φ.)

Here is another argument to the same conclusion. We have no right to expect the inferential model to be correct unless we are justified in thinking that natural languages have compositional meaning theories, theories that assign to each of the infinitely many sentences of a language some complex, compositionally determined feature that is constitutive of its

Intention-Based Semantics and Analysis of Meaning   263

meaning. But we are not justified in thinking that natural languages either have or need such theories.

Should we look beyond IBS for the correct analysis of meaning, or should we forget about trying to analyze meaning altogether?

On the one side there is the feeling that to give up now would be defeatist: "*something* about a population makes it true that their sentences and terms have the semantic properties they do—that they speak one language ... and not another" (Blackburn 1984, p. 125).[14] This is the feeling already taken note of: qua sequences of marks on paper, there is no relevant difference between

> snow is white

and

> *ı∕ ɩ̃ ⊘ʃ⅂,*

and yet the first but not the second has all sorts of semantic features. Moreover, these are features that the first sequence has only contingently: had we behaved differently in our use of the parts of 'snow is white', that sequence would have meant something other than what it now means, or nothing at all. Surely it must be possible to say *what makes it the case* that 'snow is white', but not '*ı∕ ɩ̃ ⊘ʃ⅂*', has the meaning it has.

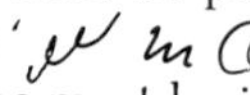

On the other side, one must be impressed by two facts. First, there does not even exist any program for the reductive analysis of meaning other than IBS, or first cousins to it, and it appears not to work. Second, although philosophers have been trying to give reductive analyses of philosophically interesting concepts since even before the time of Plato, there has not yet been one clear success. This is especially depressing when one compares the history of philosophy with that of the natural sciences. Is it that philosophy is still awaiting its Newton, or that much of it has been barking up the wrong tree?

The impulse toward analysis is a strong one; it is probably connected with an impulse toward an atomistic metaphysics, a metaphysics that insists on seeing all facts as either atomic or else built up out of atomic facts in recursively specifiable ways. But the impulse should be resisted. The failure of IBS is just one more example in the unpromising history of philosophical analysis, the search for reductions in the form of interesting necessary and sufficient conditions. It is fortunate that skepticism about such undertakings is now the prevailing conviction among philosophers.

But what about the consideration on the other side, that there must be *something* that makes it the case that some marks and sounds have the meanings they have? The philosopher's invitation to say what makes it the case that *x* is *F* is an invitation to give a correct, interesting, and noncircular completion of 'x is F iff ...', and that is what cannot be done. The moral here, as regards semantic facts, is the same as the one I drew in chapter 6 as regards Sentential Dualism and psychological facts. There, in section 6.5, I tried to relieve the itch toward analysis by speculating on the "conceptual roles" of our psychological concepts, and on the sort of cognitive mechanism we are. We are still cognitive mechanisms, noise-making physical information-processing systems all of whose movements enjoy physical explanations; we are just one kind of physical object among others—cockroaches, dogs, bananas, and grains of sand. But we are information processors, and thus we think in the "brain's language of synaptic interconnections and neural spikes" (Lewis 1983a, p. 346). The conceptual roles of our neural words—that is, the counterfactual causal properties determined for them by our belief-forming mechanisms—are ones that, one would like to think, we have because of their survival value. At the same time, they render our semantic concepts, like our psychological ones, irreducible. That we find meaning in 'snow in white', but not in '𝓮𝓷 𝓶 𝓸𝓷', is the result of our cognitive apparatus, of the conceptual roles of our semantic concepts and the way they are related to the way we are "programmed" to process productions of marks and sounds. We have the semantic knowledge we have as the joint result of our cognitive mechanism and the *physical* stimuli bombarding our receptor cells. It is ultimately the way we use marks and sounds—in a sense of 'use' describable in nonsemantic and nonpsychological terms—that, given the conceptual roles of our neural terms, explains our semantic knowledge. But the fact remains that, owing to those very same conceptual roles, the semantic knowledge we have is not knowledge that can be conveyed in nonsemantic terms.

Chapter 10
The No-Theory Theory of Meaning

10.1 Introduction

I have made clear what theories of language and thought I disbelieve, and it is time for me to say what ones are true.

None. My positive theory of meaning is the no-theory theory of meaning. What I mean is that if one were to make a list of all the things philosophers have in mind when they talk of "theories of meaning or intentional content," then I would claim that there are no true theories satisfying the descriptions on that list. The questions being asked in the philosophy of language that would require positive theories as answers all have false presuppositions.

10.2 The No-Theory Theory of Linguistic Representation

The no-theory theory of meaning has two components: one, the no-theory theory of linguistic representation, that pertains to language and to meaning in a strict sense; and another, the no-theory theory of mental representation, that pertains to the intentionality, or content, of propositional attitudes. I shall begin with the first.

One thing that would qualify as a positive theory of meaning would be a theory of what meanings are. But I deny that there are any such *things* as meanings, and I had certainly better if I am to deny the relational theory of propositional attitudes and semantic compositionality. To be sure,

[1]   'Urjvid' doesn't have a meaning

and

[2]   Harvey doesn't know the meaning of 'hemidemisemiquaver'

are true, but [1] involves no *quantification* over *entities* denoted by the "general term" 'meaning', and in [2] the "singular term" 'the meaning of "hemidemisemiquaver"' is not a *referential* singular term. Perhaps one might best paraphrase [1] by saying that 'urjvid' cannot be used to say anything, [2] by saying that Harvey does not know what would be said by an utterance containing 'hemidemisemiquaver'.

This point, that there are no such *things* as meanings, is not new; Wittgenstein is famous for it, and Oxford philosophers often made it in the fifties, J. L. Austin even going so far as to write that "the phrase 'the meaning of a word' is, in general, if not always, a dangerous nonsense-phrase" (1961, p. 24; see also Wittgenstein 1953; Ryle 1957). The point is not new, but it is not yet a commonplace. Those many propositionalists who accept the Fregean dictum that the meaning of a sentence is a function of the meanings of its parts are committed to denying it (unless, of course, they wish to maintain that the objects they would assign to words in the "meaning assignments" they would make in the course of constructing compositional "meaning theories" for natural languages are not meanings in the ordinary meaning of 'meaning'). The issue whether there are such things as meanings also has bearing on my denial of the relational theory of propositional attitudes.

Instead of [2], my example might have been

[3]   Pierre doesn't know the meaning of 'snow is white',

and my point would have been the same: in [3] 'the meaning of "snow is white"' is not a *referential* singular term. But now consider

[4]   'Snow is white' means that snow is white.

This, too, is true. But should we say that in [4] it is being asserted that 'snow is white' stands in the means relation to the entity denoted by 'that snow is white', or, as Davidson would claim, to the entity denoted by the demonstrative 'that'? (See, for example, Davidson 1968; see also the discussion in chapter 5.) Surely if that were so, then (i) 'the meaning of "snow is white"' *would* be a referential singular term, its referent the referent of 'that snow is white' (or 'that'): the meaning of 'snow is white' would be precisely that which the sentence means, viz., that snow is white; and thus (ii) [3] *would* have a reading on which 'the meaning of "snow is white"' was a genuinely referential singular term. And if [3] has a reading on which a meaning is referred to, then why would that not also be true of the other examples? But, I claim, there are no entities denoted by the general term 'meaning', and thus 'that snow is white' in [4] is not a referential singular term (and the same goes for 'that'). And if that is so, then the same is true of the 'that'-clause in 'Ralph believes that snow is white', and the relational theory of propositional attitudes is false.

Sometimes what passes as a theory of meaning is a theory that offers reductive analyses of semantic idioms. But I deny that any such correct theories can be given. If IBS cannot do it—and it cannot—then it seems to me clear that no other program will succeed in providing the elusive "analyses." Then there is the further point, often made nowadays, that one should not expect anything else, given the dreary history of analysis; if analysis is the proper business of philosophers, then philosophy is bankrupt. As I have earlier intimated, I think it is an interesting question *why* reductive, or conceptual, analysis is impossible, and perhaps we will be able to say why when we learn more about the nature of our cognitive apparatus. Also on the brighter side, there is, I think, a concessive point to be made. One can often illuminate philosophically interesting connections between a given concept and other concepts by *trying* to give an analysis of it. For example, I believe that it is possible to learn something of philosophical interest by trying to complete the schema 'x refers to y iff . . .', even though it can enjoy no true and interesting completion. Is there, then, something to be said after all for the Rylean idea that the proper business of philosophy is laying out the logical geography of our philosophically interesting concepts? (See, for example, Ryle 1949.) Not really, I should think; for "analytical" connections among these concepts will not take one very far, and after that connections are holistic in the extreme. It does seem that something interesting would emerge from omniscience about the conceptual roles of our semantic and mental concepts, but if there is anything more definite or positive to be said here, it escapes me.

In rejecting the idea that the theory of meaning should consist in "reductive analyses" of semantic notions, I do not mean to put too fine an edge on 'analysis'. I know that there are philosophers of language who take their job to be the "explication" of semantic notions, but who would vehemently deny that they are doing "conceptual" or "meaning" analysis; they would heartily endorse the negative remarks I have made about "analysis." At the same time, they may go on to define the task of the theory of meaning thus:

> Our problem in semantics is posed by a part of human behavior, the verbal part. People produce sounds and inscriptions which play a strikingly important role in their lives. Early in our theorizing about people, at about the time we attribute minds to them, we see their sounds and inscriptions as items of language: we see the items as having such semantic properties as *being meaningful*, of *referring* to parts of the world, of *being true or false*. We attribute to people complicated beliefs, hopes, desires, and so on about the world, which we think their words express, as part of our theory to explain the complicated way they behave in the world. I take the main problem of semantics to be to explain the semantic notions that appear in the theory. In virtue of what does this sound refer to that object? What is it for an inscription to be meaningful? Why is that sound true? (Devitt 1981, p. 68)

"In virtue of what does this sound refer to that object?" How can a philosopher who asks this deny that his concern is "analysis"? Surely what he is after is a completion of '*x* refers to *y* iff ...' that is true and contains no semantic terms on the right-hand side, and why is this not "analysis"? But there *is* an important difference to be discerned between two sorts of philosophers both of whom want the sort of completion just characterized. The old-fashioned champion of conceptual, or meaning, analysis does not find semantic facts especially *problematic*; he does not worry about their being incorporated into a scientific conception of the world. Rather, he feels that all concepts are either simple or else logically complex, that those that are complex can be defined in terms of simple concepts together with logical operations such as conjunction, that such reductions can be arrived at on a purely a priori, introspective basis, and that it is the business of philosophy to give such reductions. The other sort of philosopher, rightly scornful of this old-fashioned approach, differs in two respects, one motivational, the other methodological. The motivational difference has to do with physicalism. The physicalist reductionist (as we may call the second sort of philosopher) does worry about incorporating semantic facts into a scientific *Weltanschauung*.[1] This theorist is a physicalist in the sense that he denies that there can be irreducibly semantic facts; if semantic notions are to be shown to be *legitimate*, then semantic facts must be revealed to be facts statable in a nonsemantic, physicalistic (or topic-neutral) idiom; reductions of notions such as meaning, denotation, and truth must be available if these notions are really to have application. The methodological difference between the two sorts of reductionists is that the physicalist reductionist does not necessarily expect that the sought-for reductions will be discovered by introspective analysis of concepts; his model for reduction may be the scientific discovery that heat is a certain kind of thermal energy, or the reduction of valence to physical properties of atoms.

But I have argued that the enterprise of the physicalist reductionist is also misguided. There is no physicalistic or topic-neutral reduction of semantic notions, and none is needed to render them legitimate or to make them cohere with a respectably scientific outlook. There are semantic facts, in the only sense in which there are facts (the pleonastic sense), and they are irreducibly semantic.

Another thing that would count as a theory of meaning is a theory of the form that a correct "meaning theory" for a particular language would take, where a meaning theory for a particular language is a constructive theory—perhaps a compositional truth-theoretic semantics—that would specify the meaning of each word and primitive syntactical construction in the language in a way that would determine the meaning of each expression in the language. This would be a theory that "explicitly states something knowledge of which would suffice for interpreting utterances of speakers of the language to which it applies" (Davidson 1976, p. 171). But I have denied that natural languages have meaning theories. I have argued that the assumption that languages have meaning theories is not needed to explain how it is possible "that the speakers of a language can effectively determine the meaning or meanings of an arbitrary expression (if it has meaning)" (Davidson 1967a, p. 35), and that it is not needed for any other reason; and I have tried to give reasons for thinking that the assumption is false.

There is one legitimate theory that might be called a "theory of meaning," though that is not how I would choose to speak: namely, a theory of language understanding, a theory that explains one's ability to go from auditory perceptions of utterances of sentences to knowledge of what propositional speech acts were performed in them. The trouble is, however, that such a theory would not be a *philosophical* theory.

The bigger trouble is that—subject to a certain qualification—there seems not to be any important and familiar characterization of a theory of meaning that is satisfiable if what I have written in this book is correct. The questions that now define the philosophy of language seem to have false presuppositions. The qualification is this. It seems fair enough to say that the big question in the philosophy of language is, "What is the nature of meaning?", and to add that, in asking this question, it must not be assumed that a theory of the nature of meaning must take the form of any sort of reduction of meaning to something else. Now I can accept that, and can say that I have already given the theory of the nature of meaning: there are true but irreducible meaning-ascribing sentences; there are no "non-pleonastic" semantic facts or properties; natural languages neither have nor need finitely axiomatizable meaning theories—and so on, for all the other things, positive and negative, that I have written in this book. Still, one may have felt at the end of chapter 9 that having argued against this, that, and the other thing, I ought now to give *my* "positive theory of meaning." But it is just the idea that there might remain some further systematic task of "theory construction" that I am questioning.

10.3 The No-Theory Theory of Mental Representation

The same goes for theories of intentionality.

If one subscribes to the relational theory of believing, then a theory of intentionality would be, at the least, a theory of what things were the relata of the belief relation, and of what their content-determining features were. These things could be called "objects of belief"; they would be the referents of 'that'-clauses. Since 'that'-clauses would be semantically complex singular terms, their parts—for instance, 'dog' in 'Tanya believes that Gustav is a dog'—would have referents, and perhaps these things could be called "concepts." But I have denied the relational theory, and with it the idea that there are "concepts" or "objects of belief." We can of course ask what someone believes, and say that what she believes is that Gustav is a dog. But neither 'that' nor 'that Gustav is a dog' is here a genuinely *referential* singular term. And there are concepts, so to speak, but not as real entities over which one can quantify. To have the concept *dog* is just to have beliefs whose contents are correctly ascribable using 'dog'. There is, then, no theory of intentionality to be found here.

Now Tanya does believe that Gustav is a dog, and one may ask what makes it the case that she has that belief. By virtue of what does she believe that Gustav is a dog? In what does her having that belief consist? One may ask this from the point of view of the conceptual analyst or, more reasonably, from that of the physicalist reductionist. In either case the answer is the same: the question posed carries the false presupposition that one can correctly complete in nonintentional terms the schema '*x* believes that *p* iff . . .'. If one could give such a reduction, then it would certainly qualify as a theory of mental representation. But, I have argued, one cannot, and one need not. There are intentional facts, in the only sense in which there are facts (the pleonastic sense), and they are irreducibly intentional.

Having written what I have written in this book, I can think of nothing else that I might write that would qualify as a positive *philosophical* theory of mental representation.

10.4 A Defeatist Program of Despair?

One wants to know: What, Schiffer, is *your* theory of meaning? And I am disturbed by the question, for I simply do not know what could *count as* a philosophical theory of meaning and intentionality, if what I have argued in this book is correct (and if I have not already given it). Suppose one were made to give a course on the philosophy of language under the following constraints: it could not be a historical survey, and it could not consist in saying what philosophical theories of language were false; the course had to pose legitimate philosophical questions and propose positive theories to answer them. The IBS theorist would have no trouble giving this course: he would ask what meaning is and go on to give his reductions. The Davidsonian would have no trouble giving this course: he would ask what form a correct theory of meaning for a particular language must take and give his answer. But what course could *I* give? The only questions that I can think of that invite positive theories as answers all have, by my lights, false presuppositions.

I do not mean to deny that theses and arguments could be advanced that were consistent with my position and that would, if correct, be judged philosophically important. This would be the case, for example, if it could be successfully argued that only a member of a *community* of rule followers could have thoughts. That would certainly answer to a traditional concern of philosophers. But the example is an unlikely one, and likely ones are hard to find. Anyway, I have none to offer; so if the hypothetical course had to consist in a series of conceptual insights, I would still have no course to give. Besides, what one wants to find for the philosophy of meaning and intentionality, if not for philosophy generally, is a characterization of the discipline that would perspicuously define positive research programs in advance of having the positive theories that would constitute their fruition. It is this characterization that I am stuck for. I do not know how to give an *interesting* answer to the challenge to say what I do for a living. I do not know how to define myself professionally. I do not now have a further chapter to write.

Is mine a defeatist program of despair? I sincerely hope not. The "no-theory theory of meaning" is clearly not *defeatist*. That theory claims that the questions that *now* define the philosophy of language (and I use that rubric broadly to include questions about intentionality) have false presuppositions, that there can be no correct positive theories of the sort some seem to seek. How could that be defeatist if it is true? It is not as if I had got tired of looking for the theories in question. I have argued that there cannot be true such theories. It is not as if I were claiming that facts that cry out for explanation should be ignored. What that needs to be explained is going unexplained? One cannot reply, "The nature of semantic and intentional facts," without begging the question. To be sure, there are facts that do need explanation—many facts about language understanding, many about the ways in which we store, represent, and process information—but, again, these are not philosophical questions (although the skills of the philosopher would be relevant to answering them).

But if my views are not defeatist, are they *despairing*? That is a more difficult question to answer, and one that I care very much about. I do not want to think that my career is to show the fly the way out of the fly-bottle.[2] I wish that I could go on from here to raise new questions that would enable me to give my hypothetical course. But I have not been able to define those questions. I would like to think that I have not *yet* succeeded. Maybe the answer lies in some alliance with cognitive science.

Notes

Chapter 1

1. Quine's Indeterminacy Thesis runs throughout his writings, but see especially Quine 1960, Chapter 2, and Quine 1970.

2. I find 'finitely axiomatizable' too ponderous for use in informal exposition, but that is what the text's 'finitely statable' comes to. A finitely statable theory is a theory that could be expressed by a single closed sentence of finite length. It is therefore a theory that could be grasped by a finite creature.

3. This slogan is virtually omnipresent in Dummett's writings, but see especially Dummett 1975, 1976.

4. "The possibility of our understanding [sentences] which we have never heard before rests evidently on this, that we construct the sense of a [sentence] out of parts that correspond to the words. If we find the same word in two [sentences] ..., then we also recognize something common to the corresponding thoughts, something corresponding to this word. Without this, language in the proper sense would be impossible. We could indeed adopt the convention that certain signs were to express certain thoughts, like railway signals ('The track is clear'); but in this way we would always be restricted to a very narrow area, and we could not form a completely new [sentence], one which would be understood by another person even though no special convention had been adopted beforehand for this case" (Frege 1980, p. 79).

5. Chomsky is an exception; for example, Chomsky 1980. There is also a useful discussion Stabler 1983.

6. Most of these states will be "subdoxastic" in the sense of Stich 1978. A subdoxastic state is a non-belief, information-bearing state. Subdoxastic states differ from beliefs in their unavailability to consciousness and in the way they are inferentially isolated from beliefs (for instance, if you believe that if p, then q, and believe p, you are likely to infer q; but you will not make this inference if the state representing p is subdoxastic). If, as Chomsky and others claim, we have internally represented transformational grammars, then the states that represent them are subdoxastic.

7. State-*tokens* are the *particulars* (as opposed to universals) that satisfy open sentences such as 'x is a C-fiber stimulation', 'x is a pain', or 'x is a belief that the girl bit the monkey', while state-*types* are the properties expressed by these open sentences.

8. If Davidson's theory of the logical form of propositional-attitude sentences (Davidson 1969) is correct, the demonstrative 'that' is the singular term that refers to what I believe, and its referent is the occurrence, following its occurrence, of 'snow is white'. Davidson's paratactic theory—discussed briefly near the end of section 1.3, more thoroughly in chapter 5—will generally be ignored in informal glosses of the relational theory of propositional attitudes.

9. A further motivation for the relational theory can be provided for those who suppose that predicates such as 'believes that snow is white' are functionally definable. See Loar 1981, Field 1978, Schiffer 1981a.

10. The distinction between objectual and substitutional quantification is usually made with respect to formal systems. If the semantics for a formal language is such that

$(\exists x)(\ldots x \ldots)'$ is true iff some object (in a specified domain of objects) satisfies $(\ldots x \ldots)'$

and

$(\forall x)(\ldots x \ldots)'$ is true iff every object (in the domain) satisfies $(\ldots x \ldots)'$,

then '∃' and '∀' are, respectively, existential and universal *objectual* quantifiers, while 'x' is an *objectual* variable. An objectual variable has both *substituends* and *values*. Its substituends are the nonlogical constants that may be meaningfully substituted for it, and in first-order logic only singular terms can be substituends of objectual variables. Its values are the objects in the domain of discourse that it ranges over; these are the objects one inspects in determining the truth values of objectually quantified sentences. The referents of the substituends of an objectual variable will be among the values of the variable, but there may be values to which no substituends refer.

If, now, the semantics is such that

$(\Sigma X)(\ldots X \ldots)'$ is true iff some substitution-instance of $(\ldots X \ldots)'$ is true

and

$(\Pi X)(\ldots X \ldots)'$ is true iff every substitution-instance of $(\ldots X \ldots)'$ is true

then 'Σ' and 'Π' are, respectively, existential and universal *substitutional* quantifiers, while 'X' is a *substitutional* variable. A substitutional variable may have substituends, but not values (although this does not preclude substituends for substitutional variables from having references). Even in systems that are first-order as regards their objectual quantifiers, expressions of any syntactic category—singular terms, predicates, sentences—may be substituends of substitutional variables, so that, for example, from

Fa

one may infer both

$(\Sigma X)(Xa)$

and

$(\Sigma Y) Y.$

It should be clear that only objectual quantification carries "ontological commitment" (see Quine 1953a, 1969a); the ontological commitments of a substitutionally quantified sentence are only those of the substitution-instances of its quantified open sentence, which may not be any. A formal system may utilize both kinds of quantifiers. Through no fault of its own, subsitutional quantification has had a rather checkered career; see Kripke 1976 and its bibliography.

11. Whether or not this representation of [2] implies a reduction of "belief *de re*" to "belief *de dicto*" would depend on the possibility of specifying modes of presentation without reference to the objects they are of. Variants on this way of representing [2] would allow for a contextually determined reference to a particular mode of presentation, or to a particular type of mode of presentation. See Schiffer 1977, 1978, 1981b.

12. As far as I know, the Gricean program is the *only one* for reducing the semantic to the psychological; I argue for the first supposition in Schiffer 1982 and still believe that if the semantic and the psychological enjoy a physicalistic reduction, it is only via a prior reduction of the former to the latter. However, nothing in the present book presupposes the truth of this supposition.

13. See especially Bennett 1976; Grandy and Warner 1986a; Grice 1957, 1968, 1969, 1982, 1986; Lewis 1969, 1975; Loar 1976a, 1981; Schiffer 1972, 1981a, 1981b, 1982; Strawson 1964, 1969.

   Public-language semantic properties are those that supervene on use in a public, communicative language—for example, the property ascribed to 'La neige est blanche' in saying that it means in French that snow is white. The potential contrast is with ascriptions of truth or falsity to beliefs ("He has many false beliefs") or ascriptions of semantic features to expressions in an inner system of mental representation. I say "*potential* contrast" because analysis may reveal that even these latter are public-language semantic features.

14. A Tarskian definition of truth for a language prescinds from any role the expressions of the language may have in communication; if 'T' is defined for a language à la Tarski, then ⌜σ is T⌝ entails nothing about the *use* of σ in any population of speakers. See Tarski 1956.

15. The theorist must choose between mental representations and propositions as the items in the range of the belief relation; but, as will be made clear in chapter 4, this would not preclude an analysis of the belief relation that made essential reference to both kinds of entities.

16. That more than one thing may be meant by the claim that "believing is a relation to a mental representation" will be made clear in section 4.1. It may also be said that, as a limiting case, the view that propositional attitudes are relations to neural formulae subsumes the view that believing is a relation to *beliefs*—i.e., those neural state-tokens that are beliefs (and, being beliefs, are representational states that have truth values), regardless of whether or not those states have sentential structure. This, too, is touched on in chapter 4, and again in chapter 5.

17. Or perhaps not quite propositions as traditionally conceived, but properties of the kind favored by Lewis (1979). For our purposes, Lewis's theory counts as a version of the propositional theory of belief.

Chapter 2

1. David Lewis is a notable exception; although Lewis defines mental terms in terms of functional properties, he identifies mental properties with the physical properties that realize those functional properties. He has, not surprisingly, some pretty fancy maneuvering to do in order to try to accommodate multiple realization. See Lewis 1966, 1970a, 1972, 1980.

2. A first-level property is a property of particulars, things that are not properties, and a second-level property is a property of first-level properties.

3. Functional properties are also functional state-types; but I prefer the former locution because it keeps clearly in mind the fact that the bearers of those properties are physical state-tokens. Talk of functional states, while perfectly acceptable, is apt to create the confusion that functional state-tokens are something other than physical state-tokens; cf. Boyd 1980.

4. This was first made clear in Loar 1981; all references to Loar in this chapter, unless otherwise noted, are implicitly references to this work.

5. But not all functional theories are of these two types (or at least they need not be *formulated* as such). First, there may, as functionalists suppose, be psychological theories that are logically equivalent to theories of types [i] and [iii], although they are not formulated as existential generalizations. In the case of such *implicit* functional theories we obtain *explicit* functional theories by existential generalizations on the implicit theory's "theoretical" psychological terms. Second, as we shall presently note, there

are functional theories that utilize formulae (even uninterpreted formulae) rather than propositions as external indices of functional roles.

6. The values of *Bel* are *sets* of state-types in order to accommodate multiple realization; see Loar 1981, section 3.4, for the complete, unsimplified account.

7. Properly spelled out, these "definitions" would contain no metalinguistic references; see Loar 1981, section 4.2.

8. 'Rationality constraint' is Loar's expression, and he claims that the last of these generalizations belongs to that folk theory that is common knowledge among adults in our society. Paul Churchland is also quite adamant about folk psychology being a theory, and asserts that both explanations and the making of predictions presuppose laws. He also offers the following as a law of folk psychology (Churchland 1981, p. 69):

$(x)(p)(q)[((x$ believes that $p)$ & $(x$ believes that (if p then $q))) >$ (barring confusion, distraction, etc., x believes that $q)]$.

This is not a law, however, but at best a partial specification of one; one wonders how Churchland would replace 'etc.'.

9. Loar makes this point when he says that the commonsense theory fails to imply something about each belief which is true of no other belief.

10. It should be noted that the uniqueness constraint is a very weak constraint, and that satisfaction of it would not imply that *T*-correlated functional roles provided sufficient conditions in the sense in question. The following "theory," for example, satisfies the uniqueness constraint, but its *T'*-correlated functional roles do not begin to provide sufficient conditions for being in the belief states associated with them:

[T'] If p is true, then one believes p.

Because of the way in which 'p' occurs both within *and without* belief contexts, T' will imply something unique about each belief. This can be seen from the way in which it follows from the definition of $Bel_{T'}$ that $Bel_{T'}$ (that snow is white) $= N$ only if N is tokened in one if snow is white.

11. But might not one of folk psychology's platitudes be that beliefs about cats are typically caused by cats? No doubt *some* such beliefs (e.g., that one is looking at a cat) are highly reliable indicators of the truth of the propositions believed, at least among normal adults in our society; but this can hardly be elevated into a necessary condition for a state's being such a belief. Besides, Twin Earth and Burge-type counterexamples can be constructed for beliefs that are typically unreliable indicators of their truth.

12. As before, and with no greater chance of success (see section 3.5), the functionalist might try to rebut this argument with a description-theoretic construal of the content of Alfred's belief, suggesting that the content of the belief expressed by Alfred's utterance of 'I've arthritis in my thigh' is that he has in his thigh the disease called 'arthritis' in his linguistic community.

13. One might worry that Alfred in w' is not in all respects functionally equivalent to himself in w, as there will be environment-invoking functional differences owing to the way in which Alfred's use of 'arthritis' was acquired in w'. However, as Burge himself painstakingly shows, the example is easily set up so that there really are no functional differences whatever.

14. See Field 1978; Loar 1981. In the next chapter we shall find a good reason for one holding the relational theory of belief to prefer sentential objects of belief.

15. Field's point is that to state these psychological laws, believing need only be construed as a relation to uninterpreted formulae. See also Field 1986b; Fodor 1980; Loar 1981; Schiffer 1981a; Stich 1983.

16. Sometimes the fact that a given person has a certain belief is good evidence that that belief is true. A "reliability theory" of x is a theory that would tell us the ways in which

x's beliefs were, or were not, reliable indicators of external states of affairs, and it has been suggested that semantically characterized beliefs are needed to formulate such theories (see Field 1978, 1986b; Loar 1981; Schiffer 1981a; Stich 1983). The relevance of reliability considerations to the theory of belief content will be a topic of later discussion (see especially section 4.5); here it may simply be noted (i) that it is doubtful that reliability theories fall within the province of cognitive psychology (see Stich 1983) and (ii) that should "reliability theory" (such as it is) turn out to need semantically characterized beliefs, there is no evident reason that that characterization must invoke propositions (the point made in (a)). Of course I am not saying, and will not say, that beliefs do not have semantic content: my present belief that Nixon is retired is indeed true, and true iff Nixon is retired.

The *"pace"* allusions are to Burge 1986 and Fodor 1985 and 1987 where a central role for content in cognitive psychology is plumped for.

17. The metaphor is Quine's (1975, p. 91).

18. Loar 1981. Loar himself initially formulates his functionalist theory as a propositionalist theory, but then shows how propositions can be dispensed with in favor of linguistic items.

19. The fuel gauge example and the attendant claim about mental representation are taken from Dretske (1986).

20. See Schiffer 1986. See also Field 1986a and Stalnaker 1986, which, with my article, were a symposium on Stalnaker 1984.

Chapter 3

1. One other way concerns the problem of specifying modes of presentation to enter into *de re* beliefs about physical objects (see note 9 below). A second way concerns the infamous, but not well enough appreciated, Paradox of Analysis; while a third, and somewhat related, way exploits an argument in Burge (1978) to show that the principles that correctly describe substitution in belief contexts are not consistent with *any* propositionalist theory of belief.

2. As we shall presently see, the propositionalist is not committed to representing [a] as [b].

3. I am skirting issues in the philosophy of biology; not all biologists would agree that zoological species are constituted by genotypes. But that does seem to be the only view consonant with the Kripke-Putnam gloss that natural kinds are constituted by "internal" properties that account for certain observable similarities among members of the kind.

4. Why not dig in one's heels and insist that [2] and [6] *cannot* differ in truth value because the same proposition—viz., [5]—*is* referred to in both sentences (and likewise, *mutatis mutandis*, for [7] and [8])? True, someone taking this line might concede, Tanya believes, or may believe, that Gustav is not a shmog; but that merely shows that she has inconsistent beliefs, not that [6] can be false when [2] is true. True, this theorist might also concede, there is a strong intuition that these sentences *can* differ in truth value—as strong, to be sure, as the intuition that tells us that Lois Lane does not realize that Clark Kent is Superman even though she does realize that Clark Kent is identical with himself; but perhaps the significance of these intuitions can somehow be explained away.

Now one cannot coherently take this line about natural-kind terms in 'that'-clauses unless one is prepared to take what is *mutatis mutandis* the same line about singular terms in 'that'-clauses; and many believe that such an application of the 'Fido'-Fido theory to belief contexts is a position that Frege refuted nearly a hundred years ago when he pointed out that the ancient astronomer's discovery that Hesperus was Phosphorus was not the discovery of a planet's identity with itself. But in a recent book Nathan Salmon (1986) demurs from the belief of the many and defends a 'Fido'-Fido theory of belief. Not only would he maintain that the 'that'-clauses in [2] and [6] refer to the same proposition by virtue of the identity of doghood and shmoghood; he would also maintain that the 'that'-clauses in

Lois Lane doesn't realize that Clark Kent is Superman

and

Lois Lane doesn't realize that Superman is Superman

refer to the same proposition by virtue of the identity of Clark Kent and Superman; and he would maintain that my utterance of

I believe that I'm a paragon

cannot have the same truth value as my utterance of

I don't believe that he [pointing to what I fail to realize is a photo of myself] is a paragon,

as the two 'that'-clauses would, once again, refer to the same proposition, in this case the singular proposition ⟨Stephen Schiffer, the property of being a paragon⟩.

I intend to discuss Salmon's heroic stance more fully elsewhere, but will say just enough now to indicate my extensive disagreement.

Let us pretend that the Superman story is fact, and consider this utterance by an ordinary nonphilosopher, Floyd:

[A]   Lois Lane doesn't realize that Clark Kent flies.

Now Floyd would insist that [A] was true, and that in uttering it he was both asserting and expressing his belief that Lois Lane did not realize that Clark Kent flew. Salmon, on the other hand, would insist that *none* of this was true. [A] cannot be true for Salmon because, as Clark Kent is Superman, [A] is logically equivalent to

[B]   Lois Lane doesn't realize that Superman flies,

which is false: both 'that'-clauses refer to the singular proposition ⟨the person named 'Clark Kent' and 'Superman', the property of being a flier⟩. The reason why Floyd in his utterance of [A] is not asserting that Lois does not realize that Clark Kent flies is that he does not believe that, and the reason—i.e., Salmon's reason—he does not believe that is worth spelling out a bit, as it provides the essence of Salmon's solution (to use his term) to "Frege's Puzzle."

'Believes', according to Salmon, expresses a binary relation between a believer and a proposition (many of which are "singular propositions" such as the one allegedly referred to by the 'that'-clauses in [A] and [B]), but this binary belief relation is to be explicated in terms of a ternary relation, *BEL*, which holds between a believer, a proposition, and a mode of presentation, thus:

$B(x, p)$ iff $(\exists m) BEL(x, p, m)$.

In other words, x believes p *tout court* just in case x believes p under some mode of presentation or other: x may believe p under one mode of presentation, disbelieve it under another, and suspend judgment altogether under a third. Although Salmon is not sufficiently explicit on the matter, it is clear thart modes of presentation for propositions must be determined by modes of presentation for the individuals and properties that compose propositions, and in a more thorough treatment he would probably want to represent the mode of presentation for a proposition as a sequence of modes of presentation for the proposition's constituents. (I use 'mode of presentation' in the wholly neutral sense of the text and of Schiffer 1978, which presupposes nothing whatever about what modes of presentation are; Salmon's preferred terms are 'guise', 'appearance', and 'way of taking'. He offers no account of what the third term of the *BEL* relation is, but leaves that as a project for further research.) It is implicit in Salmon's exposition that a person x can believe and disbelieve a proposition p only if there are two *different* modes of presentation m and m' such that x believes p under m and disbelieves p under m'. And it is further implicit that x can believe p under m and disbelieve p under m' only if x does not believe that the two modes of presentation are modes of presentation of one and the same proposition.

It is this last point that explains why Floyd does not believe that Lois does not realize that Clark Kent flies. For Floyd does believe that Lois realizes that Superman flies, and so, given the identity, it follows (for Salmon) that he believes that Lois realizes that Clark Kent flies ('that Lois realizes that Superman flies' and 'that ... Clark Kent ...' refer to the same singular proposition). Given that Floyd does believe this proposition, the only way that he can also disbelieve it is—to abbreviate the discussion just a little—if he has two modes of presentation for Superman (i.e., Clark Kent) that he fails to realize are modes of presentation of one and the same person. But there are no two such relevant modes of presentation; for Floyd, unlike Lois, knows that 'Clark Kent' and 'Superman' refer to the same person.

Well, if [A] is false and Floyd is not asserting and does not believe the proposition it expresses anyway, then what *is* going on in his utterance of [A]? Salmon's answer, as nearly as I can tell, would proceed along the following lines.

It is common knowledge between Floyd and his audience that Lois realizes that Clark Kent flies (because, we may assume, they know that she knows that Superman flies, etc.); so there is no point in his asserting that. What he really wants to convey, however, is that there is some mode of presentation of the proposition that Clark Kent flies under which Lois fails to stand in the ternary *BEL* relation. The trouble is that English contains no verb that expresses *BEL*; so there is no direct or simple way for Floyd to say what he wants to convey. What he does, then, is to utter [A], intending his audience to recognize that the proposition that *he* wants to communicate—the Gricean implicature (see Grice 1975)—is not the one that is the literal content of the sentence uttered, but rather the proposition that there is some mode of presentation m (perhaps of a certain implicit type) such that it is not the case that BEL(Lois, the proposition that Clark Kent flies, m).

Likewise, *mutatis mutandis*, for 'Tanya doesn't realize that Gustav is a shmog'—only here the relevant mode of presentation pertains to shmoghood (i.e., doghood).

My main critical comments, baldly stated, are these:

a. Salmon's position on beliefs such as Tanya's belief that Gustav is a dog is a variant of the position I consider later in the chapter, that the complete content of Tanya's belief is a proposition that contains a mode of presentation of doghood. To that position I object that there is nothing available to the propositionalist to be the mode of presentation of doghood that enters into Tanya's belief. That objection applies straightforwardly to the treatment that Salmon would give of Tanya's belief in terms of *BEL*; and he has no reply to it, as he admits to having no account at all of modes of presentation (he really does not even know what relation his word '*BEL*' stands for, since he does not know what its third term is).

b. The main task of any 'Fido'-Fido theory of belief must be to explain away the sort of Fregean intuition according to which Tanya can believe that Gustav is a dog while not believing that he is a shmog, and according to which Lois Lane can believe that Superman flies while not believing that Clark Kent flies. But I find Salmon's use of *BEL* and Gricean implicature to account for these intuitions totally unconvincing. One cannot simply *claim* that something is an implicature of an utterance; the whole point of implicatures is that they are to be thought of as being generated by an inferential process that includes a premise about the literal meaning of the sentence uttered. But how is the implicature to be generated in the case of Floyd's utterance of [A]? Salmon offers no answer, nor does he say anything to relieve the mystery of how Floyd can take himself to be asserting and to believe that Lois does not realize that Clark Kent flies (in the nontendentious sense that if we were to ask him if he had that belief, he would say yes) when he does not have that belief, is not making that assertion, and shares with his audience the knowledge that Lois does realize that Clark Kent flies.

c. The primary motivation for a 'Fido'-Fido theory of belief is the desire to maintain a 'Fido'-Fido *semantics* for singular and general terms. But the semantics does not require the theory of belief (see Schiffer 1981b, where a 'Fido'-Fido semantics for singular terms is combined with a Fregean theory of belief ascriptions). In order to get Salmon's theory of belief ascriptions, one needs in addition to the 'Fido'-Fido semantics the hypothesis that 'that'-clauses are singular terms which refer to propositions that are semantic values of the sentence-tokens contained in them; but this assumption, traditionally denied by Fregeans for sentences like 'I believe that this is mine', is pretty much just assumed without argument by Salmon.

d. I could see pressing a Salmon-type account of 'that'-clauses if (for good reason) one wanted no truck with modes of presentation; but given that there is already a theoretical commitment to modes of presentation in the account of *BEL*, there would seem to be a much simpler and more intuitive account of belief ascriptions. One could say that a sentence such as 'Lois believes that Superman flies' expresses no proposition on its own but contains an implicit indexical component that requires reference to a contextually determined mode of presentation or type of mode of presentation; perhaps on a given occasion one uttering the sentence would mean that Superman is believed by Lois to fly under some mode of presentation which entails that he wears what we now recognize to be a woman's aerobic exercise outfit (see Schiffer 1977, 1978).

5. Here it must be kept in mind that what is at issue is the existence of a *language-independent* property of being a dog, something that could be the meaning of 'dog'. Thus the irreducibility of the *predicate* 'x is a dog' would not of itself prove that there was an irreducible language-independent *property* of being a dog but might itself be a premise in an argument to show that there was no such property. See below, 3.6.

6. 'Believes' in [a'] and [c'] *need* not be this dyadic relation. It could, for example, be construed as a triadic relation, $'B(x, \langle y_1, \ldots, y_n \rangle, P')$, which relates a believer to an n-ary sequence of items and an n-ary relation; then the propositionalist would reduce $'B$ to B. In the end, these are for the propositionalist little more than notational matters, the assumption of the text a useful expedient as well as the most plausible position for the propositionalist to take. See Schiffer 1978, 1981b.

7. Our notation for representing propositions, admitting both $\langle$Emily, cleverness$\rangle$ and $\langle m,$ cleverness$\rangle$, would be something less than perspicuous if it mattered.

8. The theorist of modes of presentation *can* represent [a'] as [d] (and [c'] as [e], though they can be ignored for the present), but need not. There are two possible ways in which he might wish to depart from this way of representing [a']. First, he might want to construe [a'] as containing an implicit indexical requiring reference to a mode of presentation or type of mode of presentation in order to accommodate a certain context relativity endemic to *de re* ascriptions (see Schiffer 1977, 1978). Second, while a theorist might agree that the mere singular proposition $\langle$Emily, cleverness$\rangle$ could not be the complete content of Ralph's belief, he might also feel that there could be no specification of that content that did not include a reference to Emily, and that, therefore, she too, along with the mode of presentation, muct be a constituent of whatever proposition was the content. For this theorist [a'] should be represented as

$(\exists m)(m$ is a mode of presentation of Emily & B(Ralph, $\langle\langle m,$ Emily$\rangle$, cleverness$\rangle$)),

$\langle\langle m,$ Emily$\rangle$, cleverness$\rangle$ being a proposition that is true in a possible world w just in case Emily is clever in w. Here m makes no contribution to the proposition's truth value, its job being to determine a functional role for the belief that secures its satisfaction of Frege's Constraint (see the next paragraph in the text and Schiffer 1978).

Although I shall later touch on the second one again, both of these complexities may be safely ignored in the present discussion.

9. In Schiffer 1977 and 1978 I plumped for a version of the description theory of *de re* thought, but I now think that that view requires people to have beliefs of a complexity and degree of sophistication that it is doubtful they can have. Thus, six-year-old Johnny has a visual memory of someone he glimpsed, and says, referring to that person, "She was a nice lady." Surely, the child believes of the woman he saw that she was nice, but it seems to me psychologically implausible that the complete content of his belief is that there is a woman who is uniquely such that his visual image is a memory image of her, and who is also nice. A number of writers have suggested that "percept-tokens" be taken to be the modes of presentation entering into perceptual, *de re* beliefs (see, for example, Bach 1982; Davies, 1982; Loar 1981; Peacocke 1981, 1983). It seems clear, however, that this view is credible only if there is some function f such that

a percept-token n is a mode of presentation of x iff $f(n) = x$,

and I am very doubtful that anyone can succeed in saying what that function is.

10. See note 8. Even though for the present discussion the option introduced by [B] can safely be ignored, however unproblematic it might be, I do think that this way of representing [2] faces difficulties over and above those facing [A]. For, first, the representation of [2] as [B] is coherent only if m need not *uniquely* determine that which it is a mode of presentation of—in this case, *Canis familiaris* (for if m did uniquely determine *Canis familiaris*, then the occurrence of the species in the proposition would be unmotivated); but, second, I do not see how a mode of presentation could satisfy Frege's Constraint if it did not uniquely determine that which it was a mode of presentation of.

11. Perhaps I should say that I can think of only two candidates that show some initial degree of promise. A candidate once entertained by David Kaplan (unpublished) which lacks the initial degree of promise would be his "characters," functions from "contexts" to "contents" (see Kaplan 1978); for in Kaplan's semantics 'dog' and 'shmog' would have the same character (as would 'Clark Kent' and 'Superman'). Perhaps I should also reiterate that as I am construing the propositional theory in a way that secures its compatibility with IBS, semantically interpreted linguistic items cannot be modes of presentation for the propositionalist. At the same time, I am not ignoring that position in logical space which does take semantically interpreted linguistic items as modes of presentation, for my objections to that position are entailed by my objections to the sententialist theories discussed in Chapter 5. In any event, taking modes of presentation to be linguistic expressions would be no more promising, and for essentially the same reason, than taking them to be Kaplanian characters: one might associate two distinct modes of presentation with an unambiguous term (cf. Salmon 1986, pp. 173–174; and Kripke's Paderewski example in Kripke 1979).

12. If stereotypes are to be modes of presentation, then they cannot without circularity be thought to be explicable in terms of beliefs with contents that are specifiable by sentences containing natural-kind terms.

Chapter 4

1. Actually, I believe that there is no way of satisfying LF, period; see note 2.

2. Why not forget about IT and go with the embedded semantic specification of R? First, it is very difficult to see what could *motivate* the view that believing is a relation to mental representations if one is then going to explicate their semantic properties in terms of the semantic properties of the public-language sentences occurring in 'that'-

clauses. Why not just take those public-language sentences as the objects of belief? Second, it is not even coherent to say that σ means in Mentalese what 'flounders snore' means in English. That would be coherent only if (i) the expression 'what "flounders snore" means in English' were a singular term that referred to some object that was the meaning of both the English and the Mentalese sentence, or (ii) the conditions for meaning such-and-such in a language of thought were the same as the conditions for meaning such-and-such in a public language. But (i) went down with the propositional theory of propositional attitudes (for what *object* other than a proposition could be the referent of 'the meaning of . . . '?), and (ii) is patently false: meaning in a public language is at least partly a matter of intention and convention, and that could hardly apply to neural formulae; moreover, meaning in Mentalese is commonly supposed to be partly a matter of conceptual role, and public-language sentences have *conceptual roles* only if one thinks as well as speaks in them.

3. This is a simplified version of Stich's account, but I believe that the counterexample I am about to give to [3] is also a counterexample to Stich's theory of content ascription.

4. Field's proposal differs from the presently dominant two-factor theory that I describe below, as he does not think that the theory of content will be able to avail itself of *intra*subjectively (as opposed to *intra*subjectively) ascribable conceptual roles. See note 23 below.

5. The SLT theorist might hope eventually to eliminate the quantification over state-of-affairs types—i.e., propositions—but too much sanguinity on this score would be naive. For he might just find that (i) he needs a causal theory of reference for general terms, in which case (ii) he will need properties to anchor one end of his word-referent causal chains; and (iii) any semantics that quantifies over properties as semantic values is, like it or not, in effect quantifying over propositions. It should be noted, however, that if propositions are needed in Mentalese semantics, this by no means opens the theory to the objections lately leveled against the propositional theory of propositional attitudes. This is because the SLT theorist would be individuating mental contents in terms of propositions *and conceptual roles.*

6. Stalnaker (1984) suggests an account of belief content that, if applied to the language of thought, would be tantamount to the Fodorian [b], but with the "when" part of the "when, and only when," removed, leaving just the "only when" part. For Stalnaker, then, one is merely infallible under optimal conditions. I do not think this is much of an improvement, however, and in Schiffer 1986 I argue, first, that the account is un-motivated, and, second, that there are good reasons for thinking that it is false (these reasons extend of course to Fodor's stronger account). See also Field 1986a; Stalnaker 1986.

7. One refinement that would have to be made would be to impose restrictions requiring the agent to be *relevantly* reliable; i.e., reliable in ways that mattered to us: we should not count an M-function as the TC function for M because it mapped each sentence of M onto the state of affairs that sugar is sweet. Perhaps an intuitively acceptable way of getting this restriction would be to restrict the notion of an M-function, and thus the vaues of 'f', to recursively specifiable functions determined by possible compositional semantics for M, each of which secured, in effect, that M had some suitable degree of expressive power. In this way the truth conditions of mental representations would be partly determined by the extensions of the nonlogical constants contained in them. I should not want to deny that SLT might founder in the attempt to spell out this "relevance" requirement precisely; my present enterprise, however, is that of making trouble for [c] even on the assumption that we are only concerned with relevant reliability, however that gets spelled out. See further Field 1978, 1986b; Loar 1981; Schiffer 1981a.

8. The question of what it might mean to say that we think in English is discussed in section 7.3. But the resolution of this question does not really matter for the present example; here one can just pretend that there are written tokens of English sentences rattling around in Ralph's head. It will also help if we further pretend that English qua Ralph's *lingua mentis* is unambiguous and without indexicals.

9. This is not quite true; Loar (1981, pp. 178–194) offers what is tantamount to an argument to show that reliability considerations will select a unique *M*-function. But Loar's argument is unsound if the objections made in chapter 2 to his functionalist theory are correct.

10. My argument presupposes that 'arthritis' in *E* means *arthritis*, and this may invite the response that one disagrees with the Burgean intuition and feels that for Alfred 'arthritis' means *shmarthritis*. Fine. We still have a counterexample to [c]; for we may now say that although *g* is the TC function for *E*, it still fails to satisfy the right-hand side of [c]. But what if one felt that the situation was indeterminate? Then it would follow from [c] that the sentences of *E* had no meaning! No doubt one could doctor [c] to get a more acceptable result, but other examples where there clearly was no indeterminacy—such as the "quaddition" example next to be discussed—would provide counterexamples to the revision.

11. John Carroll pointed out to me a simple way of setting up the Kripkean counterexample to [c] that does allow for a more sophisticated Ralph, who believes 'for any *x*, *y*, $x + y \geq x$', but does not involve nonstandard interpretations of expressions other than '+'. The trick is simply to revise the definition of quaddition so that it now reads:

$$x \$ y = x + y, \text{ if } x, y < \#$$
$$= x + y + 1 \text{ otherwise.}$$

Unfortunately, however, anyone sophisticated enough to believe that the sum of two numbers is at least as great as either of those numbers will almost certainly also believe that the sum of two numbers is never equal to itself plus 1.

12. Here one should keep in mind the restriction of *N*-functions to those determined by compositional semantics for *N*: we should not want the *N*-function that maps every sentence of *N* onto the state of affairs of Ubu's surviving in *W* to be the one that has greatest survival value!

13. For example, I know no way of stating a disquotational projective rule for sentences of the form 'Necessarily, σ'. I have also greatly exaggerated the ease of getting a disquotational reference scheme. What, for example, is the disquotational treatment of 'believes'? To answer this, one must first determine whether 'believes' is a relational predicate, a point of proper debate.

14. Field is well aware of the projectability problem. In Field 1975 it is argued that Quine's Japanese-classifier example (Quine 1969b, pp. 35–38) shows that a reduction of reference relations for languages structurally similar to English would not be adequate for determining the reference scheme for Japanese.

15. Field 1975, pp. 392–398, is suggestive in this regard.

16. To simplify the argument, I have limited it to the true-of relation, but I believe that essentially the same argument can be run on the reference relation for names and other types of singular terms.

17. A more careful statement would avoid the metalinguistic reference. See Field 1978; Schiffer 1982; and the references in chapter 2 pertaining to functional definition. For purposes of the realization of a functional relation I count a disjunction of physical relations as a physical relation.

18. I have many more objections to the idea that reference relations are functionally definable than those to be raised here. Some are implied by the discussion in section 2.5 of Psychofunctionalism. But my main objection is that I very much doubt that any sort

of causal/explanatory theory (a "reliability" theory, for example) would need to employ semantic notions of reference and truth as theoretical primitives. I think that where it may at first seem that a truth theory or M-function would be needed for devising a psychological theory (such as a reliability theory) for thinkers in M, that will turn out not to be so; and that the jobs for which semantic notions appeared to be needed can be done by substitutional quantification or by translation of M-sentences into the theory's metalanguage. These remarks should seem less cryptic after chapters 7 and 8.

19. Perhaps the theory contains generalizations like

> If α refers to a visible object and F is true of something iff it is red, then the probability that $\ulcorner F\alpha \urcorner$ is true given that one believes it is such-and-such.

20. Cf. Field 1977, where the conceptual role of a sentence is contrasted with the sentence's "referential meaning," and where to know that is to know how the sentence's truth condition is determined by the references of its parts.

21. The foregoing reason shows that a conceptual-role component is needed over and above the truth-condition component even if conceptual roles enter into the determination of truth conditions. If some conceptual roles are needed to account for the truth condition of 'Hesperus is Phosphorus', then an *additional* conceptual role will be needed to distinguish the meaning of this sentence from that of 'Hesperus is Hesperus'.

22. See Block 1986; Field 1977, 1978; Fodor 1980; Harman 1973, 1982; LePore and Loewer 1986; Loar 1981, 1982; Loewer 1982; McGinn 1982b; Schiffer 1981a, 1982; Stich 1983.

23. Field (1977) defines conceptual role in terms of an agent's subjective conditional probability function, and it is a consequence of his account that two mental representations σ_1 and σ_2 have the same conceptual role for a person just in case his subjective conditional probability function is such that, for any mental representation σ, the subjective probability of σ_1 given σ is the same as the subjective probability of σ_2 given σ. But insofar as conceptual role is wanted as an ingredient in the determination of the contents of mental states, Field's construal of conceptual role is of little use; for, as no two people (and no two time slices of the same person) have the same subjective conditional probability function, there is no obvious way on Field's account to define intersubjective sameness of conceptual role (and no obvious way to define intrasubjective sameness of conceptual role *across time*). It is true that Field is pessimistic as to there being any determinate notion of intersubjective sameness of mental content that goes beyond sameness of referential meaning. But if that pessimism is shared by an SLT theorist, he should not seek to define content in terms of Fieldian conceptual role; rather, he should argue that what is objective and determinate in ascriptions of belief content is exhausted by referential meaning.

24. Later I shall argue that the relational theory of propositional attitudes is false; but that will not help IBS, for we shall also see that it presupposes the relational theory.

Chapter 5

1. The first confrontation was reported in section 1.3.

2. Plainly, much more is required for understanding an utterance than knowing the meaning of the sentence uttered. But it is plausible that that is all that must be known as regards the language to which the utterance belongs. The rest of what we bring to bear in interpretation are truths that apply across languages. Davidson, of course, is not over-looking this platitude when he defines a meaning theory for L as a theory of L knowledge of which suffices for interpreting speakers of L.

3. Might not the extensionalist hold that believing is a relation to a mental representation (see chapter 4)? I do not think so; I think that one who holds that believing is a relation

to a mental representation, if his position is to be coherent, must subscribe to some sort of translational theory of meaning for the public language: to know the meaning of 'Snow is white' is to know that it can be used to say that snow is white; but 'that snow is white' in 'say that snow is white' for the language-of-thought theorist refers to the sentence in one's language of thought which means that snow is white. This theorist may offer an extensionalist semantics for Mentalese, but that would not make him an extensionalist with respect to natural-language semantics. Since I take the view that believing is a relation to a neural sentence to have been refuted, I shall not further explore the question raised in this note.

4. I am assuming that the sententialist shares the standard motivation for holding that 'believes' is a relation predicate: viz., that that is the only tenable way of accommodating it in a compositional semantics. Strictly speaking, however, a theorist can be a sententialist as regards belief while denying that natural languages have compositional semantics (whether such a position could be well motivated is another matter).

5. This ignores complexities arising from quantification into the position of the content sentence. The next note introduces a further possible qualification.

6. Although this is the official possition in the text of Davidson 1968, it is evidently denied in a footnote added in 1982. In that note Davidson says of his analysis of 'Galileo said that the earth moves', "Strictly speaking, the verb 'said' is here analysed as a three-place prediate which holds of a speaker (Galileo), an utterance of the speaker ('Eppur si muove'), and an utterance of the attributer ('The earth moves')" (p. 104). But this seems not to be true. Davidson's account of 'Galileo said that' commits him to holding (a) that 'that' refers to an utterance of 'the earth moves' and (b) that the ascription is true if Galileo uttered some sentence (e.g., 'Eppur si muove') with the same content as the referent of 'that'. Yet this certainly does not entail that 'said' is a three-place relation; one can certainly have a two-place relation that is defined in terms of a three-place relation (e.g., 'x photocopied y'). Clearly, the surface grammer of 'Galileo said that' favors construing 'said' as a two-place relation, as there is no grammatical slot for a third singular term (with Davidson I am ignoring implicit temporal references), and parity with 'believes' favors the dyadic construal. But nothing important turns on this issue.

7. Davidson's point, of course, is that all of the positions in, say,

   Galileo said that. The earth moves.

   are extensional, but that substitutions in the second sentence can change the truth value of the first because it will change the reference of 'that'.

8. Cf. chapter 4, note 2. It should be noticed that it is completely irrelevant to remark that the sameness-in-content relation may be taken as primitive in the construction of a theory of logical form for belief sentences. Of course that is so; but that is consistent with knowing that in the *theory of content* the relation is to be explicated in terms of nonrelative content-determining features. Surely any plausible theory of content will understand 'x has the same content as y' on the model of 'x has the same weight as y'.

9. 'That' still refers to an actual utterance, but it now no longer refers to that which Galileo believes; rather than having a primary occurrence, 'that' now has a secondary occurrence in another (implicit) singular term which does refer to what Galileo believes—the utterance-kind. Notice, too, how easily the Fregean can accept the paratactic aspect of Davidson's account: he can represent the logical form of [3] as

   B(Galileo, the proposition expressed by that).

Chapter 6

1. Consider this inference: 'Al and Betty are humble; therefore, there is something that they have in common (viz., humility)'. It would be silly to think that a nominalist about

properties must insist that this is really an invalid inference. The nominalist would be much better advised to recognize the inference as what it appears to be, trivially valid, and then seek to explain its validity in a way that does not involve an ontological commitment to properties. In this regard, one naturally thinks to understand the 'there is' of the conclusion as something akin to a substitutional quantifier. I think that this would not be too far from the mark, and I return to these issues in section 8.5.

2. Davidson (1967b). This of course may need qualification for quantum events.
3. Cf. Davidson (1974). Melden (1961) and many others have commented on the analytic, or quasi-analytic, nature of belief/desire generalizations. While I agree with Davidson (1970) that there are no strict causal laws involving propositional-attitude concepts, I do not agree with his argument, which turns on the normative status of rationality. It should also be clear that the *'ceteris paribus'* in the text has no substance but is merely tantamount to the '...' of ellipsis.
4. I do not mean to imply that all beliefs are neural states; for that would be implausible if some of one's beliefs—e.g., one's present belief that one never played checkers with Alexander the Great—are merely "dispositional" in some sense that would have to be spelled out. See the discussions of "non-core" beliefs in Dennett 1978, Field 1978, and Schiffer 1981a.
5. Those who do not may find their qualms addressed in the argument to show that there are no irreducible belief properties.
6. Jackson really only argues that qualia are epiphenomenal.
7. I trust it is clear that to object to supervenience construed as a primitive metaphysical relation is not to object to the use of 'supervene' when it simply means some other, familiar sort of dependence, such as entailment.
8. A wrong impression could be created by the Davidsonian associations of this argument. In rejecting the relational theory of believing I recognize the need to deny that 'believes' can be treated as semantically primitive within a compositional truth-theoretic semantics for English, and therefore recognize the need to deny that complex belief predicates, like 'believes that flounders snore', can be treated as semantically complex within such a semantics. That is precisely why I have emphasized that one can coherently reject the relational theory of propositional attitudes only if one rejects the hypothesis that natural languages have compositional truth-theoretic semantics. I do reject that hypothesis, and in the next chapter will try to show how we can live without it. But in denying that complex belief predicates are semantically complex *in the sense that requires that 'believes' be semantically primitive*, I am most emphatically not claiming that 'believes that flounders snore' is semantically primitive. The predicate is neither semantically complex (in the relevant sense) nor semantically primitive; and to think that it must be one or the other is to presuppose, in effect, that the language has a compositional truth-theoretic semantics, which presupposition I deny. In the argument against belief properties which I have just rehearsed, I have been concerned merely to point out, what is obviously consistent with my anticompositionality, that if there were belief properties, then complex belief predicates would be semantically primitive, and English unlearnable. I return to these issues in the next chapter.
9. In 2.4 we considered the "theory"

[T*] $(p)(q)(x)$(if x believes p & x believes q, then x believes $(p \& q)$)

and saw that its theoretical term 'believes' would be realized if [T*]'s Loar-style Ramsey-sentence

$(\exists f)(p)(q)(x)$(if x is in $f(p)$ & in $f(q)$, then x is in $f(p \& q)$)

was true. Here it was very clear that even if [T*] was realized (which is quite likely), it could not define belief, for it determines the same functional role for all beliefs with the same logical form. It should also have been clear from the discussion in 2.4 that the Loarian realization of a theory (that is, the realization of a belief/desire theory when belief and desire are construed as functions from propositions onto physical states having functional roles determined by the theory) would not be such a big deal. The real problem as regards the functional definitions of belief and desire is to find a belief/desire theory that correlates each proposition with a unique functional role.

10. 'Other things being equal' clauses are simply fudges when it is unclear what the "other things" are, or what it would be for them to be "equal."

11. The Realist of the preceding paragraph will deny that Ava is the only entity whose existence we require in order to explain the turth of [a], and will insist that that explanation must also mention the properties "expressed" by the predicates in [a].

12. I doubt that we can confidently have any stronger supervenience thesis in the absence of a principled reduction of belief properties to physical or functional properties. How is one to rule out the metaphysical possibility of disembodied Cartesian minds? And if one cannot, then one cannot claim that belief facts *must* supervene on physical facts; nor can one claim that there cannot be two physically indistinguishable possible worlds in one of which, but nor the other, someone believes that flounders snore. Second, I doubt the possibility of establishing a necessary equivalence of belief predicates with any sort of disjunction (finitary or infinitary) of physical predicates, even if disembodied minds are impossible. For in the absence of a principled reduction, there being such an equivalence presupposes what I think is ultimately incoherent: that one could, so to say, inspect each of the possible worlds in which Ava believes that a car is coming and determine, for each world, the physical fact on which the belief fact is supervening.

13. The metaphor of a formula's being in x's B-box is to be cashed out in terms of x's standing in a certain functional or computational relation to that formula. See Schiffer 1981a; Fodor 1975, 1987.

Chapter 7

1. 'Compositional semantics' is short for 'compositional truth-theoretic semantics'. I use 'meaning theory' in a way that does not presuppose that a meaning theory is a compositional semantics.

2. In *Models for Modalities* (1969) Hintikka gave an account according to which 'Ralph believes that flounders snore' is true just in case 'flounders snore' is true in all possible worlds compatible with what Ralph believes. Not only does it follow from this that Ralph believes everything entailed by what he believes, but it also follows that he believes everything if he has any inconsistent beliefs. Whether or not Hintikka's operator account could be repaired to avoid these counterexamples (see Hintikka 1970, 1975), it would still be subject to the difficulties adduced against the propositionalist account in chapter 3. In fact, it would seem that Hintikka's account is in essence little more than a notational variant of the view, associated with Stalnaker (see Stalnaker 1984), that believing is a relation to propositions construed as sets of possible worlds.

3. But see the references in note 7.

4. See the discussions of substitutional quantification in chapter 1, note 10, and in chapter 8.

5. I owe the idea of backwards English to its occurrence in Lycan 1984, where it is used to a different end.

6. The other states will be "subdoxastic" in the sense of Stich (1978); see chapter 1, note 6.

7. See Stabler 1983; Evans 1981; Davies 1981, chap. 4; Lycan 1984, chap. 10. The position I have ascribed to the CS theorist is, I believe, what Evans's account of "tacit knowledge" comes to when wedded to the hypothesis that one thinks in a language of thought.

8. Presently we shall see how, in a similar vein, we can allow for a degree of compositionality induced by truth-affecting recursion clauses for connectives and quantifiers, while also insisting that as there is no finite way of specifying semantic values for the basic predicates of the language, it enjoys no compositional semantics.

9. In a more adequate rendering there would be trade-offs with other factors, such as conversational appropriateness.

10. Not presently relevant is any argument that presupposes the relational theory of propositional attitudes, such as Frege's in the following passage:

> It is remarkable what language can achieve. With a few sounds and combinations of sounds it is capable of expressing a huge number of thoughts, and, in particular, thoughts which have not hitherto been grasped or expressed by any man. How can it achieve so much? By virtue of the fact that thoughts have parts out of which they are built up. And these parts, these building blocks, correspond to groups of sounds, out of which the sentence expressing the thought is built up, so that the construction of the sentence out of parts of a sentence corresponds to the construction of a thought out of parts of á thought. (Frege 1979, p. 225)

This is not presently relevant because our case against the CS theory is based on a refutation of the relational theory of propositional attitudes. What the CS theorist needs is an argument that does not *rely* on any relational account of propositional attitudes.

Chapter 8

1. Hintikka rejects what he calls the Principle of Compositionality, according to which "the meaning (semantic interpretation) of a complex expression is a function of the meanings (semantical interpretations) of its constituent expressions" (1984, p. 31); but, consistent with this, a game-theoretic meaning theory for a particular language would be a compositional semantics.

2. See Dummett 1973, p. 292; 1978, pp. 387, 444, 446, 454; 1975, pp. 103, 114; 1976, pp. 70, 135.

3. Dummett is actually unsure as to whether an anti-realist meaning theory should be in terms of verification or falsification conditions; but this distinction ought not to affect my later criticisms, since they should apply as well, *mutatis mutandis*, to the suggestion that a meaning theory is a recursive specification of falsification conditions. Sometimes Dummett speaks of conditions of correct or warranted assertability instead of verification/falsification conditions.

4. The non-sensible Nominalist takes the reference to a property seriously. See the nominalist positions attacked by Armstrong (1978). See also the exchange among Armstrong (1980), Devitt (1980), and Quine (1980).

5. See chapter 1, note 10.

6. But surely there are sentences of the form 'There is some property X such that ... X ...' that we are prepared to accept as possibly being true even though we recognize that the quantified open sentence '... X ...' enjoys no true substitution-instance. Consider, for example,

[A] There is some attribute, yet unthought of, that once discovered will provide the key to a unified field theory.

Or, even worse,

[B] There are properties that no one will ever think of.

It is arguable that we are able to make sense of [A] being true because we are able to imagine an enrichment of the language of physical theory that contains a predicate whose occurrence in true sentences would vindicate [A]. Something similar, I feel, is operative as regards [B], and the similar sentence, 'There are truths that our language is inadequate to express and that we are constitutionally unable to conceive'. I think that we can make sense of these sentences because we can imagine there being creatures like us, but with greater perceptual and intellectual powers, with languages that were extensions of ours, in which the alluded-to truths would be expressible. In effect, then, we should say that, strictly speaking, the quantifications in [A] and [B] are neither objectual nor substitutional (though they are like the latter in important respects). But this should come as no shock: why should we suppose that the use of quantificational idioms in ordinary language is exactly captured by some precisely defined technical notion? I feel justified in characterizing the quantification in, say, 'There is some attribute that your pants and my car have in common' as "substitutional" because (i) it is entailed by 'Your pants and my car are both black' even though (ii) the truth of this last sentence involves no ontological commitment to something referred to by the (ostensible) singular term 'the property of being black'. But I should be happy to concede that, although most of the uses of quantificational idioms with which I am concerned are correctly modeled by what is called 'substitutional quantification', there are uses—such as those exemplified in [A] and [B]—that are "substitutional" only in an attenuated sense that involves imagined extensions of the language.

7. What about ineffable thoughts? Might it not be true that

   Ralph is now thinking something

even though there was no true substitution-instance of the following sentence form?

   Ralph is now thinking that S.

It is difficult to see how, when we appreciate that substitutions for 'S' may contain demonstratives and roundabout descriptions. Thus Ralph might report his ineffable thought by saying 'I think that she has that certain *je ne sais quoi* that no words can convey'.

Chapter 9

1. I shall continue Grice's artificially extended use of 'utter', which is intended to cover any behavior by which one means something. Thus, 'In waving his hand Jones meant that the coast was clear' would be regimented as 'In "uttering" [=producing] his hand wave, Jones meant ....'

   The account of 'S means that A is to make it the case that p', for imperatival speaker-meaning, exactly parallels the account of declarative meaning, and in Schiffer 1972 I argued (certain qualifications aside) that S means something in uttering x iff, for some p and some A, S means in uttering x that p, or that A is to make it the case that p. To say, for example, that S means that A is to make it the case that A shuts the door is just a convoluted way of saying that S means that A is to shut the door.

   In Schiffer 1972, chap. 4, I tried to show how illocutionary acts could be completely defined in terms of speaker-meaning (see also Strawson 1964, where the reduction of illocutionary acts to Gricean speaker-meaning was first proposed). In Schiffer 1981b I tried to show how the various concepts of reference—speaker-reference, expression-reference, and their subspecies—could be defined within the IBS framework.

2. See Schiffer 1972, chaps. 2 and 3, where the points that follow in the text are elaborated. See also Grice 1969.

3. This is a more detailed version of a counterexample given in Strawson 1964, pp. 156–157.

4. David Lewis (1969) defined a very similar notion that he called 'common knowledge'.

290 Notes to Pages 248–271

5. I intend nothing portentous in the switch to saying; it merely reflects the fact that 'say' is much more likely to be used in describing acts of speaker-meaning than 'mean'. If there is the use of the verb 'to mean' that Griceans think they are analyzing, it is one confusedly mushed together in ordinary thought with many other uses. Ask what a speaker meant by his utterance and you are more likely to get a mini-psychoanalysis than anything else.

6. As I remarked earlier, it is not altogether clear that a noncircular set of conditions can be devised that will have this result. But to the extent that this is so, it is unclear that an IBS account of speaker-meaning is possible. In making the assumption of the text we are provisionally granting something to IBS.

7. The notion of mutual knowledge in a group G must here be interpreted, not as requiring that every member of G have knowledge of every other member of G, but rather as requiring that every member of G have the knowledge that if one is a member of G, then one knows that . . . . See Schiffer 1972, p. 131.

8. The IBS use of Lewis's idea developed in the text differs from Lewis's own account of the actual-language relation.

9. Lewis 1975, pp. 175–178. Much of what follows in explication of "grammars" is a paraphrase of Lewis, although I have taken the liberty of further simplifying Lewis's already simplified exposition. So not only shall I continue to ignore indexicality, ambiguity, and moods other than the indicative; I shall also make no attempt to accommodate "deep structure" and transformational grammars for natural languages. Trouble enough will arise for IBS even when so much is put aside.

10. Perhaps I should, more cautiously, say that I cannot see how IBS can do without the assumption that natural languages have compositional meaning theories; but the distinction between a meaning theory and a compositional semantics for a particular language will not be at issue here.

11. This is related to, but distinct from, the familiar objection that IBS definitions of speaker-meaning are psychologically implausible owing to the enormous complexity of intentions they require of speakers. I no longer find that charge so answerable as I once did (see Schiffer 1982; Loar 1981, chap. 10); but apart from that it does seem to me even more psychologically implausible that mastery of a natural language consists in propositional knowledge of a correlation of sentences with the act-type of, so to say, IBS-intending to produce in someone the belief that such-and-such.

12. It is not merely that the account requires knowledge of set theory. [L] also requires members of G to have knowledge of L as a whole; and as Loar (1981) points out, "the only non-circular way they could have this (i.e. apart from knowledge of L as 'the language of [G]') would be via an abstract description of how L recursively maps sentences onto meanings. Speakers would then have to know the semantic rules of their language, a rather strong requirement" (p. 256).

13. Both sorts of problems are raised and discussed in Grandy 1982.

14. Blackburn himself presents a considerably simplified version of the idea that x means p in G iff there prevail in G conventions conformity to which requires one not to utter x unless one means that p. But, as I pointed out above, this is not helpful unless one can say what sort of conventions would satisfy this account.

Chapter 10

1. The author of Field 1972 is a good example of a physicalist reductionist.

2. "What is your aim in philosophy?—To shew the fly the way out of the fly-bottle." Wittgenstein 1953, section 309.

References

Adams, R. (1974). "Theories of Actuality." *Noûs*, 5, 211–231.

Armstrong, D. (1978). *Nominalism & Realism: Universals & Scientific Realism*, vol. 1. Cambridge: Cambridge University Press.

Armstrong, D. (1980). "Against 'Ostrich' Nominalism: A Reply to Michael Devitt." *Pacific Philosophical Quarterly*, 61, 440–449.

Austin, J. L. (1961). "The Meaning of a Word." In *Philosophical Papers*. Oxford: Oxford University Press.

Austin, J. L. (1962). *How to Do Things with Words*. Oxford: Oxford University Press.

Bach, K. (1982). "*De Re* Belief and Methodological Solipsism." In Woodfield (1982).

Bach, K. (1984). "Default Reasoning: Jumping to Conclusions and Knowing When to Think Twice." *Pacific Philosophical Quarterly*, 65, 37–58.

Barwise, J., and Perry, J. (1983). *Situations and Attitudes*. Cambridge, Mass.: MIT Press. A Bradford book.

Bealer, G. (1982). *Quality and Concept*. Oxford: Oxford University Press.

Bennett, J. (1976). *Linguistic Behaviour*. Cambridge: Cambridge University Press.

Blackburn, S. (1984). *Spreading the Word*. Oxford: Oxford University Press.

Block, N. (1980a). "Troubles with Functionalism." In Block (1980b).

Block, N., ed. (1980b). *Readings in Philosophy of Psychology*, vol. 1. Cambridge, Mass.: Harvard University Press.

Block, N., ed. (1981). *Readings in Philosophical Psychology*, vol. 2. Cambridge, Mass.: Harvard University Press.

Block, N. (1986). "Advertisement for a Semantics for Psychology." In P. French, T. Uehling, and H. Wettstein, eds., *Midwest Studies in Philosophy 10*. Minneapolis: University of Minnesota Press.

Boyd, R. (1980). "Materialism without Reductionism: What Physicalism Does Not Entail." In Block (1980b).

Brand, M., and Harnish, R. (1986). *Problems in the Representation of Knowledge and Belief*. Tucson: University of Arizona Press.

Burge, T. (1978). "Belief and Synonymy." *Journal of Philosophy*, 75, 119–138.

Burge, T. (1979). "Individualism and the Mental." In P. French, T. Uehling, and H. Wettstein, eds., *Midwest Studies in Philosophy 4*. Minneapolis: University of Minnesota Press.

Burge, T. (1980). "The Content of Propositional Attitudes." APA Western Division Meeting; abstract in *Nous*, 14 (1980), 53–58.

Burge, T. (1982a). "Other Bodies." In Woodfield (1982).

Burge, T. (1982b). "Two Thought Experiments Reviewed." *Notre Dame Journal of Formal Logic*, 23, 284–293.

Burge, T. (1986). "Individualism and Psychology." *Philosophical Review*, 95, 3–45.

Carnap, R. (1947). *Meaning and Necessity*. Chicago: University of Chicago Press.

Chomsky, N. (1980). *Rules and Representations*. New York: Columbia University Press.

Churchland, P. (1981). "Eliminative Materialism and Propositional Attitudes." *Journal of Philosophy*, 78, 67–89.

Davidson, D. (1967a). "Truth and Meaning." *Synthese*, 17, 304–323. Reprinted in Davidson (1984); page references are to the latter.

Davidson, D. (1967b). "Causal Relations." *Journal of Philosophy*, 64, 691–703. Reprinted in Davidson (1980).

Davidson, D. (1968). "On Saying That." *Synthese*, 19, 130–146. Reprinted in Davidson (1984); page references are to the latter.

Davidson, D. (1973a). "In Defence of Convention T." In H. Leblanc, ed., *Truth, Syntax and Modality*. Amsterdam: North Holland. Reprinted in Davidson (1984); page references are to the latter.

Davidson, D. (1973b). "Radical Interpretation." *Dialectica*, 27, 313–328. Reprinted in Davidson (1984).

Davidson, D. (1974). "Psychology as Philosophy." In S. Brown, ed., *Philosophy of Psychology*. New York: Barnes and Noble. Reprinted in Davidson (1980).

Davidson, D. (1975). "Thought and Talk." In Guttenplan (1975). Reprinted in Davidson (1984); page references are to the latter.

Davidson, D. (1976). "Reply to Foster." In Evans and McDowell (1976). Reprinted in Davidson (1984); page references are to the latter.

Davidson, D. (1979). "Moods and Performances." In Margalit (1979). Reprinted in Davidson (1984).

Davidson, D. (1980). *Essays on Actions & Events*. Oxford: Oxford University Press.

Davidson, D. (1984). *Inquiries into Truth & Interpretation*. Oxford: Oxford University Press.

Davidson, D. (1986). "A Nice Derangement of Epitaphs." In Grandy and Warner (1986b).

Davies, M. (1981). *Meaning, Quantification, Necessity*. London: Routledge and Kegan Paul.

Davies, M. (1982). "Individuation and the Semantics of Demonstratives." *Journal of Philosophical Logic*, 11, 287–310.

Davies, M. (1984). "Taylor on Meaning-Theories and Theories of Meaning." *Mind*, 93, 85–90.

Dennett, D. (1978). "Brain Writing and Mind Reading." In *Brainstorms*. Cambridge, Mass.: MIT Press. A Bradford book.

Dennett, D. (1986). "The Logical Geography of Computational Approaches (A View from the East Pole)." In Brand and Harnish (1986).

Devitt, M. (1980). "'Ostrich Nominalism' or 'Mirage Realism'?" *Pacific Philosophical Quarterly*, 61, 433–439.

Devitt, M. (1981). *Designation*. New York: Columbia University Press.

Devitt, M. (1984). *Realism and Truth*. Princeton: Princeton University Press.

Dretske, F. (1986). "Aspects of Cognitive Representation." In Brand and Harnish (1986).

Dummett, M. (1973). *Frege: Philosophy of Language*. London: Duckworth.

Dummett, M. (1975). "What Is a Theory of Meaning?" In Guttenplan (1975).

Dummett, M. (1976). "What Is a Theory of Meaning? II." In Evans and McDowell (1976).

Dummett, M. (1978). *Truth and Other Enigmas*. London: Duckworth.

Evans, G. (1981). "Semantic Theory and Tacit Knowledge." In S. Holtzman and C. Leich, eds., *Wittgenstein: To Follow a Rule*. London: Routledge and Kegan Paul.

Evans, G., and McDowell, J., eds. (1976). *Truth and Meaning*. Oxford: Oxford University Press.

Field, H. (1972). "Tarski's Theory of Truth." *Journal of Philosophy*, 69, 347–375.

Field, H. (1975). "Conventionalism and Instrumentalism in Semantics." *Noûs*, 9, 375–405.

Field, H. (1977). "Logic, Meaning, and Conceptual Role." *Journal of Philosophy*, 74, 379–409.

Field, H. (1978). "Mental Representation." *Erkenntnis*, 13, 9–61. Reprinted in Block (1981); page references are to the latter.

Field, H. (1986a). "Stalnaker's *Inquiry.*" *Pacific Philosophical Quarterly,* 67, 98–112.

Field, H. (1986b). "The Deflationary Conception of Truth." In G. Macdonald and C. Wright, eds., *Fact, Science, and Morality: Essays on A. J. Ayer's Language, Truth, and Logic.* Oxford: Basil Blackwell.

Fodor, J. (1975). *The Language of Thought.* New York: Crowell.

Fodor, J. (1980). "Methodological Solipsism Considered as a Research Strategy in Cognitive Psychology." *Behavioral and Brain Sciences,* 3, 63–110. Reprinted in Fodor (1981).

Fodor, J. (1981). "Propositional Attitudes." In *Representations: Philosophical Essays on the Foundations of Cognitive Science.* Cambridge, Mass.: MIT Press. A Bradford book.

Fodor, J. (1985). "Banish DisContent." In J. Butterfield, ed., *Proceedings of the 1984 Thyssen Conference.* Cambridge: Thyssen.

Fodor, J. (unpublished). "Psychosemantics—Or: Where Do Truth Conditions Come From?" Fodor's latest thinking on these matters is presented in Fodor (1987).

Fodor, J. (1987). *Psychosemantics: The Problem of Meaning in the Philosophy of Mind.* Cambridge, Mass.: MIT Press.

Foster, J. (1976). "Meaning and Truth Theory." In Evans and McDowell (1976).

Frege, G. (1891). "Function and Concept." In *Translations from the Philosophical Writings,* tr. P. Geach and M. Black (1952). Oxford: Blackwell.

Frege, G. (1892). "On Sense and Reference." In *Translations from the Philosophical Writings,* tr. P. Geach and M. Black (1952). Oxford: Blackwell.

Frege, G. (1967). "The Thought: A Logical Inquiry." In P. Strawson, ed., *Philosophical Logic.* Oxford: Oxford University Press.

Frege, G. (1979). "Logic in Mathematics." In H. Hermes, F. Kambartel, and F. Kaulbach, eds., and P. Long and R. White, trs., *Posthumous Writings.* Oxford: Basil Blackwell.

Frege, G. (1980). Letter to Jourdain. In G. Gabriel, H. Hermes, F. Kambartel, C. Thiel, and A. Veraart, eds., and H. Kaal, tr., *Philosophical and Mathematical Correspondence.* Oxford: Basil Blackwell.

Gottlieb, D. (1980). *Ontological Economy: Substitutional Quantification and Mathematics.* Oxford: Oxford University Press.

Grandy, R. (1982). "Semantic Intentions and Linguistic Structure." *Notre Dame Journal of Formal Logic,* 23, 327–332.

Grandy, R., and Warner, R. (1986a). "Paul Grice: A View of His Work." In Grandy and Warner (1986b).

Grandy, R., and Warner, R., eds. (1986b). *Philosophical Grounds of Rationality: Intentions, Categories, Ends.* Oxford: Oxford University Press.

Grice, H. (1957). "Meaning." *Philosophical Review,* 66, 377–388.

Grice, H. (1968). "Utterer's Meaning, Sentence-Meaning, and Word-Meaning." *Foundations of Language,* 4, 225–242.

Grice, H. (1969). "Utterer's Meaning and Intentions." *Philosophical Review,* 78, 147–177.

Grice, H. (1975). "Logic and Conversation." In D. Davidson and G. Harman, eds., *The Logic of Grammar.* Encino: Dickenson.

Grice, H. (1982). "Meaning Revisited." In Smith (1982).

Grice, H. (1986). "Reply to Richards." In Grandy and Warner (1986b).

Gunderson, K., ed. (1975). *Minnesota Studies in the Philosophy of Science,* vol. 7. Minneapolis: University of Minnesota Press.

Guttenplan, S., ed. (1975). *Mind and Language.* Oxford: Oxford University Press.

Harman, G. (1973). *Thought.* Princeton: Princeton University Press.

Harman, G. (1974). Review of Stephen Schiffer, *Meaning. Journal of Philosophy,* 71, 224–229.

Harman, G. (1975). "Language, Thought, and Communication." In Gunderson (1975).

Harman, G. (1978). "Is There Mental Representation?" In C. Savage, ed., *Perception and Cognition: Issues in the Foundations of Psychology.* Minneapolis: University of Minnesota Press.

Harman, G. (1982). "Conceptual Role Semantics." *Notre Dame Journal of Formal Logic*, 23, 242–256.

Hempel, C. (1965a). "Aspects of Scientific Explanation." In Hempel (1965b).

Hempel, C. (1965b). *Aspects of Scientific Explanation and Other Essays in the Philosophy of Science*. New York: Free Press.

Hempel, C., and Oppenheim, P. (1948). "Studies in the Logic of Explanation." *Philosophy of Science*, 15, 135–175. Reprinted in Hempel (1965b).

Hintikka, J. (1962). *Knowledge and Belief*. Ithaca: Cornell University Press.

Hintikka, J. (1969). *Models for Modalities*. Altantic Highlands, N.J.: Humanities Press.

Hintikka, J. (1970). "Knowledge, Belief, and Logical Consequence." *Ajatus*, 32, 32–47.

Hintikka, J. (1975). "Impossible Worlds Vindicated." *Journal of Philosophical Logic*, 4, 475–484.

Hintikka, J. (1982). "Game-Theoretical Semantics: Insights and Prospects." *Notre Dame Journal of Formal Logic*, 23, 219–241.

Hintikka, J. (1984). "A Hundred Years Later: The Rise and Fall of Frege's Influence in Language Theory." *Synthese*, 59, 27–49.

Hornstein, N. (1984). *Logic as Grammar*. Cambridge, Mass.: MIT Press.

Jackson, F. (1982). "Epiphenomenal Qualia." *Philosophical Quarterly*, 32, 127–136.

Kaplan, D. (1978). "Dthat." In P. Cole, ed., *Syntax and Semantics 9: Pragmatics*. New York: Academic Press.

Kemmerling, A. (1986). "Utterer's Meaning Revisited." In Grandy and Warner (1986b).

Kitcher, P. (1984). "Species." *Philosophy of Science*, 51, 308–333.

Kripke, S. (1976). "Is There a Problem about Substitutional Quantification?" In Evans and McDowell (1976).

Kripke, S. (1979). "A Puzzle about Belief." In Margalit (1979).

Kripke, S. (1980). *Naming and Necessity*. Cambridge, Mass.: Harvard University Press.

Kripke, S. (1982). *Wittgenstein on Rules and Private Language*. Cambridge, Mass.: Harvard University Press.

Leeds, S. (1979). "Church's Translation Argument." *Canadian Journal of Philosophy*, 9, 43–51.

LePore, E., ed. (1986). *New Directions in Semantics*. New York: Academic Press.

LePore, E., and Loewer, B. (1985). "Dual Aspect Semantics." In LePore (1986).

Lewis, D. (1966). "An Argument for the Identity Theory." *Journal of Philosophy*, 63, 17–25. Reprinted in Lewis (1983b).

Lewis, D. (1969). *Convention*. Cambridge, Mass.: Harvard University Press.

Lewis, D. (1970a). "How to Define Theoretical Terms." *Journal of Philosophy*, 67, 427–446. Reprinted in Lewis (1983b).

Lewis, D. (1970b). "General Semantics." *Synthese*, 22, 18–67. Reprinted in Lewis (1983b); page references are to the latter.

Lewis, D. (1972). "Psychophysical and Theoretical Identifications." *Australasian Journal of Philosophy*, 50, 249–258. Reprinted in Block (1980b); page references are to the latter.

Lewis, D. (1975). "Languages and Language." In Gunderson (1975). Reprinted in Lewis (1983b); page references are to the latter.

Lewis, D. (1979). "Attitudes *De Dicto* and *De Se*." *Philosophical Review*, 88, 513–543. Reprinted in Lewis (1983b).

Lewis, D. (1980). "Mad Pain and Martian Pain." In Block (1980b). Reprinted in Lewis (1983b).

Lewis, D. (1983a). "New Work for a Theory of Universals." *Australasian Journal of Philosophy*, 61, 343–377.

Lewis, D. (1983b). *Philosophical Papers*, vol. 1. Oxford: Oxford University Press.

Loar, B. (1976a). "Two Theories of Meaning." In Evans and McDowell (1976).

Loar, B. (1976b). "The Semantics of Singular Terms." *Philosophical Studies*, 30, 353–377.

Loar, B. (1981). *Mind and Meaning*. Cambridge: Cambridge University Press.

Loar, B. (1982). "Conceptual Role and Truth Conditions." *Notre Dame Journal of Formal Logic*, 23, 272–283.

Loar, B. (1987, in press). "Truth beyond All Verification." In B. Taylor, ed., *Essays on the Philosophy of Michael Dummet*. Amsterdam: Martinus Nijhof.

Loewer, B. (1982). "The Role of 'Conceptual Role Semantics'." *Notre Dame Journal of Formal Logic*, 23, 305–315.

Lycan, W. (1979). "The Trouble with Possible Worlds." In M. Loux, ed., *The Possible and the Actual*. Ithaca: Cornell University Press.

Lycan, W. (1984). *Logical Form in Natural Language*. Cambridge, Mass.: MIT Press. A Bradford book.

McDowell, J. (1980). "Quotation and Saying That." In M. Platts, ed., *Reference, Truth and Reality*. London: Routledge and Kegan Paul.

McDowell, J. (1981). "Anti-Realism and the Epistemology of Understanding." In Parret and Bouveresse (1981).

McGinn, C. (1982a). *The Character of Mind*. Oxford: Oxford University Press.

McGinn, C. (1982b). "The Structure of Content." In Woodfield (1982).

Margalit, A., ed. (1979). *Meaning and Use*. Dordrecht: Reidel.

Melden, A. (1961). *Free Action*. London: Routledge and Kegan Paul.

Moore, G. (1903). *Principia Ethica*. Cambridge: Cambridge University Press.

Moore, G. (1942). "A Reply to My Critics." In P. Schilpp, ed., *The Philosophy of G. E. Moore*. Chicago and Evanston: Northwestern University Press.

Owens, J. (1983). "Functionalism and Propositional Attitudes." *Noûs*, 17, 529–549.

Parret, H., and Bouveresse, J., eds. (1981). *Meaning and Understanding*. Berlin; New York: de Gruyter.

Peacocke, C. (1978). "Game-Theoretic Semantics, Quantifiers and Truth." In E. Saarinen, ed., *Game-Theoretic Semantics*. Dordrecht: Reidel.

Peacocke, C. (1981). "Demonstrative Thought and Psychological Explanation." *Synthese*, 49, 187–217.

Peacocke, C. (1983). *Sense and Content*. Oxford: Oxford University Press.

Plantinga, A. (1974). *The Nature of Necessity*. Oxford: Oxford University Press.

Platts, M. (1979). *Ways of Meaning: An Introduction to a Philosophy of Language*. London: Routledge and Kegan Paul.

Putnam, H. (1975). "The Meaning of 'Meaning'." In *Philosophical Papers, vol. 2: Mind, Language and Reality*. Cambridge: Cambridge University Press.

Putnam, H. (1978). *Meaning and the Moral Sciences*. London: Routledge and Kegan Paul.

Quine, W. (1953a). "On What There Is." In Quine (1953d).

Quine, W. (1953b). "Two Dogmas of Empiricism." In Quine (1953d).

Quine, W. (1953c). "Logic and the Reification of Universals." In Quine (1953d).

Quine, W. (1953d). *From a Logical Point of View*. Cambridge, Mass.: Harvard University Press.

Quine, W. (1960). *Word and Object*. Cambridge, Mass.: MIT Press.

Quine, W. (1966). "Three Grades of Modal Involvement." In *Ways of Paradox*. New York: Random House.

Quine, W. (1969a). "Existence and Quantification." In Quine (1969c).

Quine, W. (1969b). "Ontological Relativity." In Quine (1969c).

Quine, W. (1969c). *Ontological Relativity and Other Essays*. New York: Columbia University Press.

Quine, W. (1970). "On the Reasons for Indeterminacy of Translation." *Journal of Philosophy*, 67, 178–183.

Quine, W. (1975). "Mind and Verbal Dispositions." In Guttenplan (1975).

Quine, W. (1980). "Soft Impeachment Disowned." *Pacific Philosophical Quarterly*, 61, 450–451.

Ramsey, F. (1929). "Theories." In D. Mellor, ed., *Foundations*. London: Routledge and Kegan Paul.

Russell, B. (1959). "Knowledge by Acquaintance and Knowledge by Description." In R. Marsh, ed., *Mysticism and Logic*. London: Allen and Unwin.

Ryle, G. (1949). *The Concept of Mind*. New York: Barnes and Noble.

Ryle, G. (1957). "The Theory of Meaning." In C. Mace, ed., *British Philosophy in Mid-Century*. London: Allen and Unwin.

Salmon, N. (1981). *Reference and Essence*. Princeton: Princeton University Press.

Salmon, N. (1986). *Frege's Puzzle*. Cambridge, Mass.: MIT Press. A Bradford book.

Schiffer, S. (1972). *Meaning*. Oxford: Oxford University Press.

Schiffer, S. (1977). "Naming and Knowing." In P. French, T. Uehling, and H. Wettstein, eds., *Midwest Studies in Philosophy 2*. Minneapolis: University of Minnesota Press.

Schiffer, S. (1978). "The Basis of Reference." *Erkenntnis*, 13, 171–206.

Schiffer, S. (1981a). "Truth and the Theory of Content." In Parret and Bouveresse (1981).

Schiffer, S. (1981b). "Indexicals and the Theory of Reference." *Synthese*, 49, 43–100.

Schiffer, S. (1982). "Intention-Based Semantics." *Notre Dame Journal of Formal Logic*, 23, 119–156.

Schiffer, S. (1986). "Stalnaker's Problem of Intentionality." *Pacific Philosophical Quarterly*, 67, 87–97.

Smith, E., and Medin, D. (1981). *Concepts and Categories*. Cambridge, Mass.: Harvard University Press.

Smith, N., ed. (1982). *Mutual Knowledge*. London: Academic Press.

Soames, S. (1987). "Semantics and Semantic Competence." In S. Schiffer and S. Steele, eds., *Thought and Language: Second Arizona Colloquium on Cognitive Science*. Tucson: University of Arizona Press.

Stabler, E. (1983). "How Are Grammars Represented?" *Behavioral and Brain Sciences*, 6, 391–402.

Stalnaker, R. (1981). "Indexical Belief." *Synthese*, 49, 129–151.

Stalnaker, R. (1984). *Inquiry*. Cambridge, Mass.: MIT Press. A Bradford book.

Stalnaker, R. (1986). "Replies to Field and Schiffer." *Pacific Philosophical Quarterly*, 67, 113–123.

Stalnaker, R. (1987). "Belief Attribution and Context." in R. Grimm and O. Merrill, eds., *Content of Thought*. Tucson: University of Arizona Press.

Stampe, D. (1977). "Toward a Causal Theory of Linguistic Representation." In P. French, T. Uehling, and H. Wettstein, eds., *Midwest Studies in Philosophy 2*. Minneapolis: University of Minnesota Press.

Stich, S. (1978). "Beliefs and Subdoxastic States." *Philosophy of Science*, 45, 499–518.

Stich, S. (1982). "On the Ascription of Content." In Woodfield (1982).

Stich, S. (1983). *From Folk Psychology to Cognitive Science: The Case against Belief*. Cambridge, Mass.: MIT Press. A Bradford book.

Strawson, P. (1964). "Intention and Convention in Speech Acts." *Philosophical Review*, 73, 439–460. Reprinted in Strawson (1971); page references are to the latter.

Strawson, P. (1969). *Meaning and Truth*. Oxford: Oxford University Press. Reprinted in Strawson (1971).

Strawson, P. (1971). *Logico-Linguistic Papers*. London: Methuen.

Tarski, A. (1956). "The Concept of Truth in Formalized Languages." In *Logic, Semantics, Metamathematics*, tr. J. Woodger. Oxford: Oxford University Press.

Wittgenstein, L. (1953). *Philosophical Investigations*. Oxford: Blackwell.

Woodfield, A., ed. (1982). *Thought and Object: Essays on Intentionality.* Oxford: Oxford University Press.

Wright, C. (1976). "Truth Conditions and Criteria." *Proceedings of the Aristotelean Society*, supp. vol., 50, 217–245.

Wright, C. (1984). "Kripke's Account of the Argument against Private Language." *Journal of Philosophy*, 81, 759–778.

Index